lonely 🌍 planet

Basilicata

T0283979

Potenza
Province
p97

Matera
Province
p42

Remus Carulli
Translated by Duncan Garwood

Contents

CRIPTA DI SAN FRANCESCO, IRSINA (P73)

JULIA GRIMALDI/EDT ©

CASTELMEZZANO (P109)

REMO CARULLI/EDT ©

VALERIOMEI/SHUTTERSTOCK ©

Contents

UNDERSTAND

SURVIVAL GUIDE

MARATEA (P150)

Right: Matera (p44)

VALERIOMEI/SHUTTERSTOCK ©

WELCOME TO

Basilicata

It's difficult to describe in just a few words a land that will bowl you over with its subterranean wonders and boundless open spaces, its enchanting beaches and vertiginous mountain landscapes, the sophistication of its towns and the ancestral charm of its remote reaches. But it is perhaps this, the impossibility of reducing Basilicata to a single definition, that says the most about the restless beauty of this truly eye-opening region.

Remo Carulli, Writer
For more about our writers, see p208

› Basilicata

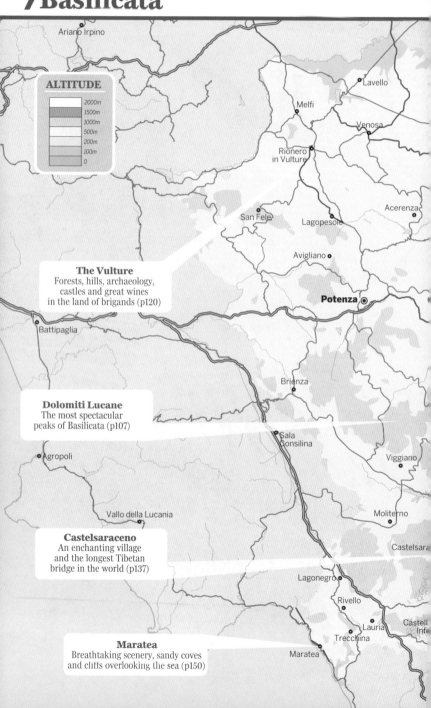

ALTITUDE

2000m
1500m
1000m
500m
200m
100m
0

Ariano Irpino

Lavello

Melfi

Venosa

Rionero
in Vulture

Acerenza

San Fele

Lagopesole

The Vulture
Forests, hills, archaeology,
castles and great wines
in the land of brigands (p120)

Avigliano

Potenza ◉

Battipaglia

Brienza

Dolomiti Lucane
The most spectacular
peaks of Basilicata (p107)

Sala
Consilina

Agropoli

Viggiano

Vallo della Lucania

Moliterno

Castelsaraceno
An enchanting village
and the longest Tibetan
bridge in the world (p137)

Castelsar

Lagonegro

Rivello

Maratea
Breathtaking scenery, sandy coves
and cliffs overlooking the sea (p150)

Lauria
Trecchina

Càstell
Inf

Maratea

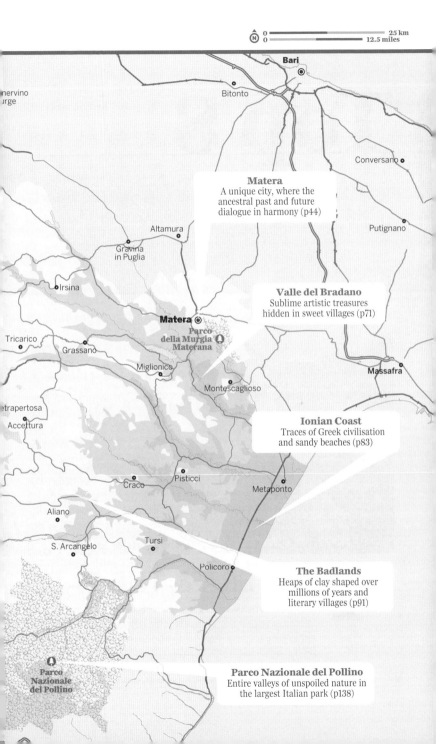

0   25 km
0   12.5 miles

Bari

Bitonto

Conversano

nervino
urge

Matera
A unique city, where the
ancestral past and future
dialogue in harmony (p44)

Altamura

Putignano

Gravina
in Puglia

Irsina

Valle del Bradano
Sublime artistic treasures
hidden in sweet villages (p71)

Matera

Tricarico

Parco
della Murgia
Materana

Grassano

Massafra

Miglionico

etrapertosa
Accettura

Montescaglioso

Ionian Coast
Traces of Greek civilisation
and sandy beaches (p83)

Craco

Pisticci

Metaponto

Aliano

S. Arcangelo

Tursi

Policoro

The Badlands
Heaps of clay shaped over
millions of years and
literary villages (p91)

Parco
Nazionale
del Pollino

Parco Nazionale del Pollino
Entire valleys of unspoiled nature in
the largest Italian park (p138)

Top 8

1 MATERA & THE SASSI

Matera can be described through poetic devices and historical narratives but nothing illustrates it better than the incredulous gaze of visitors seeing it for the first time. From the caves that pit the Sassi to its sumptuous baroque buildings, its museums and its increasingly trendy clubs, Matera and its unique cityscape captivate like few other places.

Above: Chiesa di San Pietro Caveoso (p52)

Urban Landscape

Among the many experiences Matera has to offer, nothing can top wandering its unique Sassi districts. The city is a labyrinth of stairways and you'll almost certainly get lost at some point, just as you'll be amazed by the sights that will appear before you. And it's precisely like this, by walking leisurely for hours, that you will discover the magic Matera offers up to its explorers.

Right: Staircase, Sassi, Matera (p44)

Subterranean Spaces

Matera is a city with an underground vocation. Over the centuries, the Sassi have been sculpted into their current form through thousands of human-made caves and palaces built with excavated material. The result is a mix of rupestrian (rock) churches adorned with hieratic frescoes, vast cisterns for collecting water, and ex olive oil mills transformed into restaurants and hotels – venues whose floors descend into the very bowels of the earth.

Above: Chiesa di Santa Maria de Idris (p52)

Museums

In recent years, Matera has reinforced its role as a major cultural centre by opening several museums, making a visit to the city not only an aesthetic adventure but also an unmissable opportunity for cultural enrichment. From the National Museum to the prestigious MUSMA (Museo della Scultura Contemporanea) and smaller-scale collections, the city is awash with art treasures and vestiges of its ancient past.

Above: MUSMA (p55)

2 NATURE WALKS

Basilicata occupies a large territory, yet has a smaller population than a city like Genoa. The result is a region that's still wild, with tracts of unspoiled nature, a dizzying variety of landscapes and, above all, countless opportunities for feeling like a true explorer.

Parco Nazionale del Pollino

Dense forests, deep valleys, high-altitude meadows, extraordinary biodiversity – the Pollino (pictured above) is a natural wonder. Add

in the distinctness of its cultural traditions and mind-blowing cuisine, and you have the picture of an area not to be missed. p138

The Badlands

It took millions of years for water to erode mounds of white clay and create the furrows that characterise this part of the region. Yet it only takes a moment to

be bowled over. In addition to the poetry of the landscape, the words of Carlo Levi echo through Aliano.

Top: The Badlands (p91)

The Murgia Materana

Take a path from the heart of the Sassi and in five minutes you'll find yourself catapulted into

a primeval landscape of canyons, caves and ancient rock churches – the ideal setting for a Western film. Head to the Belvedere of Murgia Timone to admire an iconic view of Matera. p69

Above: Murgia Materana (p68)

3 ADRENALINE EXPERIENCES

ADRIANO AULETA ©

In addition to signature sights such as Matera's underground wonders, the badlands and mountains, Basilicata also has a range of sites aimed at evoking thrills and emotions. Thus the region offers itself as a land dedicated to adventure.

The Dolomiti Lucane

The **Volo dell'Angelo** (p109) between Pietrapertosa and Castelmezzano, two beautiful villages set against a natural backdrop of rocky spires, is now considered an essential stop on any tour of the region. But the via ferrata routes also guarantee just the right dose of goosebumps.

Tibetan Bridges

Set in a thrilling mountain landscape in Castelsaraceno, **Ponte tra i due Parchi** (p137), is the longest Tibetan bridge in the world. The **Ponte alla Luna** (p117) in Sasso di Castalda makes up for its smaller (but still enormous) dimensions with dizzying swings. Both are stupendous.

Above: Ponte alla Luna

Maratea & the Hinterland

Maratea's **Via Ferrata del Redentore** (p148) is so spectacular that attempting to describe it is futile. The climbing walls nearby will further add to your amazement while at Trecchina's **Parco delle Stelle** (p160) you can have spine-tingling fun in the midst of stunning scenery.

4 FESTIVALS & TRADITIONS

GIUMA/SHUTTERSTOCK ©

From village festivals to religious celebrations, from rituals rooted in prehistory to Carnival festivities with masks derived from ancient times – traditional celebrations enjoy enormous popular support across the region and you'll inevitably be swept up in the festive atmosphere.

Carnival

There are many towns in Basilicata where traditional parades incorporate older cultural elements. These include Aliano (p95), with its typical horned masks, and Tricarico (p80), where you can admire the personifications of local animals.

Above: Mask at Aliano's Carnival

Arboreal Rites

The most famous event is held in Accettura (p81), but rites are held in villages throughout the region. The ancestral, propitiatory rites centre on the 'wedding' of a tree trunk to the top of a separate tree.

Festa della Madonna della Bruna

Matera boasts a full year's worth of fascinating events. But for popular participation none can top the July 2 (p58) festival of the Madonna – after the procession, the float carrying the statue of the Virgin Mary is quite literally torn to pieces.

5 PICTURESQUE VILLAGES

From Vulture to the Pollino, from the Val d'Agri to the Valle del Basento, the region is speckled with villages huddled on hilltops, nestled on mountainsides or placidly spread over the undulating countryside. Each has its own character but what unites them is the charm of these small settlements, dotted with artistic gems and animated by traditions that still live on today.

Tricarico

It may be the relics of the Norman era or the Arab districts that seduce you, or the iconic figure of former mayor and poet Rocco Scotellaro, the frescoed churches, the palazzi or the Carnival celebrations. One thing's for sure, though, Tricarico will provide you with unforgettable memories. p78

Below: Torre Normana, Tricarico

GIAMBATTISTA LAZZZERA/SHUTTERSTOCK ®

Rivello

The prettiest of the villages in the Maratea hinterland lies nestled on three hills. In addition to elegant palazzi and oriental-style churches, it boasts one of the region's most remarkable monuments. p160

Above: Rivello

Guardia Perticara

This small village in the Val d'Agri stands out for its photogenic beauty, stone alleyways and medieval appearance. In the surrounding countryside are many quality farm stays. p134

Right: Guardia Perticara

6 THE SEA & THE COAST

ADRIANO AULETA ©

GIOVANNI RINALDI/SHUTTERSTOCK ©

Maratea

If you were to determine the ratio between a territory's area and the beauty it contained, Maratea would score extremely highly – made up of numerous enchanting hamlets, it has a practically inexhaustible supply of dreamy little beaches, cliffside paths and romantic views. p150

Top left: Coast near Maratea

Ionian Beaches

They may not be as poetic as the beaches on the Tyrrhenian, but the long stretches of sand that skirt the Ionian coast evoke holiday dreams. The sea is clean, there's no shortage of small restaurants serving fresh fish, and outside of August you'll find the atmosphere very relaxed.

Left: Marina, Policoro (p87)

Riserva Naturale Bosco Pantano di Pantano

Beachside forests, marshes, sand dunes – the Ionian coast's most attractive area has a certain tropical charm. And if you look closely, you might even see monk seals, otters and sea turtles. p88

Basilicata's two short coastal stretches are very different from each other. On the Tyrrhenian side, the last offshoots of the Apennines tumble furiously into the sea, creating a coastline of rocks, cliffs and enchanting coves. In contrast, the long sandy beaches of the Ionian, bordered by aromatic pine forests, elicit an air of tranquillity. But what they have in common is that they're both ideal destinations for a great holiday.

7 ARCHAEOLOGICAL WONDERS

GIUMA/SHUTTERSTOCK ©

Metaponto & Policoro

These two localities on the Ionian coast harbour important finds from the Magna Graecia period. Their archaeological museums are fascinating, but the star attraction is the superb Tavole Palatine.

Top left: Tavole Palatine (p86)

FABIO BOCCUZZI/SHUTTERSTOCK ©

Venosa

The fact that it's the birthplace of the poet Horace is enough to put Venosa on the map of the ancient Roman world. But it also has a first-rate museum and an evocative archaeological park. p128

Left: Parco Archeologico (p129)

Museo Archeologico Nazionale, Potenza

The regional capital rarely makes it on to travellers' itineraries, but the collection showcased in its main museum is one you'll never forget. p99

Due to its crucial position on the travel routes through the peninsula, Basilicata has been a crossroads of peoples and goods for millennia. The result is a brimming chest of ancient treasures, ranging from megalithic sites immersed in woods to Roman cities, from Magna Graecia temples to rich museum collections. For archaeology fans, it's a feast for the eyes and the spirit.

8 ARTISTIC RICHES

The Sarcofago di Rapolla: Museo Archeologico Nazionale del Vulture Melfese Massimo Pallottino (p125)

Among its many attractions, Basilicata also boasts a good number of artistic masterpieces. Whether you're a fan of ancient wonders, medieval frescoes, or the architectural forms of the Renaissance, a trip to this multifaceted region will be truly rewarding.

Valle del Bradano

For an itinerary with a strong dose of art – there's the opulent Abbazia di San Michele Arcangelo in Montescaglioso (p76), a sumptuous polyptych by Cima da Coneglianoin in Miglionico (p75), and, in Irsina (p73), the only known statue by Mantegna.

Melfi

In this, the most important town of the Vulture area, you can get your fill of art by admiring the marvellous *Sarcofago di Rapolla* in the castle museum and the highly original frescoes in the Chiesa rupestre di Santa Margherita. p124

Ripacandida

Thanks to the Santuario di San Donato and its cycle of 15th and 16th centuries frescoes, the most important in Basilicata, this tiny town is an essential stop on any tour of the region's artistic jewels. p123

What's New

The Giardino del Silenzio

Among its many wonders, Matera was missing a small park (p52) with flower beds and benches. One has finally been built, in the Sasso Barisano, and it offers splendid views over the Gravina.

Vicinato a Pozzo

This multimedia route (p53) offers a brilliant opportunity to understand what life was like in the sassi caves before they were emptied.

Racconti in Pietra

For those travelling with children in tow, this interesting museum (p54) is dedicated to paleontology in the Matera area.

Palazzo Lizzadri

Boosting Tricarico's (p79) already rich artistic patrimony, this elegant palace houses museum displays of typical anthropological masks.

MAFE – Museo Archeologico di Ferrandina

Pretty Ferrandina (p80) lacked a beautiful archaeological museum: it now has one displaying finds unearthed in the area.

Essenza Lucano

Amaro Lucano is Basilicata's most iconic product (p85): you can discover its every secret at this dedicated space in Pisticci.

Basilicata Alpaca

Among travellers Acerenza has always been known for its imposing cathedral. From now on it will also be known for the farming of soft alpacas (p106), unusual in these latitudes.

Museo Laboratorio delle Arti e del Paesaggio – MuLabo

Just outside Brienza, this museum (p115) will delight both nature lovers, with an uplifting multimedia tour, and art aficionados, thanks to the fine frescoes in the adjoining chapel.

Sentiero dei Minatori

This fully equipped trail through an abandoned railway tunnel above a spectacular canyon in the Balvano area (p119) is a must for adventurous travellers.

Ancient track of the Montagna Grande di Viggiano

The first part of one of the most important pilgrimage routes in southern Italy (p133) has recently had a makeover.

MAM – Sistema Museale Aiello Moliterno

The number of museums in the tiny village of Moliterno continues to grow (p136). At the time of research there were eight.

Ponte tra i due Parchi

Since summer 2021, Castelsaraceno (p137) has been home to the world's longest Tibetan bridge.

Maratea's Via Ferrata

Overlooking the sea, the Via Ferrata del Redentore (p148) is already considered one of Italy's most exciting routes.

Parco delle Stelle

At more than 1000m above sea level and with a view of the entire coast, the location is truly spectacular. The rides (p160), on the other hand, guarantee pure adrenaline.

Month by Month

January

★ Palio di Sant'Antonio Abate

Mules and horses gallop at breakneck speed through steep (often snow-covered) alleys in Pignola (p112).

★ Le Notte dei Cucibocca

On the night of Epiphany, mysterious figures roam the historic centre of Montescaglioso (p77). Children get scared and run to bed.

February

★ Carnevale

A heartfelt event in many villages of Basilicata. One of the most spectacular celebrations is held in Aliano

(p95). Get yourself a mask and enter the fray.

★ San Valentino

The patron saint of lovers is also the patron saint of Abriola, a town that commemorates him with a party (p113).

March/April

★ Settimana Santa

Many Lucanian villages stage a Via Crucis and Passion of Christ. One of the most atmospheric processions is held in Barile (p124).

May

★ Festa di San Biagio

This Maratea ceremony might date back centuries, but the number of visitors who come for the occasion never wanes (p152).

★ Il Maggio di Accettura

This is the most important of Basilicata's arboreal rites. There are also dances and banquets to invite a fertile year (p81).

★ Parata dei Turchi

More than 900 people take part in a historical re-enactment that celebrates the patron saint of Potenza (p100).

★ Festa della Madonna della Stella

It's not every day you get to witness an event that mixes religion and folklore. In San Costantino Albanese (p143) the Madonna is celebrated and *nusazit* (traditional papier-mâché puppets) are set alight.

★ Festa del SS Crocifisso

In a tradition dating to 1238, on the first Sunday of May in Brienza (p116) a procession carries a crucifix up to a mountain sanctuary. It is brought back down on the third Sunday of September. The Madonna Nera di Viggiano follows a similar route from village to sanctuary, returning to the village on the first Sunday of September.

June

★ Festa del Mascio

Pietrapertosa hosts the evocative wedding of a Turkey oak to a holly tree (p108).

✿✿ Sagra dell'Abete

Rotonda defies nature and gets in a good harvest for the coming year (p141).

✿✿ Festa della 'Ndenna

Arboreal rites are the most typical of Basilicata's events. Those in Castelsaraceno (p137) involve the marriage of a beech tree to a pine.

✿✿ Raduno delle Maschere Antropologiche

Tricarico hosts an international gathering of different folk traditions (p80).

July

✿✿ Festa della Madonna del Pollino

One of Basilicata's most 'profane' religious festivals is staged in San Severino Lucano (p144).

☆ Rassegna dell'Arpa Viggianese

Harps and harpists are at home in Viggiano. Classical, jazz, folk, ethnic and chamber music (p133) is played to celebrate them.

☆ Maratea Scena

You'll be spoiled for choice between open meetings, fashion shows, exhibitions, theatre performances, and concerts (p152).

☆ Il Mondo di Federico II

Castel Lagopesole puts on a multimedia show to remember the man who made Basilicata central to the political life of the empire (p121). Events continue throughout August.

☆ L'Estate di Isabella

A wonderful event that continues into August. The Valsinni Literary Park sets the stage for exhibitions, concerts, shows, and plenty of food and wine (p90).

✿✿ Festa della Madonna della Bruna

A huge papier-mâché float parades through the streets of Matera to celebrate the city's patron saint. At the end of the party it's ripped to shreds (p58).

August

🍷 Cantinando Wine & Art

In the Parco Urbano delle Cantine di Barile the sound of concert music floats over rivers of wine (p124).

✿✿ Storia Bandita

Although smaller than splendours of yesteryear, Brindisi di Montagna (p106) is a choice place to learn about the history of Basilicata's brigands.

✿✿ Notte della Transumanza

Transhumance is celebrated in Rivello with dancing, music, food, and itineraries along shepherd trails (p161).

✿✿ Corteo Medievale

Do you know the history of the Cattedrale di Acerenza? To explain it, a medieval procession (p107) rolls back the years to 1080.

✿✿ Sulle Tracce degli Arabi

In memory of its ancient inhabitants, Pietrapertosa's Arabata district (p109) becomes Arab again for a day.

✿✿ Quadri Plastici

In Avigliano (p118) you can view the unusual spectacle of motionless figures representing a painting.

✗ Sagra del Vino e della Lumaca

If you love snails you can't miss this festival (p74), held under the bell tower in Irsina.

☆ Pollino Music Festival

Sleep in a campsite, party til late and listen to good music in San Severino Lucano (p145).

☆ Gezziamoci

Sounds intertwine with places as music invades the terraces, piazzas and venues of Matera and other Lucanian villages (p58).

✿✿ Sogno di una notte...a quel paese

In Colobraro (p88), the *quel paese* (unnamed land) in the event's name, this festival features exhibitions, food, wine, and dancing – all around the theme of superstition.

✗ Sagra della pasta a mano

Feasting in the streets of Oppido Lucano (p105), there's lots of handmade pasta and plenty more besides.

✿✿ Metaponto Beach Festival

A summer of music celebrated on the sandy beaches of Metaponto (p86).

Illuminations, Festa della Madonna della Bruna (p58)

☆ Vulcanica Live Festival

Live music, theatre and cinema feature at this festival held in Rionero (p121).

September

✷ Il Rito del Maggio

It might be called the Rite of May but Il Rito del Maggio is celebrated in September. Yet another of Basilicata's arboreal rites, this one is held in the town of Castelmezzano (p110).

☆ Women's Fiction Festival

For a few days each year in Matera (p58), women's (and other) literature is celebrated.

☆ MATIFF – Matera Art International Film Festival

Interesting films and a rich programme of side events (p59) in Matera.

October

✗ Sagra della Varola

The brown of Vulture colours desserts, handmade pasta, beers and much more besides. In Melfi (p126).

☆ Matera Film Festival

In a city with a strong film vocation, this extraordinary festival (p59) is for lovers of the seventh art.

✷ Giornate Medievali

Brindisi di Montagna (p106) fills with knights, fire eaters, soldiers and damsels in distress.

✷ Festival della Falconeria

In the sweet autumn of Melfi (p126), you can immerse yourself in falconry and the Middle Ages.

December

✷ Presepe Vivente

Basilicata's rupestrian (rock) civilisation forms the perfect setting for Living Nativities. Of the many staged across the region, one of the most impressive is in Matera (p58).

Plan Your Trip
Itineraries

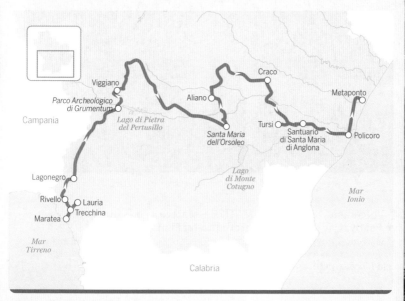

Basilicata Coast to Coast

8 DAYS

A revisiting of the classic Basilicata itinerary, celebrated by Italian cinema and symbolic of the region. En route you'll take in sea and mountains, popular culture and Greek ruins, ghost towns and fashionable cities. It's a full immersion in the region's most visceral and heartfelt depths.

First stop is enchanting **Maratea**. Here you can enjoy the historic centre, climb through the ruins of Maratea Superiore, and shiver in the shadow of the Redeemer before warming up on the beaches of the fabulous coastline, which stretches from Acquafredda in the north to Castrocucco in the south. Then turn your back on the sea and head inland to **Trecchina** to enjoy a walnut cake on a bench on the main piazza and climb up to the Santuario della Madonna del Soccorso, taking in views of sea and mountains as you go. From here, it's a short hop to **Lauria**, with its castle ruins, and **Rivello**, whose steep alleys merit exploration. Next up is sleepy **Lagonegro**, an ideal place for a lovely walk and a dip into the Middle Ages, but note that the body of water that gave it its name no longer exists.

The coast at Maratea (p148)

Now head northeast – first to explore the Roman ruins of **Parco Archeologico di Grumentum**, and then to the musical town of **Viggiano** from where you can launch a pilgrimage to the Santuario del Sacro Monte. Both will provoke intense emotions that you can process as you push on to the lunar landscapes of the badlands. Here the Convento di **Santa Maria dell' Orsoleo** will leave you speechless, but it's in **Aliano**, a town little changed since Carlo Levi was confined here, and **Craco**, with its melancholic abandoned roads, that the area expresses all its haunting charm. After a visit to **Tursi** to explore the labyrinthine Rabatana district, and to the **Santuario di Santa Maria di Anglona**, whose Romanesque architecture silently dominates its solemn surroundings, you'll finally reach the Ionian coast. Stop off in **Policoro** for a refreshing swim and a stroll through the Riserva Naturale Bosco Pantano di Policoro, and fill up on strawberries (in season). Then continue on to **Metaponto** to see what remains of the ancient Greek colony and celebrate your trip with a dinner of fresh fish.

The Best of Basilicata's Art

8 DAYS

Basilicata is best known for its wild vistas, ancestral traditions and sleepy villages. But there's another, more elegant, sumptuous side to its nature. Follow this tour and you'll discover why the region's artistic heritage can rival tha⁺ of many decidedly more celebrated parts of the Italian peninsula.

There's nowhere in the world like **Matera** and you'll need at least a couple of days to visit its fresco-clad rock churches, baroque palaces, and MUSMA museum collections. After the grottoes, tunnels and charming confines of the Sassi, the mighty dimensions of the Abbazia di San Michele Arcangelo in **Montescaglioso** will seem to grow before you. At this point, head up the Valle del Bradano. In **Miglionico** you can admire an extraordinary Renaissance polyptych by Cima da Conegliano, while in **Irsina** you'll find a sculpture by Andrea Mantegna, the only work definitely attributed to him. Before pushing on make sure you check out the extraordinarily beautiful view over the surrounding countryside and visit the Cripta di San Francesco and Museo Civico Janora. From there, head northwest to **Acerenza**, where one of the region's most striking cathedrals awaits you with a truly devotional atmosphere. Then, get lost in the alleys of Horace's birthplace, **Venosa**, before emerging to take in the town's enchanting archaeological area and superlative Abbazia della Trinità. Next up in this, the land of the Aglianico grape, is **Melfi**, with its castle, archaeological collection and aristocratic historical centre, and the **Laghi di Monticchio**, where you can rest on the peaceful banks and visit the Museo di Storia Naturale del Vulture. By now your journey is coming to an end but there's still plenty of beauty left to take in. **Ripacandida** boasts a real gem, the pictorial cycle of the Santuario di San Donato, a sanctuary twinned with Assisi. From there, turn sharply southwest, perhaps stopping at **San Fele** for a walk and a swim under the waterfalls. At **Muro Lucano**, one of Basilicata's most picturesque villages, you can round off your trip with a visit to the beautiful archaeological museum while enjoying the feeling of having lived a memorable travel experience.

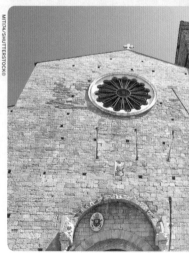

Above: L'Incompiuta, Abbazia della Santissima Trinità (p129)

Below: Cattedrale, Acerenza (p106)

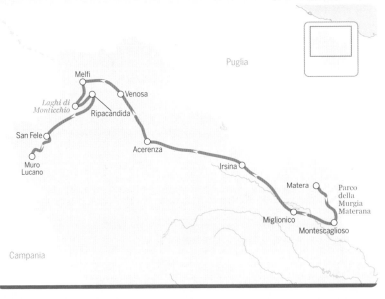

Potenza

Castelmezzano
Pietrapertosa

Laurenzana

Viggiano

Campania

*Lago di Pietra
del Pertusillo*

Castelsaraceno

▲ Monte Alpi
(1900 m)

*Mar
Tirreno*

Rotonda

San Costantino Albanese

Terranova
di Pollino

Calabria

San Paolo Albanese

*Lago
di Monte
Cotugno*

Tursi

Valsinni

Pisticci

Miglionico

Riserva Naturale
Oasi di San Giuliano

Matera

*Parco
della
Murgia
Materana*

*Mar
Ionio*

PAVLO GLAZKOV/SHUTTERSTOCK©

Parks, Villages & Nature

9 DAYS

For those who love the outdoors, views, and mountain vistas, this green itinerary traverses the length and breadth of Basilicata while also showcasing the beauty of its villages.

Start in **Potenza** by visiting the Museo Archeologico Nazionale and charging your batteries for the 40-minute journey to the Dolomiti Lucane and the splendid villages of **Pietrapertosa** and **Castelmezzano**. Surrounded by fantastical mountain spires, you can launch yourself on the Volo dell'Angelo or walk the more serene Percorso delle Sette Pietre. Then, double back a few kilometres to the entrance to the SP32 and follow it on to **Laurenzana**, where you can breathe in the pure air of its fir wood. Strike south to **Viggiano**. Depending on the season you can either ski or make the most important pilgrimage in all of Basilicata to the chapel of Sacro Monte. But don't use all your energy because after a stop in **Castelsaraceno** to cross the world's longest Tibetan bridge and enjoy a walk on Monte Ali, it won't take you long to reach **Rotonda** in the heart of the Parco Nazionale del Pollino. After visiting the historic centre, hiking out to admire a Heldreich's pine, and enjoying a fine lunch of local aubergine, you'll be ready to dedicate yourself to the eastern part of the park. And it's here that you'll find **Terranova di Pollino**, from where wonderful trails lead up to the Timpa delle Murge and Timpa di Pietrasasso, and the villages of **San Paolo Albanese** and **San Costantino Albanese** with their museums, Arbëreshë traditions and the Volo dell'Aquila – just so you don't miss anything. After so much exertion, treat yourself to a quick rest – perhaps in **Valsinni** in the company of Isabella Morra's ghost – before pushing on for the grand finale. And as you drive along the road between **Tursi** and **Pisticci**, you'll realize that views like those over the badlands are not so easy to come by. You're on the home stretch. In **Miglionico**, there's a polyptych by Cima di Conegliano and the **Riserva Naturale Oasi di San Giuliano**, but if you're not into birdwatching you could give that a miss as you follow the last few kilometres onto **Matera**. Here you can delve into rock churches and admire moving views over the **Parco della Murgia Materana**, while contemplating the wonders of your trip.

KARZOF PLEINE/SHUTTERSTOCK ©

Above: Pietrapertosa (p108)

Above: Porte tra i due Parchi, Castelsaraceno (p137)

The Best
OFFBEAT SITES

PARCO DEI PALMENTI

To some it looks like a smurf village, to others it resembles a gnome village from a Norse saga. Certainly, this cave network for processing grapes (p105) is an awe-inspiring place.

BASILICATA ALPACA

Native to the Andes, soft alpacas are certainly not indigenous to the Apennines, but you can pet them and learn about them at this Acerenza (p106) farm.

PARCO SCULTURA LA PALOMBA

This is perhaps the most overlooked of Matera's great attractions, yet the huge quarry (p71) dotted with contemporary sculpture is a jaw-dropping sight.

PARCO LETTERARIO ISABELLA MORRA

Learn about the life of Isabella Morra, a feminist before the term existed, as well as a poet and victim of a cruel fate, in her family castle at Valsinni (p90).

CASTELLO DI MONTESERICO

To reach this historic Norman manor, closed to the public, you'll almost certainly get lost in the countryside around Genzano di Lucania (p127). But what wonderfully beautiful countryside.

GIOSTRA PANORAMICA RB RIDE

In the heart of the Pollino Mountains, on a scenic hill near San Severino Lucano (p144), this is the world's slowest merry-go-round. A full ride takes a quarter of an hour, but given the beauty of the view, you might want to book a second go.

1. Castello di Monteserico **2.** Basilicata Alpaca **3.** Giostra panoramica RB Ride

The Best
FOOD & WINE

• •

CRUSCO PEPPERS

Every September, balconies and courtyards in Basilicata are adorned with long necklaces and braids of fiery red peppers hung out to dry, ready to be fried and enjoyed throughout the year.

CRAPIATA

This soup of legumes and cereals is a typical food of Matera's farm labourers. Despite its poor origins, a gourmet version can now be enjoyed in many of the city's restaurants.

BREAD FROM MATERA

Some say its secret lies in the durum wheat semolina flour, in part an ancient variety, while others insist it's the quality of the water. Either way, the memory of its texture will haunt you long after you've returned home.

AGLIANICO DEL VULTURE

Basilicata's most important native grape variety brings out its best on the slopes of an ancient volcano. It expresses all its robust intensity, both in smell and taste, in wines of extraordinary quality. It's best aged for a few years.

LUCANICA SAUSAGE

It's said that even Cicero was fond of it. You can try this tasty sausage in several versions: sweet, with fennel, or spicy. It's also great as a pasta sauce.

CHEESE

From canestrato di Moliterno, made with sheep and goat's milk and aged in typical *fondaci*, to noble caciocavallo podolico by way of pecorino from Filiano – Basilicata is a dream for cheese lovers.

1. Bread from Matera **2.** Crusco peppers **3.** Pieces of *caciocavallo* cheese

Cycle the former Ferrovia Calabro-Lucana railway (p16

Outdoor Activities

In a region where nature's vitality and creativity often surpass humanity's, the opportunities for outdoor activities are endless. From the Pollino Mountains to the Maratea coast, from the Parco Nazionale dell'Appennino Lucano-Val d'Agri-Lagonegrese to the badlands, Basilicata offers year-round adventure at every turn.

ADRIANO AULETA ©

The Best

Best Walks

➡ Gravina di Matera (p54)

➡ Santuario della Madonna del Soccorso at Trecchina (p113)

➡ Timpa delle Murge (p146)

➡ Serra di Crispo (p142)

The Most Striking Woods

➡ Abetina di Laurenzana (p113)

➡ The woods of Forenza (p131)

➡ Bosco di Tricarico (p79)

➡ Bosco Magnano (p144)

The Most Beautiful Swims

➡ La Secca (p158)

➡ Cala Jannita (p157)

➡ Dom Pablo (p86)

diverse in landscape, and in the Vulture area, particularly around the stunning **Laghi di Monticchio** (p122).

For a variation on the mountain theme, and to catch a glimpse of the sea between summits while savouring the scent of Mediterranean scrub and maritime pines on the breeze, the Tyrrhenian coast around **Maratea** (p148) provides plenty of scope for short-range trekking.

But if you prefer some art and history with your nature, don't miss trekking the trails of the **Parco della Murgia Materana** (p68) and along **Via Appia** (p127), even if many stretches are not yet practicable. In the **badlands** (p91) you'll be able to explore the area's splendid villages and their literary parks.

Finally, lovers of slow travel should know that Matera can be reached on foot from various places outside the region via the **Cammino Materano** trail network (see boxed text, p66).

Cycling

The most challenging routes for those who want to explore the area on two wheels are in the **Parco Regionale di Gallipoli Cognato e Piccole Dolomiti Lucane** (see boxed text, p81), where you can pedal along little-used back roads and perhaps take a route all the way to Matera, and in the **Parco Nazionale del Pollino** (p138) with its steep terrain and high altitudes. Two destinations that are very popular with cyclists are **Vulture** (p120), where outdoor sport can easily be combined with cultural visits and gastronomic pursuits, and the

Hiking

If you're feeling the call of the wild, the best destination is the **Parco Nazionale del Pollino** (p138).Explore woods of beech trees, silver firs and thousand-year-old Heldreich's pines; glacial lakes, rivers and streams inhabited by otters; remote peaks, and paths, paths, and yet more paths. Stunning scenery is also found in the **Parco Nazionale dell'Appennino Lucano Val d'Agri-Lagonegrese** (p132) and the **Parco Regionale di Gallipoli Cognato e Piccoli Dolomiti Lucane** (p81), both of which are extensive and

INFORMATION

To learn about Basilicata's parks, reserves and protected natural areas, check out the Basilicata section of the Italian parks website (www.parks.it). For more detailed information, see the websites of the individual parks: www.parcogallipolicognato.it, www.parcomurgia.it and www.parconazionalepollino.it. We also recommend www.viaggiarenelpollino.it, edited by guide Giuseppe Cosenza, and www.visitpollino.it.

Via Ferrata del Redentore, Maratea (p148)

Tyrrhenian coast (p148), where you can interrupt your tough climbing with a pleasant beach break. However, the absolute *must* for bike enthusiasts is the cycle path of the **ex-Ferrovia Calabro-Lucana** (see boxed text, p162), which enables you to cycle between Rivello and Castelluccio Inferiore along a former rail track.

If you're traveling to Basilicata by plane, check with your airline if there's a supplement to pay for transporting your bike and whether you'll need to disassemble and pack it. You can take a bike with you on Italian trains – depending on the type of train, you'll either be asked to stow it in a designated bike area or dismantle it and carry it in an appropriate bag. For convenience, you may decide to ship your bike separately, in which case it will arrive at your destination within a couple of days.

APT (www.basilicataturistica.it) has a freely downloadable guide to cycle tourism in the region and another on mountain bike routes.

THE BEST TIMES

➡ **December-March** For those who enjoy the snow – snowshoeing, cross-country and downhill skiing. Note, complexes are small and altitudes are not very high.

➡ **April-June** Pleasantly warm days and flower-covered hills – perfect for cycling.

➡ **July** Fans of water sports flock to the beaches, which are a little quieter than in August.

➡ **August** Peak holiday time when everything is busiest: the beaches, bike paths, trails and roads. The heat is often stifling in the Ionian hinterland but the coasts are caressed by a breeze and you can breathe fresh air in the mountains.

➡ **September-October** The days are cooler, ideal for a morning walk or bike ride. The beaches are still enjoyable.

Water Sports

In **Maratea** (p148) you'll find plenty of opportunities for boat trips, perhaps to reach one of its secluded, cliff-backed beaches, while for easy-going swimming

THE BEST DESTINATIONS IF YOU LOVE...
....

➡ **Birdwatching** – Pantano di Pignola (p112), Riserva Naturale Oasi di San Giuliano (p76)

➡ **Horse Riding**– Laghi di Monticchio (p122), Parco Nazionale del Pollino (p138)

➡ **Water Sports** – Maratea (p148), Parco Nazionale del Pollino (p138)

➡ **Gravines and canyons** – Matera (p148), Noepoli (p146)

➡ **Cycling** – Vulture (p120), Parco Nazionale del Pollino (p138), Maratea (p148)

➡ **Trekking** – Parco Nazionale del Pollino (p138), Parco della Murgia Materana (p68)

➡ **Downhill skiing** – Abriola (p112), Viggiano (p132), Lagonegro (p163)

➡ **Climbing and bouldering** – Dolomiti Lucane (p108), Castelgrande (p120), Maratea (p148)

the gentle waters of the Ionian Sea are ideal. For rafting, canyoning and aqua-trekking, the place to go is the **Parco Nazionale del Pollino** (p138). But if you prefer your water more placid, what about a nice paddleboat trip up and down the **Laghi di Monticchio** (p122)?

Adrenaline-Charged Activities

Basilicata is increasingly a reference point for thrill-seekers, to the extent that the presence of several highly appealing attractions is becoming something of a regional signature. Chief among these is the **Volo dell'Angelo** (see boxed text, p109), a zip line of more than a kilometre and a half that involves you flying through the air suspended from a steel cable at a speed of 120km/h. Adding to the giddy excitement of the experience is the amazing mountain scenery in the heart of the Lucanian Dolomites.

Still in the mountains, but further south in the Parco Nazionale del Pollino, you can try the **Volo dell'Aquila** (p147), a kind of suspended motorized hang glider that flies

you down 300m. If that doesn't quench your thirst for adrenaline, note that there are two **adventure parks** in the Pollino, one in San Costantino Albanese (p147) and one in San Severino Lucano (p144). And then there are the **Tibetan bridges of Sasso di Castalda** (p117) and **Castelsaraceno** (p137) which will provide thrills to satisfy most visitors.

Also of note is the **Parco delle Stelle** in Trecchina (p160), a sort of playground for intrepid travellers set in a panoramic position above the Maratea coast.

Vie Ferrate & Climbing

Basilicata is also a superb playground for lovers of vie ferrate and climbing. The most exciting vie ferrate is found in the **Dolomiti Lucane**, in **Sasso di Castalda** (p117), and, above all, in **Maratea** (p148), where a recently opened route allows you to climb suspended between sea and sky. Maratea is also a brilliant spot for climbing, while **Campomaggiore** (p107) is much appreciated by practitioners of bouldering (climbing on boulders).

Above: Craco (p92)

Left: Ceramic whistles, a typical souvenir from Matera (p66)

Plan Your Trip
Family Travel

Evocative settings, rituals and festivals seemingly taken from fairy tales, places of wild charm – Basilicata will certainly appeal to young travellers, especially those who love adventure.

Basilicata for Kids

In a land of adventure like Basilicata, all you need is a little imagination and you'll find numerous ways to entertain your kids on your trip. Although not all accommodation options are specifically set up to meet all children's needs (children's menus, changing tables, organised entertainment and so on), you'll find no shortage of enthusiasm and hospitality. Playgrounds can be found at campsites (always) and farm stays (often); some farm stays accept pets and some offer special kid-friendly activities. The beaches at the resorts on the Ionian coast are sandy, ideal for building sand castles, taking a ride on a pedal boat, and eating ice creams at seaside kiosks.

Where to Stay

By far the simplest solution if travelling with small children is to stay in a house, apartment or some sort of self-catering option. In some B&Bs you might have access to kitchen facilities or use of a kitchen. Also worth considering is overnighting in a farm stay, where you'll be much closer to nature. Many of those reviewed in this guide have playgrounds for children and a restaurant, which can be priceless after a tiring day of sightseeing. On the coast, campsites are very pleasant and many are situated just a few meters from the beach, most of which are equipped with everything you could possibly

A City

Unique, rocky, hidden and almost supernatural, the city of Matera (p44) mesmerizes young and old alike.

Outdoor Entertainment

You don't need to whizz down the Volo dell'Angelo to enjoy the incredible scenery of the Dolomiti Lucane (p108). You can try to spot different animals in the bizarre shapes of the rock spires, invent adventure stories in the Arabesque alleyways of Pietrapertosa, or tackle the mysterious Percorso delle Sette Pietre (p108).

Long Live Carnival!

Off-season travel can be a lot of fun sometimes. For example, head to Tricarico (p79) or Aliano (p95) for a playful immersion in one of the festivals most beloved by children.

Beaches

The mainly rocky Tyrrhenian coast is not the best place to build sandcastles, but it is easy to fall under its spell at any age. On the Ionian coast, however, the beaches and shallow waters of Policoro will delight children and parents.

need for a wonderful beach holiday. For information on accommodation, see p192.

Useful Information

Before you leave, check out www.quanto manca.com, a useful guide for people travelling with children. It's packed with valuable tips to help make your little ones' trip more enjoyable, as well as games to play and much more. Also interesting is www.babyinviaggio.it, which publishes readers' experiences of travelling with children through Europe and other continents.

Discounts

European Union citizens are entitled to discounted or free admission to museums and other sites. In general, there are three bands of discounts for children:

➡ Kids under four are usually admitted for free.

➡ Kids under 12 usually receive a discount on admission.

➡ Students up to the age of 26 often also receive discounted admission.

Entry prices for parks are often based on the height of the children.

PACKING

As you know, to enjoy a trip with children in tow, it's essential to know how to involve them. So why not start with the packing? Here are some tips.

➡ Create an electrifying air of anticipation by starting to prepare your bags a few days before departure.

➡ Ask your kids to prepare a list of things to take, perhaps one with boxes to tick off, so that they'll feel more useful when it comes time to pack everything.

➡ Let them choose their clothes to pack and help them eliminate anything unnecessary. Maybe suggest some additions.

➡ To motivate them even more, promise to buy them something new for the trip (a game, an item of clothing...) in return for their cooperation.

Highlights

Here are some activities to keep little travellers busy that you might like, too.

Face to Face with Nature

A few minutes from Castelgrande is a small **Butterfly House** (p120) inhabited by several species of colorful tropical butterflies. Children are sure to enjoy the interactive displays at the **Museo di Storia Naturale del Vulture** (p122), especially the section dedicated to the Brahmaea, an extremely rare moth that has miraculously avoided extinction for 750,000 years.

In the **beech forest of Viggiano** (p132) is a small museum dedicated to the wolf where you'll see, among other things, some stuffed examples of the animal. You can also join educational hikes through the forest. The **Riserva Naturale Bosco Pantano di Policoro** (p88) organises activities and summer stays in search of otters, turtles and the other animals that inhabit this area in what was once an ancient forest overlooking the sea. **Microworld** (p164), an interesting theme park set on the shores of a lake, takes young visitors on a journey of discovery through the planet's geological processes.

At **Basilicata Alpaca** (p106) your children can pet fluffy South American alpacas, and take them for a walk in the beautiful surrounds.

Exploring the Sky

Near the **Astronomical Observatory in Castelgrande** (p120) is a centre where it's possible to look up at the stars through a telescope with a 40cm lens. Your kids can also admire the stars and planets at the **planetarium** in Anzi (p114), a village nestled in the woods south of Potenza.

Villages

The murals scattered around **Satriano di Lucania** (p115) make the village an interesting stop for travellers of all ages. Another spectacle sure to delight travellers young and old is **Pietrapertosa** (p108) whose amphitheatre-like village-scape is framed by phantasmagorical rock spires.

If the story of the abandoned village of **Craco** (p92) is dramatic, its evocative

Carnevale at Tricarico (p80)

power is irresistible to visitors of any age, and you'll feel like you're wandering around the set of an old western movie.

Parks to Explore

There are many activities to enjoy with children in the **Parco Nazionale del Pollino** (p138), but for something special, you can turn to Viaggiare nel Pollino (www.viaggiarenelpollino.it), which organises family tours (with children aged between five and 18), rafting trips and adventure treks through the park.

Before venturing into the **Parco della Murgia Materana** (p68), it's worth stopping off at the Jazzo Gattini Visitor Centre in Murgia Timone, where numerous children's activities are offered, including craft workshops with ferula wood.

Sport & Entertainment

The **Parco Avventura del Pollino** (p144), in the Bosco Magnano (Magnano Woods) at San Severino Lucano, has three aerial rope courses and offers activities, from mountain biking and orienteering to Nordic walking and trekking. And in the forest

streams, you might just see an otter. You have to be aged 10 years or older to go on the electrifying **Volo dell'Aquila** (p147) but the nearby **Pollino Outdoor Park** (p148), still in San Costantino Albanese, is open to all ages with dedicated trails for adults, children and toddlers. The **Circolo Velico Lucano** (p88) organises sailing courses for kids every summer at Lido di Policoro. The rides at the **Parco delle Stelle** (p160) provide a truly festive afternoon after a visit to the nearby sanctuary. Finally, the **Giostra Panoramica RB Ride** (p144) may be the world's slowest merry-go-round, but we're convinced your children will love it.

From Hominids to Elephants

The paleontological park at **Notarchirico** (p130), near Venosa, will hopefully reopen soon, because the fragment of a femur from a *Homo erectus* is not something you get to see every day. Take solace in the **Museo Naturalistico e Paleontologico del Pollino** (p140), where you can round off your time in the Parco Nazionale del Pollino by examining the (almost complete) skeleton of an *Elephas antiquus*

BEACH LIFE

Maratea (p150) is an enchanting seaside resort with beautiful (though often high and rocky) coves and a string of free or serviced (not always sandy) beaches extending down the 30km of the Gulf of Policastro on the Tyrrhenian Sea. For a romantic trip, it's the best Basilicata has to offer. Families, however, might prefer the Ionian coast where the beaches of Metaponto (p85) and Policoro (p87) offer fine sand for castle building, shallow waters and kiosks for buying ice cream.

italicus and the jawbone of a *Hippopotamus amphibius.*

The Wonders of Matera

You don't need to be an art history buff to enjoy walking around the rocky walls of the **Chiesa di Santa Maria de Idris** (p45) and letting their bizarre lines spark your storytelling imagination.

The underground allure of the Sassi city is on full display in the **Palombaro Lungo** (p55). Visits to the enormous underground cistern in the bowels of the Piano district are brief and even your little ones will be impressed.

With a little imagination in your descriptions, the phantasmagorical sculptures of the **MUSMA** (p55), which are displayed in long caves, could appeal to children. Finally, the recently-opened, **Racconti in Pietra** (p54) is the only one of Matera's many museums aimed expressly at children. The idea is to have fun while learning about paleontology.

Castles

Kids will enjoy the interactive tour of the **Castello del Malconsiglio** (p75), complete with a re-enactment of the dinner at which the Conspiracy of the Barons was hatched. Meanwhile, the martial, unadorned **Castel Lagopesole** (p121) should be visited with stories of knights and battles. Inside, its Museum of Emigration is highly interactive.

Rites, Festivals & Performances

Children won't be able to resist the allure of the sassi illuminated by the Christmas lights of a **Living Nativity** (p58), whose actors will bring Galilee to life in this corner of the Murgia.

Children should beware of wandering Montescaglioso on the night of Epiphany: during the **Notte dei Cucibocca** (p77) mysterious, darkly-clad figures go round frightening children, who run to bed.

Bears, walking trees, bulls and horned masks all feature in Basilicata's **Carnevale**, notably in Aliano (p95), Tricarico (p79) and Satriano di Lucania (p115). Then there are the local **tree weddings**. These propitiatory rites are celebrated in various towns – the most engaging festivals are in Rotonda (p141), Castelmezzano (p110) and Accettura (p81).

Go and greet Podolica cows with a festive walk on the Murgia – it's the **Notte della Transumanza** (p161). End the day with songs and music around the campfire.

The **Storia Bandita** (see boxed text, p106) is a grand spectacle staged in Brindisi di Montagna and involving 500 extras in the re-enactment of Carmine Crocco's exploits. The Grancia Forest offers events of great interest to kids, with a falconry arena, petting farm, itinerant concerts and plenty of entertainment.

On the Road

Matera Province

Best Places to Eat

➡ Ego (p64)

➡ Vitantonio Lombardo (p63)

➡ Le Bubbole (p64)

➡ Trattoria Nugent (p74)

➡ Sartago (p80)

Best Places to Stay

➡ Sextantio Le Grotte della Civita (p60)

➡ Palazzo Gattini (p60)

➡ Palazzo dei Poeti (p92)

➡ San Teodoro Nuovo (p86)

➡ Marinagri (p89)

Why Go?

Matera's fame now compares to that of Italy's biggest tourist destinations, and the global interest that was unleashed in 2019 when it was appointed European Capital of Culture has become the new norm. Thus the irresistible beauty of the City of the Sassi has become the area's undisputed drawcard.

However, away from the rock churches, caves and baroque palaces of the city, the province has plenty to offer. The landscapes of the Matera area, for example, are heavenly. The Parco della Murgia Materana, just across the Gravina gorge, with its aromatic medicinal herbs, wildflowers and air of adventure; the wild, barren expanse of the badlands, celebrated by poets and writers; the woods of the Foresta di Gallipoli Cognato, where a past of remote archaic rituals goes hand in hand with human history – these all promise weeks' worth of emotion. And then there are the artistic treasures in villages such as Irsina, Montescaglioso, Miglionico and Tricarico, and evocative abandoned villages like Craco. On the Ionian coast you can split your time between days of relaxation on the popular beaches and cultural tours in search of the thrilling vestiges of Magna Graecia that abound in this ancient land.

When to Go

The Matera area promises satisfaction year-round. In summer, when the heat is often ferocious, Matera can get a bit crowded and the stalls on the Ionian beaches can mar any image you might have of a seaside paradise. However, the profusion of festivals and events is at a year-round high. Autumn is often gentle and mild, ideal for sightseeing and enjoying food and wine, while spring offers the rare chance to admire fields of an otherworldly green – the chromatic opposite of the parched summer colours – as well as opportunities for early swimming and nature hiking. There are fewer outdoor prospects in winter, but Matera is quieter and more charming than ever.

Matera Province Highlights

1 Be wowed by **Matera** (p44): it doesn't matter what criteria you use to judge a city, this one will amaze you.

2 Explore the caves, ravines and rock churches of the **Murgia Materana** (p68).

3 Take a dip in the crystal clear waters of the **Ionian coast** (p83).

4 Pay homage to Carlo Levi in **Aliano** (p94), in the heart of the badlands.

5 Explore an Arab townscape and poetic atmosphere in enchanting **Tursi** (p91).

6 Marvel at the Abbazia di San Michele Arcangelo in **Montescaglioso** (p76).

7 Discover why dozens of foreigners buy houses in **Irsina** (p71).

8 Enjoy a glass of Amaro Lucano and the charming narrow lanes in **Pisticci** (p83).

9 Wander **Tricarico** (p78), one of Basilicata's culturally rich villages.

MATERA

POP 60,521 / ALT 401M

One thing's for sure – you may have seen hundreds of photos and documentaries, listened to the accounts of friends and relatives, carefully studied its history, yet nothing can prepare you for the impact Matera will have on you. The city never fails to shock. Just look around and in an instant your gaze will go from the caves beyond the Gravina, where thousands of years ago our ancestors warmed themselves by fire, to the refined baroque architecture of the Piano district, from the intimate spaces of rock churches to the increasingly trendy atmosphere of the many clubs in the historic centre, from the triumph of indomitable nature to that of human ingenuity and adaptability. And while no words can capture the complexity of this incredible city, the way that its luminously rich architecture contrasts with its subterranean voids and the light transforms shapes as it changes throughout the day and through the seasons, makes for an aesthetically unmissable experience and a true adventure of the soul.

History

In few places is it as important as it is in Matera to study the city's history in order to understand its development. The city doesn't have a precise foundation date. Certainly the caves of the Parco della Murgia Materana (p68) were inhabited in prehistoric times and there was, perhaps, a Roman outpost here, but it wasn't until the 7th century that the city began to take on its unmistakable urban form.

The first settlement was the present Civita which, until the 16th century, was surrounded by mighty defensive walls. Over the centuries, the Sassi grew prosperous – the capacity to store foodstuffs for years in caves made it possible to profit from their price changes. Matera became a thriving town, equipped with a comprehensive canal network for sewerage and water supply. In 1663 it was elected capital of Basilicata and the Piano district flourished as baroque churches and opulent palaces, many of which can still be seen today, were built.

But decline eventually set in. The reasons for this inexorable downturn can be traced to the early 19th century – Potenza was made regional capital; the industrial revolution and improved production techniques rendered the caves less profitable places to work; and ownership of the surrounding countryside passed from the Church to private individuals, who forbade the peasantry from living there. It was this combination of events that led agricultural labourers, deprived of their homes, to live in the caves. Over time, overcrowding eventually turned the Sassi into the dramatic place described by Carlo Levi in *Christ Stopped at Eboli*. By 1950, even if only 4000 of the Sassi's 18,000 inhabitants lived in caves (the others lived in regular buildings), the rate of infant mortality had reached 50 percent and beggars were pleading for money and quinine.

After WWII, Matera became the target of choice for American propaganda promoting the Marshall Plan (which aimed to lift the European countries emerging from WWII out of poverty and ward off the spectre of Soviet influence) as well as a symbol in Italy for the need to bounce back from the dark days of fascism. And so, in 1952, the De Gasperi law ordered a complete clearing out of the districts – residents were moved to neighbourhoods built by the most celebrated architects of the day (thanks to substantial

SASSI & MISUNDERSTANDINGS

Matera is known worldwide for the Sassi, but most visitors are misled by the usual meaning of the word. The Sassi are not large excavated rocks, nor are they cave-houses. Rather the term indicates the two districts of the old city, the Sasso Barisano and Sasso Caveoso. And there are no natural caves here, only artificial caves originally dug as places for the production and storage of wine, oil and grain. The excavated material was then used to construct a building in front – in essence, behind every building in the Sassi lies a cave, which is invisible from outside. A further misunderstanding concerns the stone with which the city was built: it's not *tufo* (tuff), which is of volcanic origin, but calcarenite, which comes from the oceans. Look at the walls of buildings and you'll easily spot fossils of shells, fish bones and sharks' teeth. Thus Matera has its roots not only in the bowels of the earth but also in the depths of the sea.

THE MOST BEAUTIFUL VIEWS OF MATERA

If you have a lyrical soul and are in need of heart-wrenching contemplation, Matera is the city for you. There are many places where you can enjoy views of incomparable beauty:

Piazza Pascoli: the classic location to take a spectacular photo – even if you'll have to elbow your way through in high season – is near Palazzo Lanfranchi (p57). At dawn, the light is magnificent.

Via San Giacomo: use the MUSMA (p55) as a reference and head up the road for a further 70m. There you'll be able to look out on a view that reveals the geological make-up of the whole area – the Gravina with its layer of hard limestone, the Sasso Caveoso modelled in calcarenite, and there, where the rock finishes, the buildings and trees of the modern town.

Chiesa di Santa Maria de Idris (p52): an extraordinary spot that's both close enough and sufficiently distant to offer breadth, allowing you to take in the chaotic poetry of the Sasso Caveoso, the palaces of the Piano, and the Cathedral.

Chiesa di Sant'Agostino (p49): don't tell anyone, but the view from this sacred place embraces the Sasso Barisano, part of the Sasso Caveoso, and the wild beauty of the Gravina in a single look.

Belvedere di Murgia Timone (p69): seen dozens of times in photos, the broadest view of the city is best contemplated at sunset, when the lights are turned on and even the most anti-conformist of travellers can't help but think of a nativity scene.

U.S. funds) and the ancient area became a melancholic ghost town of ruins. Matera tried to bury its 'national shame' status and identity. Baroque palaces were torn down in the Piano neighbourhood to make way for modern buildings attesting to the change. On a social level, the new generations largely abandoned the dialect of their parents.

At the same time, however, a certain part of the population fought for the Sassi to be recognised for their extraordinary urban and cultural configuration, not just for their de-gradation. In 1993, Matera was the first place in southern Italy to become a Unesco World Heritage Site and slowly repopulation began, led by the 20 percent of former residents who had retained possession of their homes (by refusing council houses in the displacement neighbourhoods and going to live elsewhere), and by those who had been granted property by the state property office. B&Bs and restau-rants were built where old stores had once been. Then in 2019, the designation of Matera as European Capital of Culture gave the city an international visibility that helped fuel the final push of its resurrection. Matera is now firmly established as one of Italy's iconic destinations, and the challenge of the future has shifted – it's no longer how to increase tourism but how to make it sustainable.

Orientation

You cannot say you've experienced Matera unless you get lost at least once in the stairways and labyrinthine alleyways of the Sassi. Fortunately for you, it's quite hard not to. That said, after a couple of days you'll have memorised enough landmarks to orient yourself. Via Fiorentini and Via Buozzi, until a century ago traversed by streams, are the main routes through the Sasso Barisano (the more central of the two Sassi districts) and the Sasso Caveoso. Walk up them and after a few steps you'll reach the Piano (the upper part of the city), which is crossed by Via Ridola and Via del Corso. Walk down them and you'll reach Via Madonna della Virtù which runs along the canyon of the Gravina. The Civita, the rocky spur on which the Cathedral stands, and which separates the two small valleys of the Sassi districts, is at the same height as the Piano, to which it's joined by Piazza San Francesco. The entire area, which comprises the historic centre, is bound to the west by Via Lucana.

◉ Sights

Unlike other cities capable of attracting torrents of tourists and travellers, Matera doesn't count a single attraction or monu-ment that by itself justifies a visit – you don't come to Matera for a museum or a palace,

Matera Cinema
LOCATIONS

PIAZZA DEL DUOMO

James Bond lands here after a spectacular motorcycle leap in *No Time to Die*, but the space in front of the Cattedrale (p54) has starred in many films, including *War, The New Gospel* and *One Sunday Night*.

PIAZZA SAN PIETRO CAVEOSO

When you admire this square overlooked by the church of the same name (p52) for the first time, you can't help but be amazed by its scenic location on the Gravina and the somewhat eccentric solemnity of the buildings in the background. It's no coincidence that it was chosen to shoot scenes for *La Lupa, The Demon, The Sun also Shines at Night,* and *The Star Maker* among other films.

VIA MURO

Even at a first glance, the long staircase up to the Civita district recalls the Middle East. Can you think of a better place for Mel Gibson to have depicted the Stations of the Cross in *The Passion of the Christ*? A little higher up is the palace of *Ben Hur* from the remake of the famous epic.

MURGIA TIMONE

The place which commands the most iconic view of the Sassi (p69), the Murgia would inspire anyone to shoot a film, let alone cinema professionals. Among the many works to have exploited its wild beauty, *The Gospel According to St. Matthew, Ben Hur* and *The Passion of the Christ* stand out, having placed Golgotha here.

VIA FIORENTINI

The main thoroughfare of the Sasso Barisano (p48) has appeared in numerous films, including *Il vaso di Pandora* and *Italian Race*. In 1975, the Spanish director Arrabal 'abused' it while filming scenes from the Spanish Civil War for *The Tree of Guernica* but thankfully without long-term consequences.

1. Piazza San Pietro Caveoso **2.** Stuntman in the alleys of Matera during the filming of *No Time to Die* **3.** The Sassi from Murgia Timone

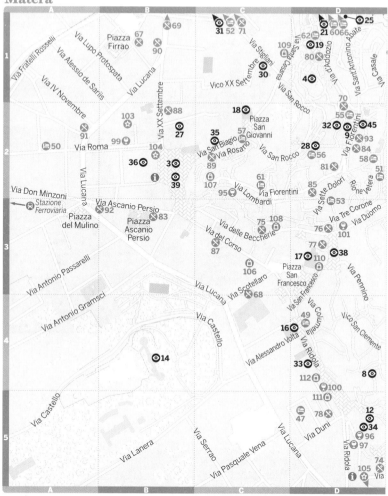

rather you come here to immerse yourself in its elusive atmosphere, one that can be brutal and violent in the summer sun, and romantic and dreamy on starry nights.

Castello Tramontano   CASTLE
(Map p48; Via del Castello) Standing on the Lapillo hill, behind Via Lucana and a stone's throw from the centre, this 15th-century Aragonese-style castle has a central keep and two massive towers. It was left unfinished after the death of Count Tramontano, who was murdered in 1514 by a group of exasperated citizens in a side street near the cathedral

– history tells of harassment and taxes imposed to fill empty state coffers, while legend refers to the practice of *jus primae noctis* by which the hated count claimed the "right" to peasants' wives. The castle, which has been under restoration for years and was still closed at the time of research, makes a striking impression with its imposing bulk and the cool gardens adjacent to it.

Sasso Barisano

The largest and most central of the Sassi is also the one with the most 'urban' look. The

exhibitions, adult/reduced €12/8) One of Matera's most jaw-dropping sites, this complex comprises dozens of caves and is capable of invoking spiritual peace and feelings of anguish, a sense of confinement and boundless leaps of thought. The 12th-century Chiesa della Madonna delle Virtù, a brilliant example of 'negative architecture' in that it was entirely excavated, bears all the hallmarks of Romanesque architecture – three naves, markedly vertical vaults, three domes framed by Greek crosses in relief. In the apse is a beautiful *Crocifissione* from the 16th century. The monastery below, bare but powerfully evocative, dates from the 10th century. Further up, the simple Byzantine Chiesa di San Nicola dei Greci stands out for its superb frescoes – in the right aisle, another *Crocifissione* (14th century); in the left apse a depiction of three saints, including St. Nicholas (13th century).

Chiesa di Sant'Agostino   CHURCH

(Map p48; Via d'Addozio) This monumental church and the Complesso Monastico di Sant'Agostino were built in the late 16th century and restored in 1747. They were later used as military barracks and a hospice for the elderly. Beyond the late baroque facade, the real reason to visit is the rupestrian Chiesa di San Giuliano, which is accessed from the interior (follow the signs in the left wing). This features 16th-century frescoes, interesting stone decorations and, best of all, a heart-rending view of the Gravina for those who climb that far.

Chiesa di San Pietro Barisano   CHURCH

(Map p48; ☑ 327 980 37 76/345 939 16 59; www.oltrelartematera.it; Via San Pietro Barisano; adult/reduced €3.50/2.50; ◷ 10am-4pm winter, 10am-7pm summer) The largest of the city's rupestrian churches will make an indelible impression thanks to the practice of its one-time resident monks to 'drain' their dead. The corpses, dressed in sacred vestments, were placed seated in special positions to allow for easy decomposition in the tiny underground rooms (if you want to enter the rooms, avoid eating too many crusco peppers the night before). The church probably dates to the 12th to 13th centuries, but it was enlarged in the 15th to 16th centuries and again in the 1700s, when it assumed its present three-aisle layout. The facade was added in 1755, complete with an unusual four-lobed rose window and two oval side openings. Most of the artworks it housed were stolen or damaged during the

caves here are never visible from outside and the harsh rocky terrain has been subjugated to meet the building needs of its inhabitants, lending the quarter a gentle, graceful appearance. Hidden in its depths, however, are several ruggedly beautiful wonders.

Complesso Monastico della Madonna delle Virtù e di San Nicola dei Greci   MONASTERY

(Map p48; ☑ 377 444 88 85; www.caveheritage.it; Via Madonna delle Virtù; ◷ 10am-1.30pm Nov-March, 10am-1.30pm & 3-6pm Apr-May & Oct, 10am-8pm Jun-Sep; rates vary depending on

Matera

decades when the Sassi were abandoned. The church now stages temporary exhibitions.

Casa Cava   CULTURAL CENTRE
(Map p48; ☎0835 33 67 33; www.casacava.it; Via San Pietro Barisano 47; adult/reduced tours €3/1.50, €2 with licensed tour guide, free under 14; ⊙10am-1pm & 3-6pm) A true symbol of the city's revival, this former quarry, once abandoned then used as a landfill, is now one of Matera's most active cultural centres. In addition to being an auditorium with extraordinary acoustics and a conference hall, it provides valuable evidence of the huge excavations that lie hidden in many Sassi buildings. It's worth a look even if there are no events on.

Museo Laboratorio della Civiltà Contadina   MUSEUM
(Map p48; ☎0835 34 40 57, 328 611 34 54; www.museolaboratorio.it; Via San Giovanni Vecchio 60; adult/reduced €3/2; ⊙9am-1pm & 4-7pm) If you want to know everything, and we mean everything, about life in the Sassi in times gone by, don't miss this very interesting museum. In the wide spaces of six connected dwellings you'll come across a barber's shop, a priest's bedroom, tons of objects, documents and artefacts that once belonged to basket makers, carpenters, saddle makers and tailors. Allow at least a couple of hours for an in-depth visit.

Casa di Ortega   MUSEUM
(Map p48; ☎3669 35 77 68; www.casaortega.it; Via San Nicola del Sole; adult/reduced €5/3.50, guided tours €20; ⊙10am-2pm Tue-Sun Sep-Jul, 10am-2pm daily Aug) José Ortega, an anti-Francoist painter and sculptor, bought this house in the 1970s. Inside are 20 powerfully expressive polychrome bas-reliefs which were made in collaboration with master papier-mâché makers from Matera. It's worth seeing, even if artistic experimentation isn't your thing, for the jaw-dropping view of the Murgia from the terrace.

THE DISPLACED NEIGHBOURHOODS

On May 17 1952, the Italian state promulgated law n. 619, ordering the complete evacuation of Matera's Sassi. But where to transfer the 18,000 people who lived there? In the following years the top architects of the age, from Quaroni and Piccinato to Aymonimo and De Carlo, set their imaginations to work to create ideal, self-sufficient neighbourhoods equipped with schools, churches, parks, shops and post offices. The most famous of these, La Martella (Map p69, A2), 7km west of the centre, was the only one designed to house farmers, with low houses equipped with stables (now often repurposed for other uses) and vegetable gardens. However, the easiest to visit is La Nera, a 15-minute walk from Piazza Vittorio Veneto along Via La Nera (the uphill road that passes Castello Tramontano on the right). It sports a more ordinary look, as does Serra Venerdì (take Viale Europa) and Spine Bianche, with its unmistakable red brick houses and a statue of De Gasperi at the crossroads between Via Nazionale and Via Manzoni. A tour of the districts, which were originally cut off from each other but are now part of the city's urban fabric, is recommended for history buffs and travellers with their own wheels, even if they're hardly thrilling in aesthetic terms.

Sassi in Miniatura ARTISANAL WORKSHOP
(Map p48; ☑0835 33 40 31; www.materasassi
inminiatura.it; Via Fiorentini 82; ⊘8.30am-7pm
Oct-March, 8.30am-9pm Apr-Sep) FREE If a map
means nothing more to you than a pleasant picture for your living room wall and
navigation in Matera remains an insoluble
enigma, help yourself by checking out this
scale reproduction of the Sassi. Measuring
twelve square meters and weighing more
than three tons, it was made in tufo rock by
Eustachio Rizzi in his workshop.

Giardino del Silenzio PARK
(Map p48; Vico Sant'Agostino; ⊘9am-5pmNov-
March, 9am-7pm Apr-Oct) This beautiful garden
with benches, flower beds and olive trees
makes an impression in the heart of Matera, partly because it's the only park in the
labyrinthine Sassi, and partly because it
juxtaposes successfully with the primordial
Murgia directly opposite. Ideal for a relaxing
break between visits.

○ Sasso Caveoso

Overlooking the wild and more typically
rocky Gravina, this is where the equilibrium

ⓘ SAVE MONEY

Three of Matera's most important churches, **Santa Maria de Idris** (p52),
Santa Lucia alle Malve (p52) and **San
Pietro Caveoso** (p52), are managed
by the **Beyond the Art cooperative**
(☑345 939 16 59; www.oltrelartematera.it),
which offers combined tickets to fans of
the rupestrian atmosphere. Admission
to all three churches costs adult/reduced
€7/5, while admission to any two of your
choice is €6/4 and entry into a single
site is €3.50/2.50. A further ticket also
gives access to the MATA (p54), the
Vicinato a Pozzo (p53) and the Casa
Grotta di Via Fiorentini (p53); it costs
€13. And if you want to add the Raccolta
delle Acque (p53), the ticket price is
adult/reduced €15.50/13. Save money
with the **Synchronos cooperative**
(☑366 935 77 68) which, through the **Ze-
tema Foundation** (☑0835 33 05 82; www.
zetema.org; Recinto Cavone 5), manages
the **MUSMA** (p55), the **Casa di Ortega**
(p51) and the **Cripta del Peccato Originale** (p68). By visiting one site you're
entitled to a reduced ticket for the others.

---

between nature and human activity becomes more extreme and unrestrained. The
southern part is occupied by the Rione
Casalnuovo (Map p48), which is expected
to host a Parco della Storia dell'Uomo in the
near future (see boxed text p57). The presence
of many caves often leads travellers to think
this is the oldest part of the city, but, as the
name implies, it's exactly the opposite. This
is, in fact, the most peripheral offshoot of the
Sassi, where immigrant peasants from the
Balkans lived in the 16th century.

Chiesa di San Pietro Caveoso CHURCH
(Map p48; Piazza San Pietro Caveoso) Overlooking the square of the same name, this
is the only church in the Sassi not hewn out
of limestone and with a normal appearance
(even if its setting on the edge of the Gravina
is hardly normal). The original building dates
to the 14th century but the facade is baroque,
the result of a 17th-century makeover. Of
note is the 16th-century tufo sculpture of
the *Madonna col Bambino* in the right aisle,
and the wooden polyptych of the *Madonna
col Bambino e i santi Pietro e Paolo* (1540)
on the high altar.

Chiesa di Santa Maria de Idris CHURCH
(Map p48; ☑3279 80 37 76, 3459 39 16 59; www
.oltrelartematera.it; adult/reduced €3.50/2.50;
⊘10am-4pm winter, 10am-7pm summer) Welcome
to one of Matera's most spectacular sights.
Carved into the side of a giant boulder,
Mount Errone (or Monterrone, or Mount
Idris), this church recalls the exotic atmosphere of Petra, the dreamlike construc-
tions of Cappadocia, and the architectural
boldness of Ethiopia's sacred sites. Before
entering, take a 360-degree look around the
rock for views over the Gravina, Cathedral,
Civita and entire Sasso Caveoso. Once inside,
check out the 17th-century *Madonna con
Bambino* on the altar, before taking the dark
corridor to the hidden church of San Giovanni in Monterrone. Here you'll find some
striking frescoes dating from the 12th century
(like the oriental-looking *Cristo Pantocratore*
on the left) to the 17th century.

Chiesa di Santa Lucia alle Malve CHURCH
(Map p48; ☑327 980 37 76, 345 939 16 59; www.oltr
elartematera.it; Rione Malve; adult/reduced €3.50
/2.50; ⊘10am-4pm winter, 10am-7pm summer)
Built in the 8th century to house a Benedictine convent, this church boasts an ornate
portal and a series of frescoes dating from
the 12th century, including a wonderfully
delicate *Madonna del latte* in the left aisle,

CAVE LIVING

If you want to get an idea of the Matera described by Carlo Levi and maybe give yourself a reason to stop complaining about the size of your apartment, a visit to one of the Sassi's cave houses is just the job. Bear in mind that there are a growing number in the city – the following list is far from exhaustive – but, to put it brutally, once you've seen one, you've seen them all. The most impressive is the Casa Grotta di Vico Solitario (Map p48; ☑0835 31 01 18; www.casagrotta.it; Vicinato di Vico Solitario 11; adult/reduced €3/2; ⊙9.30am-5.30pm winter, 9.30am-8.30pm summer), which was inhabited until 1956 by a family of 11 people, plus chickens and animals. This space, equivalent to a two-room apartment, had everything necessary for the life of an agricultural labourer, from a single table around which everyone ate to a sideboard whose open drawers served as beds for the children, from a pile of manure to a bed stuffed with corn leaves, from a mule stable to a cistern. Life would have beeen very similar in the Casa Grotta di Via Fiorentini (Map p48; ☑0835 33 40 31; www.anticamatera.it; Via Fiorentini 251; adult/reduced €2/1; ⊙9am-6pm Oct-March, 8.30am-9pm Apr-Sep), decorated with human sculptures in tuff rock, and in the five-room Casa Grotta del Casalnuovo (Map p48; ☑339 364 85 37, 333 712 62 87; www.casagrottadelcasalnuovo.com; Rione Casalnuovo 309; adult/reduced €2/1.50, €3/2 incl Cripta di Sant'Andrea; ⊙9.30am-5.30pm Nov-Mar, 9.30am-7.30pm Apr-Oct), near the Cripta di Sant'Andrea (Map p48; adult/reduced €2/1.50), which seems to descend into an abyss. Alternatively, you could opt for the Casa Cisterna (Map p48; ☑348 174 31 35; www.casa cisterna.it; Ponte San Pietro Caveoso 39; adult/under 15 €2/free; ⊙10am-7pm Mar-Oct, 10am-2pm Nov-Feb, extended opening during the Christmas period), which displays tools used during the harvest; the Casa Grotta Sassi di Matera – C'era una Volta (Map p48; ☑342 808 77 03; www.casagrottanarrante.com; Via Madonna delle Virtù 27; adult/reduced €3/1; ⊙10am-5.30pm Oct-Mar, 10am-8pm Apr-Sep), where the tone of the narration is more tender than dramatic; the Casa Grotta del Vicinato (Map p48; ☑379 185 22 92 ; www. casagrottadelvicinato.com; Via Purgatorio Vecchio 21; tickets €2; ⊙9.30am-5.30pm Oct-Mar, 9.30am-7.30pm Apr-Sep); or the Casa Grotta Senza Nidd (Map p48; ☑334 923 07 86, 339 355 67 73; www.senzanidd.it; Calata di Via Ridola 65; adult/reduced €3/2; ⊙9.30am-6pm).

and a stylised *Incoronazione della Vergine* in the right aisle. In more recent times and up until 1960, it served as a dwelling, as evidenced by the grotesque cutting of the icon wall to demarcate a kitchenette on the left. Outside, towering over the structure, is a medieval cemetery from the Lombard period. Be careful not to trip over the stones.

MOOM – Matera
Olive Oil Museum   MUSEUM
(Map p48; ☑3807 01 50 42; www.moom.bio; Vico I Casalnuovo 3; adult/reduced €5/4; ⊙by reservation) Learn how olive oil was once produced at this intriguing museum, set in a 16th-century underground mill. Exhibits cover everything used in the process, from a stable and olive storage spaces to a millstone, presses, sedimentation wells, even the bed where the miller would rest his weary limbs after a hard day's work. Note that reservations must be made at least a day in advance.

Raccolta delle Acque   HISTORIC SITE
(Map p48; ☑340 665 91 07; www.laraccoltadelle acquematera.it; Via Purgatorio Vecchio 12/13; adult/under 18 €3/free; ⊙10am-1pm Nov-March, 10am-1pm & 3-6pm Apr-Jun, 10am-6.30pm Jul-Aug) Less spectacular (and less crowded) than the Palombaro Lungo, but just as instructive, this site showcases the ingenious rain and spring water collection system used to ensure the city's water supply for centuries. Check out the cistern, canals and ubiquitous *cocciopesto* (terracotta mortar used to waterproof the walls).

Vicinato a Pozzo   MUSEUM
(Map p48; ☑346 532 98 29; www.parcostoriauo mo.it; Rione Malve; adult/reduced €5/3; ⊙10am-4pm Nov-Mar, 10am-6pm Apr-May & Sep-Oct, 10am-8pm Jul-Aug) The first accessible part of the Parco della Civiltà Contadina (see boxed text p57), this uplifting multimedia tour illustrates the peculiarities of life in a typical *vicinato* (a living space shared by several families) at the time of the sassi's evacuation. Six videos, projected in six cave-houses and

FROM THE SASSO CAVEOSO TO THE GRAVINA

In most cities of the world, you'll find greenery in pretty parks where you can play ball, watch squirrels climb trees, spread out a blanket for a nap. Not in Matera. In the city of the Sassi, it takes only five minutes to go from sipping a cocktail in a sophisticated wine bar to breathing the aromas of juniper, ferula, thyme, and oregano in a setting that wouldn't look out of place in an adventure film. If that seems over-dramatic to you, try it for yourself – from **Porta Pistola** (Map p48), about halfway along Via Madonna delle Virtù, head down path 406. In no time you'll find yourself at the bottom of the Gravina. Cross the Tibetan bridge (p69), as if you've been teleported to the Himalayas, and make the tough ascent up the other side of the canyon to the Belvedere di Murgia Timone (p69). Here you can search out the caves and soak up the primordial atmosphere and rocky beauty of the landscape. But note that you shouldn't underestimate the route – wear suitable shoes (cases of sprains and small accidents involving tourists wearing flip-flops are very common) and bear in mind that the heat can be ferocious and there's nowhere you can fill up on water. Also make sure you do not get caught out when darkness falls, otherwise you risk spending a far from comfortable night. At the time of research, access to the path was free, but that could change in the future as authorities try to control the flow of visitors to the Murgia's churches.

featuring actors playing the parts of Carlo Levi, Olivetti and other figures important for the study of Matera's social history, describe how extreme proximity resulted in solidarity and envy, mutual support and resentment. Allow an hour for a visit.

Racconti in Pietra   MUSEUM
(Map p48; ☑ 338 944 55 07; Vico San Leonardo 9; adult/reduced €2.50/1; ☉ 11am-1pm & 4-7pm Tue-Sun) Did you know that dinosaur footprints, a whale skeleton and all kinds of fossils have been found around Matera? Whatever your answer to this question, this underground paleontological trail makes a pleasant distraction from the city's better known attractions. If you're travelling with children, however, put it right at the top of your list of must-see places.

⊙ La Civita

This, the oldest inhabited part of the city, forms a kind of natural bastion that juts out defiantly between the two Sassi districts. For centuries, it was the administrative, economic and religious centre of city life. The splendour and elegance of many of its palaces attests to the fact that Matera's era of 'national shame' was just one page in the city's complex, compelling history.

Cattedrale   CATHEDRAL
(Map p48; ☑ 0835 33 52 01; www.oltrelartemate ra.it; Piazza del Duomo, entrance on Via del Riscatto; reservation €1; ☉ 9am-6pm) A far cry from the introspective beauty of the rock churches

nearby, the cathedral, built between 1230 and 1270, dominates the city with its 54-metre bell tower (which it should soon be possible to climb). The facade, an austere model of Pugliese-Romanesque architecture with hanging arches and an imposing central rose window over the entrance portal, gives no hint of the Baroque flourishes inside. Here gilded arches rest on richly carved Romanesque capitals, a suspended wooden ceiling masks the original truss ceiling, and cornices and stucco adorn the once-bare surfaces of the original structure. Just inside, to the right, is the cathedral's most significant artwork, the *Giudizio Universale* by Rinaldo da Taranto (13th century), of which the Inferno and part of the Purgatory remain. Also of interest is the altarpiece *Vergine con bambino e santi* (1580) on the high altar, the choir carved in wood in 1453 by Giovanni Tantino and, above all, the stone nativity scene sculpted in 1534 by Altobello Persio in the last chapel on the left. Access at the time of research required reservations (online or in person). If you find yourself waiting, you can use the time to visit the adjoining MATA - Museo Diocesano (Map p48; ☑ 328 211 24 81; www.oltrel artemateria.it; Via Riscatto 12; tickets €3; ☉ 10am-6pm), which has a remarkable collection of vestments, textiles, miters, sculptures and an 18th-century painting by Paolo De Matteis. Also included in the museum itinerary is the Cappella di Santa Maria di Costantinopoli, where the highly venerated *Madonna della Bruna* is kept (see boxed text, p58).

Casa Noha   MUSEUM
(Map p48; ☑0835 33 54 52; www.casanoha.it; Recinto Cavone 9; adult/15-26 years/4-14 years €6/4/2; ☉10am-5pm Mar, 10am-7pm Apr-Oct) Although of no great cultural-historical interest in itself, this FAI-owned building is the place to start a visit to Matera. Here you can watch a 25-minute film entitled *The Invisible Sassi. An Extraordinary Journey Through the History of Matera* (directed by Giovanni Carrada), which provides a comprehensive and evocative introduction to the city.

Palazzo Malvinni Malvezzi   HISTORIC BUILDING
(Map p48; Piazza Duomo; admission during temporary exhibitions free; ☉variable hrs) In addition to the interesting exhibitions that are routinely held here, this aristocratic palace, decorated between the 16th and 19th centuries, is living proof that the 20th-century narrative of absolute poverty in Matera tells only part of the historical story. In fact, its sumptuously frescoed rooms show that there were some people in the city who fared decidedly well. The view from the terrace is stunning.

★**MUSMA**   MUSEUM
(Map p48; ☑366 935 77 68; www.musma.it; Via San Giacomo; adult/reduced €7/4; ☉10am-6pm) The Museo della Scultura Contemporanea (Museum of Contemporary Sculpture) is the most important Italian museum dedicated entirely to sculpture. But if the *bravura* of the works in the 10 rooms of the 16th-century Palazzo Pomarici is slightly overshadowed by the stateliness of the setting, head to the seven underground rooms below. Here the juxtaposition of the sculptural forms with that of the caves is enhanced by the hermetic lighting of the spaces to achieve an astonishing degree of expressive eloquence. Among the many famous names represented in the 2,000 sq m of exhibition space are Manzù, Cascella, Moore and Kadish among others. Not to be missed.

◉ Il Piano

The tormented beauty of Matera suddenly gives way to the harmonious features of the Piano district – Piazza Vittorio Veneto, Via del Corso and Via Ridola constitute a parade of baroque and 19th-century magnificence, evoking aesthetic ideals more soothing than the intimate yet tortured streets of the Sassi.

Piazza Vittorio Veneto   PIAZZA
(Map p48) This, the town's salon, is where elderly folk stop to discuss the weather, tourists recharge their batteries after exploring the steep streets of the Sassi, and the sky seems bigger and bluer than anywhere else. Laid out in 1880 when the medieval walls were torn down, the piazza is home to the 18th-century **Palazzo dell'Annunziata** (Map 48) and **Biblioteca Provinciale** (☑0835 30 65 13; www.biblioteca.matera.it;☉8.30am-6.30pm Mon-Thu, 8.30am-1.30pm Fri) with its 300,000 books, small stores and cafes.

★**Palombaro Lungo**   HISTORIC SITE
(Map p48; ☑339 363 83 32; www.palombaro lungo.it; Piazza Vittorio Veneto; adult/under 18 €3/ free; ☉visits every 20 min 10am-1pm & 3pm-6pm, until 7pm Jul and Aug) This vast cistern under Piazza Vittorio Veneto is the most magnificent of the city's underground sights. Built from the 16th century onwards as a public water reserve, it comprises a labyrinth of caves, tunnels and cellars that stretches from the Chiesa di San Domenico to the Palazzo dell'Annunziata. If the term *palombaro* is a generic allusion to a place where water is collected, the *lungo* (long) is a reference to an extensive above-ground well that was built with as many as six openings. The size of the reservoir, which was essential to the

A TURINESE IN MATERA

If the Turinese doctor, painter and writer Carlo Levi hadn't been sentenced for his political activities and confined to the village of Aliano (p94), the history of Matera, or at least the narrative surrounding it, would have been very different. In his undisputed masterpiece, *Christ Stopped at Eboli*, Levi raises the age-old problem of the south with eloquence and poetic vigour, and quotes his sister in giving a merciless, dramatic description of the Sassi – 'They were like a schoolboy's idea of Dante's Inferno' – and the troglodyte houses, malaria, malnutrition, and children with swollen bellies tormented by lice and flies. It was thanks to the merits (or faults?) of this book that Matera became the 'shame of Italy' in the collective imagination and, in the post-war years, the improvement of Matera's living conditions became a national cause.

ON THE FUNCTION OF MOST CAVES

For various reasons, including the ever-increasing number of cave-dwellings set up as tourist sites (see boxed text p53), many people think that the underground caves were almost always used as homes. But this isn't the case. At least until the 19th century and the overcrowding of the 20th century, the majority of underground spaces were used to produce or store food. To clarify your ideas, it could be useful to visit the **MUde-SCA – Museo dello Scavo** (Map p48; 366 723 93 51; www.mudesca.it; Via Tommaso Stigliani 15; adult/reduced €3/2; 10am-1pm & 3-7pm) or the **MUST** (Map p48; 0835 188 33 83; www.mustmatera.com; Via San Biagio 15; adult/reduced €7/5; 10am-1pm & 4-7pm Tue-Fri, 10am-7pm Sun Nov-Mar, 10am-7pm Tue-Sun Apr-Oct). At the former, right next to the delightful 17th-century **Chiesa di San Biagio**, you'll see a press and millstone for pressing the grapes, a cellar for storing barrels and, in another room, four cisterns for collecting water. The MUST was used for similar purposes (as well as serving as a tannery for a certain period), but its museum displays are more eclectic with an unusual underground garden, a tribute to cinematic Matera and the entrance to a WWII air-raid shelter.

city's water supply until the construction of an aqueduct in the fascist era, is truly staggering – with a depth of 15 m, it could hold 5 million litres of water. These days, however, it offers visitors a glimpse of a water system of unparalleled ingenuity (one of the features Unesco highlighted when it designated Matera a World Heritage Site was precisely its water collection system), as well as entry into a dreamlike, twilight dimension. Book ahead in busy periods.

Once outside, note the covered space to your left. This looks like a tunnel that leads down from Piazza Vittorio Veneto to the Sasso Barisano but is, in fact, an ancient sacred place. The original function of the **Chiesa di Santo Spirito** can be deciphered from the aisles and a few worn frescoes.

Materasum
HISTORIC SITE

(Map p48; 331 105 40 31, 0835 33 68 52; www.ipogeomaterasum.com; Recinto XX Settembre 7; adult/reduced €7/5; 9am-1pm & 3-7pm, night tours by appointment) The exact history and function of this 1200 sq m of underground space, excavated on several layers, are not known. Don't expect any artistic wonders, but the video is interesting and the vents and underground areas are not lacking in charm.

Chiesa del Purgatorio
CHURCH

(Map p48; Via Ridola) For a blast of baroque cheer, don't miss this lovely church, inaugurated in 1756 and chock-full of skeletons, skulls and haunting references to the theme of death (as well as plenty of less macabre little angels). The green doorway, set into the sinuous convex facade, hints at the drama

to come inside. The Greek-cross interior is topped by a high dome on which the Church Fathers and Evangelists are depicted. It often hosts interesting temporary exhibitions (for which you'll have to pay admission).

Chiesa di San Francesco d'Assisi
PLACE OF WORSHIP

(Map p48; Piazza San Francesco) The church's imposing late baroque 18th-century facade clearly recalls Lecce's style of architecture. However, the building dates from the 13th century when it was constructed atop two underground churches (which are accessible via a trapdoor in the third chapel on the left but closed to the public). The interior, with its white stucco, impresses with its unmistakable southern-Italian elegance.

Piazza del Sedile
PIAZZA

(Map p48) Where's Matera's geographic centre? There's no need to check with a town planner to position it in this square, home to the eponymous palace. Built in 1540 to host town meetings, the palazzo now houses the city's Conservatory. After you've admired its bell towers and the statues of the cardinal virtues in the niches, and as violins and trumpets play in the background, you'll realise that this is where the Piano, Civita and routes to both Sassi converge.

Museo Nazionale di Matera
MUSEUM

(www.museonazionaledimatera.it) In 2020 Matera's two main museums merged to become a single institution, while maintaining their original locations and thematic features. Housed in the 17th-century Convento di Santa Chiara, the **Museo Archeologico**

Ridola (Map p48; ☑0835 31 00 58; Via Ridola 24; adult/reduced €5/2; ☉9am-8pm), named after the doctor and scholar whose private collection formed the initial nucleus of the collection, is the oldest of its kind in Basilicata (1911). Its layout fulfills the dusty expectations of those who want an archaeological museum to have display cases full of decorated pebbles from the Paleolithic age, tomb findings, wooden objects, vases and red-figure craters from the Magna Graecia period. But it also throws in some whimsical touches, such as the reconstruction of a Neolithic cave and hut, and it clearly illustrates the area's history thanks to its revamped chronological layout. It periodically hosts temporary exhibitions. Also take a look at the adjoining Chiesa di Santa Chiara where the baroque painted panels over the altar can, from a distance, be mistaken for statues.

Palazzo Lanfranchi MUSEUM
(Map p48; ☑0835 256 25 40; Piazza Giovanni Pascoli; adult/under 18 €4/2; ☉9am-8pm) A stone's throw from the proverbial terrace of Piazza Pascoli (see boxed text p45) this supreme expression of Matera's 17th-century style houses an important art collection. On the ground floor, visitors are stunned by Carlo Levi's most famous work, the enormous *Lucania '61*, a canvas of mixed styles created for the centenary of the Unification of Italy. Its six panels, assembled in sequence and with an overtly political imprint, use a vibrant expressionist language to tell of the tensions, tragedies and passions of post-World War II Basilicata and to celebrate the figure of Rocco Scotellaro (see boxed text p79), who is portrayed centre stage. On the second floor are sections devoted to local sacred art and the collection of Camillo d'Errico, with some

fine pieces attributed to Francesco Cairo and Salvator Rosa. The last part is dedicated to contemporary art and includes several portraits by Carlo Levi and a selection of works by Materano painter Luigi Guerricchio. At the time of research, the building, which was initially a seminary and later a school (where Giovanni Pascoli taught between 1882 and 1884), was undergoing renovation work. That didn't, however, spoil a tour of the museum.

Chiesa di San Giovanni Battista CHURCH
(Map p48; ☑0835 33 41 82; Via San Biagio) Standing on a graceful little piazza, this church is one of the most interesting in the city. Originally built in 1220 but revamped several times, it boasts a Romanesque exterior, a simple, stone interior imaginatively decked out with anthropomorphic, zoomorphic and floral capitals and an atmosphere charged with devotion. The 17th-century wooden sculpture of the Pietà in the left aisle is noteworthy. Perpendicular to the structure, the Ex Ospedale di San Rocco stages temporary exhibitions.

Museo del Comunismo e della Resistenza MUSEUM
(Map p48; ☑331 237 88 62; www.casa-museo-comunismo-matera.jimdofree.com; Via Gattini 4; ☉5-7pm Mon, 10am-noon & 5-7pm Wed & Fri) FREE For a departure from the 'Matera-centric' theme of most city sites, this museum showcases archival documents, photographs, posters, and scarves themed on the history of communism and anti-fascism. Thus you'll find material on the October Revolution and Mao's China, on Gramsci and Berlinguer, on Fidel Castro and Che Guevara. Of particular relevance is the focus on the Spanish Civil War.

NEW IN MATERA

The international attention Matera enjoyed in 2019, the year it was European Capital of Culture, hasn't exhausted the city's revival, which continues apace with the addition of new attractions, museums and events. The most ambitious project involves the creation of a vast multi-site museum, the Parco della Storia dell'Uomo, aimed at chronicling the area's millenary history and developing some highly representative sites. It is divided into four sections, including one on prehistory, which focuses on the Neolithic village of Murgia Timone, and one dedicated to the rupestrian churches (again in Murgia Timone), both of which are accessed through the Centro Visite Jazzo Gattini (p71). Around 10km northeast of the city, the SPARKme Space Academy boasts a planetarium and observatory, while the section on Civiltà Contadina, which calls for the restructuring of the entire Casalnuovo district (including the four rock churches of the Convicinio di Sant'Antonio), has already been inaugurated at the Vicinato a Pozzo (p53).

MATERA'S FAVOURITE FESTIVAL

If you had to pick a festival that symbolises Matera from the city's packed events calendar, it would certainly be the Festa della Madonna della Bruna. Held every July 2, it centres on a statue of the city's patron saint, which is paraded around the streets on a cart richly decorated with papier-mâché (the use of this modest material dates back to ancient times). Once the procession has ended (and the statue has been removed) the brutal and auspicious assault of the cart begins and crowds of people intent on grabbing a souvenir attack and destroy it. If you're intrigued and happen to be in the city at the wrong time, head to the MIB - Museo Immersivo della Bruna (Map p48; ✆0835 540 57 59; www.mibmatera.it; Recinto III Fiorentini 8; adult/reduced €6/3; ⊙4-8pm Fri, 10am-8pm Sat & Sun), which has a rich multimedia display and, best of all, a lifesize reconstruction of the cart.

✯✯ Festivals & Events

Living Nativity CHRISTMAS PERIOD
(www.presepematera.it) Considering that Matera is often compared to a nativity scene, it goes without saying that the version of the Nativity acted out by local Lucanian actors is a show not to be missed, even if you're not a fan of this kind of spectacle.

Festival Duni JULY-SEPTEMBER
(www.festivalduni.it) An important date for classical music, this festival is organised by the city's Conservatory and its symphony orchestra.

Sagra della Fedda Rossa e della Crapiata 31 JULY-1 AUGUST
This is a good time to venture out to La Martella district and learn more about a peculiar peasant tradition – one evening is dedicated to *fedda rossa* (toasted bread, oil and tomato), the other to *crapiata*, a soup of legumes and cereals which, before the evacuation of the Sassi, was made on one night of the year with beans, chickpeas and barley contributed by neighbourhood residents according to their means.

Matera Cielo Stellato 10 AUGUST
Imagine that every artificial light has been turned off and many small lamps have been lit. At this point it's hard for visitors to tell whether the stars are still in the sky or are being magically reflected in the Sassi. An unforgettable show.

Gezziamoci AUGUST
(www.onyxjazzclub.it) The Onyx Jazz Club has been promoting this end-of-summer festival for almost three decades. Events are staged in Matera's clubs and piazzas as well as in other regional cities.

Women's Fiction Festival SEPTEMBER
(www.womensfictionfestival.com) A few very intense days dedicated to (not just) women's literature – workshops, meetings, face-to-face appointments with editors and literary agents in a stimulating and buzzing atmosphere.

🛏 Sleeping

Matera might be the ever-growing world champion of hotel accommodation, but still you'll need to book ahead for summer (August in particular) and over long weekends. The average price is decidedly higher than in the rest of Basilicata: in high season it's almost impossible to sleep in the Sassi for less than €100 (indeed, it's not hard to find accommodation costing double or even triple that). However, rates can drop by 50% or more in the quieter periods. It should also be emphasised that even in the most sophisticated of places, the hospitality is almost always genuine. This impression was recently certified by Booking.com, which elected Matera the most welcoming city in the world for 2022.

Sasso Barisano

Sleeping in a cave in the Sassi is an experience not to be missed, and one that's usually rheumatism-proof, thanks to the effective dehumidification systems most facilities have. Many places can only be reached on foot, via narrow alleys and stairways, so bear this in mind when choosing your luggage.

Casa Vetere GUESTHOUSE €€
(Map p48; ✆333 296 67 22, 347 556 72 68, 0835 24 04 39; Via Sette Dolori 52-54; apt for 2/3/4/5 people €100/120/140/160; 🛜) This

classic accommodation in a cave buillding has charm, ample spaces, and comfortable beds. There's the possibility to cook. Ideal for groups of friends.

La Corte Vetere
B&B €€

(Map p48; ☑ 0835 33 58 11, 333 630 63 07; www.lacortematera.com; Rione Vetera 70; r €100-150) Perhaps the prices are slightly higher than elsewhere, but the care paid to each room is truly amazing – the 'Fireplace' room stands out for its artistic refinement; in the 'Grotto' room you can have the 'rockiest' pee of your life; and the noble 'Castelvecchio' apartment has four beds. Excellent breakfast.

Hotel Sassi
HOTEL €€

(Map p48; ☑0835 33 10 09; www.hotelsassi.it; Via San Giovanni Vecchio 89; s/d/ste €90/110/150; ❇☏) In a city where new B&Bs and room rentals are opening every day, being the first hotel to open in the Sassi district is quite a record. It has rooms spread over several levels and furnished in tasteful style. Perhaps a few bathrooms could do with an upgrade, but given the view and the abundant breakfast Hotel Sassi remains a recommendable option.

Le Origini
B&B €€

(Map p48; ☑ 0835 33 09 69, 391 771 86 58; www.hotelleorigini.it; Via D'Addozio 5; d/ste €150/250; ☏❇) A rising star of Matera's accommodation scene, this property near Chiesa di Sant'Agostino is renowned for its cleanliness, sophistication, original breakfasts, and suites equipped with whirlpool hot tubs.

Palazzo degli Abati
B&B €€

(Map p48; ☑0835 33 13 33; www.palazzodegliabati.it; Via San Pietro Barisano 27; standard/deluxe r €185/250; ❇☏) An institution in town, this amazing B&B is carved out of the former chapter house of the Chiesa di San Pietro Barisano. It offers everything a traveller could want – a mellow atmosphere, kind owners, clean rooms, a panoramic terrace, classy decor, and a hearty breakfast. Plus, the brand new suites are a true feast for the eyes.

Hotel Residence San Giorgio
HOTEL €€€

(Map p48; ☑0835 33 45 83; www.sangiorgio.matera.it; Via Fiorentini 259; s/d/q €160/190/250; ❇☏) The suites at this *albergo diffuso* (a hotel with rooms in several locations) may all be different, but a distinctly graceful elegance unites them. Dug out of 18th-century noble mansions in the heart of the Sasso Barisano, they wonderfully illustrate the architectural transformation of the Sassi. Special breakfasts can be prepared for guests with food intolerances.

Locanda di San Martino
HOTEL & SPA €€€

(Map p48; ☑0835 25 66 00; www.locandadisanmartino.it; Via Fiorentini 71; d €250, offers available on site; ☏❇☼) The Locanda's 33 rooms, connected by stairways and tunnels carved into the rock, have an austere, almost spiritual beauty which contrasts harmoniously with the hotel's pampering spa. Breakfast, sometimes served with background piano music, is one of the best in town. A superlative choice.

MATERA & THE CINEMA

The fact that the Città dei Sassi was chosen as a location for *No Time to Die* alerted even the most distracted of onlookers to Matera's select relationship with cinema. The list of films shot in the area since the 1950s is endless, and includes such extraordinarily successful films as Pasolini's *The Gospel According to St. Matthew*, Bruce Beresford's *King David*, *The Star Maker* by Tornatore, and Mel Gibson's *The Passion of the Christ*. After all, a city whose urban make-up seems to have sprung from a child's nocturnal fantasy rather than 21st-century reality, and which is surrounded by an untamed landscape, ideal as a setting from every era, can't not be loved by filmmakers. In addition to the constant presence of film crews, Matera's cinematic appeal is also testified to by two important events: the **Matera Film Festival** (www.materafilmfestival.it), held in October, with three international sections (feature films, short films and documentaries); and, held in September, the **MATIFF – Matera Art International Film Festival** (www.matiff.it), which focuses on eccentric themes and has a rich programme of events. If you want to take a cinema-orientated tour of the city, contact Antonio Rubino (☑329 472 77 61; www.amamatera.it; half-day guided tours €100 or per person €20).

LESSER KESTRELS

The amount of renovation work that has taken place in the Sassi in recent years has led to a notable increase in housing opportunities. Conversely, though, it has also led to a stark reduction. One of the victims of the situation is the poor lesser kestrel, which used to nest in the old city ruins between March and October having wintered in the warmth of Africa. To remedy the problem, the Province of Matera has set up a project to distribute artificial nests and install them on buildings. On your explorations you'll come across numerous signs attesting to the initiative and, simply by looking up, you'll see a few specimens of the small bird of prey circling in the sky. In the Murgia Materana area, there are a reported 2400 pairs of kestrels.

Sasso Caveoso

Accommodation here has the same characteristics as that in the Sasso Barisano, with the occasional added bonus of looking onto the primitive beauty of the Gravina.

Agli Archi RESIDENCE €€
(Map p48; ☑ 334 611 17 35; www.agliarchisassimt.it; Rione Pianelle 3/6; s/d/tr €70/90/110; 🗗 ✳) It's not as jaw-dropping as some other options nearby, but cleanliness is guaranteed, the location is stunning, and rates are honest. Plus, some rooms come with a view.

Le Dodici Lune RESIDENCE €€
(Map p48; ☑ 0835 25 63 65, 347 222 96 17; www.ledodicilune.it; Via San Giacomo 27; s/d/deluxe/ste €90/130/170/200, extra bed €25, apt per person €30-40; ✳ 🗗) Ideal for a thrilling romantic escape, this guesthouse a stone's throw from MUSMA offers beautiful soothing rooms with every comfort. Guests receive a 10 percent discount on spa treatments at the Palazzo Gattini spa.

Caveoso Hotel HOTEL €€€
(Map p48; ☑ 0835 31 09 31; www.caveosohotel.com; Piazza San Pietro Caveoso; d/ste/tr €150/200/210; ✳ @) An impeccable choice where rooms have their own entrances, ample views of the facade of the Chiesa di San Pietro Caveoso e sul Monte Idris, and a certain intimate charm. One suite is carved out of

a cave; the others are modern, comfortable and immaculately white.

Sant'Angelo LUXURY RESORT €€€
(Map p48; ☑ 0835 31 40 10; www.santangeloresort.it; Piazza San Pietro Caveoso; d from €300, variable rates, offers available on its wesbite ✳ 🗗) For an upscale caveman experience, the cave-houses of this amazing property will leave you speechless. They're immaculate in every detail and offer panoramic views of the Church of San Pietro Caveoso, Monte Idris, and on to the wild Gravina. Instead of a club, a red rose awaits you on arrival.

★**Sextantio Le Grotte della Civita** HOTEL €€€
(Map p48; ☑ 0835 33 27 44; www.sextantio.it/grotte-civita; Via Civita 28; d from €200, rates vary; 🗗 ✳ P) This is the second hotel in Italy managed by the Sextantio group and the Dom Society (the first is in Santo Stefano di Sessanio, in the province of L'Aquila, Abruzzo). The philosophy behind it is that of an *albergo diffuso* and is aimed at using tourism to revitalise buildings of so-called minor architecture (in this case an ancient Benedictine monastery). The setting is strikingly sophisticated and even travellers used to staying in the most exclusive places will be astonished by its ascetic beauty. Besides, it's not every day you get to have breakfast in a 13th-century rock church.

La Civita

The oldest part of the city has options housed in elegant mansions.

Capriotti B&B €€
(Map p48; ☑ 0835 33 39 97, 329 619 37 57, 328 186 22 11; www.capriotti-bed-breakfast.it; Recinto Annunziata Vecchia; s/d/tr €60/80/95; 🗗 ✳) Carved out of a 16th-century structure, this decent B&B offers striking views of the Sasso Barisano from its position right below the cathedral. The owners are friendly and helpful, rooms are comfortable with romantic outdoor tables and kitchenettes, and breakfast is a 'do-it-yourself' affair with produce from the kitchen.

★**Palazzo Gattini** HOTEL €€€
(Map p48; ☑ 0835 33 43 58; www.palazzogattini.it; Piazza Duomo 13; d from €190; 🗗 ✳) Let's put it this way – if you need to make up for something unforgivable and have one last, desperate chance, it would be a good idea to

book one of the sumptuous, high-ceilinged stuccoed rooms in this, the former residence of the Counts of Gattini. And if that doesn't work, you could at least enjoy the breakfast.

Il Piano & Outlying Districts

This section covers accommodation in the elegant streets of the Piano district and in more outlying areas (where prices are decidedly more accessible).

The Rock Hostel   HOSTEL €

(Map p48; ☑ 0835 68 07 07, 320 572 21 59; www. therockhostel.it; Via Santo Stefano 96; dm €20-22; 🛜) A hostel with a typically international atmosphere just outside the historic centre. It has two very clean eight-person single-sex dorms (plus a mixed room for four) and a large common room – one of the best places in Matera to meet other travellers.

Casa Vacanze Testa o Croce   B&B €

(Map p48; ☑ 329 375 88 80; Via della Croce 9/a; s/d €45/65; 🛜❄) Sure, the colour scheme is uninspiring and the fact that the private bathroom is outside the room isn't exactly the best, but you'll be a quarter-hour walk from the centre of Matera, in a comfortable space run by nice people. And what's more, the final bill will put you in a good mood.

Affittacamere Vicolo Fiore   GUESTHOUSE €€

(Map p48; ☑ 348 958 02 73; www.affittacamere vicolofiore.it; Vico Il Emanuele Duni 16; s/d standard/d deluxe/q €90/100/120/150; 🛜❄) Its four rooms are not perhaps the most character-filled, but they all have a certain sugary charm, and their cleanliness is not to be disputed. Add in the convenience of the location and the deals on the website, which offer even better rates, and it's to be promoted with flying colours.

Albergo Roma   HOTEL €€

(Map p48; ☑ 0835 33 39 12; www.albergoroma-matera.it; Via Roma 62; s/d/tr/q €80/130/160/200; 🛜❄) If the cool side of Matera annoys you and you prefer a retro atmosphere rather than a newly renovated structure that smacks of inauthenticity, this hotel has been in business since 1927. Its rooms are somewhat anonymous but they have hosted generations of travellers and their dreams.

Eden Sassi Matera   HOLIDAY HOME €€

(☑ 340 992 34 61, 347 143 40 16; www.edensassi matera.com; Contrada Belvedere; per 2/3/4/5 people from €95/120/145/170; 🛜 🅿) If, after a day of sightseeing, you feel like lounging in a garden away from the crowds, and don't

mind staying 3km from the centre, this villa near the SS7 is just the ticket. Its two apartments are modern, tastefully furnished and equipped with kitchens.

Albergo Italia   HOTEL €€€

(Map p48; ☑ 0835 33 35 61; www.albergoitalia. com; Via Ridola 5; s/d standard/d superior/tr/ste €120/160/185/220/225; ❄🛜) The fact that this historic hotel began hosting travellers in the early 1900s gives it a special charm. A recent renovation has added functionality and comfort to the atmosphere, and the quality of the fixtures ensures a peaceful night's sleep even in rooms facing the main street.

La Casa di Ele   B&B €€€

(Map p48; ☑ 389 011 73 92, 329 773 58 22; www. lacasadiele.it; Via San Biagio 26; d €200) After a nice dinner, a stroll through the starry night and a glass of Aglianico (or, better still, two or three glasses), re-entering this 18th-century palazzo will bring out the provincial aristocrat in you.

🍴 Eating

Even if the peak-season influx of tourists is comparable in scale to an invasion by Attila's Huns, the average standard of Matera's restaurants remains decidedly high. Of course, with so many new places there's always the risk of a bad experience, but on the whole, you'll be fine.

Sasso Barisano

The small restaurants in the Sassi entice not only with their menus of traditional Lucanian dishes, but especially with their romantic cave settings.

Vicolo Cieco   WINE BAR €

(Map p48; ☑ 338 855 09 84, 0835 20 46 95; Via Fiorentini 74; cialledda salad €5-6, sandwiches €5; ⊙6pm-2am Tue-Fri & 11am-2am Sat-Sun Oct-Mar, 11am-2am daily Apr-Sep) Sip on vintage regional wine at this gorgeous little spot on Via Fiorentini, where live music is played, friendliness and informality reign, and the panini are sure to win over any traveller. There's also an old-fashioned jukebox. Also perfect for an after-dinner drink.

Oi Marì   PIZZERIA, RESTAURANT €€

(Map p48; ☑ 0835 34 61 21/339 408 66 80; www. oimari.it; Via Fiorentini 66; meals €25; ⊙dinner daily, lunch Sat-Sun & holidays & pre-holidays, daily summer) In the long-running dispute over the best pizza in town, this proven Neapolitan restaurant gets a lot of votes. What's more it's an attractive spot and service is friendly.

La Talpa
PIZZERIA, TRATTORIA €€

(Map p48; ☑ 0835 33 50 86; www.latalparisto rante.it; Via Fiorentini 167; meals €30; ⊙ 7-11pm Wed, noon-3pm & 7-11pm Thu-Mon) There are tables in a small square and a pleasant rock-carved interior. Wait times can be long, but the wood-fired pizzas and spicy *spaghetti all'assassina* will kill your hunger. For an appetizing meal.

Osteria Pico
RESTAURANT €€

(Map p48; ☑ 0835 24 04 24; www.osteriapico. it; Via Fiorentini 42; meals €25-30; ⊙ 12.30-3pm & 7.30-10.30pm Tue-Sat, 12.30-3pm Sun) If you can finish a dinner comprising a Pico antipasto, a pasta dish and a main course, welcome to the Binge Olympics. The quality, moreover, is excellent. Reserve a table.

La Nicchia nel Sasso
OSTERIA €€€

(Map p48; ☑ 340 126 55 28; www.lanicchianel sasso.it; Via d'Addozio 78; meals €40; ⊙ 12-3pm & 7-10pm Mon-Tue & Thu-Sat, noon-4pm Sun) This place has long been renowned for its gracious little dining room and an atmosphere that harks back to times gone by. Recently, however, the talk has been of the culinary style of the new management – still anchored in traditional flavours but with a laudable gourmet approach. Especially appealing is the six-course tasting menu (€60).

Dedalo
RESTAURANT €€€

(Map p48; ☑ 0835 197 30 60; www.dedalomat era it; Via D'Addozio 136/140; meals €40; ⊙ 7.30-10.30pm Wed, 12.30-2.30pm & 7.30-10.30pm Thu-Mon) For labyrinthine food choices in one of the city's trendiest venues. Sculptures of Proserpina and Bacchus, subtle cross-references between menu items, and the sensuality of the excavated spaces will ensure a dining experience that's hard to forget.

Sasso Caveoso

In addition to excellent restaurants, Via Buozzi offers a slew of places that are great for both quick snacks and more substantial meals.

Panecotto
REGIONAL €

(Map p48; ☑ 0835 33 13 25; www.panecotto.it; Vico Buozzi 10, Sasso Caveoso 10; meals €20; ⊙ 11.30am-4pm & 7-10pm Tue-Sun) Renowned for its typical *cialledda* and the fact that all products are kilometre zero, this is a good spot for an informal meal, as well as picking up a jar of *lampascioni* in olive oil or a soup of fava beans and chicory. The decor is absolutely spot on.

La Lopa
RESTAURANT €€

(Map p48; ☑ 0835 165 13 70; www.lalopa.com; Via Buozzi 13; meals €30; ⊙ 12.30-2:30pm & 7.30-10.30pm Tue-Sun) It's not every day that you get to finish your meal by going down to a movie theatre set in a cave to watch a video

MATERA'S BREAD & STAMPS

Despite the variety of appetising food you can taste in Matera, the culinary product that best represents the city is without doubt its bread. Crunchy, fragrant and tasty, Matera's *pane* will work its way into your memory with the same nostalgic persistence as the city's rupestrian churches and the sunset views over the Sassi. Bakeries where you can buy it fresh out of the oven include Il Forno nei Sassi (Map p48; ☑ 0835 31 06 77; Via Buozzi 34; ⊙ 6am-noon) and the Panificio Paoluccio (Map p48; ☑ 0835 33 40 71; Via del Corso 22; ⊙ 7am-2pm & 4-8.30pm Mon-Sat), where you can also stock up on abundant focaccia. If you have problems with gluten, you can still get into the spirit of Materan bread-making by buying a typical bread stamp at a shop like Studio d'Arte Massimo Casiello (Map p48; ☑ 0835 197 03 09, 329 338 24 54; www.massimocasiello.it; Via San Francesco da Paola Vecchio 15; ⊙ 9.30am-1.30pm & 4.30-8.30pm Wed-Mon winter, 9.30am-8pm summer). The history of these objects is linked to the old practice of making bread in the city: until the beginning of the 20th century, the women of the Sassi would rush to public bakeries to cook the dough they had prepared at home. And in order to recognise their loaves, each person would mark their bread with a special stamp, consisting of a handle and a design incorporating the initials of the family name, anthropomorphic figures or animals. Now that these objects are made solely for tourism purposes, there are many more ways of customising them.

MATERA SNACKS

Matera is now teeming with restaurants of all kinds. But which are the best places in the centre for a less demanding meal? For a quick answer you need look no further than the long queues outside Sottozero (Map p48; ✉ 0835 33 36 52; Via XX Settembre 51; panzerotti €2; ⏰ 8am-1pm & 4-11.30pm Tue-Sat, 5-11.30pm Sun). To taste the legendary panzerotto served here, you'll have to be patient but it's so worth it to experience the melted cheese fillings and exceptional frying. Then considering how your continuous goings up and down in the Sassi will increase your daily vitamin requirements, a lunch based on fresh fruit might be a good idea. In this case, stop off at the market in Via Ascanio Persio, near Piazza Vittorio Veneto. If, however, you want to learn more about Lucanian cuisine, there's La Latteria Rizzi (Map p48; ✉ 328 462 67 42; Via Duni 2; ⏰ 8am-midnight Wed-Mon), recently renovated and much frequented by locals, especially at aperitif time (the cheeses are superb), and Uacciardidd (Map p48; ✉ 0835 38 51 02; Via Ascanio Persio 33; ⏰ 9am-10.30pm), which prepares amazing sandwiches with mortadella and melted *caciocavallo podolico* (as well as more elaborate dishes).

on cinema in Matera. Neither is it a daily occurrence to eat so well for such an honest price. Great ambiance and friendly service.

Francesca
RESTAURANT €€

(Map p48; ✉ 0835 31 04 43; www.ristorantefrancescasassi.com; Vico Bruno Buozzi 9; meals €35-40; ⏰ 7.30-10pm Thu-Mar, also closed Sun in winter) This renowned eatery just a stone's throw from Piazza San Pietro Caveoso serves typical Lucanian cuisine revisited with flair and originality. Expect sensational appetizers, competent service and more than convincing value for money.

L'Abbondanza Lucana
RESTAURANT €€€

(Map p48; ✉ 0835 33 45 74, 348 898 45 28; www.abbondanzalucana.it; Via Buozzi 11, Sasso Caveoso; meals €40; ⏰ 12.30-3pm & 8-10.30pm Tue-Sat, 12.30-3pm Sun) Even if the appetizer of Lucanian specialities is a moral obligation, the whole menu hits the mark here by skilfully playing with tradition, territory and innovation. The spaghetti with pistachios, mushrooms and caciocavallo cheese is sensational. Warm and engaging ambience.

★ Vitantonio Lombardo
RESTAURANT €€€

(✉ 0835 33 54 75; www.vlristorante.it; Via Madonna delle Virtù 13/14; 6/8/10-course menu €120/140/160; ⏰ 12.30-2.30pm & 7.30-10pm Mon, Sat & Sun, 7.30-10pm Wed-Fri) The formula is simple – choose freely from the menu (if you want, just primi or just main courses) and pay according to the number of courses you pick (six to 10). The result, however, is amazing in its complexity – elaborate dishes, bold combinations, great attention to the territory. Quite simply, the best restaurant in Basilicata.

La Civita

Despite its small size, this area boasts a large number of restaurants, including some of the city's most renowned.

L'Arturo Enogastronomia
REGIONAL €

(Map p48; ✉ 339 390 70 68; www.larturo.com; Piazza del Sedile 15; sandwiches €2.50-3.50, soups €5-6, cheese/cured meat platter per person €4.50-8; ⏰ 10am-3pm daily & 6-11.30pm Mon-Tue & Thu-Sat winter, until 1am summer) The location in Piazza del Sedile is for refined tastes; the robust, no-frills cuisine caters to all palates with a selection of cured meats and cheeses. Great for an aperitif, but also for deep post-dinner conversations under the stars.

La Gatta Buia
RESTAURANT €€

(Map p48; ✉ 0835 25 65 10; www.lagattabuia.eu; Via delle Beccherie 90-92; meals €35; ⏰ 12.30-3pm & 8-11pm) Apparently there was a prison on these premises until 1870. Nowadays, instead of bread and water, you'll dine on veal cheek in Aglianico and star anise sauce and Murgia-scented tempura-fried cod, in a chic, somewhat formal setting. The wine list is formidable.

L'Arco
OSTERIA €€

(Map p48; ✉ 0835 33 46 26, 339 366 58 58; www.osterialarco.it; Via Delle Beccherie 49; meals €25-30; ⏰ 1-2.30pm & 8-11pm Thu-Mar) The architectural feature that gives this restaurant its name abounds inside, as do quality dishes. On the traditional menu, highlights include caprese salad with Lucanian buffalo mozzarella and pappardelle pasta with a sauce of black summer truffle.

LA SCALETTA

We often tend to associate great artistic and archaeological discoveries with machete-wielding characters who chop their way through the jungle like Indiana Joneses, or, at the opposite end of the spectrum, with bow-tied, snobby academics. In reality, the discovery of various rock sites in the Matera area (including the sensational one of the Cripta del Peccato Originale, p68) in the 1960s and subsequent period can be attributed to the passion of a group of young people from a cultural association known as La Scaletta (www.lascaletta.net). The group is still active today, but it now mainly concentrates on the conservation and enhancement of the artistic and environmental heritage of the Sassi and Murgia. So, if you think your time has come, don't forget to pack a spade, a map and tough boots – it's whispered there are still masterpieces waiting to be found in the Murgia.

★ Le Bubbole   RESTAURANT €€€
(Map p48; ☎ 0835 197 05 62; www.palazzogat
tini.it; Via San Potito 57; meals €35-45; ⊙ 12.30-
2.30pm & 7.30-10.30pm Tue-Sun) Set in Palazzo
Gattini, this is considered the most elegant
restaurant in town. But more than its aristocratic setting and palace-worthy chandeliers,
it's the quality of the food that makes a meal
here one of Matera's don't-miss dining experiences. Excellent wine list too.

Il Piano & Outlying Districts

With a mix of tourist restaurants and places
largely frequented by local Matera folk, Il
Piano and its neighbouring districts showcase the city's most diverse culinary offerings.

Pasticceria Schiuma   PASTRY SHOP €
(Map p48; ☎ 0835 33 18 62; Via XX Settembre 10;
⊙ 7am-1pm & 3.30-9pm Wed-Mon) In business
since 1946, this is one of the oldest *pasticcerie*
(pastry shops) in town and it will delight
anyone who prefers the sight of pastries for
breakfast rather than views over the Sassi.
Try to bag one of the few outdoor tables at
the top of the ancient alleyway.

Burro Salato   BISTRO €€
(Map p48; ☎ 0835 24 04 69; Via Scotellaro 7;
meals €30-35; ⊙ 12.30-2pm & 7.30-10pm Thu-Mar)
Dining on pork chateaubriand with Aglianico wine or savoury éclairs with roquefort,
fava beans and chicory while listening to
Edith Piaf in the background is a truly special experience. Once you've tried it, you'll
undoubtedly agree that Burro Salato's atmosphere and brand of Lucanian-French food
are a real success. The crêpes are amazing.

Trattoria Lucana   TRATTORIA €€
(Map p48; ☎ 0835 33 61 17; www.trattorialucana.
it; Via Lucana 48; meals €25-30; ⊙ 12.30-3pm

Mon-Sat) Fettuccine alla Mel Gibson, named
after the actor who was apparently a regular
here while in town filming *The Passion of the
Christ*, is certainly a crowd-pleaser, but it'll
also enthuse even the most non-conformist
of diners. Like the cuisine, the atmosphere
is cheerful and homespun.

San Biagio   RESTAURANT €€
(Map p48; ☎ 0835 33 30 14, 339 793 99 26; www.
sanbiagioristorante.it; Via San Biagio 12; meals €30-
35; ⊙ 12.30-3.30pm and 7.45-10.30pm Wed-Mon)
The fact that San Biagio (St. Blaise) is the
patron saint of the throat would be enough
to recommend a visit. Once here you'll find
the elegant, pared-back ambience and impeccable cuisine will sanctify your dinner. Some
tables have a view of the Sasso Barisano. The
pasta dishes are excellent.

Alle Fornaci   RESTAURANT €€
(Map p48; ☎ 0835 33 50 37; Piazza Firrao 7;
meals €30-35; ⊙ 12.30-2.30pm & 7.30-10.30pm Tue-
Sat, 12.30-2:30pm Sun) This is where the people
of Matera come to celebrate anniversaries,
holidays and important events over a seafood meal. You'll have to forgo the nocturnal
charms of the Sassi, of course, but it will be
worth it. Cute tables outside.

Casello 75   MOZZARELLA BAR, PIZZERIA €€
(Map p48; ☎ 0835 197 50 09; www.casello75.
com; Via Rosselli; mozzarella €8.50-10, pasta dishes
€10-16; ⊙ 1-2.30pm & 7.30-11pm Tue-Sun) Given
that the category 'mozzarella bar' is rather
unusual, this place becomes even more
original when you consider its location
in a revamped railway crossing keeper's
booth. The cheese is (predictably) good and
the pizza is worthwhile. Reservations are
strongly recommended.

⭐ Ego RESTAURANT €€€
(Map p48; ☑392 90 30 963, 0835 24 03 14; www.egogourmet.it; Via Stigliani 44; tasting menu wines excluded €65-95; ⊘12.30-2.30pm & 7.30-11pm Wed-Mon) A gourmet restaurant that wouldn't look out of place in a big metropolis, with only twenty covers and a sophisticated minimalist look. And while the menu might appear pretentious, the execution of the dishes is top-notch. You can also come to enjoy a glass of wine in the small room below the main restaaurant.

Drinking & Nightlife

⭐ Area 8 BAR
(Map p48; ☑333 336 97 88; www.area8.it; Via Casalnuovo 15; drinks €5-10, tapas 6-12; ⊘7pm-2am Thu-Sun) If this metropolitan space were in New York, Cape Town or Sydney, it would leave travellers slack-jawed. But in Matera, it's like a gateway to another world. Just behind Palazzo Lanfranchi, and styled with a whimsical yet refined attention to detail, it's the perfect place to spice up your evening. The cocktails are excellent. Live music is also played.

Dai Tosi WINE BAR
(Map p48; ☑0835 31 40 29; www.enotecadai tosi .it; Via Buozzi 12) Spread over three floors, this architectural gem exudes an atmosphere that's part *Star Wars* part heightened surrealism.

Groove CRAFT BEER
(Map p48; ☑0835 197 02 89, 339 333 96 09; www.groove-matera.it; Via Roma 8; ⊘7pm-1am Mon-Sat) The clink of beer glasses is the soundtrack to this appealing minimalist bar, known for its wide range of craft brews. To accompany your drinks there are grilled meats and birramisu.

I Vizi degli Angeli GELATO
(Map p48; ☑0835 31 06 37; www.ivizidegliangeli. it; Via Ridola 36; ⊘noon-midnight Thu-Tue, daily Jul & Aug) The ice cream is exclusively artisanal, the raw materials are strictly local (the pistachios, for example, come from Stigliano), and tastiness is absolutely guaranteed. Entire poems could be recited about the mulberry, fig, milk and mint, and almond granitas.

19a buca WINE BAR, RESTAURANT
(Map p48; ☑0835 33 35 92; www.diciannove simabuca.com; Via Lombardi 3; ⊘11.30am-3pm & 6pm-midnight Tue-Sun) Who hasn't dreamed of playing golf while sipping a glass of one Italy's leading wines? Probably no one. That

said, this underground venue that retains the form of a stone cistern and with synthetic greens is a truly incredible place. Even the food is good.

Monkey Drink House COCKTAIL BAR
(Map p48; ☑392 641 74 29; Via Duomo 11; ⊘9-3am) Worth a visit if only to admire the monkey-like version of Michelangelo's *The Creation of Adam* on the wall. The quality of the cocktails will do the rest.

Charlie's Speakeasy COCKTAIL BAR
(Map p48; ☑329 429 44 33; Via Casalnuovo 12/14; ⊘7.30am-midnight Mon-Thu, 7.30pm-2am Fri-Sat, 7.30pm-1am Sun) As per local practice, the bar extends into the rocky depths. The atmosphere and music, however, are British in tone and there's a veritable hint of the dandy about the place. Try the highly original cocktails.

Quarry Lounge Terrace LOUNGE BAR
(Map p48; ☑0835 40 78 36; www.quarryresort .it; Via San Giacomo; ⊘11am-midnight Wed-Mon) The terrace of this luxury hotel, one of the Sassi's most spectacular, is open to non-guests. You can sip on champagne and excellent cocktails, and have something to eat for a very reasonable price.

☆ Entertainment

While Matera's hotel and restaurant offerings can compare with those of more established tourist destinations, the city's cultural scene still has room for improvement.

Cine Teatro Duni CINEMA, THEATRE
(Map p48; Via Roma 10) This theatre, a historical venue on the city's cultural scene, is named after the composer Egidio Romualdo Duni, who was born in Matera in 1709.

CineTeatro Comunale Guerrieri CINEMA
(Map p48; ☑0835 33 41 16; Piazza Vittorio Veneto 23) Offers an interesting selection of current films and arthouse seasons.

Casa Cava AUDITORIUM
(map p48; ☑0835 33 67 33; www.casacava.it; Via San Pietro Barisano 47) Most travellers visit even if no concerts or plays are being staged. Any scheduled performances would indeed be worth seeing.

IAC THEATRE
(Map p48; ☑338 501 70 64, 335 534 12 70; www.centroiac.com; Via Casalnuovo 156) Stages theatrical productions for both adults and children, as well as readings, dances and

A LONG WAY TO MATERA

There are many ways to reach Matera but, without doubt, the most spectacular is on foot, via the paths of the Cammino Materano (www.camminomaterano.it). The name is actually misleading as there's more than one route. At the time of research it was possible to walk from Bari (in seven stages) or Martina Franca (eight stages, the last of which is before Matera at Montescaglioso), while routes from Trani, Leuca, Paestum and Termoli were being worked on. These will also use the green and yellow signs and rely on affiliated structures. Walkers who complete the hikes will be guaranteed a *testimonial*. For more information, check the website.

various events. It's housed in a renovated olive oil mill where everything is curated with passion and enthusiasm.

Cava del Sole   OUTDOOR THEATRE
(Map p69, B1; www.cavadelsole.it; SS7) On the main road, not far from Parco Scultura La Palomba, this sensational outdoor theater is set in a disused quarry. Check the website for upcoming events.

 Shopping

Matera has plenty of shops, small stores and workshops catering to all tastes. Of these, many sell artistic handicrafts such as the ubiquitous traditional whistle (known as the *cucù*).

Mani nell'Arte   ARTS & CRAFTS
(Map p48; 0835 68 02 65, 329 203 90 91; www. angeladifonzo.flazio.com; Via Santa Cesarea 14; 10am-1pm & 4.30-8pm Mon-Sat, 10am-1pm Sun, variable hrs in winter) For jewellery, accessories and objects expertly crafted from a wide range of materials. Think bags, earrings, bracelets, paintings, trays with cups and sugar bowls, rings, and photo frames.

Vino e Dintorni   FOOD & DRINKS
(Map p48; 0835 31 07 15, 339 862 00 18; www.vinoedintornimatera.com; Via Ridola 32; 4.30-8.30pm Mon, 9am-1pm & 4.30-8.30pm Tue-Sat, 10.30am-1pm Sun) Has a formidable array of local products and more. Add to the intoxication you feel in the Sassi with some quality wine.

Schiuma Post Design   DESIGN
(Map p48; 328 143 07 04; www.schiumapost design.com; Piazza San Francesco 2; 10am-1pm Mon-Tue & 10am-8pm Wed-Sun, 10am-midnight daily Aug) If it's always been your hidden dream to have a 12cm-tall wooden puppet with your face on it for your living room, be sure to visit this shop. You can also buy furniture and handicrafts.

Crea che Ricrea   FASHION & ACCESSORIES
(Map p48; 0835 68 02 79, 329 365 51 68; www. creachericrea.wordpress.com; Via Rosario 31/32; 10am-1pm & 5-8pm Mon-Sat, longer hrs summer) A good-looking atelier selling handmade hats and garments. For the more motivated, you can brush up on your knitting at a workshop.

Amaro Lucano   FOOD & DRINKS
(Map p48; 0835 33 48 78; Via del Corso 52; 10.30am-1.30pm & 4-9pm Mon-Thur, 11am-9pm Fri-Sun Sep-Jun, 10am-9pm daily Jul-Aug) Buy bottles of Basilicata's best-known liqueur (see boxed text p85) so you can toast the memory of your wonderful trip once you get home.

Libreria dell'Arco   BOOKSHOP
(Map p48; 0835 31 11 11; www.libreriadellarco .it; Via delle Beccherie 55; 9.30am-1.30pm & 4.30-8.30pm Mon-Sat) Independent bookstore where you can find material to help further your knowledge of the local area, from architecture to urban planning, from fiction to anthropology.

ℹ Information
TRAVEL AGENCIES
Ferula Viaggi (0835 33 65 72, 328 456 16 52; www.ferulaviaggi.it; Via Cappelluti 34; 9am-1pm & 3.30-7pm Mon-Fri, 9am-1pm Sat, longer hrs in high season) Tour operator dedicated to promoting tourism in Basilicata, specialising in culture, food and wine, cycling and walking vacations.

Viaggi Lionetti (0835 33 40 33; www.viaggi lionetti.com; Via Fratelli Rosselli 14; 9am-1pm & 4-8pm Mon-Fri) This agency deals with all incoming services and has been managing the website www.sassiweb.com since 1998.

EMERGENCY
Guardia Medica (0835 26 22 60) An emergency medical service

Guardia Medica Turistica (0835 25 37 23, 329 583 26 29; 8am-8pm Mon-Fri, 24 hrs Sat

& Sun summer) An emergency medical service
for tourists.

Ospedale (Casualty ☏ 0835 25 32 12; Via Montescaglioso) Hospital about 1km southeast of the
centre.

TOURIST INFORMATION

Wandering around Matera, especially in the Pia-
nodistrict, you'll see signs for tourist information
offices. These are private agencies, which, while
often competent, will often try to sell you their
group tours (€15 to €20 for two hours).

The official **APT Basilicata Infopoint** (Map
p48, B2; ☏ 0835 40 64 64, 0835 40 88 16;
www.aptbasilicata.it; Piazza Vittorio Veneto;
☺ daily, hrs vary according to the season) is located in the prestigious setting of Palazzo dell'
Annunziata on Piazza Vittorio Veneto. Here you
can get tons of information and useful tips, as well
as a polite reception. At the time of research there
were also plans to open additional information
kiosks in other parts of the city. Note also the
official tourist website of the municipality of Matera (www.materawelcome.it).

POST

Post Office (☏ 0835 24 55 32; Via Passarelli
13/b; ☺ 8.20am-7.05pm Mon-Fri, 8.20am-
12.35pm Sat)

GUIDED TOURS

You can get a list of official guides licensed for
Sassi visits at the infopoint or on the APT Basilicata website (www.aptbasilicata.it). Alternatively,
you could contact **Guide Matera** (☏ 0835 176
60 57, 328 974 41 29; www.guidema tera.com),
which clearly lists its tour rates on its website, or
Francesco Foschino (☏ 0835 197 53 11, 347 573
64 70; www.sassidimatera.org), a passionate and
well-prepared guide who runs two group tours
each day, departing from Piazza San Pietro Caveoso at 10am and 5.30pm (€20 including tickets
to some sites). Also worth noting is **Beyond the
Art** (☏ 366 223 0517 www.oltrelartematera.it;
Via Lanera 11; ☺ 9am-1pm & 4-8pm), one of the
cooperatives that manages Matera's rupestrian
churches, and organises guided tours on request.
Its website is packed with information.

❶ Getting There & Away

Despite ever-improving links with Bari, Matera still
remains one of the hardest provincial capitals to
reach in Italy.

AIR

Thanks to the widening of the SS96 and SS99,
Matera is now less than an hour's drive from
Bari's **Aeroporto Internazionale Karol Wojtyla**.
Renting a car when you land will save you time
getting to the city and give you more freedom
to explore its surrounds. But bear in mind that
you'll have to park outside the historic centre.

Alternatively several companies operate buses to
Matera throughout the day, including **Smaldon**
(☏ 0835 0835 51 99 49; www.smaldonebus.it;
€5), **Chiruzzi** (☏ 0835 54 22 50; www.chiruzzi.
com; €5), **Cotrap** (☏ 080 579 01 11; www.cotrap.
it/www.aeroportidipuglia.it; €6), and **Cotrab**
(www.cotrab.it; €3.40). In all cases, the journey
takes about 1¼ hours, tickets can be purchased
online or directly from the driver, and the buses
stop in Piazza Matteotti, a stone's throw from the
train station. **Miccolis** (☏ 0835 34 40 32; www.
busmiccolis.it) also covers the same journey twice
a day, but stops further from the centre, at the
Villa Longo station in Via Nazionale; tickets cost
€16. Alternatively, there are private shuttles run
by car rental companies such as **Shuttle Matera**
(☏ 333 851 23 10; www.shuttlematera.it; vehicles
for 1/8 passengers €45-70/95-120). Trains run
by **Appulo Lucanian Railways** (☏ 800 050 500;
www.ferrovieappulolucane.it), also serve Matera
but are not recommended unless you're a maso-
chist – it'll take about half an hour to get to Bari
Centrale station from the airport and then another
hour and a half to reach Matera.

BUS

Buses stop in different places depending on the
company (though many stop in Via Don Luigi
Sturzo, northwest of the Sassi district). **SITASUD**
buses (☏ 083538 50 07; www.sitasudtrasporti.it)
connect Matera with Potenza (1¾ hours) and several towns in the province, including Metaponto,
on the Ionian coast (one hour). **Grassani** (☏ 0835
72 14 43;www.grassani.it) also has a few runs to
Potenza (one hour 40 minutes). **Marino** (☏ 080
311 23 35; www.marinobus.it), **Liscio** (☏ 0971 546
73;www.autolineeliscio.it), **Marozzi** (☏ 080 579
02 11; www.marozzivt.it) and **Miccolis** (☏ 0835
34 40 32; www.miccolis-spa.it) serve various
southern cities, including Taranto (€17, two hours
five minutes), Brindisi (€21, three hours), Lecce
(€22, three hours 35 minutes), Salerno (€19, 1½
hours) and Naples (€21, two hours 20 minutes). If
you're coming from a northern Italian city it's also
worth checking **Flixbus** (☏ 02 94 75 92 08; www.
flixbus.it), which operates services to/from Rome
(from €10.99, 6½ to nine hours) and Milan (from
€51.99, 12½ hours).

CAR & MOTORCYCLE

From Bari, follow the SS96 to Altamura, then the
SS99 to Matera. From Potenza, follow the SS407
and then the SS7 to the Matera exit. From Naples,
take the A1 to Salerno and then the A3 to Sicignano, exiting onto the SS407 towards Potenza. From
Rome, you can avoid Naples by taking the A30 to
Salerno.

TRAIN

It may seem incredible, but you still can't reach
Matera on a train operated by the national railway
company (Ferrovie dello Stato). On the other
hand, the city boasts a glittering station in Piazza

della Visitazione, designed by the starchitect Stefano Boeri and completed in 2019. The closest town on the national rail network is Ferrandina. You can, however, reach Bari (from €5.10, 1½ hours, frequent) on the narrow-gauge line of the **Ferrovie Appulo Lucane** (⏢ 800 050 500; www. ferrovieappulolucane.it).

Trenitalia (www.trenitalia.com) and **Italo** (www. italotreno.it) provide inter-modal connections that link the high-speed railway network at Salerno with Matera via bus.

🛈 Getting Around

CAR & MOTORCYCLE
A very strict ZTL (Limited Traffic Zone) is in force in Matera, so forget about accessing the Sassi by car. The most convenient car parks are located near Piazza della Visitazione (€0.70 per hour) and in Piazza Matteotti (€0.70 per hour). Alternatively, you could use one of the private garages located on Via Lucana (on the corner with Via Vena), Via Casalnuovo, Piazza Cesare Firrao, and Via Saragat (€0.50 per hour). You'll find a map of the various options at www.isassidimatera.com. Actually, you can still find some free parking near the Sassi, around Via Piave for example, but you'll need to be very lucky. Realistically, there's more free parking outside the centre, something worth considering if you're staying for a few days and don't need your car.

TAXI
Taxis (⏢ 0835 1835) are available 24 hours a day, but it's best to book night rides.

PUBLIC TRANSPORT
Miccolis (⏢ 0835 34 40 32; www.busmiccolis. it; ground/on-board tickets €0.80/1.50) operates city buses, which might be useful for reaching the new quarters or the Belvedere di Murgia Timone (off-limits to cars). Also useful is the Sassi Line (every 20 to 30 minutes), which runs a circular route from the Via Saragat car park, stopping off at several strategic points in the Sassi.

Murgia Materana

The allure of a city doesn't depend solely on its buildings, monuments, and people; it also comes from the timeless connection it has with the area around it. Well, like Istanbul, Lisbon, Kathmandu and New York, Matera stands out, in part, thanks to its incredible location: facing the city, over the dizzying canyon gouged out by the Gravina stream, lies the Parco della Murgia Materana (⏢ 0835 33 61 66; www.parcomurgia.it). Here wild nature – a mix of Arizona and the Rift Valley – declares its unrelenting dominion over humanity in the form of a landscape made up of desolate

WORTH A TRIP

RUPESTRIAN MASTERPIECES

For decades, the shepherds of the Murgia knew of a legend that spoke of an immense cave with frescoes so beautiful they'd outshine those of any church in the city. However, no one could ever locate its mythical position or even ascertain if it really existed. Then, the discovery – on 1 May 1963, members of the Circolo La Scaletta (see boxed text p64) stumbled upon a rocky spectacle about 13km southwest of Matera even more impressive than any described in the vaporous stories told around the campfire. The Cripta del Peccato Originale (Map p69, A2; ⏢ 320 334 53 23; www.criptadelpeccatooriginale.it, www.zetema.org; adult/reduced €10/8; ⏱ visits 9.30am, 11am, 12.30pm, 3.30pm, 5pm & 6.30pm Tue-Sun Apr-Sep, 9.30am, 11am, 12.30pm, 3.30pm & 5pm Tue-Sun March & Oct, 9.30am, 11am, 12.30pm & 3.30pm Tue-Sun Nov-Feb; by reservation only) was the place of worship of a Benedictine community in the Lombard period. Forgotten for centuries, it has 41 sq m of colourful frescoes dating back to the 8th and 9th centuries. These paintings, recently restored to their former splendour after a sophisticated restoration project, will leave aficionados speechless with the originality of their representations and symbology. In the three niches on the left wall are depicted triumvirates of the apostles, the Virgin Queen and the Archangels; on the back wall, the pictorial cycle illustrates episodes from the book of Genesis. The depictions are animated by the inclusion of carpets of bright flowers and unusual details. These include showing a fig instead of an apple to represent the fruit of original sin; the manufacture of a Lombard shield; the personification of light and darkness by two young men with their arms raised to the sky and their hands tied; Eve emerging from Adam's side, fully awake. Together the frescoes create a sensation of vigorous, almost violent holiness, a holiness bearing no relationship to tradition. To reach the crypt, take the SS7 and follow the signs for the Masseria Dragone. Note that you won't be able to access the site without a reservation. Aim to arrive half an hour before your visit time.

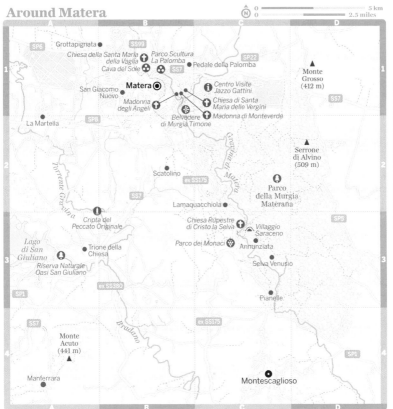

gorges, caves inhabited over the centuries by cavemen, artists and shepherds, and extra-ordinary rock churches (more than 150 have been found). The park, characterised by a pseudo-steppe that elicits exotic imaginings, covers an area of about 8000 hectares and includes sites that fall within the territory of Montescaglioso (p76).

◉ Sights

★**Murgia Timone**   PARCO DELLE CHIESE RUPESTRI
There are very few places capable of transporting travellers so far back in time, seemingly to the very confines of the human spirit, or perhaps even further back, to a time when there was no distinction between individuals and nature. The part of the Parco della Murgia Materana closest to the city is dotted with natural caves – out of which you wouldn't be surprised to see a primitive figure or ferocious beast emerging at any

moment – and constantly swept by the wind, which can be terrifying or a blessing depending on the season. The main attraction here is undoubtedly the famous Belvedere (Map p69, B1). This generally gets pretty crowded, and while it's less romantic than other viewpoints and the views it commands over Matera have been captured in thousands of standard photos, it remains a haunting place. Particularly so around sunset, when the city lights come on and you'll almost feel obliged to compare it to a nativity scene. There are three options for reaching it: walk down from Porta Pistola (p54) in Matera and up the opposite side of the canyon after the Tibetan bridge (allow about 40 minutes); use the city bus service (or join a private tour); or drive to the Centro Visite Jazzo Gattini (p71), whose planned multimedia museum will introduce you to the area, and from there follow the bike/foot path (just over 1.5km). The Belvedere is no longer accessible by private vehicle. The Murgia Timone, however, has plenty more to offer – at the time of research, the management of the area's innumerable sites of interest was under consideration. The not particularly exciting remains of a neolithic village (inhabited between 7000 and 1300 BCE) FREE near the visitor centre are set to become the central attraction of the prehistory section of the Parco della Storia dell'Uomo (see boxed text p57). The section of the park dedicated to the rupestrian civilisation will be centred on the main churches (single ticket bought at the Centro Visite Jazzo Gattini/online adult €10/8, reduced €7/5), which have all been recently restored and are accessible at set times. These churches include the 9th-century Chiesa di San Falcione, whose structure reveals its later function as a sheep pen; the Chiesa di San Vito, which overlooks the Gravina and stands near the cistern that doubled as Jesus' tomb in Pier Paolo Pasolini's 1964 film *The Gospel According to St. Matthew* (both can be visited on the walk between the visitor centre and the Belvedere); the Chiesa di Sant'Agnese, with a rectangular hall adorned with simple wall niches and cisterns for collecting rainwater; and the Chiesa della Madonna delle Tre Porte, named after the three entrance arches that give on to a superbly frescoed 15th-century hall. The latter two are located on the route to the Belvedere from the Tibetan bridge. The Chiesa di San Nicola all'Appia, decorated with graffiti, and the Chiesa della Madonna della Croce, adorned with a 13th-century Madonna Regina seated on a throne with the blessed child, are, however, a little further

EXPLORING THE MURGIA

The Murgia Timone, which constitutes only a tiny part of the Parco della Murgia Materana, offers endless opportunities for exploration. All are exciting and capable of creating indelible memories. And while it's not very simple to identify the sites of greatest interest, even just wandering around the country here, in a setting worthy of the most captivating Western film, is an exhilarating experience. However, the Murgia shouldn't be approached lightly – make sure to wear comfortable shoes and have a sufficient supply of water. It's also imperative to note that 80% of the park is private property so it's advisable to hire an authorised guide to avoid mishaps. That said, there are at least two spectacular rupestrian churches that can be visited on their own, without risking the wrath of the local landowners. To get to the Madonna di Monteverde (Map p54, B1), descend from Porta Pistola (p69) and when you reach the Gravina, follow the path away from the Tibetan bridge. After a bend in the stream you should find a wooden plank, useful for crossing the water; from there it's about five minutes (there are no signs, so try Google maps) to the church, which you'll find crowned by a bush of prickly pears and with a small bell gable. The Madonna degli Angeli (Map p69, B1) is located on a spectacular hilltop 400m to the west. To give you an idea, this is the cave with three windows that you see when looking out at the Murgia from Via Madonna delle Virtù in the Sasso Caveoso. An alternative route to the churches follows the path that descends from the Chiesa di Santa Maria delle Vergini (p71).

More challenging routes await those who venture into the southern part of the park in search of adventure. It takes about three hours to walk to the Chiesa Rupestre di Cristo la Selva (Map p69, C3), which features a remodelled 18th-century facade in the rock face and the only existing examples of confessionals dug directly into the rock. Note, however, that a guide is obligatory here. Finally, and to end with a bang, we'd recommend a guided excursion to the Villaggio Saraceno (Map p69, C3; Località Vitisciulo). The name (Saracen Village) doesn't, in fact, derive from the fact it was an ancient Moorish settlement but from the family who once owned the immense rock hamlet. Set in a small valley, the village's 90 caves house dwellings, cisterns, and the 11th-century Chiesa di Santa Maria al Visciolo (formerly San Luca). An alternative way to explore the area is to start from the Parco dei Monaci (Map p69, C3; Contrada Parco dei Monaci), which is 9km from Matera along the SP3, in the direction of Montescaglioso. For information on visiting the rock churches and other places of interest in the area, contact the Ente Parco della Murgia Materana (☏0835 33 61 66; www.parcomurgia.it).

from the main route, respectively 1km north and 1.5km southwest of the visitor centre: they will probably only be visitable with a reservation.

Chiesa di Santa Maria delle Vergini
CHURCH

(Map p69, B1; Contrada Murgecchia; ⊘ variable hrs) There are three main reasons for coming all the way out here. The first is to visit the only rock church in the Murgia that still hosts worship. The second is to take jaw-dropping photos of Matera from a different perspective – the Murgecchia plateau, separated from the Murgia Timone by the Jesce stream (a tributary of the Gravina), commands views just as spectacular as those from the better-known and more crowded Belvedere. And the third reason is to reach the churches of Madonna di Monteverde and Madonna degli Angeli (see boxed text, p70) by following the road down to the Gravina. There's also the nearby Neolithic settlement of the Villaggio Murgecchia, but you can forget about understanding this without a guide.

To get to the Chiesa di Santa Maria delle Vergini, take the SS7 and, at the crossroads 200m after the Parco Sculture la Palomba, take the first of the two roads that lead up to the right. If you make a mistake and take the second one past a long row of trees, don't worry because the 1580 Santuario di Santa Maria della Palomba (Contrada Pedale della Palomba; ⊘ 8.30am-12pm & 4.15-7pm), is well worth a stop with its delicate chapels, statues and frescoes.

★ Parco Scultura La Palomba

OUTDOOR MUSEUM

(Map p69, B1; ☑ 333 866 31 96, 328 971 61 35; www.visitmatera.it/parco-scultura-la-palomba.html; SS7 Contrada Palomba; recommended donation €1-2; ⊘ always open) Even just wandering between the immense walls of an abandoned quarry is an experience not without appeal, especially in an underground city like Matera. But if you then find sculptures by an internationally renowned artist strewn around the gigantic space, then you'll definitely want to make the 2km trip to get to the Parco della Murgia from the Sassi. Antonio Paradiso's works speak of contemporary tragedies: some are made from disused Ilva pipes, others from steel beams salvaged from the Twin Towers. All, however, have the power to jolt the traveller's imagination.

Chiesa di Santa Maria della Vaglia
CHURCH

(Map p69, B1; Via Appia SS7, km 582) Due to its size, this is considered the cathedral of rupestrian churches. Its facade is a dignified work of non-subterranean architecture, with four decorated 13th-century portals. The interior, with three naves punctuated by rock-carved columns, has frescoes from the 12th to 18th centuries. The church is 3km from Matera on the SS7, not far from the Sculpture Park.

✗ Eating & Drinking

Jazzo Gattini/Masseria Radogna
SNACK BAR €

(☑ 0835 33 22 62, 388 892 54 07; www.ceamatera.it; Contrada Murgia Timone SS7 km 583) Swept by the winds, this bucolic 19th-century sheep pen, now home to the Centro Visite del Parco della Murgia Materana, is the nerve centre for most visitors to the Murgia, as well as a good place to buy local products and tasty snacks.

ℹ Information

Park Authority (☑ 0835 33 61 66; www.parcomurgia.it; Via Sette Dolori 10, Matera; ⊘ 10am-1pm Mon-Fri & 4-6.30pm Tue & Thu) A complete list of licensed guides is available on the website.

Centro Visite Jazzo Gattini (Map p69, C1; ☑ 0835 33 22 62, 388 892 54 07; www.ceamatera.it; Masseria Radogna, Contrada Murgia Timone) This visitor centre provides information and valuable maps, as well as sells tickets for the rupestrian churches of Murgia Timone.

VALLE DEL BRADANO

It's possible to see certain elements of uniformity in the landscape that accompanies the river Bradano, the third longest in Basilicata. There are the undulating hills that soften the rough contours of the Murgia and the bare, stark panoramas in which fields and villages face off like giants on successive peaks. And there's the artistic wealth of towns that house some of the region's most important works, including rare traces of the Renaissance in Lucania. For all these reasons, the Valle del Bradano is ideal for day trips or as a base for exploring Matera.

Irsina

POP 4555 / ELEV 548M

If a pageant were held for the most eye-catching village in Basilicata, this place some 50kms northwest of Matera would be up

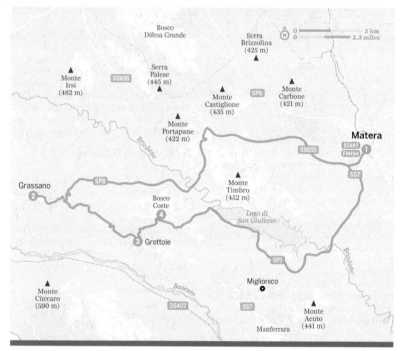

Driving Tour
A Day Out from Matera

START MATERA
END MATERA
DURATION 84KM, NINE HOURS

However charming Matera is, you may want to have a break from the rocky beauty of the Sassi after a few days of caves, tunnels and frescoes. So set out early from ❶ **Matera** and drive west for about forty minutes to ❷ **Grassano**. This village might be small but it has some special effects in store. For example, the dome of the Chiesa Madre (Via Chiesa) features a depiction of the typical eight-pointed cross of the Knights of Malta, clear evidence of the centuries-long presence – which lasted until the beginning of the 19th century – of the chivalrous order in the village. Immediately below the church, at the foot of the hill, are a series of fascinating excavated cellars, known as *cinti*, which will satisfy anyone already yearning for subterranean spaces and underground settings. Then there are the traces of Carlo Levi's presence, displayed in the form of plaques

which retrace the steps of *Christ Stopped at Eboli* through the streets. The artist, in fact, lived at the Locanda Prisco (Corso Umberto I 49) before moving to Aliano. Finally, you can check out a spectacular nativity scene by Franco Artesea at Palazzo Materi (Corso Umberto I).

Done there, jump back in your car and make for ❸ **Grottole**, where you'll probably find both the Museo delle Ceramiche Antiche (Via Nazionale) and the panoramic Lombard Castello Schinulfo (Salita Castello) closed. However, you can admire the Chiesa Diruta (Via Garibaldi) from outside. It has a certain solemn grandeur despite having lost its roof in repeated collapses and is well worth a visit. At this point it'll be time for lunch, but don't worry: 5km north of the village, in the ❹ **Bosco Coste**, the Ristorante Podus (Località Bosco Coste) has tables indoors or in a picnic area and serves mouth-watering podolica-beef steaks. Aterwards, take time for a short walk in the woods before returning happy and content to **Matera**.

for a medal. Set on a soft hill with no other inhabited areas in sight, and surrounded by a terrain that's both sinuous and terrifying, in contrast to the refined grace of its asto-nishing artistic heritage, Irsina is an incre-asingly popular destination, especially with foreign visitors. In fact, a small community of English, Germans, French, Swedes and even New Zealanders live here, drawn by the peace, good food, shady alleys and that rare-fied, out-of-time atmosphere that only certain parts of the Meridione (southern Italy) have been able to preserve. The main attraction is a unique sculptural work attributed to An-drea Mantegna, but there's enough in Irsina to make for an unforgettable day.

⊙ Sights

In its eventful history, the town, once called Montepeloso, has been inhabited by the Lom-bards, destroyed by the Saracens (in 988), and occupied by the Swabians, Angevins and Aragonese. In 1585 it was sold to a Genoese family, the Grimaldis, and a century later to the Riario Sforza family.

Museo Multimediale
'I Tesori del Bradano'   MUSEUM
(☑320 060 89 99, 327 202 42 75, 335 649 48 61; Via Ascensione; visits by appointment only) FREE
In the deconsecrated Chiesa dell'Annunziata, you can get a good introduction to the town – a film recounts the history of the artworks contained in the cathedral and there's a re-construction of Mantegna's workshop.

Cattedrale di Santa
Maria Assunta   CATHEDRAL
(☑0835 62 90 65, 334 315 22 63, 338 336 70 48; Largo Cattedrale) The bell tower is Romanesque but everything else underwent several rebu-ilds before the cathedral took on its current form – complete with a Neapolitan baroque facade and whitewashed interior – in the 18th century. The cathedral is known throu-ghout Basilicata for housing a sculpture of St. Euphemia that was recently attributed to Andrea Mantegna – what makes it even more valuable is the fact that it's the only known sculptural work by Mantegna. The statue was part of a bequest by the Irsinese priest Roberto de Mabilia, whose relations with Mantegna in Padua are well documented. Accompanying the statue when it arrived in 1454 was a reliquary with the arm of St. Euphemia, a sculpture by Nicolò Pizolo (a collaborator of Donatello) depicting a Madonna and Child, a baptismal

font in Verona marble, and a curious wooden crucifix that can be disassembled like a man-nequin and is adorned with fake hair. Also of note are the numerous Templar symbols in the crypt and the unusual pulpit supported by an eagle.

Cripta di San
Francesco   UNDERGROUND CHAPEL
(☑0835 51 83 30, 320 060 89 99; www.irsina -arte.com; Piazza San Francesco; ⊙guided tours by appointment) It's not everyday that you come across such a cycle of frescoes. Created between 1370 and 1373 in an underground chapel under the quadrangular tower of an old Norman castle (where the church of the former Convento di San Francesco now stands) they display the typical themes of the Gothic style, from the Crucifixion to the Last Supper, from the Presentation in the Temple to the Passage of the Madonna. In the four corners, you'll see symbols of the Evangelists and, in the centre of the barrel vault, the mighty face of the Creator, complete with braids. The paintings were commissioned by the Del Balzo family, lords of Montepeloso since the arrival of the Angevins in 1308.

Museo Civico Janora   MUSEUM
(☑335 649 48 61; www.irsina-arte.com; Piazza San Francesco 8; adult/reduced €2.50/1; ⊙10.30am-1pm & 5.30-8pm Tue-Sat, 10.30am-12.30pm Sun) Housed in the spacious rooms of the former Convento di San Francesco, this museum displays 300 of the 1600 artifacts collected by the Irsinian historian Michele Janora during his years of research. Vases with geometric designs and weapons and ornaments in bronze testify to the culture and customs of the peoples who occupied the area from prehistoric times to the Hellenistic period. Of particular note is a rare krater chalice from the 4th century BCE with reddish designs depicting the struggle between Bellerophon and the Chimera.

Chiesa della Madonna
del Carmine   PLACE OF WORSHIP
(Via Roma) This small 18th-century church, better known as the Chiesa del Purgatorio, harbours two paintings by Andrea Miglio-nico (San Michele e Angeli and the Madonna del Carmine) and a canvas depicting the Marriage at Cana, attributed to a pupil of Caravaggio.

I Bottini   AQUEDUCT
(☑320 060 89 99, 327 202 42 75, 335 649 48 61; www.irsina-arte.com; Contrada Fontana; ⊙free

guided tours by reservation) In a region where underground wonders are something of a hallmark, Irsina makes its contribution with I Bottini. These head-high tunnels were built in medieval times to follow the water table and channel water to an 18th-century fountain, out of which it still gushes fresh and clear. If you want to duck down into the town's depths, and you're not worried about the prospect of a few fluttering bats, book a guided tour and explore a few kilometres of this ingenious water network.

Bosco Verrutoli   WOODS
(SP209, Irsina) About 10km south of the village, on the SP209, is this small wooded spot ideal for peaceful walks along its shady paths. Sure, the road to get here is pretty rough, the deer that used to live here are all gone, and the site could be valued much better, but as a refuge from the fierce summer heat it's not bad.

⚝ Festivals & Events

Festa della Pietà   MAY
(www.comune.irsina.mt.it) This festival on the fourth Sunday of May centres on the custom of the Pizzicantò (making human towers). If you're into feats of balance, jump into the fray and help build a human pyramid. Once balance has been achieved, with five guys at the base, you all turn and sing until the pyramid collapses and the next group takes over.

Sagra del Vino e della Lumaca   AUGUST
(www.comune.irsina.mt.it) Fans of snails will rejoice at this food and wine festival held on Via Lucana under the medieval bell tower. To aid digestion, there's plenty of music and dancing.

**Festa di Santa Eufemia
e San Rocco**   SEPTEMBER
(www.comune.irsina.mt.it) This festival revolves around a symbolic procession on September 16. The townspeople give the keys of the town to the bishop and he, in turn, places them in the hands of St. Euphemia. The night before, the basements and cellars of the historic centre are filled with atmospheric candles and, decorated with white sheets embroidered by the town's elderly women, transformed into altars to display images and statuettes of St. Rocco.

🕈 Activities

Arenacea   PAINTING, COOKING
(☑335 649 48 61, 339 458 95 26; St. Piazza San Francesco 8) Every summer the sparkling

cooperative that manages the Museo Civico Janora organises painting classes in English. Their delightfully retro approach is very popular with foreign visitors. You work mainly outdoors (in the roof garden) or in the bright halls of the former Convento di San Francesco. Courses on typical southern Italian cuisine have recently been introduced as well.

🛏 Sleeping & Eating

Domus Arsia   B&B €€
(☑333 246 20 29; Via Sant'Angelo 22; r €70; 🛜❄) This B&B has two comfortable rooms, with a mini gym in the loft. Also of note is the fact that the owner asks you to put your documents (ID card or passport) in a basket which is tied to a rope and then hoisted upstairs. Instead of breakfast you get a voucher you can use at a cafe about 10 minutes' walk away.

Il Ducale   BAR, PIZZERIA €€
(☑0835 62 81 90; ilducalepizzeria.wixsite.com/il ducale; Piazza Garibaldi 1; meals €20, pizzas from €4; ☉7.30am-midnight Tue-Sun) Reliable restaurant-pizzeria, where both traditional dishes and pizzas are not to be sniffed at. What makes the difference, however, are the sensational view of the hills from the outdoor seating area.

★ Trattoria Nugent   RESTAURANT €€
(☑0835 62 81 80; Piazza Garibaldi 6, internal courtyard; meals €25-30; ☉12-3pm & 7-11pm Wed-Mon) Rustic brick-vaulted rooms chock-full of objects and old farming tools set the scene for first courses of homemade pasta, such as cavatellini with beans and wild fennel, which will win you over for ever. Undoubtedly, one of the best restaurants in the area.

Drinking & Nightlife

Bar del Commercio   BAR
(Via delle Puglie; ☉7.30am-8pm) Every Friday afternoon Irsina's foreign community gathers at this bar, which looks like something out of a 1970s movie, to cheerfully knock back one beer after another. If you're in the area, be sure to stop by.

❶ Information

TOURIST INFORMATION
For information try contacting the **Centro Turistico Giovanile** (☑320 060 89 99) or the **Arenacea** cooperative (☑335 649 48 61, 339 458 95 26; www.irsina-arte.com; Piazza San Francesco 8).

ℹ️ Getting There & Away

Irsina is on the SS96. Coming from Potenza, follow the SS7 east and then take the SS96, which traverses Basilicata as it heads on to Bari. Coming from Matera, head north on the SS655 (Bradanica) until it joins the SS96. Bus services to/from Matera are provided by **Smaldon** (☎ 0835 51 99 49; www.smaldonebus.it) which operates four daily runs. Tickets for the 1¼-hour journey cost €2.50.

Miglionico

POP 2497 / ELEV 461M

Perched on the top of a hill in the valley between the Basento and Bradano rivers, Miglionico will warm your heart on misty winter nights and cheerful summer Sundays, when locals parade up and down in their best clothes and children play in the square behind the cathedral. As well as a charming vibe, the town boasts an important artistic patrimony and, given its proximity to Matera, makes a convenient (and cheap) base for exploring the provincial capital and its surrounds.

⦿ Sights

Chiesa Madre CHURCH
(Piazza del Popolo; ⊙ 7am-7pm) The town's main place of worship impresses with its sumptuously decorated 16th-century portal, a bell tower embellished with bas-reliefs, and a majestic silhouette that's magnified by the tight knot of alleyways that surrounds it. However, these features fade into the background in the presence of a work that's as jaw-dropping as it is unusual in these southern climes – a **polyptych** by Cima da Conegliano (1499). This comprises 18 panels with centre stage given to a depiction of the *Vergine in trono con il Bambino* which shows a levity of touch typical of the Venetian Renaissance school. Next to the polyptych is the church's other highlight piece, a brutal 17th-century wooden **crucifix** by Frate Umile da Petralia. The various altars house paintings improperly attributed to Tintoretto and Guercino, and an early 17th-century *Deposizione* by Antonio Stabile which shows an angular tangle of limbs.

Castello di Malconsiglio CASTLE
(☎ 0835 55 90 05, 388 367 39 22, 327 536 51 90; www.castellodelmalconsiglio.it; Via Dante 12; €5; ⊙ by reservation) No self-respecting Lucanian village can do without a medieval cliff-top castle, complete with battlements and the remnants of its fortifications. Miglionico's

11th-century model is particularly well preserved and steeped in history and legend. Its bizarre name derives from a plot hatched by a group of barons in 1485 against Ferrante I of Aragon – it ended badly and the conspirators were all killed. The excellent tour of the castle's bare halls retraces these events – you're given a card which identifies you as one of the barons and guided by a narrator to a table where dummies impersonate those present at the conspiratorial banquet. We guarantee the ending will be less gory than the real one.

✯ Festivals & Events

Congiura dei Baroni 13-14 AUGUST
For two days a year Miglionico travels back in time to the Middle Ages for banquets, falconry shows, fire-eating, juggling, and processions. The grand finale sees a re-enactment of the barons' conspiracy, the most famous event in the history of the castle.

🛏️ Sleeping & Eating

Residenza delle Grazie B&B €€
(☎ 389 521 83 57; www.residenzadellegrazie.it; Via Poerio 24; s/d/tr/q €50/70/90/120; 🖥 ❄) Only a few rooms overlook the square of the Chiesa Madre, but all are comfortable, clean and pleasant. Excellent value for money, especially given the owner's touching helpfulness.

Hosteria del Malconsiglio PIZZERIA, RESTAURANT €€
(☎ 0835 55 99 41, 347 67 07 258; www.hosteriadel malconsiglio.it; Extramurale Castello 32; meals €25; ⊙ 7-11.30pm Wed-Sun, lunch by reservation) Great for robust pizzas and good homemade pasta. Even opponents of carbohydrates will find something to sink their teeth into in the form of delicious podolica-beef chops. The decor is trim and functional.

🛍️ Shopping

La Dispensa del Barone FOOD
(☎ 328 157 19 11, 388 939 53 31; www.ladispensadel barone.it; Via Pietro Sivilia 10; ⊙ 10am-1pm & 5-8pm Tue-Sat, 10am-1pm Sun) Miglionico is known for its figs and here you'll find them dried, in jam, and covered in chocolate.

ℹ️ Information

The **Pro Loco office** (☎ 329 122 14 45, 388 367 39 22; www.prolocodimiglionico.it; ⊙ variable) is in the Castle.

ℹ Getting There & Away

Miglionico is 20km southwest of Matera and connected by infrequent **SITASUD** buses (☑ 0835 38 50 07; www.sitasudtrasporti.it; 30 minutes).

Around Miglionico

Bosco della Monferrara   WOODS

As you leave Miglionico and take the road from the SS7 junction to Pomarico, you'll see a dense forest of Turkey oaks and Aleppo pines on your left. This is an ideal spot for beautiful walks among porcupines and badgers. If you want to make risotto for dinner, note that the area is teeming with porcini mushrooms in autumn and wild asparagus in spring.

Riserva Naturale Oasi
di San Giuliano   LAKE

(☑ 324 951 79 37; www.riservanaturalesangiuliano .business.site; Contrada Diga di San Giuliano; ☺ lake area always accessible) Modernisation can often lead to dramatic environmental disaster; other times, however, it can have positive effects. One such came when the construction of a dam on the Bradano in 1957 led several species of birds to flock to the new reservoir. To protect this area a 1000-hectare reserve was established in 1976, and today you'll see herons, cormorants and mallards fly here framed by the blue of sky and water and the green of pines and eucalyptus trees. There's a picnic area and it's hoped that the visitor centre will reopen soon.

Montescaglioso

POP 9224 / ELEV 365M

On a clear day, the view from Montescaglioso's Porta Sant'Angelo is breathtaking, stretching from the verdant Gravina to a soft succession of hills soaked in that poetic yellow that can only be achieved with parched earth. You'll see unused tuff-rock quarries and the antennas of Matera's Centro Geospaziale as well as the city of the Sassi itself, tiny from this distance. It's as if you can encapsulate both the landscape and the spirit of this magical land in a single glance. However, you don't come to Montescaglioso just to look at the view. There are, in fact, many reasons to visit, including one, the Abbazia di San Michele Arcangelo, that is truly extraordinary.

History

The origins of this town, spread over three hills (depicted in the coat of arms along with an ear of wheat), date back to the 4th century BCE. Conquered first by the Greeks and then by the Romans, Montescaglioso was a place of little importance until the arrival of the Normans. Subsequently, it thrived under the Swabians, at a time when monastic communities could obtain land bequests and considerable privileges, and the fame of its riches spread across the region's borders. This golden age proved fairly brief but still today the Abbazia di San Michele Arcangelo stands as a monumental testament to it.

◉ Sights

Even just walking through the narrow streets of Montescaglioso is a delight as its pale stone buildings evoke the more celebrated villages of Puglia.

★ Abbazia di San
Michele Arcangelo   ABBEY

(☑ 0835 20 10 16, 334 836 00 98; www.montesca glioso.net; Piazza del Popolo; adult/reduced €4/3; ☺ 10am-1pm & 3-5pm Tue-Sun Oct-Apr, 10am-1pm & 3-7pm Tue-Sun May-Sep) If after seeing Matera you think its environs can offer nothing but second-rate attractions, prepare to think again. This imposing abbey is of such seductive magnificence that it can rival anything in the provincial capital. Built, according to legend, in 534, but inhabited by Benedictines from 893, it experienced a period of splendour under Federico II and then again between 1484 and 1784, the year when the monks moved to Lecce after disagreements with the local feudal lord. A visit here is as structured as its history, passing from two refined cloisters – clear evidence of its former prosperity – to a library with 17th century grotesques, from the beautiful stuccoes of the Chiesa di Sant'Angelo to the Capitolo (Chapter House) and a 16th-century fresco of a Crucifixion scene in which Mary Magdalene sports a trendy blond hairdo. There's a small museum showcasing an archaeological collection and reconstructions of some monks' cells, a cave cellar, and an underground area with ancient Roman ruins.

The Abbey also houses the Centro Visite del Parco della Murgia Materana.

Chiesa Madre   CHURCH
(Via Chiesa Maggiore) At the end of a small side lane near the main street, the Chiesa Madre, dedicated to saints Peter and Paul, was rebuilt in the late 1700s over an earlier medieval church. Behind the facade rises a 44m-high bell tower while its bright late baroque interior harbours four 17-century canvases attributed to Mattia Preti. Adding to the church's allure is a local legend according to which it was built with a *passamano*, a kilometres-long human chain that transported material here from distant tuff caves.

Chiesa di Santa Maria in Platea   CHURCH
(Corso della Repubblica 96) This is the oldest church in town, dating back to the 11th century. The facade is simple and bare, like the single-nave interior which is decorated with seventeenth-century frescoes. It preserves a multi-material statue of a Madonna with Child, complete with necklace and daring neckline, and a papier-mâché statue of San Rocco, the patron saint of Montescaglioso.

Porta Sant'Angelo   LANDMARK
(Piazza del Popolo) Opening onto the square in front of the Abbazia, this gate commands splendid views and provides access to an area of cellars dug into the tuff rock, many of which are still used today. Outside the walls, a recently completed walkway circles the historic centre, passing by a huge megaphone on the west side, where you can shout your love for travel at the top of your voice.

★ Festivals & Events

La Notte dei Cucibocca   5 JANUARY
(www.montescaglioso.net) Be very careful if you happen to be in these parts at the beginning of January. On the fifth of the month a procession of mysterious, dark-clad characters with thick white beards emerge from the Abbey wearing hats or disk-like headwear made from the hemp used in olive oil mills. Their lovely habit is to threaten children that they'll sew their mouths shut with needle and thread if they don't keep quiet.

Carnevale Montese   FEBRUARY
(www.montescaglioso.net) The key evening is Shrove Tuesday, but the celebrations begin on the previous two Sundays. Floats are peopled by allegorical papier-mâché figures and at midnight the puppet of the 'Carnevalone' is burned as the bell of the Chiesa Madre rings 40 times.

ALTERNATIVE EXCURSIONS
....
Most travellers associate Matera with the possibility of adventurous outings into the Murgia Materana. However, Montescaglioso, 20km of caves south of the city, makes an equally convenient starting point. It too has a Centro di Educazione Ambientale (Environmental Education Centre) which organises visits and tours of the local rupestrian landscape. Bear in mind that paths are poorly signposted so it's often advisable to book a guided tour through the Centro Visite del Parco (☑0835 20 10 16, 334 836 00 98; www.montescaglioso.net; Abbazia di San Michele Arcangelo). The most interesting sites are undoubtedly the rupestrian structures spread around the Vallone della Loe, set among the canyons, oak woods and pleasant wheat fields.

Festa di San Rocco   14-21 AUGUST
(www.sanrocco.montescaglioso.net) In a region where popular devotion is as vital and vibrant as ever, the week of festivities held to celebrate the town's patron saint is awaited with baited breath. Events include processions, rituals, a concert, and a lottery whose proceeds help finance the fun.

🛏 Sleeping & Eating

Il Borgo Ritrovato   HOTEL €€
(☑0835 20 70 77, 328 367 82 20; www.ilborgoritrovato.com; Via Nicola Andrisani 25; s/d €70/120; ✸ 🅿) A beautiful portal gives access to this peaceful oasis. The rooms and apartments, all wood, arches and tuff rock, manage to combine tradition and tasteful minimalism. Make sure to ask for a look around the ancient olive mill. Excellent breakfast.

La Locanda dell'Abate   RESTAURANT €€
(☑350 090 67 30; Largo Monterrone 18; meals €30; ⊙12.30-3pm & 8-11pm Tue-Sat, 12.30-3pm Sun) Exposed stone, courteous service, and a cuisine that's both creative and traditionally-inspired are the keys to the success of this restaurant just a stone's throw from the Abbey. The starters and seafood rice and pasta dishes are truly excellent.

ℹ️ Information

The **Pro Loco** (📞 328 840 79 04; www.montesca glioso.net; Piazza San Giovanni Battista 15; ⊙ variable hours) is located in a small square near the main street, Corso della Repubblica.

ℹ️ Getting There & Away

From Matera there are frequent daily buses operated by the **Ferrovie Appulo Lucane** (📞 800 050 500; www.ferrovieappulolucane.it; €1.30; 30 minutes).

VALLE DEL BASENTO

While boasting the title of longest river in Basilicata, the Basento is today little more than a stream, in parts even a trickle, especially in summer. But in spite of its humble appearance, it profoundly shapes the geography of the entire central-eastern part of the territory. It nourishes the luxuriant and verdant woods of the Apennine slopes and passes through areas of Mediterranean maquis and barren clay soil as it flows down to the lunar landscapes of the badlands and on to the Metaponto plain. And in so doing it unites villages full of history and tradition. To follow the course of the Basento, itself a beautiful symbol of a region so seemingly poor and humble yet so rich in beauty and culture, is to look into the very soul of Basilicata.

Tricarico

POP 4929 / ELEV 698M

Given the profusion of monuments, churches, aristocratic residences, medieval traces, illustrious personalities, museums and iconic 20th-century heirlooms, it would be difficult to summarise why Tricarico is one of the province's most important centres. Quicker and more effective would be to trust us and include it in your tour of Basilicata. You won't regret it.

History

Developed in Lombard times, Tricarico was occupied first by the Saracens and then by the Normans (architectural evidence testifies to the passage of both peoples). From the late 15th century, important religious institutes appeared, where intellectuals and artists, including the painter Pietro Antonio Ferro, were trained. In the 20th century, Tricarico became the birthplace of one of the most important personalities in recent Lucanian history, Rocco Scotellaro (see boxed text p79).

👁️ Sights

Torre Normana TOWER
(📞 0835 52 61 11; Largo Santa Croce; tickets €2; ⊙ by reservation only) Soaring to a height of 27m and with its distinct corbels, this circular tower stands out as the symbol of Tricarico, the undisputed star of the town's skyline, and the only surviving evidence of the original 9th- to 10th-century castle.

Chiesa e Convento di Santa Chiara CHURCH
(Via Fuori Porta Monte; ⊙ 9.30am-12.30pm & 4.30-7.30pm Tue-Sat, 11.30am-12.30pm Sun) FREE In 1333, Tricarico's castle was transformed into an equally impregnable cloistered convent where the envied daughters of wealthy local families were sent. The adjoining church (⊙ 9am-6pm winter, 9am-7.30pm summer) stands out for its coffered ceiling and atmosphere of deep contemplation. The real highlight, however, is the Cappella del Crocifisso, which was entirely decorated by Pietro Antonio Ferro in the early 17th century. The decorative composition is extremely complex – the vault is a profusion of saints; the east wall is dominated by an Annunciazione; the west wall by a Crocifissione; and the north wall by a depiction of the Decapitazione del Battista. The frescoes compensate for their occasional lack of masterly finesse with an extraordinary narrative and chromatic vigour, capable of recalling much better-known pictorial cycles.

Palazzo Ducale HISTORIC BUILDING
(📞 0835 72 62 68; www.museopalazzoducaletrica rico .beniculturali.it; Corso Vittorio Veneto 2; ⊙ 9am-1pm Mon-Fri) FREE When the Norman castle was donated to the Poor Clares for them to make it their convent, the counts of Tricarico moved into this 14th-century building. Over the centuries it subsequently became the noble residence of the Pignatelli and Revertèra families. Today it houses a small archaeological museum, showcasing locally-found artefacts in one wing. If it's closed, console yourself with the uplifting view of the valley.

Arab Quarters NEIGHBOURHOOD
Tricarico's main attractions include the two Arab quarters of Rabatana and Saracena in the northern part of the town. The layout of the area is still legible today – the

neighbourhood is bisected by the *shari* (narrow main street), off which *darb* (side streets) branch, intertwining and leading to *sucac* (dead ends). The surrounding area, however, testifies to the ingenuity with which the Arabs dealt with the unsuitable soil conditions and managed to cultivate orchards (close to the walls) and grow vegetables (further downstream) by terracing the steep slopes and irrigating the formerly barren land.

The Gates   GATE
In addition to those in the Arab quarters, the city retains other ancient gates, such as the 13th-century Porta Fontana (Strada Boccanera), complete with its stone hinges; Porta Monte (Via Fuori Porta Monte), unusually decorated with iron spikes; the small Porta delle Beccarie (Piazza Garibaldi), through which no carts passed, only pedestrians headed into the heart of town; and finally Porta Vecchia, the most refined gate, crowned by a statue of the Madonna and Child, and also known as the Arco di Re Ladislao.

Duomo   CATHEDRAL
(Via Duomo) The scale of this massive church, consecrated to Santa Maria Assunta and rebuilt several times, testifies to the importance of the bishopric of Tricarico. In the three-nave interior, in the second chapel on the left, you'll find a 15-century triptych

---

WORTH A TRIP

A WALK IN THE WOODS

If you're suffering from an overdose of culture and history, a nice trip to the countryside could balance out your day. Take the SS7 for 13km east of Tricarico to the Contrada Tre Cancelli and you'll find the gateway to the beautiful bosco di Tricarico, a bucolic wood of Turkey oaks and oak trees. This is the ideal place for an easy-going walk, on which you might come across the scant archaeological remnants of Piano della Civita (4th century BCE). For a proverbial picnic, try to pick up a typical quiche made with sweet dough in one of the village delis.

---

and a *Trasporto al Sepolcro* by Ferro with particularly bold colours.

Museo Diocesano   MUSEUM
(☎348 972 59 68; www.mudit.it; Piazza Mons. Raffaele Delle Nocche; ☉9am-noon Tue, Thu & Fri, 3-5pm Wed, 10am-1pm & 3-6pm Sat & Sun Oct-Apr, 10am-1pm Tue & Thu, 5-7pm Wed & Fri, 10am-1pm & 4-7pm May-Sep, closed Nov) FREE More than for the collection, which nevertheless includes wooden statues, a Visione di Ezechiele by Ferro, and various liturgical furnishings, this museum merits a visit for the rich elegance of Palazzo Vescovile, in which it's housed.

THE PEOPLE'S POET

Rocco Scotellaro (born in Tricarico in 1923; died in Portici in 1953) transcended the boundaries of his hometown and of Basilicata itself to rise to prominence in post-WWII Italy. The son of a shoemaker and a housewife, he was a man of passionate temperament who, after finishing his classical studies, devoted himself to political activism in support of labourers and the poorest members of society. He founded a section of the Socialist Party in Tricarico and, in 1946, at the age of just 23, he was elected mayor. He fought fervently for agrarian reform in the south. But the events of his troubled life, cut short by a heart attack when he was only 30, take on an even greater import when seen in the light of his formidable poetic output. He wrote more than 100 poems (as well as works in other forms), creating not only a manifesto of the aspirations and tragedies of the peasantry, but also a lacerating portrayal of an intimate inner struggle between hope and despair.

The town of Tricarico has dedicated a Literary Trail to Scotellaro – along the town's streets you can read some of his verse and take a look at the house where he was born (Via Scotellaro 37). There's also a Centro Documentazion (☎0835 52 61 11; Largo San Francesco 5; ☉by reservation) housed in the former convent of San Francesco.

Following his death he received various posthumous recognitions, including a Viareggio Prize, a dedication in the form of Luchino Visconti's film *Rocco and His Brothers* and a central position in the panel *Lucania 61* created by his mentor, Carlo Levi, and now on show at Palazzo Lanfranchi in Matera (p57).

Palazzo Lizzadri

MUSEUM

(✆ 0835 52 61 11; Via Battista Laura; ☺ by reservation) FREE The Palazzo houses an exhibition of traditional Lucanian costumes and the first pieces of a museum display of anthropological masks.

★☆ Festivals & Events

Carnevale

JANUARY / FEBRUARY

Probably Basilicata's most important carnival kicks off well in advance with a parade on 17 January in honour of sant'Antonio Abate (St Anthony the Great), protector of animals. And, unsurprisingly, events involve plenty of cow and bull masks. To find accommodation in the days around Shrove Tuesday, you'll need to book well ahead.

Raduno delle Maschere Antropologiche

JUNE

Confirming the city's vocation, this sensational celebration of anthropological masks draws people from as far afield as the Pyrenees and Balkans, Greece and the most remote corners of the Italian peninsula. They come to pay homage to folk traditions that catapult visitors into another dimension.

🛏 Sleeping & Eating

Traces of Arab influence can be found in one of the town's signature dishes – *lagane*, tagliatelle pasta with stale bread, almonds and raisins.

Gianmaria

B&B €€

(✆ 320 814 15 96, 339 581 49 49; Via Fratelli Cervi 1; r €80; P �🛜) Just a five-minute walk from the historic centre, this cute little detached house offers four bright rooms, a warm welcome to your pets, and a nice little garden to relax in. Breakfasts are strictly kilometre zero.

Tre Cancelli

RESTAURANT, PIZZERIA €€

(✆ 349 459 26 74; www.trecancelli.it; Contrada Tre Cancelli; meals €20-25; ☺ noon-3pm & 7.30-10pm Tue-Sun) Tricarico's most popular restaurant is located near the town's woods. And whether you eat outdoors in summer or in front of the fireplace in winter, you'll leave fully satisfied thanks to the rustic, homemade and tasty food. The barbecued meats are excellent and the pizzas highly digestible.

ℹ Information

The **Pro Loco** (✆ 327 362 91 38, 392 560 92 84; www.prolocotricarico.it; Via Rocco Scotellaro, ☺ variable hrs) is located in the former Casa Comunale.

ℹ Getting There & Away

Tricarico can be reached by car from Matera via Ferrandina on the SS7 and SS407 (65km, about one hour) or on the SP8 Matera-Grassano road (55km, one hour). **SITASUD** (✆ 0835 38 50 07; www.sitasudtrasporti.it) operates buses to/from Matera (one hour 20 minutes to one hour 55 minutes) and Potenza (one hour 35 minutes).

Ferrandina

POP 8137 / ELEV 497M

With its houses cheekily lined up as if in pose, this elegant town seems to react with disdain to the indifference most visitors show it. Yet Ferrandina is a very pleasant place and on weekend afternoons it buzzes with a vibrancy unknown in most neighboring villages. It also boasts a series of outstanding religious buildings that lend it an air of solemnity and prestige. The most impressive of these is the massive 17th-century Monastero di Santa Chiara (Largo Palestro), which towers over the rest of town. Now that the Poor Clares have left, you can visit the Museo Comunale Civiltà Contadina e Antichi Mestieri (✆ 340 877 09 81, 328 132 71 77; ☺ daily by reservation) FREE inside and compare the grandeur of the complex with that of the nearby Convento di San Domenico. This was inaugurated at the end of the 18th century to welcome Dominican monks but was dissolved as early as 1809. Inside, the MAFE – Museo Archeologico di Ferrandina (✆ 380 781 78 89; www. civicomafe.it; Calata San Domenico; ☺ 10am-1pm & 4-7pm Mon-Thu, 10am-1pm & 5-8pm Fri-Sun) FREE displays olive oil presses from a 4th-century BCE mill and finds from a 7th-century BCE necropolis, while the adjacent church overflows with canvases (not of any great value) from the Neapolitan school. For a less austere religiosity, head to the main square to visit the Chiesa Madre (Piazza Plebiscito). Again, the scale of the building is striking – it's one of Basilicata's largest churches – as is the simplicity of the prominent facade, the baroque interior and the 16th-century sculptures of Isabella and Federico d'Aragona attributed to Altobello Persio.

✗ Eating

Ferrandina's signature food is the *majatica* olive, which is eaten dried.

Rosso di Sera

RESTAURANT €€

(✆ 0835 75 74 26; Via Dante Alighieri 6; meals €25; ☺ 12.45-2.30pm & 7.45-10.30pm Tue-Sun) The fillets of donkey meat and hearty pasta dishes will guarantee you go to bed with a full belly and a smile on your face. Good value.

⭐ **Sartagus**   RESTAURANT €€
(📞 0835 23 56 08, 334 153 60 44; www.ristorante sartago.it; Corso Vittorio Emanuele II 50; meals €35; ⊙1-3pm & 8-10.30pm Tue-Sat, 1-3pm Sun) Sartago represents a real coup for the town's dining scene. With background music and an elegant minimalist wood-and-stone ambience, it offers attentive service and bold, refined cooking – the characteristics of a restaurant that makes a mark. The desserts with matching glass of wine are superb.

ℹ️ Information
Pro Loco (Corso Vittorio Emanuele 81; ⊙hrs vary)

ℹ️ Getting There & Away
BUS
Ferrovie Appulo Lucane (📞 800 050 500; www. ferrovieappulolucane.it) operates a handful of

daily buses to/from Matera (€2.30, one hour to the village, 40 minutes to the station).
SITASUD (📞 0835 38 50 07; www.sitasudtraspor ti.it) also runs several services.
Grassani (📞 0835 72 14 43; www.grassani.it) runs buses between Matera and Potenza via Ferrandina Scalo (30 minutes for Matera, one hour for Potenza).

CAR & MOTORCYLE
Ferrandina is an important regional crossroads. By car it can be reached via the SS407 Basentana which connects Potenza to Metaponto. For Matera you have to take the SS7.

TRAIN
Ferrandina is the closest town to Matera on the **Trenitalia** (📞 800 90 60 60; www.lefrecce.it) rail network. There are direct trains to/from major cities such as Potenza (from €3.55, one hour), Naples (from €13.50, 3¼ hours) and Rome (from €45, 5½ hours). The station is located at the bottom of the valley, 10km northeast of the village.

ACCETTURA, MAY & THE FORESTA DI GALLIPOLI COGNATO

Most visitors to the Parco Regionale di Gallipoli Cognato e Piccole Dolomiti Lucane, which straddles the provinces of Potenza and Matera, are drawn by the opportunity for adventure in Pietrapertosa (p108) and Castelmezzano (p108) in the Potenza area. However, this territory barely touches the park, which extends right into the heart of the Matera province. Here the sharp sandstone peaks and deep cliffs of the Piccole Dolomiti (p107) give way to the intimate beauty of the Foresta di Gallipoli Cognato and Bosco di Montepiano. In these woods, you can explore the dense network of paths that wind through the mass of Turkey oaks, hornbeams, maples, beeches and hollies, enjoying pyrotechnic explosions of colour in spring, when anemones, cyclamens and rare orchids burst out of the undergrowth, and in autumn when the symphony of warm colours contrasts beautifully with the evergreen plants.

But the area's highlight attraction is undoubtedly Accettura. This small village boasts Italy's narrowest street, Vicolo Pozzo (just 41 cm wide), and, more significantly, hosts one of the region's most impressive events – the ancient arboreal ritual of the Maggio di Accettura (www.ilmaggiodiaccettura.it). During this festival, which derives from a pagan fertility ceremony and takes place every May, a large Turkey oak is felled and dragged by oxen to the town square, where a holly is grafted onto its top. The two 'married' trees are then righted and the strongest boys in the village challenge each other to see who can climb the highest. Similar rituals take place in other Lucanian villages such as Pietrapertosa (in June) and Oliveto Lucano (in August).

If you can't make one of these, you can make up for it by visiting the Museo dei Riti Arborei (📞 0835 67 50 05; Via del Maggio; ⊙on request) or ask for information at the Pro Loco office (📞 0835 67 52 92; www.prolocoaccettura.it; Via Roma 13; ⊙variable hrs). Finally, we'd recommend you visit the headquarters of the Park Authority (📞 347 095 79 67, 348 340 89 02; www.parcogallipolicognato.it; Località Palazzo Accettura; ⊙times vary, call ahead), 12km north of the village. Here you'll find a nature museum dedicated to the black stork, a botanical garden, the Lucania Outdoor Park (📞 348 340 89 02; www. lucaniaoutdoorpark.com; routes €6-15; ⊙10am-5pm daily Jul-Aug, variable times Sep-Jun), and access to several trails. For a short excursion, itinerary 714 is a loop of about 4km, which runs alongside a fauna-filled area populated by fallow deer.

MATERA PROVINCE FERRANDINA

BASILICATA'S STONEHENGE

One of the things that makes Basilicata so alluring is the presence of vibrant religious events dating from ancient times – pilgrimages, devotional rites, and pagan rituals. But there are also signs of an even more ancient spirituality. To find some, take the region's main axis, the SS407 Basentana, which connects Potenza to Metaponto, and exit at Calciano (or Campomaggiore, if coming from the north), following on towards Oliveto Lucano and the Parco Regionale di Gallipoli Cognato (see boxed text p81). Before entering the village, turn right and head to the Riserva Antropologica del Monte Croccia, where you'll find the remains of a fortified city from the 6th century BCE, and, best of all, the Petre de la Mola megalithic complex, whose large boulders align with the sun at noon and sunset, and on the various solstices and equinoxes. The site may not be as spectacular as its English counterpart, but then again it doesn't attract the same hordes of hippies, new age adherents and tourists. It's set in a beautiful forest of Turkey oaks and oak trees, and vibrates with a certain imperceptible energy.

Bernalda

POP 12,445 / ELEV 127M

In sparsely populated Basilicata, a small town like Bernalda takes on the dynamic and vital air of a city – throughout the day Corso Umberto I teems with activity thanks to the bars, shops and restaurants that line up behind the benches crowded with sprightly elderly people. But head south along Corso Italia and the noise of the traffic gives way to a more subdued hubbub. Here the white houses of the historic centre adhere to the stereotype of the classic Lucanian village as they lead up to the castle (SP Carrera Vecchia), characterised by two towers built by the Aragonese Bernardino de Bernaudo (after whom the town is named). Beyond, sweeping panoramas take in the surrounding countryside. Next to the castle is the Chiesa di San Bernardino, dedicated to the town's patron saint, whose domes reflect a slight Byzantine influence. Bernalda also boasts a certain glamourous appeal as the

hometown of the family of Francis Ford Coppola, to whom the town owes the restoration of Palazzo Margherita and its resurrection as an ultra-luxurious boutique hotel (☑0835 54 90 60; www.palazzomargherita.com; Corso Umberto 64; ste from €380; ❈❂P❆). Another drawcard is its privileged position between Matera and the beaches of Metaponto.

🛏 Sleeping

Sweet Holiday Home RENTAL APARTMENTS €€
(☑339 106 53 90; Via Petrarca 95 a/b; apts for 1/2/3 persons €50/70/90; ❂❈) Two pleasant little apartments a stone's throw from Corso Umberto I, both clean and comfortable. The brioches are packaged but the rates are great value for money.

🍴 Eating

In Bernalda's restaurants you can try the excellent horse meat for which the town is known.

Equineria Da Mimmo BUTCHER €€
(☑339 192 45 43; Via Albini 5; meals €25; ⊙7-11pm Mon-Sat) Of course, if you're a vegetarian this place will horrify you. If not, the quality of the horse meat and the atmosphere, somewhere between a tavern and a saloon, make for a truly superb meal.

Bernaldabella RESTAURANT €€
(☑0835 54 32 41; www.trattorialalocandiera.it; Corso Umberto I 194; meals €30; ⊙12.30-3pm & 8-11pm) Eye-catching dishes include swordfish carpaccio with green apple, cod tempura with crusco peppers, and squid ink risotto with goat cheese and shrimp tartare. There are also non-gluten options and the service is up to par. All in all, an excellent choice for a quick lunch or a more formal dinner.

ℹ Information

Pro Loco (☑0835 54 23 09; www.prolocobernalda.it; Via Anacreon; ⊙variable hrs)
You'll find plenty of useful planning information on www.visitmetapontobernalda.it.

ℹ Getting There & Away

From Matera, follow the SS7 southeast until you reach the SS407 (Basentana), then turn towards Metaponto. Alternatively, take the SS7 and SS380, following the signs to Bernalda. From Metaponto, Bernalda is 15km northwest along the SS407.

SITASUD (☑0835 38 50 07; www.sitasudtrasporti.it) runs a daily service from Matera (50 minutes), while **Chiruzzi** (☑0835 54 22 50; www.chiruzzi.it) has a few daily buses to Metaponto (25 minutes), Pisticci (25 minutes) and two to Taranto (one hour 25 minutes).

Pisticci

POP 17,602 / ELEV 389M

For centuries, life in hilltop Pisticci continued placidly above the surrounding ravine landscape (p91). But the friable clay soil that distinguishes the area and gives it its acclaimed beauty can also lead to tragedy. In 1688, a landslide destroyed almost half the town and killed 400 people. The Chiesa Madre (Piazza XI Febbraio), a Romanesque-Renaissance building overflowing with superb wooden features – statues of saints, altars, a pulpit and choir – miraculously remained standing, complete with its beautiful 13th-century bell tower. The castle (Piazza Castello), of which only a few sad ruins remain, acquired an even more heroic position, towering literally over the houses and symbolically defying the tragedy. As a result of the disaster, the historic centre was split into two parts: the surviving core, which was re-named Terravecchia, and below that, the Rione Dirupo, where rows of typical *casedde* (small white houses) were built, adding an almost Andalucian air to the neighbourhood. Among the narrow streets, the small Chiesa dell'Immacolata Concezione (Via Concezione), is worth searching out. Dating to the 16th century, it has a wooden ceiling shaped like a ship's hull, white walls and an 18th-century organ. But what makes Pisticci so evocative is the knowledge, which will hit every visitor, that it only takes a sudden and unpredictable event to totally shake up existence (in this case the life of a town).

Before leaving town, we recommend two further stops: the Museo Civico di Pisticci (☏0835 58 57 11; www.museocivicopisticci.it; Piazza dei Caduti; ☺9am-1pm Mon-Fri) FREE recently inaugurated in the town hall, with copies of vases by the Pisticci Painter (5th century BCE) and a rich multimedia display illustrating the town's history, and the Chiesa di Santa Maria del Casale (Via Vespucci 2), at the eastern end of town with an exquisite 14th-century door.

🛏 Sleeping & Eating

Antica Masseria Rullo AGRITURISMO €€
(☏391 499 50 08; Contrada Rullo; meals €30-35; ☺8pm-midnight Wed-Mon) The rural location and informal, relaxed atmosphere are typical of an agriturismo but the meat and fish dishes, while undoubtedly taking their inspiration from the local territory, display the sort of sophistication you'd normally associate with a more vaunted restaurant. The fox that roams among the garden tables in summer lends a further splash of colour. Pretty rooms (€50) and there's also a swimming pool.

L'Incontro RESTAURANT €€
(☏0835 58 24 67; Via Risorgimento 2; meals €25; ☺noon-3pm & 7-11pm Tue-Sun) Meat and fish, traditional appetizers and pizzas are served at this restaurant in the town's main square. The quality of the dishes varies but the atmosphere, thanks to a decor of arches and exposed brickwork, will give you nothing to complain about.

✹ Festivals & Events

Lucania Film Festival AUGUST
(www.lucaniafilmfestival.it) Basilicata's film vocation isn't limited to Matera. In fact, Pisticci has a long-standing relationship with film as reflected in the fact that this festival, aimed at promoting all forms of audiovisual media, has been held well over 20 times. It takes place at CineParco Tilt, in the hamlet of Marconia, 15km southeast of Pisticci.

Teatro dei Calanchi AUGUST
(www.teatrodeicalanchi.com) Absolutely spectacular theatrical performances of various kinds are held on a clay stage in the middle of the badlands. You'll find a map with the exact location on the website. Bring a good supply of water.

ℹ Information

Pro Loco (☏333 221 12 50; Piazza La Salsa; ☺9.30am-12.30pm & 3.30-8pm Mon-Sat)

ℹ Getting There & Away

Pisticci is a few kilometres off the SS407 Basentana, which connects it with Metaponto and Ferrandina. **Ferrovie Appulo Lucane** (☏800 050 500; www.ferrovieappulolucane.it) runs daily buses to/from Matera (€2.70, one hour).

IONIAN COAST

The stretch of Lucanian coast that skirts the Gulf of Taranto is short, less than 40km. Just as brief was the glorious era that gave rise to illustrious characters and opulent cities whose names remain etched into the history of antiquity. In fact, one of the main reasons visitors head to these parts is to

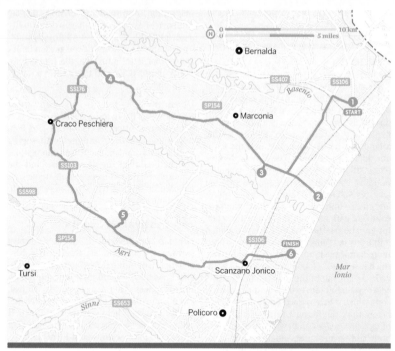

🚗 Driving Tour
Sea & the Badlands

START METAPONTO
END LUDO DI SCANZANO JONICO
DURATION 72KM, 12 HOURS

For a mix of beach relaxation and cultural and outdoor activity, this trip between the Ionian coast and its hinterland will take a whole day. At ❶ **Metaponto**, visit the archaeological museum and, after admiring its millennia-old vases and jewels, hop in the car and treat yourself to a couple of hours on the sandy beaches of ❷ **Marina di Pisticci**. Bordered by a splendid pine forest, these are among the longest on the coast. By now you'll be a bit hungry, as well as terribly hot, so it's time to head inland. After a quick glance at the more than one-thousand-year-old ❸ **Castello di San Basilio** (www.castellodisanbasilio. it; Contrada Castello di San Basilio), push on to ❹ **Pisticci** where you can wander the white-washed alleys of the Dirupo district and stop at the restaurant L'Incontro (p83). Once

you've finished lunch, take advantage of your renewed energy and continue on to ❺ **Montalbano Jonico**, one of the most haunting villages in the Matera area. Strolling along Via Carlo Alberto up to the Porta dell'Orologio, visiting the 16th-century Chiesa Madre, looking for noble coats of arms in the doorways will fill you with a melancholy that can best be consumed by exploring the ravines that surround the town, perhaps with the help of one of the highly prepared guides of the Circolo Legambiente Montalbano (legambientemontalbano.jimdo.com). By the end of the walk it will be well into the afternoon, but it's not yet time to put an end to your adventure. What better way to end your day than a nice sunset dip at ❻ **Lido di Scanzano Jonico** where the Mediterranean shrubland backs onto the sand? Nothing, except perhaps a fish dinner at the Sabbia D'Oro Beach Club restaurant (Via Lido Torre 27). This land is so varied and surprising.

explore what remains of the colonies of Metaponto, Siris and Heraclea. Another reason is to hit the sandy beaches, which, after reclamation and redevelopment work started in the 1930s, came to replace the unhealthy marshes that had infested the area for centuries. The coast doesn't always stand out for its charm, particularly in high season when the resorts are absolutely packed, but come in the quieter months and you'll be able to find remote corners where you can look out to sea, breathe in the intense aromas of Mediterranean maquis, and make out the sinuous movement of nymphs and marine deities in the rippling waves.

Metaponto

POP 1000 / ELEV 4M

As you walk the anonymous streets of this small village, part of the municipality of Bernalda (p82), you'll discover that the local architecture reflects both the grandeur of its past (from its foundation in the 7th century BCE to the 4th century BCE) and the depth of the decline that followed. Its remarkable archaeological sites bear witness to the opulence that trade brought the colony, where Pythagoras lived for 15 years (510–495 BCE) and where he's said to have hidden a mysterious treasure (if you find it, we demand a percentage for the tip). In contrast, the absence of any buildings from before the last century tells of the area's tragic abandonment following a decline precipitated by its support for Pyrrhus (272 BCE) and Hannibal (207 BCE) in their wars against Rome. After modern reclamation work, Metaponto dedicated itself to the intensive cultivation of citrus fruit, peaches and apricots, as well as beach tourism. The Lido, which teems with holidaymakers in summer but is deserted and melancholy in winter, is located 3km downstream from the main village, where the archaeological museum is located.

◉ Sights

Museo Archeologico Nazionale   MUSEUM
(☑0835 74 53 27; www.museometaponto.benicul turali.it; Via Dinu Adamesteanu 21; adult/reduced €2.50/2; ⊙9am-8pm Tue-Sun) The museum's rich collection includes artefacts belonging to the indigenous peoples who lived in the area before the arrival of the Greeks and pieces produced by the colonisers, who introduced a greater sophistication and more figurative

BASILICATA'S AMBASSADOR TO THE WORLD

Many people ignore Basilicata, overlooking even its position on a map. However, there are few who don't know its most representative product, a veritable regional ambassador to the world: Amaro Lucano. Many things have changed since Pasquale Vena invented the liqueur in Pisticci in 1894 – today 30,000 bottles are produced daily and the plant is no longer in the village but in the underlying industrial area of Pisticci Scalo. But the secret of its recipe, which is said to involve 30 medicinal herbs, has never been revealed. At the plant, there's now a visitor centre, Essenza Lucano (☑0835 46 92 07; www.esselucano.it; Viale Cav. Pasquale Vena; ⊙10.30am-7pm Tue-Sun), which has an interesting museum full of distillation stills charting the history of the company, a garden of medicinal plants, a store for direct sales, and a bar where you can enjoy amaro-based cocktails. Visits, both individual and guided, were free at the time of research, but there were plans to introduce an entrance fee – check the website.

approach to their decorations. Some tomb finds are truly remarkable. Many items are related to beauty care, including earrings, necklaces, and mirrors that will make even the most vain of travellers dream.

Parco Archeologico   ARCHAEOLOGICAL SITE
(Contrada Samson; ⊙9am-1.45pm Fri-Sun) FREE Two kilometers east of the Archaeological Museum, is the archaeological area of ancient Metapontum. Straight away, the scale of the site gives an idea of the degree of urbanization reached by the colony in the 6th century BCE. The meagre ruins, combined with a good dose of imagination, will have you dreaming of warriors and priestesses, artisans and merchants. The best-preserved structure, thanks in part to a recent restoration, is the hemicycle theatre. Over on the other side of the site are the temples, including one to Artemis, the park's most photographed, with the remnants of Ionic columns capped by a few stones. You can also make out the floor plan, with eight-columned front, of a sanctuary dedicated to Hera.

Tavole Palatine   TEMPLE

(SS106; ◔9am-1hr before sunset Tue-Sun) Leave the village and head north to pick up the SS106 towards Taranto. The first exit off this road leads to the most exciting archaeological site in Metaponto and probably the whole of Basilicata. The Tavole Palatine was built in the 6th century BCE in honour of the goddess Hera, and with 15 of the original 32 Doric columns still standing, it's a sublime place in which to breathe in history (as well as the scent of the flowers that surround the site in late spring). Come at sunset, when the sky and columns are tinged in a haunting pink.

Lido di Metaponto   BEACHES

In June and September the long stretches of golden beach offer a snapshot of wild beauty, their sands backed by Mediterranean scrub, agaves sprawling like pagan monsters, sand lilies, pine forests and rows of eucalyptus. However, in high season, the atmosphere becomes brutally chaotic as the proliferation of not particularly elegant private beach clubs (umbrella and two sunbeds €10-20) reduces the stretches of free (public) beach. But whenever you come, the clear, shallow waters make the Lido di Metaponto suitable for those travelling with children (assuming the barriers erected to limit damage from storm surges and reduce erosion are preserved).

Notable among the structures lined up along the southbound coast is the historic Lido delle Sirene (📱368 774 41 77; www.lidodelle sirenemetaponto.it; Lungomare Nettuno), which has probably been in business since Pythagoras' time (he spent the latter part of his life in Metaponto). Then there's Punta dell'Eughe (📱349 247 61 89; Lido Punta dell'Eughe), where you'll find a yoga school, Jacuzzi and restaurant. To the north, Marinella (📱333 224 71 31, 335 760 24 80; www.lidomarinella.com) stands out with its circular Hawaiian-style counter, as does the renowned Dom Pablo (📱333 368 90 00; www.dompablo.it; Via Dompablo), one of the area's most refined spots. Both are located far from the traffic in the Riserva Forestale Naturale (📱0971 41 10 64; www.ceabernaldameta ponto.it), which encompasses the mouth of the river Bradano, some beautiful dunes, and wetlands where malarial mosquitoes raged until the 1950s. The area's healthier today, and, at most, you'll meet a few otters around their habitat near the river mouth and along the reclamation channels, and, in the nesting season (June to August), some loggerhead sea turtles. In high season, you'll need to book ahead to bag an umbrella in the bathing establishments mentioned above, otherwise the free beach is very wide.

🎊 Festivals & Events

Metaponto Beach Festival   AUGUST

(www.metapontobeach.it) Held at the Castello Torremare, this is a three-day celebration of independent music, the territory and summer.

🛏 Sleeping

Tourism in Metaponto is strictly seasonal: in summer prices are high and it's best to book early; in winter it can be a challenge to find a hotel that's open.

Camping Internazionale   CAMPING €

(📱0835 74 19 16, 338 202 44 71; www.villageinter nazionale.com; Viale delle Nereide; adult/child camping €9/5; bungalow with 2/5 beds per week €480/880; 🛜 P ☀) This vacation village just 20m from the beach has a restaurant, bar, pizzeria, movie theatre, and even a gym to work out in. The bungalows are clean and comfortable, and pets are welcome.

Riva dei Greci   CAMPING €

(📱0835 74 50 14, 338 207 87 39; www.rivadeigreci .it; Via Santa Pelagina; campsite adults/children €12/7; 3-room bungalow/villa per week €1120/1400; 🛜 ❄ P) Immersed in the greenery of a pine forest, this place guarantees convenient access to a private beach – reachable on foot in 10 minutes or via a shuttle service – and delightfully retro evenings thanks to its piano bar and amphitheatre for cabaret shows. There's also a tennis court/football pitch, restaurant and market.

Hotel Turismo   HOTEL €€

(📱0835 74 19 18; www.hotelturismometaponto .it; Viale delle Ninfee 5; B&B/half-board/full-board per person in standard rooms €60/80/90, in superior rooms €80/100/110; ◔Apr-Sep; ❄ 🛜 @) Clean, simple, overlooking the central square and very close to the beach. The staff are friendly and helpful and have smiles that are brighter than many of the rather gloomy communal areas.

⭐ San Teodoro Nuovo   AGRITURISMO €€€

(📱0835 47 00 42, 366 573 64 77; www.santeodoro nuovo.com, www.tenutavisconti.com; Contrada San Teodoro, Marconia; s/d €100/160; ◔year-round; ❄ 🛜 P 🐕) The historic farmhouse of Duke Visconti di Modrone-d'Oria (still inhabited by the family) is surrounded by 150 hectares of citrus orchards and olive groves. Its 10 apartments are furnished with memorabilia and antiques and guarantee aristocratic comfort. It's possible to organise excursions on horseback or rent bicycles; or you can head off to the sea 8km away or take a day trip to Matera and the Lucanian Apennines. Dogs are welcome.

Magna Grecia Hotel Village RESORT €€€
(☑0835 74 56 61; www.magnagreciavillage.com; Via del Lido 1; full-board per person €155; ☺mid-Jun–mid-Sep; ✳ 🎇 🖃) With three swimming pools, an amphitheatre for outdoor shows, tennis and volleyball courts, a football pitch, a gym and aerobics classes, as well as a shuttle service to its private beach, a playground for children and a spa for adults, this resort is for those who prefer comfort over atmosphere. The accommodation units are furnished in a modern style.

✗ Eating

There are a lot of bars on the beach and restaurants in hotels and holiday villages, but relatively few restaurants on the sea, at least fewer than you'd expect at a seaside resort.

Ristorante Le Sirene PIZZERIA, RESTAURANT €€
(☑333 409 85 34, 346 863 54 77; Viale delle Sirene 12; meals €25-30; ☺lunch May-Sep) The TV in the dining room, the tables on the terrace and the style of the furnishings aren't exactly encouraging, but the freshness of the fish and the competitive prices dispel any fear. A stone's throw from the beach.

ℹ Information

Metaponto's **Pro Loco** (☑0835 23 61 82, 328 421 39 33; www.prolocodimetaponto.it; ☺9am-2pm Mon-Sat & 3pm-6pm Tue-Thu) is located in Piazza Giovanni XXIII. More convenient for holidaymakers is the summer **infopoint kiosk** (☑328 421 39 33; ☺9am-noon Mon-Sat Jun-Sep) in the clearing where the rides are located. There's also useful information on www.visitmetapontobernalda.it.

The **Centro di Educazione Ambientale Bernalda e Metaponto** (☑329 419 44 11, 391 791 52 15; www.ceabernaldametaponto.it) highlights the development of the territory and social tourism. It organises (sometimes free) guided tours and educational activities focusing on the area's archaeological and natural heritage.

ℹ Getting There & Away

BUS
SITASUD (☑0835 38 50 07; www.sitasudtrasporti .it) buses connect Metaponto with Matera (one hour), Taranto (25 minutes) and Policoro (20 to

45 minutes). **Chiruzzi** (☑0835 54 22 50; www. chiruzzi.it) operates frequent services to Bernalda (25 minutes) and a Friday night bus to Milan (13 hours).

CAR & MOTORCYCLE
From Matera, take the SS7 and then the southbound SS407 (Basentana); allow about 40 minutes' driving for the 48km. Metaponto is on the SS106, 50km southwest of Taranto.

TRAIN
The Taranto–Reggio Calabria railway line runs parallel to the coast and the SS106. **Trenitalia** (www.trenitalia.com) trains connect Metaponto with Taranto (from €3.40, 35to 55 minutes, approximately half-hourly) and Potenza (from €6.05, 1½ hours, 10 daily). From the station, which is located 3km west of Lido di Metaponto, a regular **SITA-SUD** (☑0835 38 50 07; www.sitasudtrasporti.it) bus service runs to the beaches.

Policoro

POP 17,788 / ELEV 25M

Evidence that Policoro was once the Greek settlement of Heraclea and the site of a famous battle in 280 BCE between a Roman army and Pyrrhus and his elephants, can be found in the town's archaeological museum and in the names of its waterfront streets, 5km east of the centre. The town's appearance, however, is decidedly less evocative. Policoro has been growing since the 1950s and is still expanding – in contrast with the increasing de-population of the inland villages – after a long decline that began as far back as the imperial age. But despite its lack of looks, Policoro is a destination worthy of note, both for history lovers and fans of beach life, as well as travellers greedy for strawberries, a local speciality much admired across the south. And unlike Metaponto, there's life in Policoro throughout the year, and even on the darkest winter evening you'll be able to find someone in the bars of Piazza Heraclea with whom to reminisce about the deeds of the great figures who made the history of this land thousands of years ago.

⊙ Sights

Museo Archeologico Nazionale della Siritide di Policoro MUSEUM
(☑0835 97 21 54; www.museosiritide.beniculturali. it; Via Colombo 8; adult/reduced €2.50/2; ☺9am-8pm Wed-Mon) The wealth of Heraclea and the pre-existing Siris (founded in the 7th century BCE) was extolled in ancient times

THE VILLAGE WITH NO NAME

If you Google *quel paese* (that town), surprisingly, and despite the vagueness of the term, you'll be directed to a specific place, Colobraro. The name of this village – set in a dizzying position in the Valle del Sinni, virtually opposite Valsinni (see boxed text p90) and accessible via the SP154 from Tursi – hasn't been spoken since time immemorial, not by Lucanians nor by anyone from southern Italy, for to do so would be to invoke bad luck, dark influences, the evil eye. The origin of this superstition isn't known for sure. Some claim that Colobraro (don't say it out loud, you never know) has always been home to professional sorceresses while some stories tell of an infallible *jettatore* (bringer of bad luck) originally from the village. Certainly the superstition's ubiquity is so deeply rooted that it has even influenced common parlance – the exhortation to *andare a quel paese* (literally 'go to that town' but really 'go to hell') is a current curse. However, for some years now the village inhabitants have been able to revive a sense of belonging thanks to a truly distinctive event. The Sogno di una notte... a quel paese (☎349 115 13 94, 340 323 40 14; www.colobraro.basilicata .it) is a theatre and arts festival that brings music, dance and feasting to the village every August. And so, if anyone tells you to go to hell, at least in these parts, you know they're being entirely benevolent.

by Archilocus and Herodotus. And needless to say this very interesting museum has much to say, particularly regarding the town's heyday between the 3rd and 4th centuries BCE. Tomb finds abound, with crowns, necklaces, earrings, breastplates, belts, pendants, and totemic objects, many chiselled out of transparent drops of amber. There are also tombs complete with skeletons and spears and javelins from the Roman period. However, the collection's highlights are the terracottas painted by the 'Policoro Painter', which reveal a surprising dexterity in their depiction of heroic themes. Behind the museum is the Parco Archeologico Siris Heraclea (entrance included with the museum ticket), where you can see foundations of the city's ancient buildings. But unless you're a real aficionado, the site is more interesting for the sweep of the landscape and the lizards that shelter among the uneven stones than for the archaeology. Worthy of note are the remains of a mosaic depicting a sea monster.

Castello Baronale Berlingieri   CASTLE
(Largo Castello) This 14th-century fortified farmhouse, later transformed into a Jesuit monastery and a noble residence, is on a hill in the northeastern part of town. For centuries it was the only resting place for travellers in this formerly marshy, inhospitable area. Near the castle look out for the *borgo dei casilini*, a series of terraced houses built after the land reform of the 1950s, in a period when the state had expropriated Baron Berlingieri's residence and transformed it into accommodation for farm labourers. Now, the restored baronial building hosts exhibitions, events, offices and a few restaurants.

Riserva Naturale Bosco Pantano di Policoro   NATURE RESERVE
(☎0835 182 51 57, 340 728 79 94; www.oasiwwfpoli coro.net; Centro Visite: Piazza Siris 1, Località Idrovora; ⏰9am-12.30pm & 4-7 pm, guided tours 9.30am, 11am, 4pm & 5.30pm Sun Apr-mid Jun, 9.30am, 10.15am, 11am, 5.30pm & 6.30pm Sun-Fri mid-Jun-mid-Sep; tours by appointment 8.30am & 5pm Sat & Sun) The Pantano Woods have been enchanting visitors since the time of the Grand Tour with their 21 hectares of wetland beachside forest, marshes, sand dunes (the monk seal has been spotted here), and distinctly tropical atmosphere. Cover yourself up to guard against mosquitoes.

Lido di Policoro   BEACHES
Okay, culture is a good thing, but when the sun is scorching and the surf beckons, there's nothing better than a nice day at the beach. As in Metaponto, there are bathing establishments and stalls in high season (and even a few fashionable bars where you can have a drink, especially on the south side of the promenade), but the white-sand beaches are longer here and the sea waters deeper.

🏃 Activities

Sailing
The core business of the Circolo Velico Lucano (☎0835 91 00 97; www.circolovelicolucano.it; Via Lido; 📶) is hosting sailing, nature and sports vacations for youngsters (weekly and bi-weekly, with lodging in the club's facilities).

It also organises sailing and kitesurfing courses, suitable for passing visitors.

Sleeping

Policoro Village   CAMPING €
(☎0835 91 01 68, 347 687 63 94; www.policoro vilage.net; Via Aristarco 1; tent pitch for 3 people €40, 4-person bungalow per week €1100) Abutting a sandy beach, this campground is situated in a poetic pine forest. But the atmosphere is decidedly more prosaic in high season, when pitches are lined up one against the other. All the amenities are here, from a convenience store and mini-club to a barbecue and restaurant. Bungalows of various sizes and comfortable teepees are also available.

Apricot   B&B €€
(☎349 147 36 43; www.apricotlucania.com; Via Ricciardulli 5; d/t/q €80/90/130, apt for 3-5/5-7 persons per week €1200/1600; ☎P☀) The Bosco Incantatp (Enchanted Forest) room has tree decorations on the walls and a chandelier made from a tangle of branches. The other rooms and apartments are equally as appealing, as is the verdant location in the countryside 5km west of the village. Breakfasts are made with organic products.

Hotel Heraclea   HOTEL €€€
(☎0835 91 01 44; www.hotelheraclea.com; Via Lido 100; B&B per person in double room €90, 2-bed apt with kitchenette per night €250; ☀☎P☀) The hotel is hardly beautiful but it is functional and rates are good value for money. It's located a short distance from the beach and there are bikes available for guests to explore the surrounding bike paths. Facilities and services include a swimming pool, spa, gym, football pitch, children's games, kids' club and summer entertainment.

★Marinagri   HOTEL €€€
(☎0835 596 02 01, 392 327 36 93; www.hotel marinagri.it; Via San Giusto, Località Torre Mozza; d from €200; ☀☎P☀) With its harbour and small houses overlooking the water, this is the only place in Basilicata where you can feel like you're in Dubai. The property, set in a nature reserve, is truly luxurious, with bars, restaurants, a private beach and aqua spa. There are few amenities in the surrounding area, but then again you won't need them.

✖ Eating

L'Altro Impero   TRATTORIA €
(☎340 623 16 38; Viale Salerno 82; meals €20; ◷noon-3pm Mon-Sat) Well known locally, this cheerful little trattoria prides itself on its wholesome, home-style cuisine. Fish and pasta dishes are the stars. Exceptional value.

Il Chioschetto di Petty   KIOSK €€
(☎333 863 91 95; Via San Giusto, Località Torre Mozza, Policoro; meals €25; ◷Apr-Sep) Just a stone's throw from the Marinagri residence, this rustic kiosk draws customers from far and wide with its super-fresh fish dishes, sausages, porchetta, and the opportunity to provoke a fine bout of indigestion by diving into the water straight after your meal.

Ristò la Francese   RESTAURANT €€
(☎393 632 96 14; Via Largo Castello; meals €35-40; ◷8-11.30 pm Mon-Sat, 12.30-3pm Sun) What many consider to be the best restaurant in Policoro is located in the baronial castle (p88). In summer, you'll eat in the courtyard, complementing the picturesque location with refined seafood dishes.

Sfizi del Palato   STEAK HOUSE €€€
(☎0835 97 26 19; www.sfizidelpalato.com; Via Siris 156; meals €50; ◷7pm-midnight Mon-Sun) From Angus to Kobe beef, from Florentine to Argentine steaks, the menu offers the best meat lovers could wish for. A special mention also for the end of the meal with rum, chocolate and cigars.

ⓘ Information

The **Pro Loco** (☎347 086 1184; www.proloco policoro.com; Piazza Heraclea, at the library) is the place for tourist information. To organise a guided tour of the archaeological sites and the museum, you can contact **Archeoart** (☎0835 90 21 65, 338 130 09 72; www.archeoart.eu; Via Giulio Cesare 4). It also runs educational activities and workshops.

ⓘ Getting There & Away

Policoro is located 21km south of Metaponto, on the SS106. **SITASUD buses** (☎0835 38 50 07; www.sitasudtrasporti.it) run along the coast from Metaponto (20 to 45 minutes), but connections are frequent only in summer. Alternatively, you can use the train, but the Policoro-Tursi station is 2km from the town and to reach it you'll need to take the shuttle bus (for Metaponto €1.80, about 20 minutes, frequent).

Rotondella
POP 2538 / ELEV 576M

No, you haven't overdone the Amaro Lucano if walking through the village you get the impression the streets aren't straight. The spiral pattern around the hill is, in fact, what characterises Rotondella, 14km from the Ionian coast, along with the intoxicating 360-degree panorama that swings from the blue of the sea to the brown-green of the Sinni river valley, and from the woods to the surrounding hills. Nowadays the town is best known for its Marina, one of the Ionian's main seaside resorts, and for its apricots.

◉ Sights

A brief stop here is pretty satisfying. There's no need to search for any one sight in particular, but soon after arriving, you'll find the doorways of the aristocratic edifices, the masks and noble coats of arms will start to quieten your aesthetic cravings. Notable among the places of worship is the Chiesa Madre (Via Umberto), with its 17th-century chapels commissioned by the village's most important families, and the soothing Convento di Sant'Antonio (Piazza Plebiscito 23), immaculately white and with a wooden ceiling. But Rotondella's headline sight

is the terrace on Via Garibaldi, which is extraordinary even in a region of such high panoramic standards as Basilicata.

Once you've admired the sea from afar, head there on the Strada Provinciale della Trisaia, and perhaps rent an umbrella at the Lido Splash (☑ 349 283 93 73; Lido di Rotondella), from where you can see the Calabrian coastline sloping southwards.

✦ Festivals & Events

Sagra dell'Albicocca   JULY

Enjoy music, meetings, debates, and stands at Rotondella's apricot fair, a yearly event for well over 20 years now. Above all, the fair is an occasion for sumptuous feasting on the delicious fruit.

⬛ Sleeping

A' Ferachiusa   HOTEL €

(☑ 0835 50 42 83, 389 681 81 02; Vico Cervaro IV 12; r per person €35; ☺ year-round) An *albergo diffuso* with six rustic apartments, some of which are panoramic but all of which are sober and

---

A POET'S GHOST

For sensitive souls, the small village of Valsinni, set in a panoramic position in the Valle del Sinni on the SS653 (which links it to the Ionian coast and the Pollino), could be a highlight of your trip to Basilicata. Not so much for its admittedly attractive tangle of alleys and covered passageways, but for the tragic story of the poet Isabella Morra (1520–46), to whom a literary park (☑ 392 392 25 51; Via Carmine 20; ☺ 10.30am- 1pm & 4pm-7pm winter, 11am-1pm & 5-10pm summer) is dedicated along with the Estate di Isabella festival (☑ 392 392 25 51; www.parcomorra.it), which animates August evenings with art exhibitions, minstrel shows and storytellers. The unfortunate woman, daughter of a local nobleman who fled to Paris to avoid persecution by Charles V, spent her life closed in the town's domineering castle (☑ 392 392 25 51; www.parcomorra.it; tickets €2; ☺ 10am-1pm & 4-6pm winter, 9.30am-1pm & 4-7.30pm summer) in the overbearing custody of her brothers. From her confinement she turned her gaze to the luxuriant nature of the surrounding area and wrote 13 remarkable poems, railing against fate, invoking Christian spirituality and pagan elements, conversing with the mountains and Sinni river.

In a happy turn of events, Isabella fell in love with the Spanish baron Diego Sandoval de Castro and hope suddenly blossomed in her life. But unhappiness had only eased its grip for a while – her brothers intercepted some letters between the lovers and brutally murdered her, claiming she had tarnished the family name. Her ghost is said to still haunt the rooms of the castle. However, as part of the castle is inhabited today, it's more likely that the footsteps that are sometimes heard belong to the current owners, rather than the restless Isabella. The castle itself is not particularly interesting but the guide's passionate narration and the plaques bearing Isabella's verses make a visit well worth it. To round off your visit to Valsinni, treat yourself to a good lunch at the medieval-style La Fontana del Borgo (☑ 0835 81 70 76, 342 121 60 27; lafontanadelborgo.it; Via Mentana 18; meals €25; ☺ noon-3pm & 5-10.30pm Tue-Sun Sep-Jul, dinner daily Aug) and a walk in the woods where a tormenting wind often blows, just like it once did to inspire Isabella's restlessness.

cosy with kitchenettes and bathrooms. Great if traveling in a group. It scores extra points for the sweeping view from the adjoining restaurant, Le Lamie (meals €20).

Eating

Rotondella boasts several culinary specialties with unpronounceable names, including the *durableu pastizz r'tunnar* (a calzone filled with eggs, cheese, minced meat, olive oil, salt and pepper), the delicious *frizzùli ca' middiche* (homemade pasta rolled with a wire and topped with meat sauce, preferably kid, or cheese), and the commendable *p'pòne e savizizzèdde'* (dried pepper cooked with sausage).

Il Pago AGRITURISMO €€
(☑ 338 322 22 95, 388 471 20 23; www.ilpago.eu; Via Piano del Forno 7; meals €25, s/d/tr €55/90/130; ☺ by reservation) ⚓ If you have a car, the restaurant of this organic farm is worth the trip. The educational farm produces fruit, honey, tomato puree and jams, and supplies many local companies. Needless to say, the specialties are local and, especially in summer, there's never any shortage of grilled meat. There are also four rooms with bathrooms and free wi-fi.

Locanda Pane e Lavoro TRATTORIA €€
(☑ 0835 50 40 32; www.locandapaneelavoro.it; Via Papa Giovanni XXIII 28; meals €25-30; ☺ noon-2pm & 8-11pm Tue-Sun) Featuring a bookshelf stocked with wine, a fireplace and exposed stone, this restaurant sports the kind of shabby chic flair that makes such a good impression. The local cuisine, from traditional antipasti to meaty main courses, really lives up to the hype. One of the best restaurants in the area.

ⓘ Getting There & Away

By car, Rotondella can be reached from Matera via the SS7, SS380, SS175 and SS106 roads (92km, about 1¼ hours). It's located 23km from Policoro via the SS106 and Strada Provinciale Trisaia. Buses to Policoro (one hour) are operated by **SITASUD** (☑ 0835 38 50 07; www.sitasudtrasporti.it).

THE BADLANDS (LATERRA DEI CALANCHI)

Wild mountains and long sandy beaches, expanses of cultivated fields and verdant hills, dense forests and sheer sea cliffs – Basilicata boasts a rich, varied landscape. But nowhere has the iconic significance of the region's

ROMAN BATHS

If you have time for a small detour on the way from the village of Rotondella to its beaches, we'd recommend a stop at the **Vasche di Sant'Alessio** (Località Sant'Alessio, Nova Siri; ☺ 24hr). It's an ancient baths complex of Roman origin, made up of six connected stone baths filled with transparent water and delicious bubbles. As well as visiting the curious site, where legend holds a local friar and nun would once meet in passion, the refreshing view in the scorching Lucanian summer will supercharge your desire to dive into the blue Ionian Sea as quickly as possible.

badlands. Like an immense canvas on which nature has traced a rambling web of lines and arabesques – the work of surface-water erosion on mounds of million-year-old white clay – this area represents the true identity of a region where lyricism and tragedy are perpetual bedfellows. Exploring the badlands in the southwestern corner of Matera province, you'll bounce from feeling like you're in an inhospitable place to revelling in the glorious literature it has nurtured, and feeling insignificant in the presence of so much grandeur to feeling relief for your sunburned heart and body. And so, while it's not always easy travelling in this part of the region, it's always an unforgettable experience.

Tursi

POP 4808 / ELEV 243M
Even from below, the view of the steep cliff on which the oldest part of the village is located is truly remarkable. As you walk slowly uphill, savour the words of the poems by the town's favourite son, Albino Pierro (1916–95), which you'll find written on plaques and signs – if you don't read Tursitan, ask a local elder for help, though they may well then need help to translate them into Italian. Continuing up, you'll realise that you don't need to be a poet to admire the bizarre slopes dotted with prickly pears, the enigmatic shapes of the Rabatana quarter, and the interesting religious architecture. And even if you don't pen any verse in its honour, Tursi will remain etched on your mind as a place steeped in eloquent exoticism.

History

It was probably the Goths who, in the mid-5th century, first chose to live here among the deep, inaccessible gullies that furrow the terrain. They were followed by the Saracens who, imagining the unassailability of such a rocky ridge, built the Rabatana quarter. After them came the Byzantines, Normans, Swabians, and Angevins. Tursi experienced its heyday during the 16th and 17th centuries and began to decline towards the end of the 18th century. Between the late 19th and early 20th centuries, misery and unemployment drove thousands of inhabitants to leave in search of better shores.

⊙ Sights

The Rabatana   NEIGHBOURHOOD

Tursi's Arab quarter is perhaps the most beautiful in all of Basilicata. Built in the 10th century during the period of the Saracens, it can be reached by passing through the modern lower part of town, climbing the clay plateau between the Agri and Sinni rivers, and ascending a steep and scenic road known in the local dialect as *a pitrizze*. The quarter is an authentic little maze, made up of houses that look as if they might crumble at any moment, narrow alleyways, and steep stairways, all huddled around a castle of which few traces remain today.

Alternatively, and less romantically, you can drive up along a well-signposted road a couple of kilometres long.

Chiesa di Santa Maria Maggiore   CHURCH

(Via Duca degli Abruzzi) Fairy-tale in its pastel pink, with a time-worn portal and an arabesque bell tower on which traces of vague and confusing symbols can be made out in the stone, this church sits in the heart of the Rabatana district. Inside, it preserves a 14th-century triptych centred on a depiction of a *Madonna in trono col Bambino*. In the crypt, the Cappella De Georgiis is decorated with 16th-century frescoes which some people have attributed to Giovanni Todisco. Also of note is Altobello Persio's 16th-century stone nativity scene and a similarly-aged marble sarcophagus. Legend has it that there's an underground passage connecting the church to the castle ruins, but we didn't find it.

Centro Studi e Parco Letterario Albino Pierro   CULTURAL CENTRE

(☑ 333 640 16 29; www.albinopierro.it; Corso Umberto I 4; ⊙ by appointment) **FREE** Tursi's most eminent son, Albino Pierro, was one of the

greatest dialect poets of the 20th century. He wrote almost exclusively about his hometown and childhood in Tursi's ancient dialect. This study centre, which aims to promote the memory of his works, is housed in his home, where there's a photo exhibition and a small picture gallery with works created by Lucanian artists on the 10th anniversary of his death. The poet's library and study can also be visited. In the village alleyways you'll come across numerous plaques with verses from his poems.

🛏 Sleeping & Eating

★ **Palazzo dei Poeti**   HOTEL, RESTAURANT €€

(☑ 0835 53 26 31; www.palazzodeipoeti.it; Via Manzoni; tasting menu €35; s/d €70/110; ⊙ Dec-Oct; ❄ 🛜) In perfect harmony with the sinuous forms of the Rabatana, this ancient stately home, once attached to the castle, offers dreamy stone rooms, with vaulted and wood-beamed ceilings, and a restaurant serving refined cuisine. A dinner on the panoramic terrace will inspire you to ardent verse. Not to be missed.

❶ Information

In summer you'll find a **Pro Loco tourist office** (☑ 333 640 16 29; Piazza Maria Santissima di Anglona; ⊙ hrs vary Jun-Sep) in the centre of the village.

❶ Getting There & Away

Tursi is located about 70km south of Matera and can be reached via the SS106, which runs parallel to the Ionian coast, or from inland by way of Miglionico, Ferrandina and Pisticci – in both cases, allow at least an hour and a quarter. From Metaponto, head south along the SS106 and exit at Policoro, 24km from Tursi. If you're travelling by bus it won't be easy to get around, but **Grassani e Garofalo** (☑ 0835 90 14 43; www.grassaniegarofalo.it) has one service a day to Matera (one hour 20 minutes).

Craco

POP 643 / ELEV 391M

In 1963 Craco was one of an endless number of villages in the region set on top of a hill with a modern part sat at the foot of the slopes. It had more than two thousand inhabitants, mostly farmers, and children played in the streets as old people watched time go by from their balconies. A Norman tower, subsequently amplified by Federico II, testified to its glorious past. Then tragedy

WORTH A TRIP

THE SANTUARIO DI SANTA MARIA DI ANGLONA

The chimerical landscapes of Tursi (p91) find a form of definitive union 12km from town, towards Policoro. Here, a blissful oasis of pine, olive and eucalyptus trees seems to miraculously transform the brutal terrain of the badlands while also providing the setting for this solitary 12th-century sanctuary (☑ 351020 86 46; ⊙ , 8am-6pm, to 8pm summer, sometimes closed at lunch). It's a breathtaking sight and not just for the contrast between the graceful contours of the setting and the rippling roughness of the surroundings. The sanctuary, made of tuff rock and travertine, features an austere facade and a portal surmounted by an arch decorated with bas-reliefs depicting the four evangelists and lamb. And these, along with the Romanesque-style bell tower, take us straight into the heart of the Middle Ages. Inside, a series of 13th-century frescoes depicting the *Episodes of Genesis*, the *Episodes of the Ark*, the *Offering to Melchizedek*, the *Sacrifice of Isaac* and the *Blessing of Jacob,* adorns two levels above the central nave. These paintings, one of Basilicata's most important pictorial displays, add a sense of beguiling splendour to the air of alienation that surrounds the church. Once outside again, make sure to admire the timeless panorama. More prosaically, the site is equipped with shady tables and bathrooms, and is ideal for a picnic.

struck and the village was reduced to ruins by a series of landslides, caused by excessive building and the construction of a retaining wall to aid the retention of water in the underground clay. Craco became a ghost town. Silently, and with no deaths to cause a scandal, no inquiries to punish the guilty, no clamour for the hundreds of people whose lives were uprooted and who were forced to move to the anonymous centre of Craco Peschiera, a little further downstream, where there's a pharmacy, a post office, two grocery stores, a tobacco bar, a kiosk selling sandwiches and an air thick with melancholy. In a deafening silence, broken only by the circumspect footsteps of looters who slowly took everything, Craco continued to stand naked and proud above the surrounding landscape. Today, in that same silence, Craco has risen again, as a symbol of the destruction inherent in the indiscriminate pursuit of modernity, as a warning of the dangers that can threaten other Cracos, and as an emblem of a region whose authentic charm lies in its mix of beauty and desolation.

◉ Sights

Whether you drive in from the east or west, get your camera ready well before you reach the village – Craco is one of the region's most scenic villages, and it's best appreciated from a distance. At the time of going to press, visits to the abandoned village had been suspended. Phone the Parco Museale Scenografico (see below) to find out if they're running again.

Parco Museale Scenografico   MUSEUM PARK
(☑ 338 160 22 05; www.prolococraco.it; Craco card with guided tour €10) The car park and ticket office are located on the northwestern edge of the village, a few hundred metres from where guided tours lead visitors (complete with safety helmets) into the abandoned village. The secure areas are gradually extending, thanks to funding. But you only need walk along the first stone road, which has been perfectly restored, to feel a sense of dazed amazement – the houses look like they were lived in until yesterday and you half expect to see a housewife lean out of a window and hang up her laundry or a farmer to come out of a door on his way to the fields. However, once you reach what remains of the main square, the sense of devastation takes over – it's a large space surrounded by ruins where donkeys graze and elderly inhabitants sometimes go in search of *lampascioni* for a nutritious evening soup. From there, you climb several stairways up to the crumbling Chiesa di San Nicola and its majolica bell tower. You'll see stone decorations and damaged wooden panels and, through the glassless windows, the faded frescoes of ancient noble palaces. The visit lasts about an hour, but it will touch you for days. To complete your tour, check out the multimedia installation at the MEC (☑ 338 160 22 05; www.prolococraco.it/www.cracoemotion.org), which tells the story of Craco. It's housed in the 17th-century Convento di San Pietro, at the village entrance on the Craco-Montalbano Jonico municipal road.

CRACO & THE CINEMA

You don't have to be a studious cinephile to realise that Craco makes a perfect film set. Many directors have exploited its otherworldly atmosphere to shoot films here. The best known of these include Francesco Rossi's *Christ Stopped at Eboli*, *King David* by Bruce Beresford, *The Passion of the Christ* by Mel Gibson (this is where Judas' suicide was filmed), and, of course, the region's signature film, *Basilicata Coast to Coast* by Rocco Papaleo.

At the time of research, visits to Craco had been suspended for bureaucratic reasons. Before planning a trip, though, check the Pro Loco website for the latest information.

Sleeping & Eating

Il Calanco AGRITURISMO €€
(☑ 0835 46 21 91, 340 280 11 34; www.ilcalanco.it; Contrada Santa Lucia, Pisticci; d €80; meals €25) The abandoned state of Craco is attested to by the absence of any sleeping or eating options. This agriturismo, 12km towards Pisticci, is the most convenient option if you want to take some time visiting the village. It serves good, plentiful food, prepared with ingredients of the highest quality, and children will enjoy feeding carrots to the horses in the stables.

Information

For tourist information contact the **Craco village council** (☑ 0835 45 90 05; www.comune.craco.mt.it; Via Monsignor Mastronardi 2) or the **Pro Loco** (☑ 338 160 22 05; www.prolococraco.it).

Getting There & Away

Craco is about 50km southwest of Matera. It's a half-hour drive from Pisticci on the SP176 and from Montalbano Jonico on the SP103. You can also get there by a daily **SITASUD bus** (☑ 0835 38 50 07; www.sitasudtrasporti.it) from Pisticci (30 minutes) or Matera (one hour).

Aliano

POP 909 / ELEV 498M

There are many who argue that if Carlo Levi hadn't been confined in Aliano during the fascist period, the village would probably have slipped into oblivion. But maybe without the inspiration of the lunar beauty in which this amazing village is shrouded, his masterpiece *Christ Stopped at Eboli* wouldn't have held such vivid expressive power? Today, the natural stage on which the sleepy life of its inhabitants plays out reveals the same brutal and inclement harshness that it did in 1935, while simultaneously exuding the sort of irresistible allure that can only be felt in places where the balance between human life and the environment is so precarious. Other things have changed, while remaining the same – local living conditions are certainly less dramatic than those of Levi's 'Gagliano' and malaria is no longer a threat, but unemployment, the ongoing wounds of the 1980 earthquake, and the isolation of the village still render life in Aliano pretty tough for its inhabitants. In contrast, visits to the village are steeped in poetry. You can see the vertiginous Fossa del Bersagliere (where, Levi tells us, a Piedmontese *bersagliere* is said to have been thrown for harassing some local women) and observe how the shimmering green patches of shrubland interplay with the unpredictable, twisting lines of the land; you can watch hawks in flight and check out the deserted main street in a silence broken only by the bells of grazing cows; you can glance at the profiles of women dressed in black in the windows and read a few pages of the book as the sunlight fades, gently relaxing the first surly impressions evoked by the landscape. It won't take eight months to bond with Aliano, as it did for Levi. Half a day will suffice.

Sights

Obviously, visits to the village revolve around Carlo Levi and the literary park dedicated to him. However, Aliano does have some additional attractions. The Casa del Malocchio (Piazza Garibaldi), right in front of the Town Hall, is an evocative testimony to popular superstition – its structure is shaped like a human face (with a fireplace in the place of the nose, windows as eyes, and the door serving as the mouth) to keep away negative influences. There's a second similar place in front of the amphitheatre. The Chiesa di San Luigi Gonzaga (Via Roma) houses a beautiful central baroque altar and a particularly rough, enigmatic Madonna with Child. Finally, at the highest point of the village is the cemetery (Via Mercato), which marked the point beyond which Levi wasn't allowed to

EXCURSIONS IN THE BADLANDS

When the sun loosens its grip in summer, the badlands are a popular destination for brief outings and hikes – as well as an inexhaustible subject for contemplation. However, avoid the immediate vicinity of the village – the descent to the base of the Fossa del Bersagliere, which starts next to the bridge, is considered dangerous. Instead, head to Località Frattine di Capobianco – drive 2km south along the road to Alianello, then follow the turn-off, where there are two suitably signposted circular trails: the Don Carlo trail (20 minutes), which is ideal for a taste of the area, and the Don Luigino trail (50 minutes), another simple route suitable for those who don't want to overdo it.

go. Here the artist would paint, contemplate the landscape and meditate. Since 1975 his remains have rested here, in a tomb to the left of the main entrance marked by two rows of bricks.

Parco Letterario Carlo Levi   PARK

(☑ 0835 56 85 29; www.parcolevi.it; Via Plebiscito; adult/reduced incl Pinacoteca, Museo Paul Russotto, Casa di Confino di Levi & Museo della Civiltà Contadina €5/3; offices ☉ 10.30am-12.30pm & 3.30-6pm winter, 10.30am-12.30pm & 4.30-7.30pm summer, closed Mon; guided tours 11.30am & 4.30pm winter, 11.30am & 5.30pm summer) There are numerous plaques in the village streets marking the most significant places in Levi's novel, but if you want to squeeze every ounce of magic out of Aliano you'll really need to visit this literary park (one of 17 created in southern Italy to promote the territory that inspired *Christ Stopped at Eboli*). It harbours the Pinacoteca Carlo Levi, a picture gallery exhibiting writings, documents and paintings by the author (including seven interesting lithographs from the book *Christ Stopped at Eboli* that he donated to the museum a few months before his death) and the Casa di Confino di Carlo Levi. This is the house where the author spent seven months between 1935 and 1936; it has its original floors and the most beautiful terrace a confined person has ever had in history. In the old olive oil mill below Levi's house is the Museo della Civiltà Contadina, full of agricultural and domestic tools and utensils, as well as instruments used for craftwork. Displays illustrate ancient crafts such as wool spinning and brick baking, as well as showcasing masks used to ward off evil influences and musical instruments used during Carnival. And finally, there's the Museo Paul Russotto, which houses a fine collection of paintings by the American artist Russotto, who was a master of abstract expressionism.

Alianello Vecchio   ABANDONED VILLAGE

As you approach Aliano on the road from the SS598, you'll come across the hamlet of Alianello Nuovo. Leave the car here and you can visit the ghost town of Alianello Vecchio, which was completely abandoned after the earthquake of 1980. The site is shrouded in that twilight atmosphere typical of abandoned places and is perfect for playing hide and seek with friends. One kilometre to the north, in the direction of Aliano, the Belvedere dei Calanchi offers superb views of the tortuous clay formations.

✹ Festivals & Events

Carnevale delle Maschere Cornute   FEBRUARY

As in many other towns in the region, preparations for Carnival are in full swing in Aliano in February. The standout feature here are the masks – described exhaustively by Levi and characterised by pronounced horns and long hanging noses – which are worn under voluminous and colourful hats. The most important festivities are held on Sunday and Shrove Tuesday when you can try typical dishes such as rafanata, *frazzul* and chiacchiere. The cheerful tradition here is for groups of young people to go around the streets with their *ciuccigni* (sort of flexible truncheons) beating anyone they find, including nobles and lords. The spectacle is exciting and worth a few blows.

La Luna e i Calanchi   AUGUST

Thousands of people flock to this annual landscape festival directed by Franco Arminio and featuring performances, poetry readings, debates, and shows that narrate and exalt the area's beauty.

🛏 Sleeping & Eating

Taverna La Contadina Sisina   TAVERN €€

(☑ 0835 56 82 39, 327 046 72 63; Via Roma 13; s/d €30/60; fixed menu €25; ☉ Thu-Tue) Aliano

THE ALIANO OF THE FUTURE

Given its small size, Aliano already presents itself as a destination of considerable cultural value. And the future would seem to prospect even more initiatives – at the time of research, there was talk of opening new museum itineraries, dedicated to photography, carnival and Carlo Levi. The village even put forward (and then retracted) its candidacy for Italian Capital of Culture for 2024. Which is not so strange, after all: the village is just a few kilometres from the city that has transformed itself from being a 'national disgrace' to being one of Italy's top travel destinations, so the fact that a village lost in the badlands should aspire to become an important artistic destination does make sense.

seems to emerge from times long past, and this tavern on the main street confirms that feeling with its wooden ceilings, fireplace and old photos on the walls. Obviously there's no written menu and dishes are strictly from the peasant tradition. Upstairs there are five very basic guest rooms.

Palazzo Scelzi GUESTHOUSE €€
(☏ 338 361 57 28, 340 370 30 28; www.palazzoscelzi.it; Piazza San Luigi Gonzaga 1/A; s/d/tr €40/65/80; ☏ℙ) The rooms are simple and basic, but the 17th-century building will give your stay an ineffable touch of grace. Overall, excellent value for money.

ℹ️ Information

Visitor centre of the Parco Letterario (☏ 0835 56 85 29; Via Plebiscito; ⊙ 10.30am-12.30pm & 3.30-6pm Tue-Sun winter, 10.30am-12.30pm & 4.30-7.30pm summer)

ℹ️ Getting There & Away

If you don't have a car, reaching Aliano can be a real undertaking.

BUS

Taking the **SITASUD bus** (☏ 0835 38 50 07, 0971 50 68 11; www.sitasudtrasporti.it) from Matera you'll have to change at Sant'Arcangelo, while from Potenza the scheduled stop is in Stigliano.

CAR & MOTORCYCLE

Aliano can be reached from Potenza (about 100km) by taking the SS407 Basentana towards Salerno, then exiting at Tito Scalo towards Brienza, and following the SS598 towards Taranto until the Aliano exit. From Matera, 85km to the northeast, take the SS7, then the Basentana towards Metaponto, exiting at Pisticci Scalo. Finally, if you're coming from the Ionian coast, continue south along the SS106 then join the SS598 near Policoro and exit at Aliano.

Potenza Province

Include ➡

Best Places to Eat

➡ Antica Osteria Marconi (p102)

➡ Bramea (p107)

➡ Ristorante Tipico Luna Rossa (p147)

➡ Al Becco della Civetta (p111)

➡ La Villa (p127)

Best Places to Stay

➡ Atmosfera Bubble Glamping (p115)

➡ La Voce del Fiume (p116)

➡ Difesa d'Ischia (p135)

➡ Mulino Iannarelli (p145)

➡ Il Castello dei Principi Sanseverino (p143)

Why Go?

To get an idea of what it means to travel in the province of Potenza, it helps to cite a few figures: the province has a population of less than 400,000, the same as a medium-sized city, yet its surface area is more than 6000 sq km, making it one of Italy's largest. Add to this the predominantly mountainous terrain – which helps to explain the lack of an efficient infrastructure – and the variety of landscapes, traditions and cultures, and it becomes clear that a visit to these parts is a real adventure, a trip more like an expedition of discovery than a holiday in its capacity to stretch time and space out of all proportion. From the capital's surrounds, dotted with sleepy villages frozen in time, to the cultural and wine delights of the Vulture and the castles of Federico II; from the cellars of Aglianico to the wonderful towns of Melfi and Venosa; from archaeological finds to the atavistic devotional rituals of the Val D'Agri; from Maratea's soaring coastline to the adrenaline-soaked thrills of the Volo dell'Angelo, Ponte tra i Due Parchi and Parco delle Stelle and silent hikes through the highlands of the Parco Nazionale del Pollino – the province offers so many compelling places that you'll only be able to cover some of them. And it's precisely this diversity that characterises this wild, wonderful, indomitable territory.

When to Go

Obviously, if you want to enjoy the sea, take long walks in the mountains, and regret the day you were born on the Volo dell'Angelo, you'll want to come in summer, when most of the festivals take place. The pyrotechnic colours of spring and autumn give the villages of Vulture and the Pollino valleys a special charm, while winter is recommended for ski enthusiasts, who can take to the slopes of Monte Sirino, Abriola and Viggiano.

Potenza Province Highlights

1 Explore the fascinating **Museo Archeologico Nazionale** (p99).

2 Admire castles, cellars, lakes, churches, art and poetry in the magical **Vulture** (p120).

3 Release your inner thrill-seeker in the **Volo dell'Angelo** (p109) then unwind in the

villages of **Pietrapertosa** (p108) and **Castelmezzano** (p109).

4 Traverse the longest Tibetan bridge in the world in **Castelsaraceno** (p137).

5 Hike trails for all levels in the **Parco Nazionale del Pollino** (p138), Italy's largest national park.

6 Try to find an adjective that describes the beauty of the **Maratea** coast (p148).

7 Discover the charming landscapes and villages suspended between sea and mountain in the **Maratea hinterland** (p159).

POTENZA

POP 64,960 / ELEV 819M

Most travellers tend to bypass Basilicata's capital, the highest regional capital in Italy. After all, the city hardly has the *physique* of an unmissable destination with its hillside tower blocks, ugly, unharmonious urban sprawl and shabby contemporary architecture. Yet there's something profoundly intriguing about Potenza's resigned profile – it's as if the city embodies the travails, torments and labours that have worn down this part of Italy for centuries and stands as a symbol of it and a necessary key to the understanding of it.

Already inhabited in Roman times, and later repeatedly sacked and passed from one family to another, the city was ravaged by earthquakes on numerous occasions. But every time – in 1273, 1694, 1857 and then again in 1980 – it managed to rise up again. Neither poverty nor its subordinate role in the territory could defeat it. The city faltered, but never gave in to the challenges of being elected regional capital in 1806, on the initiative of Giuseppe Bonaparte, nor did it bow to the trials caused by the unification of Italy and brigandage. The sense of lacerating precariousness that history has conferred on it can also be detected in its urban development. Suspended between several peaks, it rises vertically through steep streets, stairways and futuristic escalators, which connect the railway station and modern districts with the historic centre, and which together make up Europe's longest escalator network. As well as these varying splendours there are also several cultural attractions, fragments of the city's indomitable past, such as its medieval gates, interesting churches, and a sense of hospitality that goes beyond the superficial. Ultimately, Potenza might not be one of the most graceful destinations you visit on your trip to Basilicata, but it will certainly be one of the most significant.

◉ Sights

Via Pretoria   STREET

This long pedestrian street, which traverses the historic centre in an east–west direction, is not only where locals come to relax after work or take a romantic hand-in-hand stroll, but it's also a good-looking spot with some elegant buildings, pleasant open spaces, small piazzas, and trendy cafes, all of which go to brighten the dour appearance of the rest of the city. In particular, Piazza Pagano,

home to the 19th-century Teatro Stabile, creates a somewhat elegant atmosphere on starry nights, while the presence of the Tempietto di San Gerardo adds a refined air to Piazza Matteotti. Most sites of interest are located in the adjacent streets.

Escalators   ESCALATOR

(☑800 8935 75; www.trotta.it; 2 rides/8 rides/20 rides €1.50/3/5) What do Potenza and Tokyo have in common? Certainly not Zen temples, onsen and fish markets that burst into life at dawn. Rather it's the record for the world's largest city escalator system (Basilicata's capital is currently in second place with 1.5km). In addition to simplifying mobility, the escalators have also created a tangible identity for the city – in fact, Potenza can now proudly claim the title of 'stairway city'. Four lines are currently in operation (but new openings are planned): the Basento line (⊙7am-7pm) connects Potenza Centrale railway station with the offices of the Mobility Centre in Via Nazario Sauro; nearby, the Prima escalator (⊙7am-10pm, until 11pm summer) connects Viale Marconi with Piazza Vittorio Emanuele II in the historic centre, saving your legs a lot of work. Then there's the Via Armellini-Via Due Torri escalator (⊙7am-10pm, until 11pm summer), which descends towards the northern districts, and the Santa Lucia line (⊙7am-10pm, until midnight summer), a mammoth 26 ramp structure, which can be covered in about 20 minutes from the Poggio Tre Galli district (though you can go halfway up to near Viale dell'Unicef where there's a car park). The escalators, which are sometimes a little shabby, host temporary exhibitions and give the city a pleasant underground touch.

However, traditional staircase purists shouldn't worry. Potenza abounds with steep flights of stairs where you can curse your healthy habits – the 19th-century Scala del Popolo (Via del Popolo) is the finest example.

Museo Archeologico Nazionale   MUSEUM

(☑0971 217 19; www.musei.beniculturali.it; Via Serrao 11; adult/reduced €2.50/2; ⊙2-8pm Mon, 9am-8pm Tue-Sun) The region's most important museum, dedicated to the Romanian archaeologist Dinu Adamesteanu (1913–2004), has been housed in Potenza's most majestic historic building, Palazzo Loffredo, since 2005. Here you can get a comprehensive introduction to the area with exhibits ranging from artefacts of indigenous 9th-century BCE peoples to finds from Roman times. The collections are extremely varied and interesting even for those who aren't huge archaeology fans. The exhibition is spread over 22 rooms and two floors. Highlights to look out for among the Gorgon masks, vases, headdresses, amphorae and bronze helmets include jewellery found in the tomb of the 'child princess' (who died aged seven in the 6th century BCE), an imaginative bronze foil depicting a Nereid riding a dolphin from the 4th century BCE, and the floor of a Roman villa.

Cattedrale   CATHEDRAL
(☑0971 224 88; Largo del Duomo; ☉7.30am-12.30pm & 5-8pm) The city's main religious monument dates to the 12th to 13th century but was rebuilt towards the end of the 18th century. Of note is the 20th-century decoration which adorns the dome, transept and vaults. This, clearly influenced by traditional iconography, gives the cathedral an unusual air of modernity. Decidedly older are the remains of San Gerardo housed in a Roman-era sarcophagus in the right transept. Note the beautiful bronze portal sculpted by Giovanni Niglia in 1978, and the sturdy five-order bell tower.

Behind the church, the Museo Diocesano (Via Vescovado; ☉10am-1pm & 5-8pm Tue-Sat, 5-8pm Sun) houses paintings by local artists, a 15th-century illuminated Bible, and a 16th-century reliquary.

Chiesa di San Francesco   CHURCH
(Via Alianelli; ☉7.30am-noon & 5-7pm) This introspective, single-nave church near Piazza Pagano, founded in 1274, resembles a long, unadorned hallway, but actually houses two major works: on the left is a fresco depicting St. Sebastian by the superstar of 16th-century Lucanian painting Giovanni Todisco, while on the right, the *Pietà* (1608) by Lucanian painter Giovanni di Gregorio (known as Pietrafesa) captivates with the disruptive intensity of its expression.

Chiesa di San Michele Arcangelo   CHURCH
(Via Rosica; ☉7am-noon & 5.30-8.30pm) With its harmonious blend of stone and wood, this is probably the most striking church in the city. Its 1849 remodeling did not, in fact, soften the austere Romanesque rigour of the original 13th-century construction. Furthermore, the *Annunciazione* (1602) by Pietrafesa and an 18th-century wooden sculpture of St. Michael the Archangel reinforce its spiritual aura, especially on gloomy days.

Museo Archeologico Provinciale MUSEUM
(☑0971 44 48 33; Via Lazio 18; ☉9am-1pm Mon-Fri, 2.30-5.30pm Tue & Thu) **FREE** The displays at this museum north of the centre are less compelling than those of the Museo Archeologico Nazionale (p99) and will mainly be of interest to fervent archaeology aficionados. The collection of local artefacts spans the period between the prehistoric age and Roman times. Of particular note is an alabaster statuette of the enthroned goddess Persephone, dating to the 6th or 5th century BCE.

Ponte San Vito   BRIDGE
(Via dell'Elettronica) Built by Diocletian in the late 3rd century, this bridge is the finest Roman relic in the city. The structure itself doesn't really merit the drive from the centre (some 3.5km to the southeast) but what does is the prospect of a stroll on the verdant banks of the Basento river.

★ Festivals & Events

Parata dei Turchi   MAY
This festival, involving more than 900 participants, has been held in Potenza for over four centuries to celebrate the city's patron saint, Gerardo da Piacenza. According to legend, the saint drove out a group of Turks who, one night in 1111, sailed up the Basento river (even if the river wasn't navigable at the time). Recognised as a Patrimonio d'Italia per la Tradizione (Traditional Heritage of Italy), the celebration starts at the Cattedrale and continues with a parade of characters from the legend, including Saracens on horseback and archers with banners.

🛏 Sleeping

Even if Potenza is regional capital, it doesn't have a huge supply of accommodation. However, the hospitality it offers is wonderful.

Il Pozzo di San Lorenzo   B&B €€
(☑346 685 78 69; www.pozzodisanlorenzo.com; Via Pretoria 63; d/tr €70/90; 🛜) The cleanliness, the creaky parquet floors, the modern bathrooms and pleasant guest rooms makes this place easy to recommend. Breakfast is served in a nearby bar.

Leucos   B&B €€
(☑0971 193 13 15, 339 264 56 32; www.myleucos.com; Piazza Vittorio Emanuele II 14; s/d/tr/q €55/70/85/100; 🛜) This beautiful B&B, at the end of the Marconi escalator, is the hands-down winner of the prize for the most original

Potenza

and colourful decoration in the city. Its rich breakfast also deserves a special mention.

Taverna Centomani　B&B €€
(☎320 929 75 02; www.tavernacentomani.it; Via Tora 304; s/d/tr €70/85/115; ☎ⓟ) ✐ If you have your own wheels and fancy staying in the rarefied atmosphere of the Lucanian countryside, we'd recommend this amazing inn, built on an ancient cattle track and continuously inhabited since the Middle Ages. The rooms have been built into old sheep pens according to the principles of

bio-architecture, while breakfast and dinner (the latter on request) are served in what was once the stable. In the barn there's a shop selling farm produce.

Al Convento
B&B €€
(☑ 348 330 76 93, 329 816 95 79; www.alconvento potenza.it; Largo San Michele Arcangelo 21; s/d €60/90; ☎) Housed in a 19th-century convent in front of the Chiesa di San Michele Arcangelo, this B&B offers a monastic atmosphere revisited with charm and elegance. There's also the possibility to use a garage (€10 a night). Excellent value for money.

Grande Albergo
HOTEL €€
(☑ 0971 41 02 20; www.grandealbergopotenza. it; Corso XVIII Agosto 46; s/d/ste €87/105/180; ✱ ☎ P) It's central and undoubtedly convenient and comfortable with marble floors, wood-panelled walls and black leather sofas setting the tone. The view over the Valle del Basento from the terrace and some rooms is a further plus. However, it doesn't really stand out for warmth and atmosphere. Rates are lower on weekends than weekdays.

La Primula
HOTEL €€
(☑ 0971 583 10; www.albergolaprimula.it; Via delle Primule 84; s/d from €80/90, junior ste & ste €100-150; ✱ ☎ P ⚟) Outside the city centre is this impeccable hotel with a garden, gym and swimming pool. Rooms are bright, spacious and comfortable. And for those folk who don't want to go back to the centre for dinner, there's a highly-rated restaurant (€30) serving revisited traditional dishes.

✕ Eating

Tiri
CAFE, BAKERY €
(☑ 0971 30 95 91; www.tiri1957.it; Via del Gallitello 255; slice of panettone €3.50; ☉ 7am-9pm Mon-Fri, 7am-10pm Sat, 8am-1pm & 4-9pm Sun) The panettone served year-round at this historic Lucanian company is considered among the best in Italy. In fact, all the leavened desserts are a delight. For a breakfast with a capital B.

Taverna Oraziana
TAVERN €€
(☑ 0971 27 32 33; Via Orazio Flacco 2; meals €20-30; ☉ 12.30-2.30pm & 7.30-10.30pm Mon-Sat) The atmosphere is rustic and the floral tablecloths questionable, but the fireplace in the centre of the room lends this restaurant a graceful touch. The homemade pastas are the star attraction, but whatever you eat you'll leave full and satisfied.

Antiche Torri
RESTAURANT, PIZZERIA €€
(☑ 0971 180 11 82; Via Due Torri 8; meals €25-30; ☉ 7.30-11pm Wed-Mon) People come here to enjoy the pleasant setting, with arches and exposed stonework, the pizzas (among the best in the city), and the impeccable regional cuisine. It's small so you'll need to reserve at the weekend.

C'era una Volta
RESTAURANT €€
(☑ 0971 60 12 17; Via Valle Paradiso 94; meals 25-30; ☉ 12.30-3pm & 5.30-10.30pm Mon-Sat, 12.30-3pm Sun) The nostalgic name (Once Upon a Time) is reflected in the retro look – wooden tables, trumpets, violins and a blackboard – and the traditional cuisine. However, the quality of the meat will ensure that your meal is far from melancholic. And the excellent value for money will make you want to come back. It's located 6km west of the centre.

★ Antica Osteria Marconi
RESTAURANT €€€
(☑ 0971 569 00; Via Marconi 233-235; menus €30-40; ☉ 12.30-2.45pm & 8-10.30pm Tue-Sat, 12.30-2.45pm Sun) For many people, this is the best restaurant in town, thanks to its well-curated dining areas (the outdoor space is lovely), the superb quality of the ingredients used in the dishes, and the creativity of its traditionally inspired but orientally-influenced cuisine. Feel free to choose at will from the menus.

🍷 Drinking & Nightlife

Da Vito
CAFE
(Via San Luca; ☉ 7am-6pm Mon-Fri, 7am-1.30pm Sat & Sun) A veritable institution of the city's football scene, this cafe behind the Museo Archeologico Nazionale is the place to partake in fans' discussions. But if Potenza lost on Sunday, we'd recommend you watch what you say.

0971
LOUNGE BAR
(☑ 0971 361 01; Via Pretoria 310-312; ☉ bar 6.30am-3am, kitchen 12.30-2.30pm & 7-11.30pm; meals €25) A trendy place where you can drink a beer at the bar, philosophise outside over a cocktail, and enjoy a rich and interesting aperitif. It's also not bad for dinner.

Goblins Pub & Restaurant
PUB
(☑ 0971 210 01; www.goblinspub.com; Via Rosica 82/Piazza Mario Pagano 9; ☉ noon-4pm & 7pm-1am Mon-Fri, 7pm-1am Sat & Sun, closed Sun Oct-May) This popular, centrally located Irish-style pub serves good cheap food and gets very busy on weekend evenings. Both beers and pizzas are good.

⭐ Entertainment

While it's no New York, Potenza is still the most important city in the area and there's no shortage of cultural spaces and entertainment opportunities.

Cinema Due Torri   CINEMA, THEATRE
(✆ 0971 219 60; www.potenzacinema.it; Via Due Torri 5) This central cinema-theatre is located next to the escalators. See the website for the upcoming programme.

Cineteatro Don Bosco   CINEMA, THEATRE
(✆ 0971 44 59 21; www.cineteatrodonbosco.com; Piazza San Giovanni Bosco 11 bis) Together with the Teatro Stabile, this is the main venue for performances during Potenza's theatre season. It also puts on film screenings.

Teatro Stabile   THEATRE
(✆ 0971 27 30 36; Piazza Mario Pagano) Built as a likeness of Naples' Teatro San Carlo and inaugurated in 1881, the Teatro stages the province's top theatrical productions.

ℹ Information
EMERGENCY
Hospital (✆ 0971 61 11 11; Via Petrone, Contrada Macchia Romana)
Local Police (Mobility Offices: ✆ 0971 41 57 54; Via Sauro)
Post Office (Via Pretoria 253-259)

TOURIST INFORMATION
The **IAT tourist office** (✆ 0971 41 50 80; www.basilicataturistica.it; Via Cesare Battisti 22; ⏱ 9am-1pm & 3-6pm Mon-Sat), not far from the Museo Archeologico Nazionale, has plenty of free maps and material.

ℹ Getting There & Away
BUS
The main bus station is in Viale del Basento, near the railway station. **Grassani** (✆ 0835 72 14 43; www.grassani.it) runs a bus service to Matera (€5.90, 1½ hours, six daily) via Ferrandina. **SITASUD** (✆ 0971 50 68 11; www.sitasudtrasporti.it) has daily connections with many towns in the area, including Melfi (1½ to two hours), Castelmezzano (one hour 10 minutes) and Maratea (three hours). Other companies serve places outside the region: **Liscio** (✆ 0971 546 73; www.autolinealiscio.it) connects Potenza with Perugia (€30, six hours 50 minutes) and Rome (€25, 4½ hours); **Miccolis** (✆ 0835 34 40 32; www.busmiccolis.it) serves Naples (€19.90, two hours), Brindisi (€27.40, three hours 25 minutes) and Bari (€21.40, 3¼ hours); **Flixbus** (✆ 02 94 75 92 08; www.flixbus.it) operates direct services to Milan (from €24.99, 13 hours).

CAR & MOTORCYCLE
Potenza is connected to Salerno to the west by the A2 autostrada (motorway). Metaponto is located southeast of the city along the SS407 Basentana. For Matera, take the SS407 then turn north onto the SS7 at Ferrandina.

PUBLIC TRANSPORT
Potenza's attractions are in the old city at the top of the hill. Apart from the escalators (p99), visitors are unlikely to need public transport, which is managed by Trotta (✆ 800 8935 75; www.trotta.it); single-ride tickets cost €1.50. **Taxis** (✆ 0971 17 71; ⏱ 24 hours) are also an option.

TRAIN
The **Ferrovie dello Stato** (✆ 89 20 21; www.trenitalia.it) manages the stations of Potenza Superiore and Potenza Centrale, while the **Ferrovie Appulo Lucane** (✆ 800 05 05 00; www.ferrovieappulolucane.it), which operates buses to many neighbouring towns, serves Potenza Inferiore, Potenza Città and Potenza Santa Maria. From Potenza Centrale station there are regular connections to Ferrandina (from €3.55, 50 minutes), Metaponto (from €6.05, 1¼ hours), Taranto (from €9.50, two to 2½ hours), Salerno (€7.05, 1½ hours), Naples (from €9.80, two to 2½ hours) and Foggia (€7.70, two to 2½ hours). Substitute buses leave from the square in front of the station. To reach Matera (from €9.70, three hours), you'll have to take one of the sluggish trains of the Ferrovie Appulo Lucane and change at Altamura, or a substitute bus (direct). Trains to Bari (from €11, about four hours, often replaced by bus) leave from Potenza Santa Maria station (right in front of Potenza Superiore) and require a change at Gravina in Puglia. Again, these are sometimes replaced by direct buses.

THE POTENTINO

A few kilometres are enough to leave the architectural melancholy of the capital and enter an enchanted world. This is a land of small country roads – where you half expect brigands to appear at any moment – of villages lost in time, sanctuaries quivering with devotion, Roman ruins, cathedrals of rock, woods of oaks, beeches, larches, and firs, and Don Quixote-like wind turbines that frame the landscape rich in variety and emotion.

Northeast of Potenza

Leaving Potenza, most travellers head north towards the alluring contours of the Vulture or east towards the Matera area. In between lies a land whose unassuming appearance belies its complex, glittering history.

❶ Getting There & Away

BUS

A few **SITASUD** (☎ 0971 50 68 11; www.sitasud trasporti.it) buses connect Potenza with Acerenza (one hour 20 minutes). There are slightly more services to Pietragalla (30 minutes) and Oppido Lucano (one hour). Palazzo San Gervasio can be reached from Potenza (2½ hours) and Venosa (30 minutes).**Grassani e Garofalo** (☎ 0835 90 14 43; www.grassanigarofalo.it) operate buses to Vaglio di Basilicata (30 minutes).

CAR & MOTORCYCLE

The SS169 runs from Potenza to Pietragalla and Oppido Lucano; for Acerenza you must then take the SP6. Vaglio can be reached on the SS7.

Vaglio di Basilicata

POP 1934 / ELEV 954M

From a geographical point of view, it's only about 15km from Potenza to this small village in the upper Basento valley. But in terms of atmosphere you could be aeons away. As you stroll through the silent alleyways around the Chiesa Madre (which harbours a 1582 *Madonna del Rosario* and a 1580 *Sacra Famiglia* by Antonio Stabile, but is often closed) you'll find yourself catapulted into a slow, sleepy world. To wake yourself up, you need only stop by the fascinating Museo delle Antiche

ARCHAEOLOGICAL TOURS

As well as chestnut, olive and beech trees, the countryside around Vaglio di Basilicata is scattered with archaeological ruins. At **Serra San Bernardo**, 4km east of town (follow Via Paschiere), you'll find the archaeological area of the same name. Back around the 5th century BCE there was an acropolis-style settlement here but all that's visible today are the bases of its house walls. Some 7km to the north, **Rossano di Vaglio,** harbours the solemn ruins of a temple dedicated to the seductive pre-Roman goddess Mefite (4th century BCE), to whom waters and springs were sacred. There are no longer any fountains or springs here but the site retains a certain evocative power. In summer, both sites should be open at the same time as the Museo delle Antiche Genti di Lucania (p104), but to be safe, or if you happen to come outside these hours, call ahead.

Genti di Lucania (☎ 0971 48 78 71; Via Dinu Adamesteanu 1; ⊙ 10am-1pm & 4-7pm Mon-Sun), one of the most original and significant museums in the area. The highlight of its collection is the *Tavola Lucana*, an autographed self-portrait attributed to Leonardo da Vinci. The painting, which dates to the end of the 15th century, is often away on loan, but the reconstruction of 75 machines designed by the great man will make up for its absence. On the ground floor there's a small archaeological section, with finds from Serra San Bernardo and Rossano di Vaglio. The more conventional Museo della Civiltà Rurale (☎ 338 986 31 84; www.museoruralevaglio.it; Via Roma 28; ⊙ 6-8pm Tue & Fri, noon-1pm Sun summer, other days by reservation) **FREE** illustrates peasant life with displays of objects and work tools, as well as barrel organs and suitcases used by emigrants between 1800 to 1950 to set off in search of new worlds.

🛏 Sleeping & Eating

⭐ **La Dimora dei Cavalieri**   AGRITURISMO €€

(☎ 340 374 57 30; www.dimoracavalieri.it; Contrada Tataseppe 1; r €85; tasting menu €35; 🐾 P 🏊) One of the most acclaimed spots in the Potentino is this agriturismo, nestled in a splendid rural set-up where the bleating of sheep will accompany your every thought, the cheese is terrific, and you can breathe the smell of hay. What's more, the swimming pool guarantees refreshment after a lovely walk along the farm's paths. Fair prices.

❶ Information

Pro Loco office (☎ 0971 590 51; www.ilpercorso divaglio.it; Piazza Tamburrino 1; ⊙ 6.30-8pm Mon-Sun)

Oppido Lucano & Around

POP 3710 / ELEV 670M

Surrounded by pleasant olive-clad hills, Oppido Lucano doesn't exactly fit the stereotype of a fairy-tale village where you stroll around gasping in admiration at every corner. Even the main attraction, the Museo Etnografico (☎ 0971 94 55 39, 338 190 52 12; Via Unità d'Italia 33; ⊙ 6-8pm Mar or by reservation) **FREE** and its well curated collection of artisanal, shepherd and farm tools is housed in an ominous looking building (look for the AVIS headquarters). However, for daring travellers with wheels, there are adventures to be had around here courtesy of the remarkable attractions in the surrounding countryside. So set your compass and head towards the most important artistic site, the 15th-century Convento di Sant'Antonio (☑ 0971 94 50 02; SP35), which boasts biblical frescoes by Giovanni Todisco (1558) in three rooms. In the adjacent church, you'll find a superb 16th-century wooden choir, complete with armrests carved in the shape of a dolphin, as well as a late 16th-century polyptych and triptych by Antonio Stabile. To get to the sanctuary from the town centre take the SP35 towards Tolve or ask for the cemetery. For a more hermetic atmosphere, search out the Chiesa rupestre di Sant'Antuono (Contrada Pozzella), dedicated to Sant'Antonio Abate and decorated with 14th century frescoes. To find the church, follow the SS169 towards Genzano and after about 3km take the downhill road right at the first large crossroads. After a few hundred metres you'll see signs for the church, along a dirt road through the olive trees.

If you want to go even further back in time, you can visit the remains of two 1st-century BCE Roman villas. Villa San Gilio can be reached by continuing along the SP35 towards Tolve – make sure to leave your car at the foot of the hill otherwise you risk destroying its axle shaft. The Masseria Ciccotti, complete with the remains of an aqueduct, is located near the SS96 bis, after the crossing with the SS169. You can locate it with Google Maps, but don't follow the directions as they'll send you down the wrong roads. For the latest information on the opening hours of the churches and sites, contact the Pro Loco (www.prolocooppidolucano.it, www.visitoppido lucano.it; Via Palermo 12; ⊙ variable hrs) or ask (in the morning) at the local Comune (☑ 0971 94 50 02; Via Bari 14).

✪ Festivals & Events

Sagra della pasta a mano   AUGUST
Food stands and stalls appear in the historic centre in the third weekend of August for this festival of handmade pasta. Pasta dominates, but there are plenty of other delicacies. Bring a plunger to aid digestion.

Pietragalla

POP 3992 / ELEV 834M

If you're coming from Potenza, before reaching the countryside around Oppido Lucano you'll come across this pleasant village on the road. Sadly known for a brigand raid on the night of 16 November 1861, its territory now hosts three interesting historical sites.

The first is in the village centre, the Palazzo Ducale (☑ 0971 94 43 11; Piazza Pafundi; ⊙ variable hrs) FREE. Originally dating to the Middle Ages but since remodelled several times, the edifice lends an air of nobility to the village with its massive, austere presence. About 15km to the northwest is the archaeological site of Monte Torretta (Frazione San Giorgio) FREE, with the meager remains of a 4th-century BCE fortified settlement – ask the locals for information as it's not well signposted. Lastly, the dramatic Parco dei Palmenti (⊙ 24 hrs) FREE, stands out among the village's modest attractions. Located just beyond the last houses to the east on the SS169, the park owes its name to the ancient term *paumentum* or perhaps *pavire*, meaning 'to press' in Latin. Technically it's not a park but a vast network of caves (about 200, dating to the second half of the 19th century) which was used for processing grapes. You can make out the tanks used for pressing, positioned higher up, and those for fermentation into which the liquid from the pressed grapes would flow. Rigorous historical explanations aside, you'll find yourself in a sort of Lucanian smurf village. Many caves are open, and you can wander around at your leisure.

❶ Information

Pro Loco (☑ 370 145 63 61; www.proloco-pietra galla.it; Via Roma 14; ⊙ variable hrs)

Acerenza

POP 2268 / ELEV 833M

Of all the villages in the area – in fact, of all the villages in Basilicata – Acerenza is one of the most spectacular. Perched on a strategically located hill, its profile dominated by the sumptuous form of its cathedral, it has an ancient, articulated and solemn history. It was originally founded by the Oscans and was later occupied by the Romans in the 4th century BCE, the Lombards in the 7th century CE and, from 1061, by the Normans, to whom it owes the construction of its walls and the architectural marvel for which it's still famous today. Next came periods of Swabian, Angevin and Aragonese domination (13th-15th centuries). Finally, at the behest of Philip II, Acerenza became a duchy in 1593. Few monumental traces exist of this sparkling succession of rulers, but a leisurely stroll through the medieval-tinged alleys of the historic centre certainly won't disappoint.

⊙ Sights

★ Cattedrale   CATHEDRAL

(📞0971 74 15 11; Largo Duomo 5; ⊘9am-noon & 4-7pm) Whether you see it from miles away as you arrive from the main road, or from a few metres as you admire the portal, marble columns and pedestals embellished with sculpted human figures and monsters, or even from the bare stone interior, you'll be left speechless by the grandeur of this extraordinary cathedral, consecrated in 1080 and dedicated to St. Mary of the Assumption and St. Canius. Acerenza became an episcopal see in 1059, and Archbishop Arnaldo, the abbot of Cluny who arrived here in 1067, used French craftsmen to build and assert the architectural values of the Cluniac congregation. Further enhancing the structure's sense of soaring momentum is the contrast with the intricate network of lanes that surrounds it, and the simplicity of the decoration in the bare naves. The cathedral was restored after an earthquake in 1456, but it retains its original Romanesque layout, with the ambulatory (behind the altar) surmounted by cross vaults onto which three chapels open. Of particular note are the two works by Antonio Stabile housed in the transepts: on the right, a polyptych depicting the *Madonna del Rosario* (1583) and on the left, framed by a sublime stone aedicule, a *Deposizione* (1570). Even more remarkable is the Renaissance crypt beneath the presbytery, frescoed during the 16th century (the walls probably by Giovanni Todisco). However, according to some esoteric theories, the cathedral's real highlight would be none other than the Holy Grail.

Museo Diocesano di Arte Sacra   MUSEUM

(📞0971 74 12 99; www.diocesiacerenza.it; Largo Seminario 2; tickets €1; ⊘10am-12.30pm Mon-Sun) Among the sacred artefacts and ceramic finds look out for a bust of Julian the Apostate dating from the 4th century CE, and liturgical vestments.

Museo della Civiltà Contadina   MUSEUM

(📞329 423 34 65; Via Albini 20; ⊘9.30am-12.30pm & 4-6pm Tue-Sun) FREE This is effectively a reconstruction of a traditional farmhouse. If you haven't visited a similar museum in the area, it could be interesting. To visit, ask at the Pro Loco office.

Basilicata Alpaca   ALPACA FARM

(📞340 524 94 74; Contrada Alvanello; activities with animals adult/reduced €11/8; ⊘10am-6.30pm Tue-Sun, start of activities at 11.30am & 5pm, also 10.30am Sat & Sun) A corner of South America in the heart of Basilicata. At this unusual farm you can pet the soft Andean animals and take them for walks. There are about twenty alpacas and unlike llamas they don't have the habit of spitting. You can also buy a sweater in the shop (Via Umberto I 27; ⊘10.30am-1.30pm & 4.30-7.30pm Tue-Sat, 10.30am-1.30pm Sun) in the centre.

WORTH A TRIP

THE STORIA BANDITA

Of Basilicata's many summer festivals, the Storia Bandita (📞351 588 26 97; www.parco grancia.it; Parco della Grancia, Brindisi di Montagna) was for several years the most eagerly awaited. Imagine an immense scenic area of 25,000 sq m where 400 extras perform a multimedia re-enactment of one of southern Italy's most controversial historical chapters (and one that's deeply rooted in the Lucanian identity) – the era of brigandage. The voices of Michele Placido, Orso Maria Guerrini, and Paolo Ferrari animate the controversial figures of Carmine Crocco and his bandits, who, in the years after Italian unification, put Basilicata to fire and sword, often with the support of the local population. In recent years the festival has taken place in a reduced form, but the hope is that the colossal event will soon return to its former glory. If not, the village of Brindisi di Montagna can still provide satisfaction. The Castello Fittipaldi Antinori (📞0971 98 50 02; Via del Castello; ⊘variable hrs) FREE, perched on a classic peak-top, exudes grandeur and has an excellent multimedia itinerary inside. And should you happen to come here during the Giornate Medievali (www. brindisimedievale.it), usually at the end of October, you'll be able to challenge knights and soldiers in the village streets. For information, contact the Pro Loco (📞347 548 79 72; www. prolocobm.it; Via Estramurale Basento; ⊘variable hrs). To drive to Brindisi di Montagna from Potenza, take the SS407 and SP37 (about 30 minutes). Bus services are run by Allegretti (📞0971 98 50 19; 30 minutes).

 Festivals & Events

Corteo medievale AUGUST 11-12
A great theatrical performance acts out the history of Acerenza's cathedral. Then the medieval procession swings into action, with dances, fire eaters and street artists.

Eating

Al Duomo RESTAURANT €
(☑0971 74 14 02; Largo Glinni 13; meals €20; ⊙12.30-3pm & 8-11pm Wed-Mon, daily summer) People come here to sample the village's signature homemade pasta, *z'zridd* and beans, here served in homely abundance. The restaurant, right next to the Cathedral, doesn't stand out for its attention to detail or refinement, but the out-of-town trattoria atmosphere is quite pleasant.

ℹ Information

TOURIST INFORMATION
Pro Loco office (☑329 423 34 65; www.proloco acerenza.it; Via Umberto I 3; ⊙9.30am-12.30pm & 4-6pm Tue-Sun)

Palazzo San Gervasio
POP 4590 / ELEV 485M
Suspended between the Vulture and the Pugliese border, between Potenza's satellite towns and the Materano area, this small village lies in the Alto Bradano. Few make it here except for walkers on the Via Appia (see boxed text p127) and some passing travellers, and while its historic centre is less photogenic than average in these parts, it reveals a certain cultural dignity in the form of a significant museum. The **Pinacoteca D'Errico** (☑0972 444 79; www.pinacotecaderrico. it; Corso Manfredi 110 ; ⊙10am-1pm & 5-7pm) **FREE**, which periodically swaps around its exhibited works, showcases a collection – part of which has been transferred to the National Museum of Matera, p56 – amassed by the intellectual and patriot Camillo D'Errico. Inside there's also a small archaeological section displaying a striking Samnite helmet.

🛏 Sleeping & Eating

Torraca B&B €€
(☑0972 448 53; www.complessolatorraca.it; Contra-da Crognale; r €60; ☽❋P) This is an unusual place for an overnight stay – it has a public swimming pool (adult/reduced half-day €6/4, full day €10/6), a children's play area, a bar-pasticceria, a pizzeria, and there's movement and cheer at all hours. That said, the rooms

are decidedly ordinary, though comfortable and clean, and there's a beautiful courtyard open for guest use.

★**Bramea** RESTAURANT €€€
(☑0972 20 94 88; www.bramearistorante.it; Viale Villa D'Errico 10; meals €35, menus €40-90; ⊙7am-midnight Wed-Mon) Though not all the flavours are perfectly balanced, if you love creative cuisine this place is a must. The daring combinations, the intensive research into raw materials and the pyrotechnic presentations make this restaurant, set in the converted stables of the D'Errico family's summer villa, a veritable temple of avant-garde cuisine.

The Dolomiti Lucane
One of Basilicata's top destinations, the increasingly popular Dolomiti Lucane (Lucanian Dolomites) stand in the northwestern part of the **Parco Regionale di Gallipoli Cognato e Piccole Dolomiti Lucane** (☑0835 67 50 15; www.parcogallipolicognato.it; Località Palazzo, Accettura) about 50km southeast of Potenza. It's a place of prodigious evocative power – bizarre rock spires soar above rounded peaks, reminiscent of those in Trentino and seemingly conjured from a child's dream, inspiring playful and inexhaustible efforts to compare them to objects and animals. The villages are cinematically beautiful, halfway between reality and fantasy, in parts rough and smooth, and suspended between the earth and a sky constantly furrowed by falcons, red kites and storks. And, speaking of the sky, there's also the astounding Volo dell'Angelo (see boxed text p109), one of the most popular outdoor attractions in the entire region.

Campomaggiore
POP 794 / ELEV 808M
If you didn't know the history of this small village on the edge of the park, it would be impossible to imagine that it was here that the most ardent human ambitions once found concrete form. At the end of the 18th century Count Teodoro Rendina met the architect Giovanni Patturelli, a pupil of Vanvitelli, in Siena, and together they decided to put into practice their utopian ideas, inspired by the theories of Owen and Fourier. Thus construction began on the Utopian City, a city for 1600 people with houses arranged in grids around a central square, a church and baronial palace, a plot of land

for each inhabitant, a cemetery, mills where the men could make olive oil and a fountain where the women could wash their clothes. But fate was cruel to Campomaggiore, and in 1885 a landslide destroyed the entire village, along with the chimerical vision that had created it. Nowadays, Campomaggiore Vecchio (☑0971 98 26 61, 347 953 98 90; www.campomaggiorecittadellutopia.it; adult/reduced €4/2.50; ⊙10am-1pm & 4-8pm Sat & Sun, daily Aug) is a set of run-down ruins, melancholy like all ghost towns. Recently, however, a lively multimedia itinerary was set up, in which a description of the pre-landslide town from the romantic viewpoint of a young girl, fires the imagination. But that isn't to say that a walk past the Rendina castle, the Casino della Contessa and the church won't also inspire ideas for a better world.

To complete your visit, the Museo dell' Utopia (☑0971 98 26 61, 347 953 98 90; Corso Umberto I), in the modern village 4km southwest of Campomaggiore Vecchio, documents its history in great detail.

🏃 Activities

Pietra del Toro   CLIMBING
(www.pietradeltoro.com) Fans of bouldering (climbing on boulders) will find two areas near the town. Enthusiasts consider them to be among the most spectacular in southern Italy. Look out for the sign on the SP13, about 6km south of the village.

ℹ️ Information

Pro Loco office (☑346 855 60 84; Via Regina Margherita 62; ⊙variable hours)

ℹ️ Getting There & Away

From Potenza, Campomaggiore can be reached by car on the SS407 or SS7 and the SP13 Castelmezzano road. Allow about 45 minutes. Bus connections to/from Potenza (50 minutes) are operated by **Savitour** (☑0971 98 20 43; www.savitour.it), which also runs a daily service to Castelmezzano (45 minutes).

Pietrapertosa

POP 965 / ELEV 1088M
The highest municipality in Basilicata, Pietrapertosa creates memories that will creep into your heart on wintery nights. You'll think back to the narrow alleys of the Arabata, the oldest part of the village where the Saracens led by Bomar took refuge in the 9th century, and where clothes hang in the sun like flags.

You'll remember the solemn form of the Castello Normanno Svevo (Pro Loco ☑320 833 78 01; adult/reduced €3/1.50; ⊙10am-7pm Aug & first half of Sep, & in conjunction with the opening of the Volo dell'Angelo), dug into the rock and inhabited over the centuries by noble families. You'll recall the light and rarefied atmosphere of the small village churches and the Convento di San Francesco (Via Sant'Angelo), dating back to 1474 and adorned with beautiful frescoes in the presbytery and a 16th-century polyptych by Giovanni Luce. But more than anything what you'll think back to are the fanciful shapes of the majestic rock spires that preside over Pietrapertosa, their silent but tangible presence recalling the elderly folk who sit in the doorways of the houses. Unless, of course, you've come to experience the sensational Volo dell'Angelo (right), in which case, all your suffused perceptions will be blocked by the burst of adrenaline through your veins, even months after you've left the village.

🏃 Activities

Percorso delle Sette Pietre   HIKING
If you don't want to travel between Pietrapertosa and Castelmezzano by car, or in the air (see boxed text, right), the old 2km sheep track that links the two villages is a more reassuringly pleasant alternative. The walking trail features artistic installations based on the book *Vito ballava con le streghe* (Sellerio, 2004) by Mimmo Sammartino, itself inspired by the area's traditional oral tales, and offers glimpses of real beauty, especially when you reach the stream. To follow the narrative order it's best to begin your walk in Pietrapertosa.

🎉 Festivals & Events

Festa del Mascio   JUNE
Pietrapertosa's most important festival, celebrated on the Sunday following 13 June in honour of St. Anthony, is one of Basilicata's many arboreal rites. It's divided into four phases: the felling of a Turkey oak (known as the Mascio) and a holly tree (known as the Cima); the transport of the trees by, respectively, a team of oxen and a pair of young cows with a yoke; the grafting of the two trees, as if they were a man and woman celebrating a spring wedding; and finally the raising of the Mascio with a system of ropes. The bravest villagers then try to climb it, and eventually everything concludes with music and fireworks.

FLY THROUGH THE MOUNTAINS

The extraordinary Angel's Flight zip line is now one of Basilicata's must-sees, or rather must-do's. Of course, it takes a certain sang-froid to descend 400m, prone and tied to a 1550m-long steel cable at speeds of up to 120km/h. But it would be a shame to back out after you've travelled so far. After all, the flight only takes a minute, and harnessed as you are, you'll be able to curse yourself for your madness without risking anything. Besides, it shouldn't be so hard to banish the thought that once you reach your destination, you'll have to steel yourself for the return trip. The **Volo dell'Angelo** (✉ 331 934 04 56, 345 597 13 09, 334 788 00 84; www.volodellangelo.com; single €35-63, couple €40-72; ☉ 9.30am-6.30pm Sun May & Oct, 9.30am-6.30pm Sat & Sun Jun-mid Jul & mid Sep-end Sep, 9.30am-6.30pm daily mid Jul-mid Sep; Castelmezzano ticket office ✉ 0971 98 60 42; Via Roma 28; Pietrapertosa ticket office ✉ 0971 98 31 10; Via Garibaldi 4) is a kind of human funivia that connects the villages of Pietrapertosa and Castelmezzano in a simply fabulous natural setting. But let's be clear: as electrifying as the experience is, it doesn't present any risk. And to relieve you of any practical concerns, and let you enjoy your fears to the max, there's a shuttle service from the villages to the arrival and departure stations. Only at Castelmezzano is there a short 20-minute walk to the departure station – you could perhaps use this time to slip in an extra prayer or two. Wear comfortable shoes.

POTENZA PROVINCE THE DOLOMITI LUCANE

Sulle Tracce degli Arabi AUGUST
(www.comune.pietrapertosa.pz.it) This August festival might be a bit kitschy but it's certainly spectacular. To commemorate its ancient inhabitants, the Arabata district adopts its former Moorish look in a whirl of noise, music, fabrics, clothes, food stalls, markets and itinerant shows.

🛏 Sleeping

La Casa di Penelope e Cirene B&B €€
(✉ 0971 98 30 13, 338 313 21 96, 345 771 39 19; Via Garibaldi 32; s/d €50/80; 🐾) An atmospheric B&B with refined furnishings and splendid stone arches in the village centre. The owner is a wealth of local information and it offers convincing value for money.

Il Palazzo del Barone B&B €€
(✉ 339 586 93 43; www.ilpalazzodelbarone. it; Piazza Garibaldi 8; s/d/tr €50/100/120; 🐾) Impeccable cleanliness, simplicity, grace and courtesy in one of Pietrapertosa's most popular accommodation options. There's also a delicious pizzeria (✉ 345 979 92 80) in the same building.

🍴 Eating

La Locanda di Pietra RESTAURANT €€
(✉ 0971 98 31 81, 368 386 58 63; www.lalocandadipietra.com; Via Garibaldi 58; meals €25-30; ☉ 12.30-3pm & 8-11pm Thu-Tue May-Oct) In an elegant early 20th-century building this restaurant boasts a terrace overlooking the Luca-nian Dolomites, and hearty food that will

re-awaken your appetite after the thrills of the Volo dell'Angelo. The km0 meat is excellent (lamb from the Dolomites, pork from local black pigs and veal from Podolica cows) as is the soppressata salami and cheese.

ℹ Information

In summer you'll find a **tourist information kiosk** (☉ 9am-noon & 4-7pm Jun-Sep) in the car park at the village entrance, but you can also get informative material at the **Pro Loco office** (✉ 320 833 78 01; www.prolocopietrapertosa.it; Via della Speranza 159; ☉ variable hours) or the Volo dell'Angelo ticket office (p109).

ℹ Getting There & Away

From Potenza take the SS407 Basentana towards Metaponto and exit at Campomaggiore; from there continue for 11km to Pietrapertosa. If you're coming from Matera, take the SS407 towards Potenza, then the Campomaggiore and Pietrapertosa exits. Keep in mind that there are no petrol stations in Pietrapertosa. But if you have the misfortune to be travelling without your own means of transport you'll have to resort to the **Autolinee Renna** (✉ 0971 47 16 36; www.fratellirenna.it), which runs several daily buses from Potenza (50 minutes).

Castelmezzano

POP 792 / ELEV 750M
If there's a poet hiding in you and you're looking for inspiration to awaken your dormant creative fervour, then Castelmezzano is not to be missed. With its houses stacked gently on the sandstone ridges, its rock spires

sporting even more whimsical and bizarre shapes than those in neighbouring Pietrapertosa, and with that sense of enchantment that reaches a peak of moving intensity at sunset when the light tinges the stone pink and warms the spirits, Castelmezzano is Basilicata's tourist Olympus.

◉ Sights

Adding to the village's charm are traces of the presence of the Knights Templar. The order's seal is reproduced on the village's coat of arms (two knights, one of whom is a Moor, on a single horse), while a cross pattée has been found on an external wall of the Chiesa Madre.

Chiesa Madre di Santa Maria dell'Olmo CHURCH
(Piazza Caiazzo) This 13th-century church, which overlooks the village's central square, houses several enigmatically beautiful polychrome wooden sculptures, including one depicting Santa Maria dell'Olmo. Enjoy the wonderful view from the belvedere in front of the church.

Castello RUINS
The name of the village ('Castrum Medianum') derives from this castle, situated halfway between Pietrapertosa and Albano di Lucania, which the Normans built in the Middle Ages to guard the territory. Little remains of the original structure, which lies beyond the western end of the village, except for the ruins of the outer walls, but the sight of them is one that will leave an impression long after you have left. Photo opportunities abound.

✪ Festivals & Events

Il Rito del Maggio SEPTEMBER
Here in Castelmezzano the Festa del Maggio is also held in honour of St. Anthony, but it takes place on 13 September. The rite is very similar to that of the Festa del Mascio (p108) in Pietrapertosa.

🛏 Sleeping

Some accommodation options in the village are open only in summer.

La Grotta dell'Eremita AGRITURISMO €
(☑0971 98 63 14, 335 687 48 45; Contrada Calcescia 1; www.grottadelleremita.com; r only/half-board/full-board per person €35/55/70; 🛜 ❄) To get bored here would require application and commitment what with horse riding, an educational farm, and opportunities for excursions (with the option of babysitting for your children) providing plenty of diversions. The restaurant, specialising in home-produced dairy products and fresh pasta, is open to everyone. The farm is about 5km north of the village.

La Perla nelle Dolomiti B&B €€
(☑0971 98 63 73, 329 376 19 98; www.dolomitiluca nebb.it; Vico Castello 2; s €35-40, d €60-70; 🛜) More than a B&B, this is an ideal apartment for a couple or family (it sleeps up to four). In addition to a kitchenette, it offers a panoramic balcony and breakfast with an impressive jam tart. Impeccably clean.

La Casa di Giulietta B&B €€
(☑333 488 45 79, 338 981 16 84; www.lacasadi giulietta.net; Via Garibaldi 16; d/tr/q €77/106/120; 🛜 ❄) We don't know of any Shakespearean characters that have lived in these parts however, a stay at Juliet's House, just a few

---

VIE FERRATE, A NEPALESE BRIDGE & AN ANCIENT STAIRWAY

Opportunities to get your adrenalin fix in the Dolomiti Lucane aren't limited to the Volo dell'Angelo. For additional thrills you can tackle the **Via Ferrata Salemm**, on the Castelmezzano side, and the **Via Ferrata Marcirosa**, on the Pietrapertosa side (about 1700m each), with a scenic Nepalese-style hanging bridge of about 70m providing the icing on the cake. The starting point of the via ferratas is in a clearing by a stream about halfway along the Percorso delle Sette Pietre (Seven Stones Route; p108). If you don't have the necessary kit, you can use the rental service at the Volo dell'Angelo ticket offices (€20 per day). The ancient gradinata normanna (Norman stairway; for guided climbs ☑0971 98 60 42, 331 934 04 56; www.volodellangelo.com; 1/2 people €8/13; ⊙Jul-Aug) allows you to combine dizzying emotions with edifying historical insight – the 54 steps were, in fact, carved into the rock by the area's 12th-century rulers in order to reach a lookout on the walls of the Castello di Castelmezzano (p110). And even with no enemy sightings on the horizon, your attention will be captivated by the superb view.

meters from the castle, might just fire up some romantic impulses. Its five rooms are spacious and some come with beautiful views. Electric bikes are available to hire (€25 for three hours).

✖ Eating

Castelmezzano's specialities include *crost'l*, a wedding pastry made with honey and oregano. Keep in mind that in the low season it can be difficult to find places open for lunch.

Dal Vecchio Scarpone RESTAURANT €€
(📞333 732 56 40; Corso Vittorio Emanuele 3; menus €20-25; ☺noon-3pm & 7-9.30pm, closed Tue Oct-Apr) This small restaurant in the village's narrow streets is rustic and very inviting (especially on the upper floor). There's a family atmosphere and the food, which is served in quantities sufficient to meet your weekly calorie count in a single sitting, is good.

★Al Becco della Civetta RESTAURANT €€
(📞0971 98 62 49; www.beccodellacivetta.it; Vico I Maglia 7; meals €30-35; ☺open lunch & dinner from the Sunday before Easter to 2 November, variable hrs in winter) Foodies reckon this is one of the best restaurants in Basilicata. Boasting an exhilarating view from its windows and terrace, it cooks up a menu that combines substance and sophistication to leave you thoroughly satisfied. If, after the fig ice cream with fennel seeds, you can't face getting in your car, above are the 24 rooms of the hotel **La Locanda di Castromediano** (Via Volini 50/a; s/d €70/100; ✳🛜).

🍷 Drinking & Nightlife

Luciano BAR
(Corso Vittorio Emanuele II 9; ☺6-2am) Ladies and gentlemen, welcome to the beating heart of the village. Come at any time of day and you'll find someone to chat with or ask for information. Just be careful not to challenge any of the regulars to scopa (an Italian card game) or your self-esteem could take a beating.

ℹ Information

For information, you can contact the local **Comune** (📞0971 98 61 66; Via Roma 28).

ℹ Getting There & Away

From Potenza, take the SS407 towards Matera and exit at Campomaggiore. **SITASUD** buses (📞0971 50 68 11; www.sitasudtrasporti.it) run to the village four times daily (one hour).

CYCLING ADVENTURES

Considering the spectacular natural scenery, it's not surprising that the **Ciclovia delle Dolomiti Lucane** (www.basilicataturistica.it) attracts many bike lovers in summer. In reality, there's no actual cycle path, rather a set of routes that take advantage of the paved roads and scarcity of car traffic. For example, there's a nice 25km loop through Pietrapertosa and Castelmezzano, or you can pedal off to Accettura (see boxed text p81). If you're moderately fit, however, there's nothing to stop you from crossing the park boundaries and tackling the 114km from Pietrapertosa to Matera in two or three stages. You'll find maps on the website.

The Potentine Mountains

When talking about travel and describing places that are particularly quiet or detached from life's frenetic rhythms, it's quite common to refer to a slowing down, or even a suspension, of time. Well, head south from Potenza on the SP5, visit the villages and explore the woods, and you'll realize that just sometimes these references aren't merely narrative devices.

ℹ Getting There & Away

Pignola and Abriola are respectively 10km and 18km south of Potenza on the SP5. For Calvello you must then take the SP16. **Ferrovie Appulo Lucane** (📞800 05 05 00; www.ferrovieappulo lucane.it) buses run from Potenza to Laurenzana (1½ hours), passing through Pignola (20 minutes), Abriola (45 minutes) and Calvello (one hour). Reckon on three departures a day.

Pignola

POP 6996 / ELEV 927M

A small village perched on a hill, like all the villages in these parts, Pignola stands out from its neighbours thanks to a distinguishing architectural peculiarity. The *paese dei cento portali* (town of a hundred portals), as it's known, features an enviable collection of stone portals carved and embellished with caryatids and masks. These adorn many of the period buildings that line the narrow streets and steep alleyways that lead up to the village's highpoint. Some of the most notable

WINTER & SUMMER IN POTENZA'S MOUNTAINS

You know those immense Alpine ski complexes that take entire days to explore and have slopes for all tastes? Well the Sellata-Pierfaone ski area (www.skisellata.it; Contrada Pierfaone; weekday ski pass half/full day €13/19, 2hr/half/full day ski pass €15/20/30) is nothing like those. After all, you are in Basilicata, not Sestriere. However, the approximately 7km of pistes offer different levels of difficulty, snake down a beautiful beech forest, and will keep you happily occupied for a whole day. In summer, the Pierfaone becomes a paradise for fearless cyclists due to its bike park, a real rarity in these parts.

overlook the irregular main square, Piazza Vittorio Emanuele. Chief among the village's religious buildings is the panoramically-sited Chiesa Madre (Via Dante Alighieri 23), which houses two paintings by Pietrafesa – though the erudite parish priest disagrees with this attribution – and the remains of the artist (in a pillar to the left of the presbytery), who died in Pignola in 1653. Ask at the caretaker's house for someone to let you in. The Pro Loco harbours a small Museo Scenografico del Costume e della Civiltà Rurale (☑0971 42 14 10, 346 694 38 89; Via Garibaldi 1; ⊙ variable hrs) at its location a few hundred meters below the church. Before leaving the village, stop by the Branca & Mecca dairy shop (☑0971 42 10 02; Via Umberto I 46; ⊙ 8am-1.30pm & 5-8pm Mon-Sat) to pick up a mozzarella you'll remember for a long time.

✯ Festivals & Events

Palio di Sant'Antonio Abate   JANUARY
Every January 16, mules and horses compete in a mad race through the village's steep and slippery alleys, which are often covered in snow.

🏃 Activities

Oasi WWF Pantano
di Pignola   BIRDWATCHING
(www.wwf.it; Contrada Petrucco; ⊙ closed at the time of research) For bird lovers, this lake 4km west of Pignola is a true paradise – in addition to the 158 species of migratory birds that pass through here, you can also look out for the 37 resident species (as well as mosquitoes as big as eagles) from the observation huts. Unfortunately, at the time of research, the area was closed, but the cycle/pedestrian path that circles it was still open for pleasant walks.

🛏 Sleeping & Eating

There aren't many places to eat in the area. In fact, hotels are often the best choice for sleeping and eating.

Hotel Giubileo   HOTEL €€
(☑0971 47 99 10, 366 721 68 03; www.giubileomaison.it; SS92 Località Rifreddo; r from €70; 🅿 P ❄) A four-star hotel immersed in the woods about 15 minutes' drive from Pignola. It has 80 rooms (some a little dated), a spa and fitness area, and a good restaurant (meals €30). It may not stand out for atmosphere, but as a base for exploring the surrounding area it does the job perfectly.

La Taverna del Boscaiolo   AGRITURISMO €€
(☑0971 42 02 19; Contrada Arioso; menus €25; ⊙10am-4.30pm Tue-Fri & Sun, 10am-4.30pm & 7pm-midnight Sat) You'll eat well, helpings are generous and there's a view as vast as your stomach will feel at the end of lunch. It also has a nice outdoor space where children can play in summer.

Abriola

POP 1329 / ELEV 957M

Art lovers head to this small town in the heart of the Lucanian Apennines, just 40 minutes' drive from Potenza, to explore the birthplace of Giovanni Todisco, Basilicata's most important 16th-century painter. Here they can visit the small Chiesa di San Gerard (Via San Gerardo 2), adorned with fragments of frescoes, the Chiesa della SS Annunziata (Via Annunziata), which showcases some significant pictorial pieces from the 13th to 15th centuries in the highest part of town, and, most notably, the Chiesa Madre (Via Sarli 35), which incorporates the contemporary look of the bronze door panels by Antonio Masino, the baroque vapidity of the *Donazione della stola a sant'Idelfonso* (1622) by Pietrafesa, and the popular devotional purity of the enigmatic wooden madonnas. To access the churches send a WhatsApp message to the Pro Loco (☑338 118 36 53; Via Marinelli; ⊙ variable hrs). Sportier travellers pass through the village on their way to the ski resort of Sellata-Pierfaone or, in the summer months, to saddle up and throw themselves around the bike park at breakneck speed. Then there are those who come to combine outdoor exercise and culture – the Santuario della Madonna di Monteforte can be reached in just over an hour along a footpath that starts at the cemetery (though you can also drive up from the Sellata pass). Inside, you'll find Marian frescoes by Giovanni Todisco and an 11th-century Christ Pantocrator in the apsidal basin. Here too, as in Brienza, San Severino Lucano and Viggiano, a statue of the Madonna is kept in the Chiesa Madre in winter and in the mountain sanctuary in summer.

Of course, you can always come to Abriola for no specific reason at all, just to sit on a bench and listen to the silence, to slip into the slow rhythms of the elderly locals and watch as clothes flap above the tranquil, sleepy dogs lying in the doorways. In fact, this is probably the best way to get to know Abriola.

✯✧ Festivals & Events

Festa di San Valentino   FEBRUARY, AUGUST
It's said that while St. Valentine was travelling from Rome to Puglia he stopped near the town which was suffering a famine at the time. He healed people and sent for wagons of wheat to feed the population. As the village counts so few souls in winter, the feast of February 14 is repeated on August 16, when bonfires are lit on the streets and people eat together and play music.

Calvello

POP 1940 / ELEV 730M

As you walk through the steep uphill streets of the historic centre and spot some ugly buildings in the more modern part of town, you might think that Calvello is just like all the other pleasant villages in the area. However, it has a very specific identity, which has its roots in a centuries-old tradition – the decoration of ceramics. This artisanal tradition is kept alive in a series of workshops, including Arte Ceramica Val Camastra (☑328 767 61 36; www.arteceramicaval camastra.it; Via Roma 27; ⊙10am-1pm & 5pm-8pm) and La Bottega di Faenza (☑329 636 46 38; www.gallicchio.eu; Largo Plebiscito 28; ⊙9am-1pm & 5-8.30pm, but call ahead).

In the evocative setting of the medieval castle (which later became a noble residence) is the Museo della Ceramica (☑0971 92 19 11; Via Sant'Anna 10; adult/reduced €3/2) where you can attend an interesting workshop (adult/reduced incl museum admission €7/5). Also worth a look is the Convento di Santa Maria de Plano (Largo Garibaldi 1). Frescoed in the 17th century, the beautiful Franciscan cloister now houses, among other things – in one of the most daring associations in the history of Italian museology – the Museo della Canzone Napoletana (☑0971 92 19 11; ⊙variable hrs), which exhibits sheet music of Neopolitan songs and period photos. You can get information by calling the Pro Loco office (☑347 216 42 98; ⊙variable hrs) or checking www.visitcalvello.it.

POTENZA PROVINCE THE POTENTINE MOUNTAINS

THE ABETINA DI LAURENZANA

Laurenzana, 35km south of Potenza on the SS92, is known for the ominous ruins of its castle. Originally constructed in the 1200s, but rebuilt in the 16th century, this sits atop a vertiginous rock as if in a Gothic novel. However, the main reason for stopping by these parts is to visit the equally romantic Riserva Regionale Abetina di Laurenzana. At this nature reserve you won't know whether to look up to the tops of the white fir trees, some of which reach heights of 40m, or down to the undergrowth, where wild orchids, cyclamens, and hawthorns abound and the rustling of hares and dormice stirs the sacred stillness of the forest. For walkers, a beautiful circular trail starts in Acqua del Prosciutto (from Laurenzana take the SP60 southwest). This woodland path, which is well signposted from the fountain where you can leave your car, is about 12km and takes about four and a half hours. You'll walk through solemn beech and oak trees until you meet your first *abeti bianchi* (white fir trees) after a couple of kilometres. Alternatively, a second 7km path starts at the Rifugio Fontana dei Pastori (☑0975 196 62 55, 349 415 88 48; Via Fontana dei Pastori 2, Viggiano) and passes through a vast beech wood (with fragrant expanses of flowering garlic at various times of the year) until it joins up with the first trail.

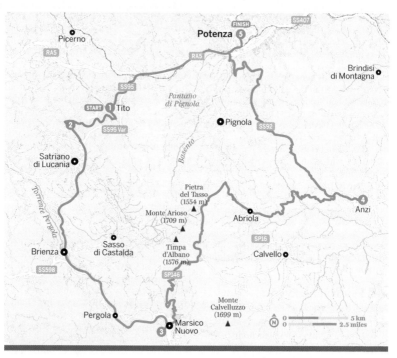

🚗 Driving Tour
A Cheerful Sunday in Potenza

START TITO
END POTENZA
DURATION 124KM, NINE HOURS

When the sun shines and the call of the road becomes impossible to resist, a tour of the Potentino's less frequented parts will help sate your wanderlust – not that the district's other areas are exactly teeming with travellers. From Potenza take the Raccordo Autostradale 5 (RA5) towards Salerno and exit at Tito. Continue on to the cloister of the 16th-century **❶ Convento di Sant'Antonio** (☑348 969 64 00; Largo del Convento; ⊙by reservation), which boasts a lively cycle of frescoes (1606) by Pietrafesa illustrating the life of St. Antonio. From there follow the SS95 and take a small well-signposted detour off to the left. This will lead you to the **❷ Torre di Satriano** (☑329 458 87 95, 340 269 79 57, 389 962 42 61; www. torresatriano.it; Località Torre di Satriano; adult/reduced €3/2; ⊙by appointment 10am-11.30am, 11.30am-1pm & 5-7pm), whose upland setting comes as close as anything in Basilicata to the Scottish highlands. The history of the

medieval-but-repeatedly-demolished-and-rebuilt tower, is told in the small museum inside. Now that you've felt like the Lucanian king of the castle, you might be starting to feel a bit peckish. So, push on southwards on the SS95 and SS598 to **❸ Marsico Nuovo**. Home to the HQ of the Parco Nazionale Appennino Lucano Val d'Agri-Lagonegrese, there are several agriturismi that make an ideal lunch stop. If you go to **Agriturismo Vignola** (☑0975 34 25 11; www.agriturismovignola.it; Contrada Capo d'Acqua 23; meals €30) you'll realize that the term 'Vignola' (meaning little vineyard) doesn't quite work, given the huge size of the portions. To digest your meal, you can drown in rivers of Amaro Lucano or drive an hour up to **❹ Anzi** (via the Abriola–Anzi road) and its futuristic **observatory** (☑340 469 49 09; www.planetario anzi.wixsite.it; Via Salita Rosario; planetarium visits €5, planetarium & observatory €10; ⊙by reservation), positioned on Monte Siri. Next to the observatory, the **Chiesa di Santa Maria** houses 16-century frescoes by Giovanni Todisco. After such a varied day, return to **❺ Potenza** with your heart brimming with beauty.

Valle del Melandro

Heading west from the regional capital means entering a wild land, where the drama of the titanic precipices is tempered by the grace of the villages that dot the hilltops. For decades the area has been ignored by tourism, despite harbouring several cultural and naturalistic attractions, but things have begun to change thanks, in part, to the appearance of a structure with the potential to kickstart things, the Ponte alla Luna.

❶ Getting There & Away

The SS95 and SS95VAR both run south of Potenza and traverse the whole valley. For Sasso di Castalda you have to take the SP39 from Brienza. From Satriano di Lucania the SP12 deviates westwards and runs to Savoia di Lucania. A few daily **SITASUD** buses(📞 0971 50 68 11; www.sitasudtrasporti.it) connect Potenza to Brienza (one hour) via Satriano (50 minutes).

Satriano di Lucania

POP 2321 / ELEV 635M

It's certainly worth making the trip to this eclectic village about half an hour's drive from Potenza, especially when the sky is blue and the green of the surrounding trees sparkles with a festive light. A top reason is because Satriano can cheer up young and old people with the colourful murals (for guided tours book via whatsapp at 📞 340 234 18 92; €25) which brighten the facades of many houses. Visitors hungry for local culture will find plenty to keep them busy. The 18th-century Palazzo Loreti, which belonged to a rich noble family, houses a small Museo Archeologico and a Museo della Civiltà Contadina (📞 0975 38 37 15; Via De Gregorio 23; ⊙ both closed at the time of research). Travellers who cultivate the spirit and pursue beauty will enjoy the fact that Satriano was the birthplace of Giovanni De Gregorio (aka 'Pietrafesa'), the indisputed star of 17th-century Lucanian art. The Museo Virtuale del Pietrafesa (to visit contact Satriano's town council 📞 0975 38 37 15; Rocca Duca di Poggiardo) illustrates the painter's art with the aid of 40 digitized works, while the Cappella di San Giovanni (Via San Giovanni) houses one of his frescoes with angels and cherubs (1626). Finally, before rushing off to lunch, we'd recommend a preparatory stop at Pepem Fabuleum (📞 347 877 62 80; Via De Gregorio; ⊙ by reservation), a museum above the Infopoint which recounts the hottest secrets of the chili pepper.

🛏 Sleeping & Eating

⭐ **Atmosfera Bubble Glamping**   GLAMPING €€€

(📞 379 263 25 15; www.atmospherebubbleglamping.it; Contrada Le Piane; bubble room for 2 people €260; 🛜 ❄ P) Sure, it's not cheap, but the experience of sleeping in a transparent bubble immersed in an oak forest, with a private outdoor hot tub, is undoubtedly unique. Book well in advance.

Sotto la Torre   RESTAURANT €€

(📞 0975 38 36 30; Contrada Passariello; meals €35, tasting menu €40; ⊙ 6.30-11.30pm Tue-Sat, noon-4pm Sun) Probably the best restaurant in the valley given the elegance of its location and the quality of the dishes which fully complement the ambitions of the refined menu. If available, try the truffled egg. It's located just north of the historic centre.

✪ Festivals & Events

Carnevale   FEBRUARY, MARCH

One of the region's most important carnival celebrations centres on the *rumita* (hermit), a man covered in green branches who, on the last Sunday before Shrove Tuesday, goes around town rubbing the *fruscio* (stick) on house doors.

Information

Infopoint (📞 0975 38 37 15; Via De Gregorio; ⊙ variable hrs)

Pro Loco office (📞 393 974 96 49; www.proloco satrianodilucania.wordpress.com; ⊙ variable hrs)

Brienza

POP 3873 / ELEV 713M

There's no denying that Brienza exudes a certain fading charm – the Castello Caracciolo, founded by the Angevins and around which the whole village twists and turns, fires fantasies of feasts and court banquets; the uninhabited historic centre, dotted with a few fine aristocratic palaces, shrouds visitors in silence; while to cap it all off, there's the desolate, ever-present atmosphere of a provincial Lucanian village. To get the most out of your visit, contact the Pro Loco, which organises guided tours (voluntary donation; ⊙ by reservation at 11am & 3pm Sat & Sun winter, 11am & 6.30pm Sat & Sun summer) of the old part of Brienza (including the castle), which is normally out of bounds.

Some 1km from the centre along the SS95 towards Potenza, the Museo Laboratorio delleArti e del Paesaggio-MuLabo (📞 342

698 25 65, 348 158 24 29; www.mulabo.it; Contrada Madonna degli Angeli; adult/reduced €4/3), gives access to the Cappella della Madonna degli Angeli, complete with frescoes by Pietrafesa, and a trail that showcases the area's amazing nature. And if the museum's multimedia presentations whet your appetite for grand landscapes, you can experience them for yourself at the Faggeta del Lago, 15-minutes' drive southwest of the village. Here you'll find picnic areas and well-marked routes through an area which local legend holds is teeming with jovial witches.

★ Festivals & Events

Festa del SS Crocifisso   MAY, SEPTEMBER
Since 1238, every first Sunday of May, a crucifix is carried up the mountain to the sanctuary of the same name. It then makes the return trip on the third Sunday of September, when a solemn procession takes it back to the Chiesa Madre. On the same day, the ritual of the *volo dell'angelo* (flight of the angel) is is staged – a child dressed as a cherub flies across the piazza hanging from a cable stretched between two buildings.

⌴ Sleeping

★ La Voce del Fiume   B&B €€
(☑ 339 229 06 30; www.lavocedelfiume.it; Vico del Carmine 7; s/d €100/130; 🛜❄) The river can indeed be heard at The Voice of the River B&B. But what sets this period house apart are its superb stone rooms, with wooden floors and refined details. The breakfast, too, is remarkable. Not to be missed if you're a romantic traveller.

ⓘ Information

Pro Loco (☑ 348 937 48 63, 324 798 03 09; Piazza Unità d'Italia) As well as visits to the historic centre and the castle, it organises events at the Parco Letterario Francesco Maria Pagano (www. parchiletterari.com), a literary park dedicated to the great jurist who was born here in 1748.

Sasso di Castalda

POP 766 / ELEV 940M

This charming little village 7km from Brienza is now a fixed point on the region's tourist map. Until a few years ago, few travellers hung out in these parts, despite the stone houses that evoke a northern European atmosphere on autumnal evenings. Nowadays, however, it can be hard to find parking space on summer days thanks, in the main, to the amazing Ponte alla Luna (see boxed text

right) and the village has started to enjoy a certain popularity. Adding to its appeal is its rich supply of walking trails and the poetry of the surrounding landscape.

◎ Sights

Area Faunistica del Cervo   WILDLIFE AREA
(Via San Rocco) Head up the village's narrow streets, and when the houses end, follow the fence around to the left until you see a hut – this is the best point to try and spot the deer that live in this 18-hectare wildlife reserve. Bring some apples with you and you'll make the animals very happy.

⟁ Activities

Arenazzo   VIA FERRATA
A path starting from the historic centre of the village leads to the bed of a stream and from there to the via ferrata, which crosses two hanging Tibetan-style bridges. Near the village, there's also a second via ferrata, called the 'Belvedere'. You can rent equipment (€15) at the Ponte alla Luna ticket office (see boxed text, right).

Sentiero Frassati   HIKING
This 22km hiking circuit (which includes a short link road) is one of the most spectacular in Basilicata. En route you'll come across abandoned farmyards, mills, chapels, farms, forests of pine, beech and fir trees, and fountains – and with them all, the memory of the roads that for centuries linked the community of Sasso di Castalda to the mountains. Allow eight hours from the historic centre. If you don't have time to walk the path, drive to the wonderful La Costara beech forest, which stands as lyrical as a cathedral, 3km east of the village. If, however, you want to go Nordic walking, contact local guide Donato Filippi (☑ 328 646 91 89; €20-40).

⌴ Sleeping & Eating

Guarda che Luna   B&B €€
(☑ 320 041 81 02; www.guardachelunabeb.com; Via San Nicola 18; s/d/apt for 4 people €60/80/100; 🛜) This small, pretty structure is located at the entrance to the Ponte alla Luna. The round window overlooking the gorge in one of the rooms is a real gem. The cleanliness of the place and the kindness you'll receive are worthy of applause.

Pizzeria Restaurant 85   PIZZERIA, RESTAURANT €
(☑ 0975 38 51 06; Via Carrara 26; meals €15; ⏱ noon-2.30pm & 7.30-10pm Tue-Sun) Beautiful it's not, and once you enter the restaurant

LUNAR ADVENTURES AT SASSO DI CASTALDA

Going up the streets of Sasso di Castalda, at a certain point you'll find yourself in front of a deep chasm in a mountain landscape of sublime beauty. Hanging between the two banks is a 90m-long Tibetan bridge, suspended at a height of 27m. Your legs will tremble, your heart will start beating crazily, and you'll contemplate going back. And this is just the test bridge (known as the Petracca), where you can familiarise yourself with the void, the swinging, that mix of fear and excitement. The real **Ponte alla Luna** (Bridge to the Moon; ☑ 347 097 9181; www.pontetibetanosassodicastalda.com; ticket office in Via Roma; €20; ⊙ vary according to the period & weather conditions: call or consult the website) is just beyond it – you'll see it by slightly turning your gaze and running your eyes over its 300m length. Some 102m below a stream flows, its gurgling providing a soundtrack for your progress (at least between autumn and spring). And the experience really can be recommended to everyone (over 14 years old), especially because any anxiety attacks you might get or regrets you might feel for not having made a will, will usually manifest themselves in the first few metres of the Petracca bridge, after which things get decidedly easier. However, if you really would prefer something similar but slightly more easy-going, you could opt for the Castelsaraceno bridge (p137), about an hour's drive away in the Val d'Agri. There you won't feel any rocking and it'll be easier to maintain a sense of being in control.

you may feel suspicious of our recommendation. However, eat the strascinati pasta with crusco peppers and ricotta and you'll quickly change your mind. Bargain prices.

 Drinking & Nightlife

Time Bridge PUB
(☑ 331 976 44 84; Via Provinciale 5; ⊙ 7.30pm-3am Wed-Mon) People come here from far and wide to have a beer on stormy nights. Typically British atmosphere. One caveat: the hot dogs are longer than the Ponte alla Luna.

 Information

Pro Loco Il Nibbio (☑ 328 745 51 67; Via Rome; ⊙ variable hours)

Savoia di Lucania

POP 1114 / ELEV 720M

One of the symbolic characters of Basilicata's history is undoubtedly Giovanni Passannante. The youngest of 10 brothers, he was born in Savoia di Lucania in 1849, when it was still called Salvia di Lucania. He experienced all the hardships of poverty but was driven by a passion to raise himself and his people from their plight, and so, on November 17 1878, he attempted to assassinate King Umberto I on a visit to Naples. He failed, though, and his stabbing only slightly wounded the monarch. Charged with this heinous act, Passannante was imprisoned and locked up in a cell situated below sea level in the Portoferraio prison on the island of Elba. After years of confinement in inhumane conditions, he was transferred to a criminal asylum where he eventually died. However, his fame was destined to live on, and he was praised by intellectuals (including Pascoli, who wrote an *Ode a Passannante*) and celebrated over the decades. There were even consequences for his birthplace and the name of the small village was changed to Savoia di Lucania, as a token of submission to the royal authority. To learn more about these events, visit the **Museo Salviano** (☑ 0971 71 10 00/328 754 62 75; Via Garibaldi 14; ⊙ by reservation), which also houses numerous relics from the Fascist era.

History apart, Savoia enjoys a scenic location which offers wild views – which do, in effect, inspire dignified rebellions of the spirit – and nature walks. Take the road to Vietri and then the well-marked dirt road on the right just after the village, and you'll reach the unspoiled **Bosco Luceto**, thick with Turkey oaks and hornbeams with roots as big as Nasa missiles, and the **Vallone del Tuorno**, an off-shoot of the Melandro. Head up this and you'll come to some roaring waterfalls – but note that some parts are a bit exposed, so bring suitable shoes. If you don't fancy going it alone, contact **Savoia Sport Adventure** (☑ 3484 24 87 28; www.savoiasportadventure.it; Via Vittorio Emanuele 12).

Savoia di Lucania is 15km west of Satriano di Lucania, to which it's connected by three provincial roads, and 30km from Potenza.

The Marmo Platano

The name (in English, The Platano Marble) comes from two features of the landscape – Monte Marmo, near the village of Balvano, and the Platano stream, which runs for a long stretch along the regional border with Campania. However, the reason for including it on a Lucanian travel itinerary is that it harbours some interesting sites and boasts one of the region's most beautiful villages.

❶ Getting There & Away

The Marmo Platano is crossed by the SS7, which connects the main centres to Potenza. For San Fele you'll need the SP381, which continues on to Atella and the heart of the Vulture. Alternatively, **Autolinee Liscio** (☑ 0971 54 673; www.autolinee liscio.it) runs daily buses from Potenza to Muro Lucano (one hour) and on to Castelgrande (one hour 20 minutes).

Muro Lucano & Around

POP 5211 / ELEV 600M

In terms of its ability to make a striking first impression, Muro Lucano rivals any centre in Basilicata. Like many, the town is elevated above the valley floor and features a tangle of arduous alleyways and staircases. It also has a medieval castle (Via Castello), dating to the 10th century and with a history of betrayals, conspiracies and assassinations (including that of the ruler of Naples, Giovanna d'Anjou, in 1382), as well as lavish noble palaces, small churches and lyrical, romantic vistas from viewpoints such as the Belvedere Torrione (Via Raia 16). However,

unlike the usual hillside old towns, Muro Lucano manifests a certain intangible and subtle elegance, courtesy of a series of buildings that spread in an amphitheatre-like pattern which, in the morning haze, seems to resemble a Tibetan monastic complex, and the many small squares that give the town a sense of greater space.

All in all, it's a place that should absolutely be included on any tour of Basilicata.

◎ Sights & Activities

Sentiero delle Ripe e dei Mulini WALKING TRAIL
The Borgata Pianello, just below the Cathedral, is the oldest part of the town. From there you can observe the bridge of the same name, built at the time of World War I and positioned as if on the set of an adventure film, and take this medieval path. Gouged out of the limestone rock, the trail is equally cinematic as it descends towards the valley, passing the remains of several water mills and a Romanesque bridge.

Museo Archeologico Nazionale MUSEUM
(☑ 0976 717 78; Via Seminario 6; ⊙ 9am-1pm & 2-4.30pm Mon & Tue, 9am-1pm Wed-Fri, 10.30am-12.30pm & 5.30-8pm Sat & Sun mid-March–Oct) **FREE** Focused on the Romans and the Peuketian people who lived here before them, this museum exhibits armour, jewellery, ritual vases and household utensils from a period ranging from the 7th century BCE to the early Middle Ages. The most interesting part is a section that illustrates the Roman villas of northern Basilicata, while ladies searching for a whimsical look for Saturday night can

THE CURIOSITIES OF AVIGLIANO

Even without mentioning that it's a pretty hilltop town, a description you could apply to most places in Basilicata, Avigliano merits a stop between Potenza and the Marmo Platano for several reasons. Firstly, there are the Quadri Plastici (www.quadriplasticiavigliano. it), representations of sacred scenes or artistic masterpieces created by immobile performers. These come to life on the first Sunday of August and are considered one of the region's most spectacular events. Secondly, the town is renowned for its excellent craftsmanship: Vito Aquila (☑ 335 834 40 29; www.vitoaquila.it; Via Don Stolfi; ⊙ variable hrs), for example, produces the celebrated balestra aviglianese, a very sharp dagger that for centuries was carried by bandits and any aspiring killer worthy of respect in these parts. Annangela Lovallo (☑ 0971 70 03 75; www.annangelolovallo.it; Via Santa Maria del Carmine 18; ⊙ 9am-1pm & 5-8pm Mon-Sat), an embroiderer of national fame, has set up a small textile museum next to her workshop. Finally, people come to Avigliano to sample its signature baccalà (salted cod), as you can do in many different recipes, at the Osteria Gagliardi (☑ 0971 70 07 43; www.osteriagagliardi.it; Martiri Ungheresi; meals €25; ⊙ 1-3pm & 8-11.30pm Wed-Sat, 1-3pm Sun).

take inspiration from the displays of ivory combs and bone pins. Once outside, pay attention to where you put your feet: the Scala della Poesia, a staircase made of coloured stones, starts right in front of the museum.

🛏 Sleeping & Eating

Hotel delle Colline   HOTEL, RESTAURANT €
(✆ 0976 22 84; www.hoteldellecolline.com; Via Belvedere; d €55-70; meals €20-25; 🛜 🅿) Despite its considerable appeal, Muro Lucano doesn't have many places for lunch. This hotel's restaurant may not be the fanciest place to eat, but the food is reliable and filling.

ℹ Information

Pro Loco office (✆ 380 475 65 67; www.proloco murese.it; Piazza Don Minzoni)

San Fele

POP 2966 / ELEV 920M

Halfway between the Marmo Platano and the Vulture, in a small basin between two spurs of rock, lie the houses of San Fele. These once sat in the shadow of a mighty fortress, built by Otto I of Saxony (969 CE) and later enlarged by Federico II. But only ruins now remain of the castle, just as there are few vestiges of the historic centre which was almost destroyed by a landslide in 1968 and was hit by an earthquake in 1980. However, the suggestion of a village is still intact and this, today as in the past, sits in symbiotic harmony with the nature that surrounds it.

⊙ Sights

U Uattënniérë   WATERFALL
The major natural and ethnographic attraction in this area is undoubtedly these waterfalls on the Bradano stream. The name – if you can pronounce it correctly, you'll have our undying respect – derives from the dialect term for a fulling mill, a machine used in factories built close to waterfalls to beat wool and make it more compact and less rough. There are 10 'serviced' waterfalls – some paths can be covered in 10 minutes from the village (including one that leads to the highest waterfall, U Urtone, at the mouth of which is a drinking fountain); others will require up to seven hours. Whichever you take, the landscape is picturesque and, in summer, some of the waterfalls are suitable for swimming. One such is the Paradiso, which has a well with a depth of more than six meters.

THE GOLE DEL PLATANO

The village of **Balvano**, about 25km south of Muro Lucano, is less known for its environmental value than for a terrible railway disaster that left more than five hundred people dead in 1944, intoxicated in a tunnel. However, the two things are no longer at odds, at least not since it's been possible to walk the **Sentiero dei Minatori** (www.goledelplatano.it/attivita/sentiero -dei-minatori/), a path dug to facilitate the excavation of the tunnel in which the disaster took place. To tackle the route, which overlooks a spectacular canyon and is fitted with a fall arrest line for more than a kilometre, use the Tibetan bridge of Balvano as a reference for Google Maps, and check www. goledelplatano.it for information.

Badia di Pierno   SANCTUARY
(✆ 0976 982 50; www.montepierno.it; Località Santuario di Pierno) Nine kilometres east of the village on the Strada Comunale Bosco della Pietra stands this important Marian shrine, a popular pilgrimage destination. Its spectacular isolated position, set on mountain slopes, inspires asceticism and recollection, even if the profusion of mushrooms in the chestnut and oak woods that surround the site will elicit less elevated and more edible thoughts in some visitors. The monastery was probably founded by San Guglielmo da Vercelli in 1189, but the basilica dates to 1515

🛏 Sleeping

La Costa del Sole   HOLIDAY RENTAL €/€€
(✆ 347 945 01 67; www.lacostadelsole.it; Corso Vittorio Emanuele II 33; per person per night, minimum 2 people €35; 🛜 ❄ 🅿) Has various apartments, all of different sizes but all equally pleasant. Located in the village alleys, with a view of the valley. Pets are not accepted.

🍴 Eating & Drinking

La Locanda del Bosco   RESTAURANT €
(✆ 0976 982 26, 338 344 16 47; Località Pierno; tourist menu €15; ☺ best to call before, especially out of season) After a visit to the Badia, there's nothing better than a nice lunch of home-made pasta, cured meats, provola cheese and mixed grilled meats. The atmosphere is rustic, the food authentic.

ROCKS, STARS & BUTTERFLIES

Castelgrande, about 10km northwest of Muro Lucano, may not be one of the Potentino's prime artistic or cultural destinations, but there's no shortage of interesting things to do. You can start by taking a contemplative look over the valley from the top of the village before heading to the **Butterfly House e Parco dei Colori** (☑ 347 793 05 30; Via Fuori Corso Gasparrini 36; ⊙ by reservation 4-7pm Mon-Fri, 10am-1pm & 3-7pm Sat & Sun Apr-Sep; ♿) where different species of tropical butterflies flutter around, as if in a fairy tale – there's also a selection of native species. You'll need to keep your gaze up and look skyward at the **Astronomical Observatory** (☑ 0976 44 81, 351 981 9348; Località Toppo; ⊙ by reservation only), where there's an immense telescope with a 40cm diameter mirror. Then, to return back to earth, you can enjoy yourself climbing one of the 100 limestone rocks at the **Boulder Area l'Agrifoglio** with the guides of **Basilicata Sport Adventure** (☑ 320 606 23 54, 320 792 58 23; www.basilicatasportadventure.com; Vico Castello, Pescopagano; bouldering tour per person €20). This outfit also organises tours, trekking and canyoning in the area.

POTENZA PROVINCE THE VULTURE

The Oliver St. John
PUB
(☑ 0976 948 30; Corso Umberto I 197; meals €15; ⊙ 5pm-1am Wed-Mon, also lunch on Sunday) The decor is typical of a pub, as are the beer and background music. The menu, on the other hand, resembles that of a restaurant. Good pizzas.

ⓘ Information
'U Uattënniérë' Association (☑ 347 518 73 98; www.cascatedisanfele.it; Via Umberto I, in the former offices of an accounting department) Organises guided excursions.
Pro Loco (☑ 328 287 85 39)

THE VULTURE

There's something magical about this area in the north of the Potenza province, which transcends even the highest of expectations. It's as if the volcano (1326m), which has been extinct for tens of thousands of years and which gives its name to the area, continued to burn in the spirit of the people who lived here (and still visit), firing their imagination and fuelling their poetic impulses. Vulture is the land of Aglianico, one of Italy's most prestigious vines, which thanks to the lava in the subsoil attains extraordinary levels of expression. It's also the homeland of Horace, the poet of *Carpe Diem*, whose message lives on in the form of fleeting sunsets, vineyards, olive-cloaked slopes, orchards in ever-precarious colours, and villages shrouded in sensuality. It was a source of pleasure and creativity to the great Federico II, who penned hunting manuals and legislative works in Castel Lagopesole and Melfi. And the list goes on, potentially for a long time, as Vulture has given rise to lakes set in mountains like diamonds in stone, forests where brigands took refuge and churches adorned with artistic masterpieces. However, maybe it's just easier to hit the road and seek inspiration for yourself.

Rionero in Vulture
POP 12.596 / ELEV 676M
Re-populated in the 15th century by Albanian peasants and Italian-speaking settlers after it had beeen abandoned for more than a hundred years, Rionero is a melancholy place, yet one steeped in a fierce pride. This is perhaps due to the earthquakes which devastated it on several occasions (at the end of the 17th century, in 1930, and again in 1980), but from which it was always able to bounce back. Or perhaps the town's personality was forged by the character of the restless brigands who were born here (see boxed text, p122), or by Aglianico wine, which has its main production centre here. Whatever the cause, don't come expecting a postcard-pretty town (indeed, the outskirts are rather ugly), rather come to tour its cellars (see boxed text p124) and visit the **Museo della Civiltà Contadina** (☑ 0972 08 25 74; Via Garibaldi 2; ⊙ 10.30am-12.30pm & 4.30-6.30pm Mon-Sat) **FREE** in the 18th-century **Palazzo Fortunato**, and in the former Bourbon prison, the strange **Museo del Brigantaggio** (☑ 0972 08 25 74; Largo Mazzini; admission/guided visits €1/3; ⊙ 10am-12.30pm & 4.30-7pm Fri-Sun Apr-Oct), which has a rich multimedia display and a section dedicated to female brigands. Both museums merit your attention.

✈ Activities

La Valle dei Cavalli
HORSE RIDING

(☑ 340 645 03 14, 366 460 56 87; www.lavalledei
cavalli.com; Contrada Piani di Carda Atella; per
1h/2h/3h/day €30/40/60/90, multiday trek €359-
390) Horses are serious business in Vulture,
and have been since at least the times of
Federico II's cavalry. So, whether you choose
a brief ride or a multi-day trek you're sure
to come into contact with the spirit of the
territory. This place is located 15km south of
Rionero, immersed in beautiful countryside.

✯ Festivals & Events

Vulcanica Live Festival
AUGUST

(☑ 348 565 56 27; www.associazionevulcanica.
it) This live music, theatre and cinema festival is the flagship event of the Vulcanica
cultural association, founded in 1999 by a
group of university students and conservatory graduates.

☰ Sleeping & Eating

La Pergola
HOTEL, RESTAURANT €€

(☑ 0972 72 18 19; www.ristorantelapergolarionero.it;
Via La Vista 27-31; d/tr/q €70/80/100, meals €30;

(⌨ P) In the middle of town, La Pergola has a
large, somewhat anonymous hall and rooms
that are functional, if lacking in charm. At the
restaurant, the quality is perhaps not what it
once was, but the dishes are rich in typical
local flavours.

Pasticceria Libutti
BAR, PASTRY SHOP €

(☑ 0972 72 10 63; www.pasticcerialibutti.it; Via
Garibaldi 25; ⊙ 7am-2pm & 3-9pm Wed-Mon,
7am-2pm Tue) This patisserie, the pride of
the town, has been in business since the
mid-19th century, when pastries were made
with honey and almonds (sugar wasn't yet
widely available) and cooked in communal
ovens. Today's specialties include its homemade ice creams (they once made granitas
by mixing snow with fruit juice and spices),
dry pastries, Aglianico chocolates and, above
all, its cannoli.

ℹ Information

Pro Loco office (☑ 0972 08 25 74; www.proloco
rioneroinvulture.it; Via Garibaldi 2; ⊙ 10.30am-
12.30pm & 4.30-6.30pm Mon-Sat).

POTENZA PROVINCE RIONERO IN VULTURE

CASTEL LAGOPESOLE

Want to start your Vulture tour with a bang? Then head to Castel Lagopesole, some
25km north of Potenza along the SS93. You don't need to be a military commander
to appreciate the village's extraordinary strategic position. This was first exploited by
the Byzantines, who built a fort here. This *castrum* was subsequently enlarged by the
Normans and, in the mid-13th century, it was transformed into a home where Federico II
could indulge his leisure pursuits, including falcon hunting. He was actually staying here
when he wrote *De arte venandi cum avibus*, a monumental work outlining his thoughts,
his insatiable thirst for knowledge, and his drive to dominate not only humankind but also
nature. The building was later owned by the Angevins (until 1280), the Caracciolos, and
the Dorias (from 1513), before eventually reverting to the State. Nowadays, the village's
ancient forests no longer exist, but its castle (☑ 0971 860 83, 338 715 52 11; www.castello
dilagopesole.com; Via Sotto il Castello), survives in all its martial grandeur. With its massive
rectangular structure and two courtyards, it looks like a gigantic medieval lego model, the
ideal setting for legendary chivalric epics. The interior, closed at the time of research for
renovation work, boasts several attractions. Regular visits take in the small archaeological museum and its collection of medieval porcelain, oyster shells and deer horns used at
imperial banquets, as well as the Palatine Chapel. More intriguing, however, is the Museo
Narrante, which peoples the castle with figures from the life of the great sovereign, and
the Museo dell'Emigrazione Lucana, which uses multimedia presentations to tell of
the hopes and tribulations of the thousands of people who emigrated from Basilicata
in previous centuries. In summer, the castle also hosts numerous events, including Il
Mondo di Federico II, a show with special effects and holographic projections on the
castle's courtyard walls. For more information, contact the Pro Loco (☑ 0971 862 51,
333 866 39 01; www.prolocolagopesole.it; Piazza Federico II 22), while for an on-theme meal,
the Osteria Medieval (☑ 340 900 47 47; Via Leopardi; meals €20; ⊙ 12.30-2.30pm & 7.30-
10.30pm Wed-Mon) could fit the bill.

THE BRIGAND'S BRIGAND

One of the Vulture's most complex historical figures is undoubtedly **Carmine Crocco**. Born in Rionero in 1830, he was, depending on your point of view, a patriot, a brutal bandit, a romantic revolutionary, or a local Robin Hood. What's sure is that after he'd participated in uprisings during the Risorgimento (in the hope of an amnesty for his long list of crimes), in 1861 he formed a band of a thousand or more men and set up camp in the woods around the Monticchio lakes. He was subsequently arrested after countless exploits and sentenced to life imprisonment. But, in the end, what happened in reality is of little importance because the name of Carmine Crocco belongs less to history than to legend, to popular fantasy, to the hope for social redemption that has never died down. And just as in life he escaped military and gendarmes, so too today he continues to evade being pinned down, avoiding any moral judgment that tries to impose an unequivocal definition on him.

ℹ Getting There & Away

Rionero is about 40km north of Potenza, which can be reached on the SS658 (45 minutes). **SITA-SUD** (☑ 0971 50 68 11; www.sitasudtrasporti.it) buses run from Potenza (one hour to one hour 40 minutes) and continue on to Melfi (25 minutes). It's easier to get a **Trenitalia** (www.trenitalia.com) train to Rionero in Vulture from Potenza Centrale (€2.80, about one hour, frequent).

Laghi di Monticchio

Aeons ago when the erupting crater of Vulture spat out fire and flames, the surrounding landscape must have been bare and lyrically desolate. The mountain's wrath has since subsided and in its wake have emerged two pretty lakes (652m) surrounded by a thick forest of alder trees and Turkey oaks. There's a serenity and sweetness to the area, at least out of season. But come summer the vibe is decidedly less than peaceful: it becomes noisy, chaotic and crowded as a string of bars, stalls and tourist restaurants appears on the narrow isthmus that separates the two bodies of water.

The white and solemn form of the 18th-century Abbazia Benedettina di San Michele (☑ 0972 23 81 40, 0972 23 87 12; www. badiasanmichele.it; ⊙ times vary, call at least three days in advance to book a visit), built over caves inhabited by Basilian monks, is reflected in the smaller of the two lakes as it keeps a strict and inscrutable watch over the comings and goings of pedal boats and the crowds of noisy holidaymakers who have taken the place of the pilgrims of yester-year. In rooms once occupied by the convent you'll find the Museo di Storia Naturale del Vulture (☑ 0972 73 10 28, if closed, call the

Museo Provinciale Archeologico di Potenza ☑ 0971 44 48 33; www.museodelvulture.it; adult/reduced €3/1; ⊙ 9am-1pm Wed-Thu & Sat, 9am-1pm & 2.30-5.30pm Tue, Fri & Sun Nov-Easter, 9am-1pm Wed, Thu & Sat, 9am-1pm & 2.30-5.30pm Tue, Fri & Sun Easter-Oct). Here, entomology enthusiasts will be able to gasp at the Bramea, a very rare moth dating back to the Miocene period which has a life span of a week. In addition to the educational and interactive set-up, which children, in particular, will appreciate, you can admire medieval frescoes in the chapel dedicated to Saint Michael and remarkable views from the windows of the abbey.

🏃 Activities

There are plenty of activities and excursions available around the lakes – though swimming is not one of them as bathing is not permitted in the lake waters. For an easy-going workout you could rent a pedal boat on the shores of the small lake, or walk up the steps to the ruins of the Abbazia di Sant'Ippolito (10th to 13th century) on the isthmus that separates the two lakes. You could take spectacular photographs of the white water lilies on the western side of the large lake or walk one of the 'brigand' paths from the Abbazia di San Michele – there are signs with maps nearby – which lead, in a few minutes, to the caves where the brigand Carmine Crocco (see boxed text, above) hid with his gang. More demanding routes lead to the summit of Monte Vulture (which is a military area and therefore out of bounds to travellers), and follow through the oak woods of the nearby Riserva di Grotticelle (where a Giant Bench by Chris Bangle stands out about 7km west of Lago Grande), as well as snaking over to Rionero (3½ hours).

🛏 Sleeping & Eating

Parco Naturale Camping Europa　　　　CAMPING €
(☑ 349 368 23 48; Via Lago Grande 28, Monticchio Lakes; two adults & camper €25, each additional person €5; ⊙ mid-Mar–early Nov) For those who prefer a tent under a willow tree to a good bed, this campsite a stone's throw from the lake guarantees a comfortable stay. There's a lawn equipped with tables, benches and a barbecue, and a lakeside solarium.

Il Casale dell'Acqua Rossa　　AGRITURISMO €€
(☑ 0972 73 10 72; www.casaleacquarossa.it; Strada Monticchio Sgarroni; s/d/tr €50/70/90; P 🗪) The rooms at this villa surrounded by greenery 2km from the lakes are simple, comfortable and have a private bathroom and TV. There's also a restaurant offering meals for around €30, with drinks included. The supplement for small pets is €30.

Borgo Villa Maria　　　　HOTEL €€
(☑ 0972 73 13 02, 347 340 32 05; www.borgovilla maria.com; Monticchio Laghi; d/tr €90/110; ⊙ Mar-Nov; 🗪 P 🏊) This hotel a stone's throw from the lakes has many strong points: the rooms are simple but large, the two swimming pools guarantee splashing afternoons of relaxation, and the kitchen of the adjoining restaurant, Il Setaccio (meals €30), cooks up appetising dishes from the lake (and beyond).

ℹ Getting There & Away

From Potenza, exit the SS658 at Rionero in Vulture and follow signs for the Laghi di Monticchio, which are about 12km from the town. In summer, the area near the two lakes might be closed to cars – if that's the case you'll have to follow signs for Monticchio Sgarroni and take one of the free shuttle buses from there.

Ripacandida
POP 1691 / ELEV 620M

Even if the village houses are no longer as white as the name would suggest, Ripacandida can still evoke pure thoughts thanks to the presence of one of Basilicata's most important artistic sites, the Santuario di San Donato (☑ 347 934 50 93; www.sandotoripacan dida.net; Viale Regina Margherita 268; ⊙ 8am-6pm). This single-nave Franciscan church is entirely covered in 15th- and 16th-century frescoes – in fact, so rich are its decorations that it deserves to be called the 'Assisi of Basilicata'. The pictorial narration begins in the third bay with depictions of the creation and

Noah's Ark stories, while in the second bay it ranges from the tale of the Tower of Babel to the Sacrifice of Isaac and the story of Joseph and his brothers. As you can tell from a change in style, the first bay is the most recent, created towards the end of the 16th century and dedicated to classic subjects from the New Testament, such as the Annunciation, the Visitation, the Nativity and, on the left and right walls, the Last Judgment and Hell. But while the individual scenes are capable of capturing the imagination and arousing curiosity – why, for example, do the corner panels in the second bay show three vases of flowers and a monkey drinking an egg? – it's the overall effect that leaves you slack jawed. To recover from the aesthetic shock, take a stroll in the adjacent garden, which is spread over two levels and has reflective, well-kept paths where once Franciscan monks meditated in the shade on the great questions of existence, and today the town's young hide away to kiss furtively among the branches. There's also a 500 year-old Aleppo pine tree.

Ripacandida is also known for the production of honey. You can buy different types at Oro dei Fiori (☑ 320 184 97 50; www.orodeifiori.it; Via Contrada San Pietro; ⊙ 8.30am-1pm & 3-7.30pm Mon-Sat, 8am-1pm Sun).

ℹ Information
Pro Loco office (☑ 340 423 09 53; Via Aldo Moro 35; ⊙ variable hrs)

ℹ Getting There & Away
Ripacandida is on the Horatian highway that connects the SS568 at Rionero in Vulture to Venosa. A single daily SITASUD bus (☑ 0971 50 68 11; www.sitasudtrasporti.it) covers the route, leaving Rionero at 5.15am (15 minutes).

Barile
POP 2708 / ELEV 664M

Most travellers see two sides to Barile, both seemingly at odds with each other. The first is the somewhat ungainly architectural development and the ugly 20th-century buildings which hardly make a visit to the town memorable. The second are the superb cellars dug out of the tuff rock in the attractive area below the town. These date to the 15th century and create a striking urban landscape. The fact that the town maintains its Arbëreshë ethno-linguistic traditions (like San Costantino Albanese and San Paolo Albanese, p147) only really becomes

THE CELLARS OF THE VULTURE

Followers of Bacchus, prepare yourselves for a swirl of emotions. The Vulture is a land deeply rooted in wine, and while its landscapes don't display the elegiac beauty of the Langhe or Val d'Orcia, and its vines are interspersed with other crops, a tour in search of the secrets of the Aglianico can compare with any you might undertake in those more celebrated areas. The following are some of the Vulture's most important wineries.

Le Cantine del Notaio (☑0972 72 36 89; www.cantinedelnotaio.it; Via Roma 159, Rionero in Vulture; tour incl tasting €10-30; ☺by reservation 9am-1pm & 5-8pm Mon-Sat) Locally renowned, this winery owes its fame to the 17th-century caves dug by Franciscan friars (and before that by the Albanians), where crosses carved into the rock watch over the aging of the wine. The tour and tasting is truly comprehensive.

Elena Fucci (☑320 487 99 45; www.elenafuccivini.com; Contrada Solagna del Titolo, Barile) Even if Aglianico is a wine for aging, this vineyard's award-winning Titolo label manages to draw the best out of the vine even after a few years. The cellars have been built according to the dictates of bio-architecture and have tables and chairs made from old barrels.

Pater Noster (☑0972 77 02 24; www.paternosterwine.it; Contrada Valle del Titolo, Barile) Another historic label that has contributed to making Aglianico an elite wine. The winery, which cleverly combines antiquity and tradition, is located at the exit of the state road. Its flagship wine, Don Anselmo, is amazing.

Cantina di Venosa (☑0972 367 02; Via Appia 86, Venosa; ☺8am-1pm & 3.30-6.20pm Mon-Fri, 9am-1pm Sat) This renowned winery may be less impressive than the others to visit, but it produces quality wines for all budgets. It's located in the outskirts of Venosa, before the centre if coming from Barile or Rionero.

Carbone (☑328 281 43 44; www.carbonevini.it; Via Nitti 48, Melfi) Located in the historic centre, it has a truly magical cellar dug out of tuff rock. Reservations are required for tours and tastings.

clear to most visitors during the town's two main events.

★ Festivals & Events

Via Crucis   GOOD FRIDAY
(www.viacrucisbarile.it) This sacred representation, the oldest in Basilicata (17th century), is prepared for weeks in advance. Events kick off with mass at 3pm on Good Friday after which the procession winds its way through the historic centre, led by Roman centurions and the Marys followed by Christ and the Ecce Homo. Distinguishing Barile's procession from the others are the characters of the Zingara (a Roma woman) and the Moro (Moor).

Cantinando Wine & Art   AUGUST
The underground cellars, used by Pasolini as a location for the first part of *The Gospel According to St. Matthew* (1964), serve as the venue for this dizzying event dedicated to art and music. The main protagonist, however, is the local Aglianico wine.

🛏 Sleeping

Grand Hotel Garden   HOTEL €€
(☑0972 76 15 33, 346 623 06 94; www.grandhotel garden.com; Località Giardino SS93 km 75; s €60-70, d €85-110; ☎✳☀❄Ⓟ) 🍴 It's difficult not to notice this colossal hotel which received a major award for bio-ecological architecture in 2004. Built on top of a hill, it has spacious rooms with views of the valley (which turns red in spring as poppies burst into flower), a fitness area, a panoramic swimming pool and a restaurant.

Melfi

POP 16,985 / ELEV 562M

Melfi has everything to captivate at first sight. There's a castle to inspire instant reveries of court intrigues, receptions and battle plans, and a cathedral bell tower which projects a sense of majesty for miles around, as well as a compact and mighty ring of walls. If you have time for a more sedate exploration of the town, you'll find the dreamy atmosphere of the narrow streets, with their low-lying houses, wrought iron balconies full of flowers, and noble 15th- to 17th-century palaces, evoke more nuanced but equally gratifying feelings. All of which,of course, goes to make the Vulture's largest town a destination not to be missed.

History

Melfi boasts a glorious history, though it's often overshadowed by the presence of the FCA factory (fortunately far from the historic centre), for which the town is best known today. Melfi's golden age came in the Middle Ages when Federico II stayed in the town's majestic castle to promulgate the *Constitutiones Augustales* or Melfi Constitutions, a single code of laws for the entire Kingdom of Sicily. This, the first organic legal text written in the Middle Ages, was a work of extraordinary importance in the history of law. The town was also an important religious centre as can be attested to by the size of its cathedral and the fact that several papal councils were held here (including the one in 1089 when Pope Urban II established the league that would later lead the first Crusade). Subsequent centuries saw the town fall into slow decline after the 1528 'sack of Melfi' in the Franco-Spanish conflict, and a series of merciless earthquakes.

Sights

The 15th-century walls preserve one of the town's six ancient entrances, the only one to have survived the earthquake of 1851. **Porta Venosina** (Via Commenda di Malta), built in the 13th century as part of an extension ordered by Federico II, retains its original pointed arch and has two cylindrical towers dating from the 15th century. Originally, a tablet was affixed to the gate announcing the town's greatness. This has since been replaced by a copy, and its design now serves as the symbol of the **Parco Letterario Federico II** (www.parcofedericosecondo.it), which organises interesting cultural events. Another town icon is the **Fontana del Bagno** (Via Bagno), a not particularly pretty fountain where millions of clothes have been washed and which has watered all the horses in the history of Melfi.

Castello CASTLE

Close your eyes and imagine an impregnable castle. Well, apart from crocodiles in the moat, your mind's eye will probably have created something not too dissimilar to this monumental bulwark, with its eight towers and brick bridge. The castle's fame preceded the arrival of Federico II in 1230. In fact, it was here that the Norman knight Robert Guiscard was crowned duke of Puglia and Calabria by Pope Nicholas II in 1059. Later, the Angevins took control, arriving in 1266 and digging the moat, followed by the Caracciolos in 1416, and then, in 1531, the Dorias. Inside is the **Museo Archeologico Nazionale del Vulture Melfese Massimo Pallottino** (☎0972 23 87 26; Via Castello; adult/reduced €2.50/2; ⏰2-8pm Mon, 9am-8pm Tues-Sun) and its collection of shining armour, refined jewels, candelabra, helmets and the usual repertoire of pottery from the populations who lived in the north of Basilicata between the 7th and 3rd centuries BCE. The rooms, with their coffered ceilings and golden stucco, are also worthy of note. The museum's highlight is the Sarcofago di Rapolla, a marvellously sculpted marble sarcophagus from the 2nd century CE, attributed to artists from Asia Minor. There's also a

WORTH A TRIP

SPA & WINE

While the name **Rapolla** comes from the Latin word *rapum*, meaning a 'place full of thorns', this town between Barile and Melfi is best known for its thermal waters. These have long been recommended as a cure for rheumatism, sciatica, laryngitis and any other ailment that might afflict travellers to Basilicata. The **hotel** (☎0972 76 01 13; www.termedirapolla.it; Via Melfi 170; s/d/tr €50/80/110; 📶P❄), incorporated into the thermal baths complex, doesn't stand out for charm but it guarantees relaxation and comfort. Check the website to get an idea of the packages (starting from €39), on offer at the spa, which is open between May and October. After dedicating yourself to body care, look after your soul with a visit to the massive 13th-century **cathedral** (Via Marconi), adorned with remarkable bas-reliefs on the right side, and the **Parco Urbano delle Cantine** (☎0972 64 02 73; www.parcourbanocantinerapolla.it; Via Monastero), a set of cellars cut into tuff rock which, one October weekend, provide the location for a grandiose party based on wine, good food and music.

small picture gallery and some interesting canvases in the Cappella Doria.

Cathedral
CATHEDRAL

(☎0972 23 81 80; Piazza Duomo) It's enough to enter the square and have a quick look at the church to grasp the complexity of its history. In front of you, to the left, the Norman bell tower (tickets €1; ⊙9.30am-12.30pm, best to call in the afternoon) was built by Noslo di Remerio in 1153. Almost miraculously it has survived the various earthquakes that have devastated the region and it retains its original exotic features – note the two griffins next to the last mullioned window, the symbol of the Norman dynasty. Further to the right, the 18th-century baroque facade displays more bombastic and familiar, but no less valuable, forms. The interior boasts a beautiful coffered ceiling in gilded wood above the central nave and four frescoes by Andrea Miglionico in the vault above the refined wooden choir and organ. In the left arm of the transept, there's a Byzantine-inspired fresco of a Madonna with child from the 13th century.

Episcopio
MUSEUM

(Largo Duomo 12) Unlike most towns in Basilicata, Melfi exudes a kind of aristocratic charm. Next to the cathedral, for example, the baroque Palazzo del Vescovado recalls eras of sumptuous pomp with its long and harmonious facade, grand staircase and stupendous Italian garden dotted with marble busts. Its frescoed rooms house the Museo Diocesano (☎0972 23 84 29; adult/reduced €2.50/1.50; ⊙10am-12.30pm & 4-6pm Fri-Sun Nov-Mar, 10am-12.30pm & 5-8pm Fri-Sun Apr-Oct), which displays silverware, vestments and, on the main floor, an art gallery with works from the 15th to the 18th centuries.

Museo Civico
MUSEUM

(☎0972 25 12 25; Vico Rispoli 15; ⊙closed at the time of research) FREE If you still have time to stroll around the historic centre, and in case the museum has reopened, the collections housed in the 17th-century Palazzo Donadoni

---

---

include works in Vulture lava stone by the Melfi-born sculptor Poppa. Upstairs there are temporary exhibitions.

Convento dei Cappuccini
MONASTERY

(Via Cristoforo Colombo) Adjacent to the church of the same name, this monastery isn't required viewing from an artistic point of view, but its hilltop position a stone's throw from the historic centre makes it an excellent spot from which to enjoy a truly superb panorama or for a moonlit declaration of love.

Chiesa rupestre di Santa Margherita
CHURCH

(☎0972 23 97 51, 335 639 36 75, 339 733 23 09; SS303, Km 1; adult/reduced €8/5; ⊙guided tours every day by reservation at the Pro Loco, at 10am, 11.30am, 3.30pm Oct-March, 10am, 11.30am, 4pm & 5.30pm Apr-Sep) When it comes to Basilicata's rupestrian churches, thoughts immediately turn to Matera, but this 13th-century church a couple of kilometres south of the centre towards Rapolla , rivals any in the region's rocky landscapes. The frescoes adorning the single nave – off which, there are four side chapels – combine traditional Byzantine splendour with unusually macabre themes. It's said that Federico II is depicted in the Contrasto dei Vivi e dei Morti as a squire in hunting gear. Nearby, the Chiesa di Santa Lucia (Contrada Giaconelli) is a single-space church with a frescoed barrel vault.

✸ Festivals & Events

Festival della Falconeria
OCTOBER

This festival, a wonderful dive into the Middle Ages, attracts falconers from all over Europe. Archery competitions are held in the castle moat, while a procession is peopled by jesters, minstrels, crusaders and fire-eaters who follow in the footsteps of Federico II. It's held on the last weekend in October.

Sagra della Varola
OCTOBER

(www.prolocomelfi.it) A dutiful celebration of the delicious marroncino del Vulture (a chestnut known as the Varola), collected in the hillside woods around Melfi. Chestnut cakes, desserts, chestnut ice cream, aromatic beer and fresh pasta with chestnut flour await.

🛏 Sleeping

Il Tetto
HOTEL €

(☎0972 23 68 37; www.hosteliltetto.com; Piazza IV Novembre, Palazzo del Seminario; s/d/tr/q €40/50/70/90; ⊛) This hotel-hostel managed

THE APPIAN WAY IN BASILICATA

It is still largely impassable, but the Appian Way (Via Appia) – antiquity's most important road which led from Rome to Brindisi through Basilicata – seems destined to live again. At the time of research it was already possible to walk the leg between Venosa and Palazzo San Gervasio, albeit with a diversion. However, for the other sites of interest, you'll really need a car and an adventurous spirit. In the territory of Lavello, 20km northeast of Melfi – and a few kilometres north of Via Appia – you'll find the Casa del Diavola (Località San Francesco), an imperial-era Roman villa complete with a thermal baths complex. To reach it, exit the SS655 and follow towards Lavello's industrial area; then, with the help of Google Maps, continue on foot along the dirt road. In the countryside around Palazzo San Gervasio (p107) you can visit a recently rediscovered Roman bridge. You have to enter 40°57' 31.2" N 15° 57'31.1"E on your navigator and you might have to take a few steps through mud if the weather's bad, but at least you'll be guaranteed recognition as an 'explorer' by your frends. Finally there's the Castello di Monteserico (Via Monteserico, Genzano di Lucania), of Norman origin and renovated by Federico II, 20km southeast of Palazzo San Gervasio (and in this case easily accessible by car). You can't go inside but that won't bother you as its panoramic position on an expanse of sparsely inhabited, rounded hills will amply repay you, and might turn out to be one of the unexpected highlights of your trip. You can get up-to-date information on the state of Via Appia on www.appia.beniculturali.it and www.camminodellappia.it.

by a cooperative is housed in a former 18th-century convent adjacent to the cathedral. The accommodation is unpretentious, but the rooms have all the necessary comforts and the location is great. It's particularly suitable for travelling families.

Relais la Fattoria HOTEL €€
(☑0972 247 76; www.relaislafattoria.it; SS658; s €75-90, d €91-130; 🕾�=P) Known locally as the hotel where FCA engineers stay, the Relais has spacious rooms and a beautiful swimming pool. Its fours stars, however, owe little to the charm of its location. To explore the surroundings, bike hire is free, and the restaurant (meals €25 to €30) gives a pretty good account of itself.

🍴 Eating

Delle Rose PIZZERIA, RESTAURANT €€
(☑0972 216 82, 335 161 36 51; www.pizzeriaristorantedellerose.it; Via Vittorio Emanuele 29; menus €15-35, meals €25-30; 🕙noon-4pm & 7pm-midnight Mon-Sun) Expect no frills and lots of substance at this restaurant-pizzeria with a leafy courtyard. Sure there are more glamorous establishments, but for a meal between sightseeing it's not bad. Good meat.

Ristorante Lucano RESTAURANT €€
(☑0972 23 73 91; 29 Via Floriano Del Zio ; meals €25; 🕙12.30-3pm Wed-Sun, 7.30-10 pm Thu-Sun) Robust, no frills – you'll leave with a full belly

and a pleasant sense of torpor. The ambiance is nice and welcoming.

Destino Ristorante Espressioni Rurali RESTAURANT €€
(☑0972 23 81 34, 379 112 83 81; Via Carmine 13; meals €30; 🕙12.45-2.30pm & 8-10.30pm Thu-Tue) A rising star among the city's restaurants, this place stands out for its modern, elegant atmosphere and its successful reinterpretation of traditional cuisine. The cod in gazpacho is excellent. Take a look at the beautiful cellar.

★La Villa AGRITURISMO €€€
(☑0972 23 60 08; Località Cavallerizza; meals €30-35, tasting menu €50; 🕙12.45-2.30pm & 8-10.30pm Tue-Sat, 12.45-2.30pm Sun) Excellent produce, respect for the local territory and a typical farm house atmosphere go hand in hand with a surprisingly creative menu at this very popular agriturismo. It's undoubtedly one of the best recommendations in the area, so it's always best to book.

☆ Entertainment

Cine-Teatro Ruggiero II CINEMA, THEATRE
(☑333 200 00 62; Via Vittorio Emanuele) If you happen to be in Melfi in the evening, check out the billboard of this cinema-theatre. Built in 1856, it hosts screenings and a good-quality programme of theatre.

❶ Information

The **Pro Loco office** (☎0972 23 97 51, 335 639 36 75; www.prolocomelfi.it; Piazza Umberto I 14; ⊙9am-noon & 5-8.30pm summer, variable hours winter) is centrally located in the Palazzo della Corte, one of Melfi's many 16th-century buildings. If you're looking for a good guide for Melfi and the Vulture, ask for Michelangelo Levita (☎339 710 16 87) or Lina Moscaritolo (☎339 733 23 09).

❶ Getting There & Away

Melfi is 53km north of Potenza on the SS658. **SITASUD** (☎0971 50 68 11; www.sitasudtrasporti. it) runs frequent daily buses from Potenza (1½ hours), while **Trenitalia** (www.trenitalia.com) operates trains from Potenza (€3, about one hour) and Foggia (€4.85, one hour), with stops at Rionero (€1, 12 minutes).

Venosa

POP 11.488 / ELEV 415M

It's easy to fall in love with Venosa on summer evenings, when the streets fill with life, the heat subsides and a quiet, enigmatic calmness descends on the town as darkness falls. It's also easy to fall for the town when you discover its artistic heritage – church by church, ruin by ruin, Venosa towers over every other town in the Vulture. Or maybe you'll be won over by the words of Quinto Orazio Flacco (Horace), Venosa's favourite son, reproduced on plaques to create a veritable literary itinerary. And so, in the call to live every moment intensely, it will be the town itself that invites us to celebrate its beauty while savouring the sense of discovery that animates every journey.

History

The history of Venosa can't be separated from the pleasantness of the woods where the Latin poet Horace spent his childhood. Conquered by the Romans in 281 BCE, the town flourished thanks to its strategic position on Via Appia, the road which connected Rome with its eastern provinces. For the same reason, when the emperor Trajan diverted the road further north, the town began a slow and ruinous decline, which was aggravated by barbarian invasions, and only later mitigated by the Norman conquest in the 11th century and the enlightened reign of Federico II. However, the town retained its artistic significance, as if its tie to the goddess Venus (it was called 'Venusia' in antiquity), a symbol of love and beauty, was never broken. In the 16th century, for example, it was the birthplace of a certain Prince Carlo Gesualdo (1566–1613), a composer of madrigals and sacred music – and also an insanely passionate lover – who killed his wife and lover in a fit of jealous rage. Nowadays, the town seems to live its passions through its own imperishable cultural heritage.

◉ Sights

Looking closely at the elegant palazzi in the centre, you might notice parts of capitals, statues arranged in unusual positions, and stone blocks with ancient engravings. This is because, over the centuries, the town's Roman ruins were 'recycled' for the construction and restoration of buildings.

Castello di Pirro del Balzo   CASTLE
(Piazza Umberto I) Built in 1470 by Pirro del Balzo Orsini as a defensive fortress, this castle is one of the most deeply rooted symbols of the town's identity. As in Melfi, the structure is surrounded by a deep moat, though here it's more martial in appearance than romantic, and inside there's the interesting **Museo Archeologico Nazionale** (☎0972 360 95; www.museovenosa.beniculturali.it; adult/reduced incl Parco Archeologico €2.50/2; ⊙2-8pm Tue, 9am-8pm Wed-Mon). Housing finds from Venusia and the Samnite and early medieval periods, the museum has recently been updated with the addition of multimedia features. The collection's highlight is the *Testa del Diadumeno*, a 2nd-century marble copy of a famous sculpture by Polycletus. On leaving the castle, take a look at the unusually sober 17-century baroque facade of the **Chiesa del Purgatorio** (also known as San Filippo Neri).

Cattedrale di Sant'Andrea   CATHEDRAL
(Largo Vescovado) After one, two or even three glasses of Aglianico in one of the many cafes on the main square, take Via Vittorio

---

AGLIANICA WINE FESTIVAL

This travelling festival centres on Basilicata's iconic wine and takes place in different towns in the Vulture. Exhibition booths, displays, stages, and tasting areas are set up in autumn to celebrate the Dionysian nectar. More information is available on the Aglianica Wine Festival Facebook page.

TRAVELS WITH HORACE

If there was a rulebook for travellers, a visit to Venosa would undoubtedly be prohibited without a volume of Horace's works in your backpack. In fact, the great poet, born here in 65 BCE, provides words of wisdom for every type of journey. The most famous concern the irreversibility and precariousness of the time we have at our disposal, and culminate in what is arguably the most famous aphorism ever written, *Carpe Diem*, taken from the eleventh poem in the First Book of the Odes. But just as he invites us to get the most out of every moment of our travels, so he exhorts us to seek a frame of mind focused on the right measure, on an *aurea mediocritas* (Ode 10 of the Second Book). This is a feeling alien to travellers who try vainly to tick off every site and attraction but rarely enjoy any of them, or who think their trip is ruined in case of bad weather. Our hero also teaches us not to harbour excessive expectations for a trip because "*they change their sky, not their soul, who rush across the sea.*" (Letter 11, First Book of Epistles).

A top spot to read, ideally with a bottle of wine to hand, is under the statue dedicated to him in Piazza Orazio, perhaps the most romantic spot in town.

POTENZA PROVINCE VENOSA

Emanuele II (where immediately on the left you'll see the first of many panels showing excerpts from Orazio's works) and after a few minutes you'll come to the Municipio (Town Hall) and, opposite that, the cathedral. Completed in 1502, and built over the ancient Greek church of San Basilio, it houses, under the beautiful trussed ceiling, a 13th-century painting depicting the *Madonna dell'Idria*, and, in the right aisle, a remarkable 16th-century portal. The atmosphere of solemn devotion becomes even more intense in the crypt where you'll find the tomb of Maria Donata Orsini, wife of Pirro del Balzo, who originally commissioned the building.

Parco Archeologico   ARCHEOLOGICAL SITE
(☑0972 360 95; www.museovenosa.beniculturali.
it Località San Rocco; adult/reduced incl Museo Archeologico Nazionale €2.50/2; ☺9am-1hr before sunset Wed-Mon) This archaeological park, the best place to imagine Venusia's ancient splendour, is in the eastern part of town, where the countryside starts and olive trees rustle in the wind. The park's route takes in the *domus*; a baths complex, complete with a *frigidarium* sporting a refreshing mosaic of marine animals in the waves; a residential complex; an ancient 5th-century basilica; and, over the road, an amphitheatre (closed at the time of research). Other than these, only some street ruins remain, as the rest of the material was stripped down and reused for the construction of later buildings. However, the scenery is vast and very impressive. From the park you can also access the Incompiuta (p130).

⭐ **Abbazia della Santissima Trinità**   ABBEY
(Padri Trinitari: ☑0972 342 11; Località San Rocco; ☺8am-noon & 4-6.30 pm summer) In a contest for Basilicata's most important sacred site, this extraordinary thousand year-old abbey would be a serious contender. Built in the 11th century over an earlier 5th-century Paleochristian structure, it has survived earthquakes, glorious visions of grandeur, dramatic periods of decline, and changes of ownership, from the Benedictines who founded it in 1046, before the arrival of the Normans, to the Knights of Malta who resided here until about 1800. Today it is a place of irresistible allure, like an orchestra comprised of different styles that come together to create a unique architectural symphony. Seen from outside, its 5th-century lions might not go unnoticed but the irregular facade gives little hint of the magnificence that awaits inside. The wonder starts in the atrium, where Palmerio's swirling, Arab-influenced 1287 portal gives on to the church. Next to the door is the famous 'friendship column' – according to an ancient legend any two people who hug the column and reach around it to hold the other's hands will remain bound by an eternal bond of friendship (though we disclaim any responsibility in the case of failure). Inside, you will see the church has a classic early Christian layout with a wide nave and a crypt under the chancel. Immediately to the left of the entrance, you'll find the first mosaic floor and an extraordinary holy water font carved from an 11th-century capital and decorated with the theme of the creation. By now you'll have gone slack-jawed at the sight of the marble Tomba di

UNCERTAIN OPENINGS

At the time of research, two intriguing sites near Venosa were unfortunately inaccessible: the **Catacombe Ebraiche** (Jewish Catacombs; ☑ 0972 360 95; Località La Maddalena), dating back to a period between the 4th and 6th centuries, and the palaeontological park of **Notarchirico** (☑ 0972 360 95; Località Notarchirico), with fossils and bones hundreds of thousands of years old. Before trying to visit, call ahead to check if they're open.

Alberada (in the left aisle), the tomb of the repudiated wife of Robert of Altavilla (aka Guiscard), who rests, along with other family members, in the **Tomba degli Altavilla** (in the right aisle). Also noteworthy are the precious **frescoes** in the central nave dating from the 13th to 16th centuries, which include a 13th-century depiction of St. Apollonia (on the column opposite the Altavilla Tomb), and the baroque altar at the end of the right aisle. This was made with money donated by Abruzzi shepherds in the 17th century and is significant for the face of the crucified Christ which is unusually turned towards heaven. But the best is still to come. In the 12th century, the Benedictines planned to enlarge the church, to extend it from the apse and create a colossal structure. Building work began, with material from the local Roman ruins, but it was never completed as Pope Boniface VIII suppressed the monastery. The result is the exhilarating **Incompiuta** (same ticket and hours as the Parco Archeologico), the ruins of the unfinished church. Here you can admire walls, columns, capitals, and arches, as well as the daring of the dreamers who designed it. And with its floor of grass instead of marble and vaults of sky rather than stone, maybe this is how the Abbey has attained full spiritual realisation, in spite of its name (the 'Unfinished').

Porta Coeli   GALLERY

(☑ 0972 364 34, 348 582 97 89; www.portacoeli.it; Vico San Domenico 1; ⊗ 9am-2pm & 3.30-6.30pm Mon-Sat) FREE In a town whose tourist appeal is largely based on beauties from the past, the presence of an art gallery that looks to the contemporary is a pleasant surprise. It organises exhibitions and courses.

Vicoli degli Angeli   AREA

(Vico San Pietro) The narrow streets of this part of the historic centre have been adorned with colourful drawings of angels, both stylized and detailed, in a successful example of urban renewal. Check every wall as the angels are numerous and sometimes in inconspicuous places.

Casa di Orazio   MUSEUM

(☑ 339 480 74 31; Vico Annunziata; ⊗ by reservation) FREE If you should happen to see some unhappy tourists while walking around Venosa, rest assured that the reason they're upset will not be that they didn't visit Horace's house. For one thing, it's quite likely that the patrician residence, in which baths dating to the first century have been identified, never had anything to do with the poet. The museum tour doesn't offer anything particularly interesting but the guides do provide a lot of useful information.

🛏 Sleeping

Ai Rosoni   APARTMENT €

(☑ 333 997 46 22, 333 915 95 47; www.bebairoso nivenosa.it; Largo Baliaggio 5; apt €60; 🛜) True, the location below street level can feel a bit claustrophobic, but the apartment is lovely, with exposed stonework, delightful furnishings, a handy kitchenette and a modern bathroom. What's more, the owner knows all the hidden secrets of Venosa and the town's surrounds.

Hotel Orazio   HOTEL €€

(☑ 0972 311 35; www.hotelorazio.it; Via Vittorio Emanuele II 142; s/d/tr/q €50/70/95/115; ❄🛜 P) Housed in a 16th-century residence, formerly the seat of the Balì dei Cavalieri di Malta, this is Venosa's best-known hotel. Marble floors, ancient majolica tiles, and a panoramic terrace recall the buildings sumptuous past. The rooms, however, are fairly short on charm. Good value for money.

Ca' del Borgo   GUESTHOUSE €€

(☑ 338 383 21 75; Largo Marcello 4; r €110, superior apt €140; 🛜) This place has personality as well as comfortable, spacious rooms (the one with wine-themed decor is particularly attractive). Excellent location and impeccable cleanliness.

Venusia   HOTEL, RESTAURANT €€

(☑ 0972 323 62, 0972 329 16; www.hotelvenusia.it; Via Accademia dei Rinascenti 68; s/d/q €60/80/120; meals €20; 🛜 P 🐾) If you're not too obsessed with aesthetics, you'll appreciate the comfort of this straw-yellow hotel just outside the centre. Facilities include a car park, swimming pool, pizzeria-restaurant (discreet and well-priced) and a garden shaded by palm trees. Staff are efficient and very kind, and the rooms are spacious. If you forego breakfast, you get a €5 discount.

✖ Eating

Il Brigante   RESTAURANT, PIZZERIA €€

(☑0972 37 42 03; www.ilbrigantevenosa.it; Via Colonnello Ruggiero Albergo 1; meals €20-25; ☺12.30-3pm & 8-11pm Thu-Tue) Simple, reliable cooking, with a mile-long pizza list taking up the lion's share of the menu. Informal atmosphere.

Al Baliaggio   RESTAURANT €€

(☑0972 350 81, www.hotelorazio.it; Via Vittorio Emanuele II 136/142; meals €30; ☺12.30-2.30pm Tue-Sun, 8-10.30pm Tue-Sat, open daily Aug) An ever-present point of reference for town dining, the restaurant of the Hotel Orazio serves creative cuisine (including fish dishes) in a contemporary-styled dining room. Excellent value for money.

If, on the other hand, you just want to have a drink or order a platter, immediately to the right as you leave the restaurant is the Balì (platters €15 to €16), with good music and a refined ambiance.

L'Incanto   RESTAURANT €€€

(☑0972 360 82; Discesa Capovalle 1; menus €30, meals €40-45; ☺12.45-2.15pm & 7.45-10pm Tue-Sat, 12.45-2.15pm Sun) Set amid small, charmingly decadent houses a stone's throw from the castle, this restaurant's elegant glass-walled terrace makes a striking first impression. No less surprising are the aromas of perfumed candles and traditionally-inspired dishes cooked with flair. The menu also offers tasting courses.

ℹ Information

TOURIST INFORMATION

There's no information office as such in Venosa, but you can contact **Minutiello Viaggi** (☑0972 325 69; www.minutielloviaggi.com; Via Vittorio Emanuele II 12; ☺9.30am-12.30pm & 5-8pm Mon-Fri), which also organises good tours in the area, or the **Pro Loco Venusia** (☑380 636 04 17; Via Roma 22-25; ☺variable hrs).

ℹ Getting There & Away

We don't recommend trying to get to Venosa by train as routes, including services from Potenza (€6.05, at least two hours 20 minutes, with a change at Rocchetta S. Antonio Lacedonia), are complicated, and the Venosa-Maschito station is about 3km from the centre. Even by bus, things aren't exactly simple: **SITASUD** (☑0971 50 68 11, www.sitasudtrasporti.it) services require a change at Melfi (45 minutes). Really, the best way is to drive: from Potenza head north on the SS658 and exit onto the SS93 at Barile. From Rome and Naples take the A16 and come off at Candela; from Bari follow the A16 north and exit at Cerignola. There are free parking spaces behind the castle.

VAL D'AGRI

To pin down the character of the Vald'Agri is a hard task. It's an elusive land made up of plains and mountain ridges, genuinely unspoiled areas and drilling platforms for extracting hydrocarbons, religious traditions from the past and modern bar discussions about water contamination, villages steeped in poetry and recently-added tourist attractions. Its very position in the province is also indefinable, suspended as it is between the Pollino in the south and the northern valleys, the regional borders with Campania in the west and the badlands to the east. And so, as you head head down the SS598 and its offshoots south of Potenza, you'll come across archaeological sites, renowned food

---

THE WOODS OF FORENZA

With creeping urbanisation around Venosa, the woods so dear to Orazio have progressively got smaller. However, about 20km south of town along the SP10, in the territory of Forenza, the pagan Bosco Grande (Contrada Derricelle), is an uncontaminated pocket of secular Turkey oaks and oak trees where sightings of nymphs and fauns are the order of the day. Once in these parts, it's worth popping into the village to visit the Casa Contadina (Peasant's House; ☑338 947 75 11; Via Roma 75; ☺variable hrs) FREE, which has multimedia displays and a classic collection of rural objects. For further information contact the Pro Loco (☑338 947 75 11; www.prolocoforenza.it).

and wine centres, closed ski resorts, slightly squalid villages, and ancient convents. And as you go, you'll suddenly realise that this multi-faceted territory deserves all the time that you're dedicating to it.

Viggiano

POP 3269 / ELEV 1023M

Unless you know Viggiano's history, you're unlikely to realise you're in one of Basilicata's most emblematic villages as you walk its sleepy streets and stairways. For Viggiano is a pilgrimage destination for devotees from across southern Italy, who come here in droves to celebrate the Black Madonna (see boxed text, right). In addition, the village has been known for its music for centuries. Following the example of villagers who would go to Naples in the 17th century to play bagpipes at festivities, the locals developed a reputation for making and playing the harp in the period after the inauguration of Naples' Teatro San Carlo. They constituted a kind of cooperative that lasted until after World War I and still today you will come across craftsmen in the narrow lanes of the historic centre. Finally, it goes without saying that Viggiano, surrounded as it is by sumptuous natural scenery, has always been a popular destination for mountain enthusiasts.

◉ Sights & Activities

In the village there are several panoramic terraces offering dizzying views over the valley. Climbing the alleyways, sooner or later you'll arrive at the ruins of the medieval castle (Larghetto Cima Castello).

Chiesa Madre CHURCH
(☑0975 611 13; Via Rome; ☉7am-7pm) This 18th-century church wouldn't be particularly interesting if it weren't for the painting of St. Cecilia in the right aisle – as befits a town consecrated to music – and the beautiful panorama it commands over the valley. However, what makes it an absolute must-see is the 13th-century statue of the Madonna Nera (Black Madonna) housed here from September to May.

Museo del Lupo MUSEUM
(☑347 081 28 82, 349 365 04 70; www.aceaviggiano.it; Contrada Fontana dei Pastori; ☉10.30am-5pm Sun & holidays, call for other times; ⊞) FREE On the Montagna Grande, not far from the turning to the sanctuary (see boxed text, right), this small wooden building sits at an altitude of 1400m in a beautiful beech forest. It serves as a kind of Basilicata wolf research centre and displays a few stuffed specimens. Check about the possibility of joining a hike into the woods.

Museo delle Tradizioni Locali MUSEUM
(☑347 081 28 82, 349 365 04 70; www.aceaviggiano.it; Via del Convento 17; ☉10am-1pm & 3.30-6.30pm Sun) FREE Housed in the suggestive setting of an ancient convent, this lovingly tended museum illustrates the area's local traditions. There are interesting multimedia features and tons of artefacts.

Pietra del Pertusillo LAKE
A few kilometres from Viggiano on the eastbound SS598, is the reservoir known as

THE PARCO NAZIONALE DELL'APPENNINO LUCANO VAL D'AGRI-LAGONEGRESE

In a land of ancient traditions, Italy's most recent national park is also one of its most diverse and varied. In fact, its jagged borders – which encompass 29 small municipalities between the territories of Val d'Agri and Lagonegrese – make it difficult to conceive of it as a single unit. Far easier is to perceive the presence of some of Basilicata's highest mountains – Monte Papa (2005m), Monte Sirino (1907m), Monte Volturino (1835m) and Monte Raparo (1764m) – which tower over vast tracts of woodland, in particular beech and fir woods (such as that of Laurenzana, p113), pastureland and cultivated fields. Its fauna is also pretty varied, ranging from wolves to spectacled salamanders and otters. The Centro Visite del Parco (Park Visitor Centre; ☑0975 34 42 22; www.parcoappenninolucano.it; Via Manzoni 1; ☉10am-1pm Mon, Wed & Fri, 3.30-5pm Tues & Thur) is housed in a former convent in the upper part of Marsico Nuovo. Here you can peruse a permanent exhibition on biodiversity and pick up information material; the website also has a list of official guides.

THE QUINTESSENTIAL PILGRIMAGE

On the first Sunday of May, the statue of the Madonna Nera (Black Madonna) is joyfully transported from Viggiano's church to a chapel on Sacro Monte, where, according to legend, it was found in the 14th century – the return journey then takes place on the first Sunday of September. If you happen to be in these parts in summer, follow this centuries-old tour for an unforgettable experience. Start at the point (well indicated by Google Maps) where an ancient droving track branches off the Madonna di Viggiano municipal road, 3km north of the village. (Note that the trail was recently restored along with a Roman-era tomb stone and a bridge over the Alli stream). From this point, at an altitude of 800m, the climb becomes increasingly steep as it passes fountains and distant farmhouses en route to Piana Bonocore (where you'll find space to park your car). From there the last, most sacred, leg of the hike takes about 45 minutes. By now you'll have left the forest behind and willl be walking along highlands whipped by mystical winds until you finally spot the Santuario (⊙8.30am-6.30pm May-1st Sun of Sep), at an altitude of 1725m. Allow three to four hours in total, and factor in rivers of sweat, unmeasurable quantities of lactic acid in your legs, and endless beauty at every turn.

POTENZA PROVINCE VIGGIANO

the Lago di Pietra del Pertusillo – the dam, built between 1957 and 1963, can be seen from some panoramic points in the village. At the lake you can walk, lunch on panini in the picnic area, and go birdwatching.

★ Festivals & Events

Unsurprisingly, given Viggiano's musical heritage, the main village events are highly musical. Happily, the Teatro Miggiano (☑0975 611 37; Via Roma 30) has recently been inaugurated.

Rassegna dell'Arpa Viggianese   JULY, AUGUST
A three-day event dedicated to the Viaggianese harp and the village's centuries-old artistic tradition. As well as concerts and workshops, you can enjoy musical aperitifs.

✦ Activities

Montagna Grande   SKIING
As well as spiritual value – assured by the presence of the Sanctuary – the Montagna Grande is also of interest to sports fans with a few kilometres of ski runs (☑346 243 40 84; Strada Comunale Madonna di Viggiano; daily €18). These are more runs suitable for beginners than for expert skiers. At the time of research, the nearby ski areas on Monte Volturino (☑393 801 27 72; Località Monte Volturino), in the municipality of Marsicovetere, had been closed for some time.

🛏 Sleeping

La Dodicesima Notte   B&B €€
(☑377 470 28 00; Via Regina Elena 19; s/d €50/70; 🛜) The location in the village centre is excellent, the cleanliness impeccable, and the view an added bonus. Overall, a reliable option.

Il Castelluccio   AGRITURISMO €€€
(☑339 428 79 99; www.ilcastelluccioagriturismo. it; Contrada Castelluccio; apts for 2-4 people €160-240 per day; 🛜P) If you are thinking about droping everything and moving to the countryside, these three idyllic self-catering properties will help you get used to the idea. Small pets are allowed and there's a barbecue area for guests' use.

🍴 Eating

Theotokos   RESTAURANT €
(☑0975 614 09; Via Don Francesco Romagnano; meals €15-20; ⊙12.30-2.30pm & 6-9.30pm) The simple restaurant of this hotel-hostel doesn't disappoint with its generous helpings and quality meat. Check that it hasn't been taken over by the groups of pilgrims that periodically crowd the place.

Pantagruel   RESTAURANT, PIZZERIA €
(☑0975 615 20; Via Ida Sallorenzo 12; meals €20; ⊙12.30-3pm & 7.30-11pm Tue-Sun) The name (a reference to a gigantic fictional prince) is, in fact, justified by the abundant size of the portions. And, with its informal atmosphere, it's a perfect place to mingle with the locals. Good pizzas.

BASILICATA'S WOODEN STATUES

When you think of the great expressions of sacred art, your thoughts don't usually turn to Basilicata. Yet, between the Middle Ages and the 18th century, the region raised the art of wood carving to such remarkable heights, and produced so many wooden sculptures, that it has become something of a signature art form. In the Potentino, a lot of churches have depictions of Madonnas with Child, many of which are moved in summer to mountain sanctuaries such as those in Viggiano, Abriola, Brienza and San Severino Lucano. Some works are crude but vigorously striking while others are surprisingly refined. Viggiano is home to the most celebrated statue of all, the Madonna Negra, whose composition and chromaticism resemble that of a goddess.

ℹ️ Information

Pro Loco office (☎ 347 720 80 82; www.proloco viggiano.it; Viale Vittorio Emanuele II 22; ⏲ variable hours)

ℹ️ Getting There & Away

Good luck to anyone without their own transport. By car it takes 1¼ hours to get to Viggiano from Potenza (68km) via the SS95, SS598 and SS276. Taking **SITASUD** (☎ 0971 50 68 11; www.sitasud trasporti .it) you'll have to change at Villa d'Agri and catch the only daily bus which leaves at 2.25pm. Allow three hours in total.

Around Viggiano

Twelve kilometres south of Viggiano, the Area Archeologica di Grumentum (⏲ 9am-1pm Tue-Sun) and the Museo Archeologico Nazionale dell'Alta Val d'Agri (☎ 0975 650 74; www.museoaltavaldagri.beniculturali.it; Località Contrada Spineta 1, Grumento Nova; adult/reduced €2.50/2; ⏲ 8.30am-7.30pm Tue-Sun) showcase the remains of ancient Grumentum, the site of a bloody 215 BCE battle between Hannibal's troops and the Roman legions. The museum, whose collection includes a tusk of *elephas antiquus*, a marble bust of Livia Drusilla, Augustus' third wife, and some statues of nymphs, and some recently added artefacts from the imperial age, serves as the prelude to a visit to the archaeological area. Here you can survey the ruins of an amphitheatre, a *domus*, complete with the remains of some mosaics, and the bumpy decumanus which you can walk with the proud, bellicose gait of an ancient warrior (if that's your thing). Beyond the site's obvious historical-archaeological value, it's also a pleasant place for a stroll – the air is thick with the smell of grass while poppies flourish and the village of Grumento Nova perches in the background. The ruins are sometimes used to stage plays produced by the Teatri di Pietra (www.teatridipietra.org), so check their website for upcoming shows.

Nearby, the highly recommended Agriturismo Parco Verde (☎ 338 509 28 98; www.agri turismoparcoverde.it; Contrada Spineta 50; Grument Nova; meals €30; ⏲ Jun-Sep) offers further opportunities for time travel in the form of traditional food and a 700-year-old oak tree in the garden.

Guardia Perticara

POP 524 / ELEV 750M

Of Basilicata's many municipalities, Guardia Perticara is undoubtedly one of the most photogenic, and most controversial. 'The village of stone houses' has an architectural coherence that you won't see anywhere else, yet the overall effect seems somewhat fake, artificial even. This visual hegemony came about after the 1980 earthquake, when the local administration decided to finance a renovation of many existing houses, even though the village had suffered minimal damage. The end result being that the houses plastered with sand (in dialect, *reina*) that Francesco Rosi featured in his 1979 film *Christ Stopped at Eboli* no longer exist, having been replaced by a medieval-style mix of small columns, arches and balconies. You can reflect on the transformations of time by visiting the village's small churches and strolling through the steep alleys and stairways, and contemplate the continuity of existence by admiring the surrounding landscape, which is superb in every direction.

👁️ Sights

Start your exploration by walking along Via Garibaldi to the beating heart of the village, Piazza Vittorio Emanuele, where at any hour of the day you'll find some old boy sitting on a bench watching the clouds roll past. From there, pass under the Arco, an ancient medieval gate that bordered the castle, and continue on the elegant Via Diaz to Piazza Europa, flanked by the Chiesa Madre, entirely rebuilt after an earthquake in 1857, and the 17th-century Palazzo Montano. Then search out the early 17th-century Chiesa di Sant'Antonio (Viale Principe Umberto), which merits a visit to see its two 16th-century stone lions in the presbytery. Spend the rest of your time strolling slowly and aimlessly through the silent alleyways.

🍴 Sleeping & Eating

⭐ **Difesa d'Ischia** AGRITURISMO €€

(☎0971 965 248, 338 843 00 42, restaurant 333 265 04 73; www.agriturismodifesadischia.it; Contrada Difesa d'Ischia; s/d €60/90, meals €30; ⊙restaurant lunch & dinner daily by reservation; 🛜🖥🅿) About 8km from Guardia Perticara's historic centre, this bucolic stone structure has nine rooms and a restaurant that serves the farm's own produce (cheese, salami, wine and oil), as well as a playground for children. It also boasts a swimming pool, an area for bocce, a tennis court and a football pitch. For those travellers who are feeling really energetic, there's also the possibility of helping out with farm work, going fishing or hunting for thrushes and hares.

ℹ️ Information

There's no tourist office, but you can contact the Comune (☎0971 96 40 04), which will quickly find you a free guide for a pleasant walk around the village.

ℹ️ Getting There & Away

Guardia is signposted to the right off the SP103, from Viggiano to Craco. Rare bus services are operated by **SITASUD** (☎0971 50 68 11; www. sitasudtrasporti.it; 2½ hours to Potenza).

Roccanova & Around

POP 1345 / ELEV 648M

Very few travellers make it to Roccanova, even if its sleepy streets and the slightly worn signs of the barber and fishmonger in the central square, will enamour it to lovers of all things vintage. Roccanova is known locally as the 'city of wine', thanks to the excellent local Grottino DOP (made mainly from the sangiovese grape). The wine is little heard of, even by aficionados, but it can often be really pretty good. So, anyone wanting to show off to friends on their return home, could consider an afternoon of tastings. The Cantina Cervino (☎347 672 91 85; Contrada Marchese; ⊙9am-12.30pm & 3.30-6.30pm Mon-Sat) is the first winery you come to if driving in from the SS598 – it's near the kart track on the SP133. The Cantina Graziano (☎348 695 16 12; www.cantinegraziano.com; Contrada San Iorio; ⊙9am-1pm & 3-6pm Mon-Sat) is on the road that joins Roccanova to the SS92. Finally, at the entrance to the town, the Cantina Torre Rosano (☎0973 83 34 27; www.torrerosano.it; Via Vittorio Emanuele 28; ⊙9am-1pm & 4-7pm daily) ages its reds for three years in Italian oak barrels, then six months in barriques. At this point, and with your senses heightened by the precious nectar, you could take a small detour to Castronuovo di Sant'Andrea, 6km southwest of Roccanova, to visit the MIG – Museo Internazionale della Grafica (☎0973 83 50 14 ; www.mig-biblioteca.it; Piazza Marconi; ⊙5-8pm Tue-Sun) FREE, with its rich collection of graphic art and a permanent exhibition of nativity scenes. Temporary exhibitions are also often organised.

ℹ️ Getting There & Away

SITASUD (☎0971 50 68 11; www.sitasudtrasporti. it) buses connect the village of Roccanova with

POTENZA PROVINCE ROCCANOVA & AROUND

DELICACIES OF THE VAL D'AGRI

There are certainly more famous destinations in terms of art and culture, but when it comes to food and wine the Val d'Agri is one of Basilicata's prime areas. Its list of quality products is truly formidable. First up, obviously, is the region's culinary icon, Senise's crusco pepper, a kind of pepper chip that is served with many dishes (but which is similarly satisfying just munched). Sarconi's beans, just a step below in terms of celebrity, are particularly appreciated for their quick cooking time. Other specialities include pecorino cheese from Moliterno (p136), *caciocavallo podolico* cheese from Viggiano, ham from Marsicovetere, and olive oil from Missanello. As for wine, as well as Grottino (p135) from Roccanova, Terre dell'Alta Val d'Agri (www.terredellaltavaldagri.it), produced from cabernet sauvignon and merlot grapes, deserves a mention.

SANTA MARIA DELL'ORSOLEO

Sant'Arcangelo is a town in the eastern foothills of the Potenza province and Val d'Agri that commands beautiful views over the badlands but has a few too many concrete pylons near its historic centre. It's not an especially pleasant place in itself, but it nevertheless boasts one of the area's most artistically intriguing sights, the Convento di Santa Maria dell'Orsoleo (☑ 349 454 65 76; Località Orsoleo; adult/reduced €5/3; ⊙ 10am-1pm & 3-6pm Sat & Sun, by reservation Mon-Fri), which sits nestled in isolated hills reminiscent of Tuscany. Built from 1474 by the local lord Eligio della Marra – who, according to legend, was helped by the Madonna to defeat a dragon that haunted the area – and later entrusted to the Franciscans, it impresses with its grandeur and cloister frescoes by Giovanni Todisco (1545). Inside, there's a Museo Scenografico, housed in the cells, refectory and various rooms, which tells the story of everyday monastic life, and, with the help of films and images, the history of many of Basilicata's rupestrian churches. Also on display are the fangs and jaw of the dragon killed by the convent's founder. The warmly-coloured adjacent church reveals a beautiful choir and several wooden statues. To reach the convent from the village of Sant'Arcangelo, turn left onto the SS598 in the San Brancato neighbourhood. For a good meat-based meal, I Sapori dei Briganti (☑ 345 260 05 32, 340 526 07 41; Contrada San Vito; meals €15-20; ⊙ 10.30am-3.30pm & 5.30pm-midnight Wed-Mon) is a grillhouse on the main road styled as a sort of Lucanian saloon with buffalo horns over the entrance.

some localities in the area, including Sant'Arcangelo and Moliterno. By car, take the Roccanova-Aliano exit off the SS598.

Moliterno

POP 3663 / ELEV 879M

We don't know if it's a record, but six museums in a small village of not even four thousand people is quite a lot. As well as an artistic outlook, this pleasant locality 17km south of Viggiano can also claim a gastronomic product of excellence, the mouthwatering canestrato cheese.

◉ Sights

The MAM – Sistema Museale Aiello Moliterno (☑ 339 572 50 77; www.aiellomusei.com; cumulative ticket €12; ⊙ 9.30am-12.30pm & 4.30-7.30pm) boasts a comprehensive offering that will delight art lovers. The Museo Michele Tedesco e dell'Ottocento Lucano (Via Arcivescovo De Maria; tickets €2) showcases paintings by the main Lucanian artists of the 19th century, while the Museo del Paesaggio (Largo Chiesa Madre; tickets €3) exhibits canvases by landscape painters from Campania, painters on the Grand Tour, and Divisionists, in a historic building that is, in itself, a worthy sight. The Museo della Ceramica (admission €3) and the Museo del Novecento Lucano (admission €3) are located in the same building on Via Mazzini, the village's main street. Then there's the multifaceted Museo d'Arte

Moderna (Via Amendola 66; tickets €3), with a comprehensive collection of design objects, paintings and vintage radios, and the Museo d'Arte Contemporanea (Via Rosario 15; tickets €2), with some works by artists of the stature of Hans Hartung, Antoni Tàpies and Pablo Picasso.

By this point you won't be able to avoid visiting Moliterno's last attraction, the medieval castle tower (☑ 339 572 50 77; Via Panoramica; tickets €1; ⊙ by reservation), to end your day with a breathtaking view.

🛍 Shopping

Mircantella Formaggi e Sapori   FOOD & DRINKS

(☑ 333 272 40 90; Via Petruccelli della Gattina; ⊙ 8.30am-1pm & 4-8.30pm Mon-Sat, 8.30am-1pm Sun) Here you can buy foodie delicacies including the original canestrato, a cheese made from goat and sheep's (at least 70%) milk and aged in a specific *fondaco* (a special curing space).

ℹ Information

Pro Loco office (☑ 339 572 50 77; Piazza Vittorio Veneto; ⊙ variable hours)

ℹ Getting There & Away

It takes more than two hours, but SITASUD (☑ 0971 50 68 11; www.sitasudtrasporti.it) has at least a couple of daily buses to/from Potenza. For those coming by car, the SP103 connects Moliterno with the SS598.

Castelsaraceno

POP 1243 / ELEV 916M

What would happen if you hung the world's longest Tibetan-style hanging bridge in an unknown village immersed in nature on the border between the Val d'Agri and the Pollino? Come to Castelsaraceno and you'll find out.

◉ Sights

Almost everyone who comes to Castelsaraceno comes for the bridge or for the outdoor activities in the surrounding area. Nonetheless, the village is very pretty, with stone houses and a pleasant central square. The Museo della Pastorizia (www.visitcastelsaraceno.info; Via dei Mille; tickets €5, or incl in Tibetan bridge ticket; ⊘10am-6pm Nov-Mar, 9am-7pm Apr-Oct) is worth a visit. Aiming to highlight the knowledge built up by generations of local shepherds, it displays a *skavuratèddu* (a mould for ricotta cheese) and other traditional objects, as well as showing video interviews discussing how beef is raised and collars are made. There's also a multi-sensory room where you can smell the fragrances of different mountain herbs.

★ **Ponte tra i due Parchi**   BRIDGE
(www.visitcastelsaraceno.info; Via Portella; online/at the infopoint €25/30; ⊘daily) The 586 metres of this record-breaking Tibetan-style bridge makes this futuristic structure, which seemingly leaps into the void as the upper village peters out, the longest in the world. Despite this striking record, don't expect an obstacle course for tightrope walkers or professional adventurers, because, unlike the more electrifying bridge in Sasso di Castalda (p116), this one doesn't swing, thanks to a system of steel cables that anchors it to the mountains. This makes it easy to walk and suitable for everyone, provided, of course, that the idea of being at a height of 80m doesn't provoke undue anxiety. If you can cope with that, you're free to concentrate on the mind-blowing terrain – the stream that runs along the bottom of the canyon, the infinite shades of green that cloak the rock faces and the mountains that rise in every direction. Once you reach the other side, you can happily return to the startpoint via a path on the western side of the gorge. The time you'll need to cross the bridge varies – it can depend on how many selfies the people in front of you want

to take – but allow at least half an hour. A harness is included in the ticket, but note that in winter the ropes get very cold, so remember to bring a pair of gloves.

⚡ Activities

The area around Castelsaraceno lends itself to splendid excursions and original experiences, many of which are detailed on the village website (www.castelsaraceno.info). You can scale the summits of Monte Alpi (which marks the border with the Pollino) and Latronico by following part of the Sentiero Italia CAI; you can stroll merrily among the beech trees of the mountain-side Bosco Favino, or descend from the village into the canyon to look up at the bridge from below and reach a short via ferrata.

✦ Festivals & Events

Festa della 'Ndenna   JUNE
This is one of Basilicata's typical arboreal rites. Held on the first three Sundays of June, events centre on the union between a beech and a pine tree.

🛏 Sleeping & Eating

Castelsaraceno has become a tourist destination virtually overnight and in high season the number of restaurants isn't sufficient to meet the demand – though the sandwiches from the food shop in the piazza are great. The situation is better for accommodation – there's a list of options at www.castelsaraceno.info. Reckon on an average of €30 per person per night.

Continanza   B&B €€
(☑347 835 94 61, 340 982 82 45; Via Piave 4; apts for 1/2/3 people €40/80/120; 🛜) A very pleasant place in the village alleys. It's spacious, clean and has a crackling fireplace in front of which you can relax at the end of the day. The cakes served at breakfast might well be addictive.

Lutipico   BISTRO €
(☑349 806 95 66, 392 357 99 34; www.lutipico.it; Via De Gasperi 18; platters per person €6-8; ⊘10am-3pm Sat & Sun, 5-8pm Fri-Sun) As long as you're not a vegetarian or vegan, a plate of the grilled local sausage '*nnuglia* from Lutipico will send you home with a smile. They don't serve full meals but the cured meats and cheeses (which you can buy to take home) are all excellent.

ⓘ Information

The **tourist office** (www.visitcastelsaraceno.info; Piazza Piano della Corte; ⊙10am-6pm Nov-Mar, 9am-7pm Apr-Oct) serves as the ticket office for the bridge and is brimming with useful material.

ⓘ Getting There & Away

SITASUD (☑ 0971 50 68 11; www.sitasudtrasporti .it) buses serve Moliterno, Latronico and Lagonegro. By car, take the SS598 from the north or the SS653 from the south.

PARCO NAZIONALE DEL POLLINO

In a region where mountains, wilderness and unspoiled natural scenery are the norm, the area around the Pollino massif is still exceptional, its beauty greater even than its towering heights. The 192,565-hectare Parco Nazionale del Pollino (www.parco nazionalepollino.it), spread between Calabria and Basilicata, encompasses lush forests of alder, oak, maple, beech, chestnut and fir trees, high-altitude grasslands and windswept karst plateaus. It is not only Italy's largest national park but also but one of the most varied in terms of landscape. As well as extraordinary views, you will find villages where isolation, in an already remote region, has allowed for the preservation of cultural traditions whose origins date back to a past as deep as the canyons and valleys that furrow the land. And then there are the area's foodie treasures, small museums, festivals, and outdoor pursuits such as trekking, rafting and mountain biking. There are poems to be written at sunset on the banks of bubbling streams as eagles glide overhead through the peaks. And everywhere you look, so much beauty, in all its many forms.

Orientation

Given its size, the presence of as many as five main valleys, and the winding nature of its mountain roads, it's important to decide in advance where you want to access the park. The Valle del Sinni to the north, traversed by the SS653, provides a convenient gateway to both Latronico (to the west) and Senise (to the east). From Senise, or Valsinni if you're coming from the Ionian coast or Matera, you can also reach the Valle del Sarmento, the area's easternmost valley through which the SP92 runs to Terranova di Pollino. Bear in mind that the roads that run from there

to the Mercure and Frido valleys, in the western part of the park, are really slow and steep, albeit scenic. Given this, it's best to access the valleys from Rotonda, where the park authority is based. Rotonda can be accessed by the A2 (Laino Borgo, Lauria Sud or Campotenese turn-offs), especially if you're coming from Potenza, or by the SP4 from the SS653.

Maps

The *Carte escursionistiche – Cuore del Parco* hiking maps (1:20,000) can be purchased at the various bars, hotels, and B&Bs listed on the park website.

🏃 Activities

Pollino is like a huge natural amusement park.

Hiking

The park's main attraction is undoubtedly its dense network of trails. You can head out alone or contact an official park guide (around €100/150 for a half-/full-day hike) or a private agency such as Wilderness Life Adventure (☑ 329 342 16 03; www.escursioninel pollino.it; Piazza Vittorio Emanuele III, Rotunda).

Snowshoeing

In winter, there are plenty of snowshoe trails. For information and guidance, some hotels can offer assistance, or you can contact guides at Info Pollino (☑338 233 38 88; www.infopol lino.com; Via Fiumara 2, Viggianello) or Wilderness Life Adventure (☑329 342 16 03; www.escursioninelpollino.it; Piazza Vittorio Emanuele III, Rotonda) .

Mountain Biking

Given that there are few facilities for cyclists and distances between them are considerable, you would do well to bring your own maintenance kit. To get the lowdown, two publications are available at tourist offices or downloadable online – *Cicloturismo in Basilicata* and *MTB/Trekking/Walking Basilicata*, edited by APT Basilicata (www. basilicataturistica.it). Both outline some routes in the Park.

If you don't have a bike, some accommodation options have mountain bikes to rent and can provide guides for a tour. One such is the Rifugio Fasanelli (p141).

Rafting, Aqua Trekking & River Tubing

To go rafting you'll have to cross the regional border to Calabria – many hotels indicated

Parco Nazionale del Pollino

POTENZA PROVINCE VALLI DEL FRIDO & MERCURE

in this guide offer packages. In Laino Borgo there are several centres, including Lao Canyon Rafting (☑0981 856 44, 338 639 36 36; www.laorafting.com; Corso Umberto I 120). In Basilicata, guides from Info Pollino (☑338 233 38 88; www.infopollino.com; Via Fiumara 2, Viggianello) offer acqua trekking itineraries for families and true adventurers (www.pollino acquatrekking.com), as well as tube descents of the Mercure-Lao river.

ⓘ Information

TOURIST INFORMATION

Ente Parco Nazionale del Pollino (☑0973 66 93 11; Strada Provinciale Calabra 12; ⊘variable hrs, call ahead) Pollino National Park Authority

Official guides of the Parco Nazionale del Pollino (www.parconazionalepollino.it) Consult the website for a list of the park's official guides.

Valli del Frido & Mercure

Flowing down from the slopes of the Pollino Massif are the rivers Frido, which laps the village of San Severino Lucano, and the Mercure, which slides down the floor of the wide valley overlooked by the villages of Rotonda, Viggianello, Castelluccio Superiore and Castelluccio Inferiore. Many people consider these the park's most spectacular valleys; they're certainly the most accessible and popular.

ⓘ Getting There & Away

Give up any idea of visiting the park without your own transport. No trains serve the area and bus services are extremely limited or even non-existent outside the summer season.

BUS

There are no direct buses from Potenza or Matera to the Pollino National Park. If you really have to, use **SITASUD** buses (www.sitasudtrasporti.it). Whether you leave from Matera (☑ 0835 38 50 27) or Potenza (☑ 0971 50 68 11) you'll have to get to Senise and from there to San Severino Lucano. The **Società Lagonegrese Automobilistica** (☑ 0973 210 16; www.slasrl .eu) operates one bus a day from Rotonda to Naples (four hours) via Lagonegro (1½ hours).

CAR & MOTORCYCLE

To reach the village of Rotonda, the main centre, from Potenza, traverse the Valle del Melandro on the SS95 and SS95VAR, then take the A2 and come off at Laino Borgo. If you're travelling on the A2 from Calabria, take the SS19 and exit at Campotenese. From Matera and Metaponto follow the SS653 westwards to Francavilla in Sinni. Come off here and take the winding SP4, or continue as far as the junction with the A2 and follow on to the Laino Borgo turn-off.

Rotonda

POP 3282 / ELEV 626M

Home of the main Park Authority, this pleasant village, immersed in greenery, makes an excellent base for exploring the park's most far-flung corners, as well as

THE PARK'S SYMBOL

The pino loricato (Heldreich's pine) is a vary rare tree species found nowhere else in Italy. And even travellers uninterested in flora will be impressed by its size, by its plated bark that resembles ancient Roman armour, and by its twisted forms, expressions of its heroic struggles against frost, wind, and lightning. Dating back to the last glaciation, this arboreal monument can be found on rocky ridges in certain, well circumscribed areas. Walking the paths that start on Monte Impiso you'll be able to admire some of the most astonishing specimens, such as the thousand year-old Patriarch (at the edge of a beech forest on the Pollino peak), and the petrified Zi Peppe (between the Serra delle Ciavole and the Serra di Crispo, see boxed text p142). This was set on fire a few years ago by a group of hooligans and has become, after long being considered the park's symbol, an icon of human stupidity.

an interesting destination in its own right. The small historical centre retains traces of a more illustrious past, when the fiefdom was ruled by the noble De Rinaldis family (special dignitaries of the court of Charles V) and the town huddled around a small castle, of which a few ruins are still visible today (and whose position commands amazing 360° views). Even if the glories of the past have long since gone, wandering through the alleys in search of sculpted portals and fountains, some of which are particularly imaginative (such as the one in the shape of a sheep on Via Principe Umberto), can be a pleasant and edifying experience after a day of hard walking in the mountains. Of note are the Chiesa Madre (Via Garibaldi) and Chiesa del S.S. Rosario (Via Principe Umberto) which feature interesting stone decorations, evidence of the centuries-old tradition of Rotonda sculpture.

Rotonda is also known to foodies for its two PDO (Protected Designation of Origin) products: white beans (www.fagiolibianchidi rotondadop.it) and the curious red aubergine, a small, purple variant of the vegetable (www. melanzana rossadirotondadop.it).

◉ Sights

Museo Naturalistico e
Paleontologico del Pollino   MUSEUM
(☑ 0973 66 10 05; Via Roma 12; ⊘ 9am-1pm Mon, 9am-1pm & 4-7pm Tue-Sun) It's not every day that you get to admire the remains of an elephant dating back to the Pleistocene epoch (from 400,000 to 700,000 years ago). And then to be faced with the intact skeleton of a hippopotamus. The finds were unearthed a few kilometres from the village.

Complesso Monumentale
Santa Maria della
Consolazione   MUSEUM, SANCTUARY
(Strada Provinciale Calabra 12) As well as the headquarters of the Pollino National Park Authority (p139), the Complesso Monumentale di Santa Maria della Consolazione, 2km south of the village, also houses an ecomuseum (☑0973 66 93 11; ⊘variable hrs) **FREE**, with interactive paintings illustrating the park's flora and fauna, and the purely devotional Museo del Culto Mariano (☑338 493 65 22; www.museomarianorotonda. it; ⊘variable hrs) **FREE**, which includes a sanctuary where a miraculous statue of the Madonna is kept.

✿ Festivals & Events

Sagra dell'Abete   8-13 JUNE

Rotonda's most eagerly awaited festival has much in common with that of Accettura (see boxed text p81) and mixes the paganism of the 'arboreal wedding' with devotion to St. Anthony. After a nighttime procession up to the 1350m-high Piano Pedarreto, a beech tree is felled and dragged into the village by 13 pairs of oxen. A silver fir is then grafted onto it, after which the 'married' trees are raised on the village square. To conclude the festival, religious services are held, along with dancing and folk performances.

🛏 Sleeping & Eating

In most of the indicated agriturismi it's possible to have lunch even if you're not staying at the property.

Agriturismo A Civarra   AGRITURISMO €

(Map p139, B4; ✎ 333 635 54 54, 388 445 08 69; Contrada Valli 5; B&B per person €35; 🛜 P) Some 4km from Rotonda, and with a panoramic view over the town, this six-hectare farm grows olives, fruit, vegetables and cereals while offering comfortable rooms and an incomparable atmosphere. The restaurant and pleasant open spaces will tempt you to stay longer than you planned.

Rifugio Fasanelli   REFUGE, HOTEL €

(Map p139, B4; ✎ 0973 66 73 04, 349 875 84 17; www.rifugiofasanelli.it; Località Pedarreto; half/full board per person €75/95; 🛜 P) A real institution in the area, this refuge sits at an altitude of 1350m and offers 12 pleasant rooms (each named after a nearby locality), mountain cuisine and comfort far superior to the standards of most mountain refuges. It also organises excursions. Check the website for special offers.

Terra Verde   AGRITURISMO €

(Map p139, B4; ✎ 389 948 3678, 338 189 10 08; www.agriterraverde.it; Contrada Daniele; overnight stay/half/full board per person €45/60/75; ⊙ Tue-Sun; 🛜 P) This farm stay in the countryside outside Rotonda is a convincing option. Rooms are large, the cuisine is substantial, there are horses and, in summer, you might see some fireflies. For dinner, ask for the Rotonda aubergines in oil.

Masseria Senise   AGRITURISMO €€

(Map p139, B4; ✎ 328 844 31 32; www.masseria delpollino.it; Località Castellano; B&B/half/full board per person €30/50/70; menu €15-25; ⊙ Tue-Sun;

MINI-EXCURSIONS FROM ROTONDA

If you prefer digestive walks to exhausting treks but still want to enjoy Pollino's gripping landscapes, the Sentiero Paraturo is the trail for you. Starting in the centre of Rotonda (take Via Roma as your reference point, just behind the town hall), it takes about 20 minutes to get to a pleasant river site, complete with picnic area. The Cascata del Diavola (Devil's Waterfall) adds a wild touch that makes all the difference on such a short trip. The path is well signposted and on its return it passes the Fontana i Susu, one of the most beautiful fountains ever built by Rotonda's stonemasons.

P) For some R and R in the midst of wild nature, this agriturismo sits at an altitude of 1000m, surrounded by beech woods and with an enviable view of the Valle del Mercure. Cheeses, cured meats and meats come from their farm. They also organise outdoor activities and excursions.

Il Borgo Ospitale   HOTEL €€€

(✎ 0973 66 11 70; www.ilborgoospitale.it; Via Mordini 1; s/d €70/120; 🛜) The most sought-after hotel in the area offers elegant rooms in the heart of Rotonda's historic centre. One of the structure's properties houses the Centro Benessere Eufrasia (✎ 345 435 69 82). Check the website for interesting packages that include excursions, relaxation treatments and dinners with overnight stays.

A Rimissa   RESTAURANT €

(✎ 0973 66 12 02; www.arimissa.it; Via Vittorio Emanuele III 8; meals €25-30; ⊙ 12.30-2.30pm & 7.30-10.30pm) People come to this restaurant, named after its former function as a car park, to enjoy typical local food, a good wine list, and, best of all, meat grilled on a wood-burning fireplace and served on lava stones. On Fridays, a cod-based menu is served at dinner. Highly rated locally.

Ristorante Da Peppe   RESTAURANT €€

(✎ 0973 66 12 51; Corso Garibaldi 13; meals €30; ⊙ noon-3pm & 7.30-10pm Tue-Sat, 12.30-3pm Sun & Mon, daily Aug) A place that's far from ordinary. The setting is atmospheric, the cuisine showcases local products and the smiling,

HIKING ON THE POLLINO

Whether you find yourself in Rotonda or Viggianello, if you're after adventure, the place to be is Colle Impiso (1575m). Like the apex of a triangle, this is almost equidistant from both towns, about 20km to the east, and is the startpoint for the Pollino's most thrilling hikes. From there you can go up to the Piana del Pollino, where the scenery starts to become ethereal and majestic and paths lead off to the Serra di Crispo (2053m) and Serra delle Ciavole (2127m), revealing astonishing Heldreich's pine trees (see boxed text p140) en route. From Colle Impiso, calculate three hours for the ascent of Serra delle Ciavole and three and a half hours for Serra di Crispo. Also starting at Colle Impiso is the route for the summit of Monte Pollino (2248m), where you can spy eagles and peregrine falcons. Bear in mind that the trails require a certain level of fitness. A decidedly less demanding route, and one suitable for everyone, starts at the Rifugio De Gasperi (Località Piano Ruggio), 4km west of Colle Impiso along the Ruggio-Visitone road. It leads through a dense beech forest to the Belvedere Malvento, from where you can see as far as the Castrovillari plain in Calabria.

polite welcome will put you and your stomach in a good mood. Of the first courses, try the spaccatelle pasta with Rotonda red aubergines and the bean soup with powder of Senise red pepper.

🍷 Drinking & Nightlife

Pollino Divino   WINE BAR
(📞 340 172 89 69; Corso Garibaldi 4/7; ⊙ 9am-2pm & 5.30-9.30pm Tue-Thu, 9am-2pm & 5.30pm-1am Fri & Sat, 9am-2pm & 5.30pm-midnight Sun) The wooden ceiling and exposed stone are the only reminders that you're in a mountain village. Otherwise, the decor is worthy of a trendy big-city venue. Good selection of wines, not just local.

ℹ️ Information

For information, you can contact the local village authority, the **Comune** (📞 0973 66 10 05; www .comune.rotonda.pz.it; Via Roma 56), message the Facebook page of the **Associazione Operatori Turistici di Rotonda**, or ask the staff of the Museo Paleontologico (p140).

Viggianello

POP 2790 / ELEV 500M

Legend has it that one day long ago a barbarian queen bent down to drink water from the River Mercure and as she did so she lost her wedding ring. She desperately looked for it, but in vain, so she begged one of her faithful servants to help her look. At a certain point, the moon lit up the river and the servant shouted: "*Vidi anello regina!*" ("I saw the queen's ring!"). Hence Vidianello. Then Viggianello.

◎ Sights

The village, 8km northeast of Rotonda on the SP4, is pretty and steeply-sloped, and almost consumed by the dense woods that surround it. In May it's pervaded by the faint smell of flowers – not for nothing is it called *il paese delle ginestre* ('the town of brooms'). On a rocky spur above the village stands the 15th-century Castello dei Principi Sanseverino, now a hotel, p143. Also in the upper part of the village, the Chiesa dell'Assunta (Via San Francesco), merits a look for its essential architectural lines and splendid wooden door carved in squares and dating to the 16th century. Other interesting places include the Cappella della Santissima Trinità (SP Pedali-Viggianello 13), with its 16th-century Byzantine dome, and the Chiesa Madre (Piazza Umberto I), home to a beautiful 19th-century organ.

However, you don't really come here for its cultural sights, rather you come to hike and explore its fantastic territory. In addition to several demanding routes (see boxed text, above), the Area Faunistica del Cervo can be reached along a well-signposted path that strikes off left from the SP4 a few hundred metres outside the village towards Rotonda. After walking for 15 minutes you'll find the special wooden observation posts and, with a pinch of luck and a little patience, you might see some splendid specimens – reintroduced since 2006. Doubling back and continuing along the SP4, after 2km you'll reach the crystal clear Sorgenti del Mercure. You won't be able to dive in, unfortunately, but you can still fill your water bottle.

 Festivals & Events

Festa della Madonna
del Carmelo
AUGUST

On the third Sunday of the month, the hamlet of Pedali celebrates a rite linked to the fertility of the fields. The faithful offer the Madonna wooden sheaves decorated with ears of wheat and coloured ribbons – the so-called *cirii*. Then, while the women dance to the rhythm of the tarantella and raise the *cirii* above their heads, the farm labourers stage a 'dance of the sickle', miming the harvest.

🚌 Sleeping & Eating

La Locanda di San Francesco
HOTEL €

(📞 0973 66 43 84, 347 182 85 83; www.locanda sanfrancesco.com; Via San Francesco 47; s/d/tr €45/70/98, half-board s/d/tr €70/120/168, full-board s/d/tr €80/140/196; 🛜) This elegant 19th-century building with spacious rooms decorated in pastel shades and exposed beams offers splendid mountain views and hearty cuisine, also available to non-guests. They also organise snowshoe hikes and various excursions. A good option.

⭐ Il Castello dei Principi
Sanseverino
HOTEL €€€

(📞 350 032 43 38; www.castellodelprincipe.it; Via Marconi 6; s/d/tr €70/100/130, half-board €95/150/200; 🛜 🅿) The ideal place to realise your dream of sleeping in a real castle, complete with fireplaces, a library full of esoteric books, and secret passageways (even if we haven't found them). The rooms also reveal a certain noble refinement. The solarium is amazing, positioned in the crenellations of the old tower. Be sure to check the website for offers.

Masseria Campolerose
AGRITURISMO €

(Map p139, B3; 📞 335 171 29 31; www.masseria campolerose.it; Località Campolerose; meals €25; ⏱ noon-3pm & 7-10pm Wed-Mon; 🛜 🅿) The timeless atmosphere, the fields and animals, the genuine and abundant (really abundant) cuisine to be enjoyed outdoors, the extreme kindness, the possibility of excursions, the availability of local produce to buy and the chance to stay overnight (doubles €70) all combine to make this one of the best options in the area. It's 3km from the village along the SP4.

ℹ️ Information

Pro Loco (📞 334 384 92 59; www.prolocoviggia nello.it; SP4; ⏱ variable hours) The information point is near the municipal amphitheatre.

Castelluccio Inferiore & Castelluccio Superiore
POP 1955/739, ELEV 495M/680M

The western gateway to the park, 12km northwest of Rotonda on the SP4, is often overlooked by travellers longing for higher altitudes. Yet a stop here is warranted, as it harbours several attractions unique to the park. In particular, Castelluccio Inferiore's baroque sights stand out, especially when contrasted with the rough mountain terrain that surrounds the village. The Chiesa Madre (Piazza San Nicola) is the most lavish church in the Pollino, with stucco embellishments and a fresco cycle (1731–35) depicting stories from the Old and New Testaments. The Chiesa di Santa Maria delle Grazie (Largo Marconi), annexed to the 16th-century Convento di Sant'Antonio da Padova and sporting some interesting baroque flourishes, also adds to the coherence of the village identity, as do the portals of various stately buildings. Just outside the village, the modest Chiesa di Santa Maria della Neve (Località Madonna della Neve) also merits a mention. Here, in the rooms of the former rectory is a Museo della Cultura Contadina (📞 0973 66 33 93; ⏱ by reservation) `FREE`.

Of an entirely different tenor is the urban development of Castelluccio Superiore, with its steep alleys (even by Lucanian standards) and the upper part of the village largely abandoned. Local pride of place goes to the Santuario della Madonna del Soccorso (Località Madonna del Soccorso), located a windy 5km to the north of the village, at an altitude of 1103m. From here you can enjoy a wide view of the Valle del Mercure.

🚌 Sleeping & Eating

Sette e Mezzo
HOTEL, RESTAURANT €€

(Map p139, A3; 📞 347 350 65 83, 0973 66 32 74; www.hotelsetteemezzo.it; Via Aldo Moro 30, Castelluccio Superiore; s/d €65/90; 🛜) The building and the rooms are a bit anonymous, but the location is excellent and from the terrace you can enjoy a beautiful view over the valley. The attached restaurant, the Taverna Lucana (meals €15 to €20), offers traditional dishes and a few extra-territorial options.

THE DIFESA WOODS

The locals' venue of choice for any self-respecting barbecue, the **Bosco Difesa** is 3km east of Castelluccio Superiore along the SP46. In spring the expanse of tall Turkey oaks is softened by wild orchids, while in autumn the colour show is truly sensational. If you don't want to worry about charcoal, the Chalet Bosco Difesa (☑ 340 946 89 54; Località Difesa; ⊙ from 5pm, seasonal opening) sells sandwiches, pizzas and earthy traditional dishes.

San Severino Lucano

POP 1419 / ELEV 877M

This pretty village in the valley of the Frido river, on the SP4 between Viggianello (17km away) and Francavilla in Sinni, is a must for anyone visiting the surrounding area. It takes its name from the ancient feudal family of Sanseverino that ruled the town in the 15th century. The local nerve centre is the 16th-century Chiesa di Santa Maria degli Angeli, which guards the Byzantine statue of the Madonna del Pollino in winter. The other sights are outside the village.

◎ Sights & Activities

**Santuario della
Madonna del Pollino**   SANCTUARY

This, the most venerated sanctuary in the Pollino, stands at 1573m, on the spot where the Madonna is said to have appeared to a shepherd boy. The church is not of any special interest, but the presence of the Madonna del Pollino throughout the summer is the source of intense devotion and contributes, along with the breathtaking views over the Valle del Frido and the grace of the setting, to making it one of the park's most popular attractions. The sanctuary is 16km south of San Severino on the SP4. If you want to walk, leave your car in Mezzana near the Mulino Iannarelli (p145) and hike for around four hours. Otherwise you'll need to drive up the hairy mountain road.

Bosco Magnano   WOODS

You can feel a slightly graceful pagan air in this 1000-hectare wood of maples, hornbeams, alders and Turkey oaks. Bubbling streams course through the area, and you might just catch sight of an otter, an elf or

even a nymph intent on bathing. From the village, take the road to Francavilla in Sinni and after 5km park your car at the first stalls.

**Museo Laboratorio
della Fauna Minore**   MUSEUM

(☑ 0973 57 61 32, 333 572 92 84; Frazione Mezzana Frido; ⊙ 10am-1pm Sat & Sun) FREE It takes more than a quarter of an hour to drive here from San Severino (head southeast) but if you're passionate about butterflies and invertebrates it will be worth it. Of note is a section on how humans have depicted them in art, myth and poetry.

**Giostra Panoramica
Rb Ride**   FAIRGROUND RIDE

(☑ 0973 57 61 32, 0973 85 94 55, 340 678 68 65; www.artepollino.it; Località Belvedere Giostra; voluntary donation; ⊙ variable hrs) What are you going to meet on a lookout surrounded by woods, 4km east of a small village in the Pollino? Without pausing too much you might think of a farm, an agriturismo, a refuge even. Instead, here you will find yourself in front of a colourful car-ride carousel created by artist Carsten Holler. What's more, the structure boasts a rather curious record – it's the slowest in the world, taking a quarter of an hour to complete a full revolution. An ideal way to force yourself to contemplate the landscape.

**Parco Avventura
del Pollino**   ADVENTURE PARK

(☑ 377 381 19 74; www.parcoavventurapollino.it; Località Bosco Magnano; courses €7-20; ⊙ 10am-5.30pm Sun & holidays Apr-Jul & Sep-Oct, 10am-6pm daily Aug 🏍) The park offers aerial courses that will amuse children and adults with Tarzan tendencies, as well as being a point of reference for many other outdoor activities, from MTB and orienteering to Nordic walking and trekking.

✸ Festivals & Events

**Festa della Madonna
del Pollino**   SPRING, JULY, SEPTEMBER

The event takes place on three different occasions. The first, in late spring, sees the statue of the Madonna del Pollino carried in procession from San Severino to the Santuario della Madonna del Pollino. The second, and liveliest, appointment comes at the beginning of July. For three days the sanctuary is at the centre of celebrations as pilgrims play accordions and bagpipes and dance the tarantella. The final installment, in September, marks the return of the statue to San Severino.

Pollino Music Festival
AUGUST

(www.pollinomusicfestival.it) This festival, a yearly appointment since 1996, marks an important occasion for coming together and promoting tourism in the park. You can buy tickets on the website, which also has plenty of useful information on eating and sleeping options (there's even an area for free camping).

🛏 Sleeping & Eating

Albergo Bosco Magnano
HOTEL €€

(Map p139, B3; ☑346 360 12 73, 0973 57 6472; www.albergoboscomagnano.it; Località Bosco Magnano; half/full board per person €60/70; 🛜 🅿) Perhaps the location is not as fairy-tale as the extraordinary scenery in which it's immersed, but the food is good, the basic rooms are clean, and the owners will point you towards the best places for picking chestnuts in autumn.

⭐ Mulino Iannarelli
HOTEL, RESTAURANT €€

(Map p139, B3; ☑0973 57 02 05, 340 792 88 21; www.mulinoiannarelli.com; Mezzana Salice; s/d €70/100, meals €30; ⊙noon-3pm & 7.30-10pm; 🛜 🅿) One of the most spectacular accommodation options in the Pollino, suitable for romantic travellers or those looking for inspiration for a historical novel. The hotel is housed in a renovated 18th-century mill, obviously on a stream, surrounded by stone walls and full of period furniture. The restaurant is open to all but it's best to book.

Crescente Antonio
AGRITURISMO €€

(Map p139, B3; ☑347 249 48 05; Contrada Mezzana Cianci; menu €25, meals €20; ⊙year-round) If you can eat your way through the menu without your stomach exploding you're ready for the food olympics. Featuring high-quality ingredients, an enchanting setting surrounded by greenery, and the chance to eat outdoors in summer, it's absolutely worth the 11km drive to get here – follow south from the village of San Severino.

LATRONICO – THERMAL BATHS & TREKKING

It's said that the therapeutic virtues of the waters of Latronico have been known since prehistoric times. They are certainly appreciated today, and this in a region that's not usually renowned for its thermal spas. And so the Terme Lucane (☑0973 85 92 38; www.termelucane.it; Contrada Calda, Latronico; wellness packages per day €55-90; ⊙7am-noon & 4-6pm Mon-Fri, 7am-noon Sat May-Oct) attract cheerful visitors, even if their function, atmosphere and proposed treatments are mainly health-orientated. Adding to their appeal is the fact that a stone's throw from the facility is a mammoth work by the contemporary artist Anish Kapoor (www.artepollino.it; ⊙24 hrs), as well as a path leading to some delightful waterfalls.

The hamlet of Contrada Calda (5km from Latronico) also offers further attractions. Don't expect the spa-town atmosphere of a 19th-century novel, but there are several sights that merit a brief stop. The Museo del Termalismo (☑0973 85 94 55, 340 678 68 65; www.ceasindra.it/mula; Vico I Stabilimento; ⊙4-7pm Fri, 10am-1pm & 4-7pm Sat, 10am-1pm Sun, by reservation Tue-Thu Oct-Apr; 10am-1pm & 4-7pm Fri-Sun, by reservation Tue-Thu May-Sep) FREE occupies a former factory and is recognisable by the unmistakable smell of rotten eggs. Then there's the Museo Civico Archeologico (Contrada Calda 1), with a two-room collection of classic tomb finds, and, in the same building, the Museo delle Arti, dei Mestieri e della Civiltà Contadina (Museum of Arts, Crafts and Rural Life), which displays almost 800 objects and reconstructions of traditional environments. Immediately beyond the upper part of town there are some natural caves that resemble prehistoric dwellings.

As well as reviving yourself with a sauna and Turkish bath, and taking in cultural sights, you come to these parts to hike up Monte Alpi (1900 m). From Piazza Umberto I in Latronico – which is reachable via the SS653 and the Lauria exit on the A2 autostrada – you can summit the mountain (climbing about 1000m). En route you'll see some fine examples of Heldreich's pine trees. Allow about eight hours to get to the top and back and continue on to Castelsaraceno (p137). At the outset, you can save yourself a couple of kilometres by parking at the start of a path. For more information, ask the locals or contact Arte Pollino (☑0973 85 94 55, 340 678 68 65; www.artepollino.it; Via Falcone 3; 1hr/half/full day hikes €15/100/150; ⊙9am-1pm & 3-6pm).

ℹ Information

Pollino Pro Loco office(☏ 0973 57 63 32; www.
prolocodelpollino.org; Via Nicola Germano 18;
☉ daily Aug, variable rest of year) Serves as the
visitor centre for the Pollino national park.

Valle del Sarmento

The eastern section of the Parco del Pollino
captivates with its wild, harsh, sometimes
even brutal beauty. Uninhabited for centuries
because of how difficult it was to work the
land, the area was re-populated in the 16th
century by Albanian refugees, whose traditions are still maintained today. As well as its
cultural peculiarities, the Valle del Sarmento
offers adrenaline-charged attractions and
outdoor itineraries.

ℹ Getting There & Away

BUS
The main destinations in the valley can be reached
from Senise by **SITASUD bus** (☏ 0971 50 68 39;
www.sitasudtrasporti.it). Five daily buses pass
through Noepoli (20 minutes), San Costantino
Albanese (45 minutes) and Terranova di Pollino
(one hour 10 minutes).

CAR & MOTORCYCLE
From Senise, the SS92 crosses the entire valley.
To reach the eastern parts of the park, take the
sometimes bumpy road for Mezzana Frido.

Terranova di Pollino & Around
POP 1065 / ELEV 926M

The valley's main centre, this charming
village surrounded by beech and chestnut
trees at the foot of Monte Calvario is the
startpoint for many hikes in the area. The
village itself is not particularly interesting,
but on holidays the cheerful atmosphere in

WORTH A TRIP

BASILICATA'S GRAND CANYON

Comparisons with the landscapes of
Arizona abound in the area, however
improbable. Yet, there's no denying that
the 270° view from Piazza Marconi in the
village of Noepoli is remarkable, and
merits a contemplative stop en route
to the Albanian towns and Terranova di
Pollino. To reach the village, pick up the
SS92 at Senise (see boxed text, right)
and continue for 16km.

the bars and main street is contagious. If it's
open, pop into the **EcoMuseo** (☏ 0973 930
09; Via Convento 85) **FREE**, which has displays
dedicated to bagpipes and traditional music.

🏃 Activities

In summer, the detailed trail sign next to the
town hall is often crowded with travellers
pondering which route to take for the day.
The area is, in fact, a veritable maze of more
or less demanding routes. Some of the most
popular start at Casa del Conte, a rural settlement 6km east of town. From there you can
take the rather bumpy road to **Lago Duglia**,
the startpoint for the path to Serra delle
Ciavole and Serra di Crispo (4½ hours; see
also boxed text p142). If, on the other hand,
you fear for the safety of your car, you can
park in the clearing about 1km from Casa
del Conte and continue on foot to the bizarre
rock formations of **Timpa delle Murge**
(one hour) and **Timpa di Pietrasasso** (1½
hours). Equally spectacular, though wetter,
is the **Garavina path**, which runs along the
bottom of the homonymous canyon under
tall holm oaks seemingly set to spy on your
steps. Unless you're very experienced, it's
advisable to tackle this route only in summer.
You should leave your car at the Piano della
Tranquillità, 3km from Terranova. Finally,
if you want something pretty easy-going,
the climb from the village centre to the
Madonna della Pietà (Località Madonna della
Pietà) is steep, suggestive and takes no more
than half an hour.

🛏 Sleeping

BioAgriturismo La Garavina AGRITURISMO €
(Map p139, C3; ☏ 0973 933 95, 388 471 94 36;
www.lagaravina.it; Contrada Casa del Conte; half/
full board per person €60/80) ⌀ This farm stay
with certified production of organic produce,
guarantees genuine vegetables and home-
produced meat. The rustic furnishings and
farmhouse-style rooms are impeccable, and
there's a breathtaking view. Trails start from
outside the front door and you can call on a
team of three official Park guides.

Hotel Picchio Nero HOTEL €€
(☏ 0973 931 70; www.hotelpicchionero.com; Via
Mulino 18; s/d €70/90, meals €30-35; 🐾) This
chalet-style hotel in the centre of Terranova
has wood-panelled rooms, a small garden
overlooking the valley, and a recommended
restaurant. The owners are generous with
hiking tips and can contact a guide for you.

SENISE

On your Basilicata travels, you'll probably hear Senise named on several occasions. The birthplace of Nicola Sole, a Unification-era poet, the village is best known as the home of the *crusco* pepper (p135) – and following the August harvest every window in the village will be adorned with hanging chains (*serte*) of drying peppers. But it's is also known for the controversial Monte Cotugno dam. Opposed by a large part of the local population (the water supplies towns in Puglia) the reservoir offers sensational summer views as its waters contrast with the surrounding golden wheat fields. Senise's position, halfway between the Val d'Agri and the Pollino on the SS653, also makes it a convenient stopover on longer journeys. If you decide to stop by, check out the Chiesa di San Francesco (Corso Vittorio Emanuele), which features a polyptych by Simone da Firenze (1523), and the Museo Etnografico del Senisese (☑ 0973 68 65 76; Via Rinaldi; ⊙ closed at the time of research) FREE. From the village you can continue on to Terranova di Pollino or overnight at the Hotel Villa del Lago (Map p139, C2; ☑ 0973 68 67 35; www.villadellago. it; Contrada Chianizzi; s/d €60/80; 🛜 ✳ 🅿), one of the main options for visitors to the Valle del Sarmento.

POTENZA PROVINCE VALLE DEL SARMENTO

🍴 Eating

★ Ristorante Tipico
Luna Rossa   RESTAURANT €€
(☑ 0973 932 54, 347 856 73 85; www.federicovali centi.it; Via Marconi 18; tasting menu €25-35, meals €25; ⊙ 11.30am-3pm & 7-10pm Thu-Tue, always open summer) The reputation of this panoramic restaurant in the centre of Terranova is legendary and some ardent fans even claim it's the best in the province. Certainly, the flavours and aromas of the typical local cuisine, which makes use of ancient culinary traditions from the Middle Ages to the Renaissance and is cooked with passion, will leave you fully satisfied. Make sure to book.

San Paolo Albanese & San Costantino Albanese

POP 226/624, ELEV 800M/650M

Built on the wide basin of the Sarmento by groups of Albanian refugees fleeing Turkish invasions in the 16th century, these two tiny villages, just 7km apart, represent an immense cultural heritage rooted in the depths of time. Due to their isolation and pride in their own traditions, the Arbëreshë communities (the Albanian peoples who have settled here and in other parts of southern Italy) have managed to preserve the language, traditions and customs of their homeland. The layout of San Paolo Albanese (Basilicata's smallest parish), for example, is typically organised in blocks with a central clearing overlooked by houses and their access stairways. Walk around the streets here and it's perfectly normal to meet women in brightly coloured traditional costume (the manufacture of lace and fabrics is a widely practised artisanal craft). And then there's the music played on handcrafted instruments, and the Greek-Orthodox influenced food – typical of which are the *pettulat* (soft fritters cooked on a red-hot stone slab) – and the religious ceremonies, celebrated according to the Greek-Byzantine rite. To learn more about the traditions and history of the Pollino's Albanian peoples, visit the Museo della Cultura Arbëreshë (☑ 0973 943 67; www.museoarbereshe.it; Via Regina Margherita; adult/reduced €2/1; ⊙ 9am-1pm & 3-6pm or 4-7pm Mon-Sun), in San Paolo Albanese, and the Etnomuseo della Cultura Arbëreshë (☑ 0973 911 26, 349 231 60 43; Via Demostene 3; ⊙ 10am-1pm daily & 4-7pm Sat & Sun) FREE in San Costantino Albanese. In San Costantino, you can also check out the 17th-century Chiesa Madre (Piazza Plebiscito), which has majolica tiles on its facade and a beautiful iconostasis, and the small Museo d'Arte Sacra in the the former rectory.

🏃 Activities

Volo dell'Aquila   HANG GLIDER SIMULATOR
(☑ 0973 911 26; Località Torretta, San Costantino Albanese; ⊙ closed at the time of research) Less well known (and less ecological) than the Volo dell'Angelo (p109), this motorised hang-glider simulator is one of Basilicata's great outdoor attractions. The most electrifying part is the climb, during which you can easily find yourself making all sorts of oaths and promises in return for a safe descent – and all this despite a reduced ascent speed of

55km/h. The 80km/h descent is usually more enjoyable, offering as it does amazing views of the valley as you fly down 300m in altitude. The Volo dell'Aquila can be tackled alone or in groups of up to four people, aged 10 and up. The startpoint is near the sports field. At the time of research, the site had been closed for a while, so check if it's reopened before you organise your trip.

Pollino Outdoor Park ADVENTURE PARK
(☑ 340 597 25 99, 342 599 27 56; www.pollinopark.wixsite.com; Località Tumbarino, San Costantino Albanese; ☺ 9am-6pm Sat & Sun Apr-Jul & Sep-Nov, 9am-6pm daily Aug) To reinforce the adventurous vocation of San Costantino Albanese, this new park offers seven aerial courses, three of which are for children.

✨ Festivals & Events

Festa della Madonna della Stella MAY
A pyrotechnic procession in San Costantino Albanese accompanies a statue of the Madonna on the second Sunday of May. Events culminate in the explosion of characteristic papier-mâché puppets known as *nusazit*.

🔒 Shopping

Zampogne Pollino Quirino BAGPIPES
(☑ 340 411 06 51; www.zampognepollinoquirino.it; ☺ call for an appointment) If you don't know the difference between zampogna bagpipes, shawms, reeds and surdulina bagpipes, you can learn all about them at Quirino Valvano's workshop, where you might find an instrument to suit you. They're all handcrafted.

MARATEA & THE TYRRHENIAN COAST

After so much mountain terrain, Basilicata's Tyrrhenian coast is truly fleeting, stretching for a mere 30km between Calabria and the Cilento in Campania. Yet, the endless sequence of views to feast your eyes on, the many coves and inlets that capture the very essence of the sea, and the harmonious co-existence of idyllic villages and the Apennine's last slopes, encapsulate the beauty of entire continents.

🏃 Activities

Hiking
Although most travellers come to these parts to lie back on the beach, Maratea's amazing landscapes – a disorientating mix of sea views and spectacular mountain scenery –

can best be appreciated on foot. Popular routes include the Monte San Biagio circuit, which climbs up to the Redentore from Piazza Buraglia and returns to the town centre in five very steep kilometres, and the Madonna della Pietà trail, which winds up from Piazza Buraglia to the homonymous church and continues up the Marinella road to the Grotta delle Meraviglie (p157) and Scalinatelle, before descending for 2km to the port. If, however, you're a hiker with a capital H, don't miss the Maratea Skyline, a panoramic 48km route between Acquafredda and Castrocucco, or the inland trail up to Trecchina (about 20km from Acquafredda), which crosses the Passo della Colla, following the course of several drystone walls.

Via Ferrata
Inaugurated in summer 2021, the Via Ferrata del Redentore has attained Olympus-like status among enthusiasts. From the centre of Maratea, take the Monte San Biagio circuit (p148) in an anti-clockwise direction and then follow the signs. The first section is not particularly challenging, but the view is already superb. The second, which includes two Tibetan-style hanging bridges, features some vertical sections on exposed walls.

Climbing
Two wild walls make Maratea a popular destination for climbing fans. The Capo La Grotta crag can be reached in 10 minutes on foot from Piazza Europa. The Falesia San Biagio, with 25 aided routes, can be accessed via the path that goes up to the Redentore.

Bike Tours
Cyclists can download the information brochure *Cicloturismo in Basilicata* from the website, www.aptbasilicata.it. If you're fit, you could consider cycling from Maratea to Rotonda (p140), in the Parco Nazionale del Pollino. If you don't have your bike with you, the easiest solution is to cross the regional border into Calabria and check out the shops in Praia a Mare. Try Freewheeling (☑ 339 250 49 82; Via Longo 103) or Bike Motor Point (☑ 340 677 24 13; www.bikemotorpoint.com; Via Armando Diaz 1).

Boat Trips &Kayaking
Nautilus Escursioni (☑ 334 354 50 85; www.nautilus-boat-excursions.business.site; SP Maratea-Castello, Maratea) runs group and individual tours lasting 3½ hours, during which you can swim in otherwise inaccessible coves and secret caves. Similar services are provided

by Marvin Escursioni (☎ 338 877 78 99; www.marvinescursioni.it; SP Maratea-Castello).

With a kayak from Fly Maratea (☎ 333 795 72 86; www.flymaratea.it) you'll be able to reach caves not even accessible by boat.

Beaches

Maratea's main draw is its spectacular rocky coastline and azure sea waters – hence most travellers come here for the beach life. But don't come expecting long, immaculate stretches of sand. The sand here is rough, pebbly even, and often grey-black, and the beaches are backed by cliffs and mountainous spurs. Heading north from Maratea you'll come to Fiumicello, then the small bays of Cersuta (p154), set in a spectacular stretch of rocky coastline, and finally the wide sandy spaces of Acquafredda (p154). To the south, you'll find the beaches of Marina di Maratea (p157) and Castrocucco (p157), the widest on the entire Lucanian seaboard. They're easily reachable by car and dominated by the Torre Caina which stands on a rock overlooking the sea.

Most of the beaches, framed by thick vegetation, have lidos where you can hire water sports equipment (kayaks, windsurfs, pedal boats), as well as umbrellas and deck chairs. There are almost always stretches of free beach while the smallest and most difficult to reach coves are best for those who can do without their creature comforts. If you don't mind getting up early, in high season you'll be able to get in some quiet time on the beach before 10.30-11am, when most people arrive. The pre-evening hours are rarely so quiet as many people stay on the sand until sunset.

Maratea

POP 4837 / ELEV 300M

We don't know why the ancients called the town Thea Maris (goddess of the sea), but being disposed to aesthetic contemplation we can say that the name is still completely appropriate today.

History

The territory was inhabited in prehistoric times, as evidenced by the discovery of tools from 40,000 years ago in the coastal caves. For a long time, Maratea Superiore (p152) was a commercial nerve centre and important water supply post, as well as an impregnable stronghold, at least until its surrender to Napoleonic troops in 1806 and its consequent abandonment. Since then, Maratea Inferiore, the current town, which was built in the late Middle Ages in a position invisible from the sea and so sheltered from Saracen raids, has become increasingly important. In the post-war period, the town's history took a turn, thanks in part to Stefano Rivetti di Val Cervo (1914–88), an industrialist from Biella who, in the 1960s, decided to transfer his interests from his native valleys to the Gulf of Policastro. His wool mill turned out to be a flop, but he had great success in the tourism sector, renovating streets and squares, planting conifers and bougainvillea, and building the Hotel Santavenere (p156) in Fiumicello, and the statue of the Redeemer (p151).

Orientation

Finding your way around the area takes a bit of time, but once you understand the position of the various centres you'll be able to move around as if you were in your own living room. The main difficulty lies in the fact that the name Maratea refers to both a municipal area – comprising the entire coastal strip and its various hamlets – and Maratea Inferiore, the main town and seat of the municipal institutions. This is located on the slopes of Monte San Biagio, at the top of which you'll find the ruins of Maratea Superiore and the statue of the Redeemer.

Head towards the sea from Maratea Inferiore, which is located some 3km from the coast, and you'll immediately reach the Porto di Maratea (Port of Maratea). About 3km south of the Port, on the SS18, is Marina di Maratea, and a further 6km beyond that, Castrocucco, at the southern end of Basilicata's Tyrrhenian coast. Heading north from the port on the SS18 towards Campania, you'll reach the hamlets of Fiumicello (1.5km), Cersuta (5km) and Acquafredda (10km). Finally, the hamlet of Massa is some way from the sea, a twisting 8km drive east of Maratea Inferiore.

◉ Sights

Maratea Inferiore, or more simply Maratea, is a delightful little town with a maze of cobbled streets, colourful little houses, noble palaces with portals adorned with stone or tuff rock coats of arms, and small squares ringed by cafes and stores. Because of its size and the fact that you can't see the sea from here, on dreary winter evenings you could easily confuse it with a more threadbare internal town. However, in high season, the atmosphere takes on a glamorous air unknown anywhere else in the province, and it can become something of a challenge to bag a table at one of its many restaurants. The heart of town is the stretch between Piazza Vitolo, with its modern bronze statue of a mermaid, and Piazza Buraglia, chock-full of bars and small clubs.

Chiesa di Santa Maria Maggiore CHURCH
(Map p151; Largo Santa Maria Maggiore; ⊙ Sunday for mass, variable hrs other days) Of the 44 religious buildings scattered across the Maratea area (most of which are generally closed to the public), this church is the most impressive. Built between the 13th and 14th centuries, and remodeled several times, it houses a wooden choir in its baroque interior, considered one of the region's most beautiful, as well as some wooden statues and oil paintings.

Chiesa dell'Addolorata CHURCH
(Map p151; Via Salita dell'Addolorata; ⊙ variable hrs) Facing the obelisk (1788) of the same name, this 17th-century church was renovated in the 19th century and displays a sense of freshness that's so typical of many southern Italian churches with coloured majolica

Maratea

Maratea

floors, Neapolitan-made marble altars (note the beautiful silver tabernacle in the main altar), a wooden choir loft and white walls.

Chiesa dell'Annunziata   CHURCH
(Map p151; Via San Pietro) This church houses the area's most important painting, a delicate 16th-century *Annunciazione* by Simone da Firenze. Outside is the marble Colonna di San Biagio, dating to 1758. According to tradition, it was found at sea near the island of Santo Janni. Its base is engraved with Maratea's coat of arms and that of the Bourbons.

Palazzo DeLieto   MUSEUM
(Map p151; ☑ 0973 87 76 76; Via Gafaro; ⊙ by reservation, 3-9pm Sat & Sun Jul & Aug) FREE You

can't say this museum lacks originality, with its collection of anchors, amphorae and artefacts found on the seabed around the nearby island of Santo Janni, and, on the second floor, a collection of 20th-century paintings by Angelo Brando. The building itself also has its charm – it was built in the 18th century to house the town's first hospital.

★ Redentore (Redeemer)   STATUE
(Map p149, B3) Having exhausted the gentle delights of the town, it's time to stir your emotions. The enormous white concrete and marble statue of Christ, completed in 1965 by the Florentine sculptor Bruno Innocenti, is the undisputed symbol of Maratea, standing at a height of 22m and with an arm span

of 19m – though given the size of the views below, it's easy to lose sight of its cyclopean dimensions. The reference to the better-known Christ on Mount Corcovado in Rio de Janeiro (with which Maratea has recently twinned) is inevitable, and while there's no samba dancing here, the comparison is not so far fetched, at least in terms of landscape. The statue, erected to replace an early 20th-century iron cross that had been knocked down by stormy weather, will be a soothing presence during your stay in Maratea, even if you don't go up to it. Its silent silhouette, in fact, looks down on the holiday comings and goings along the entire coastal stretch. And at night, when it's illuminated in the darkness of the mountain, it inspires even more reverence.

To get to the statue, follow the 5km of hairpin bends up from Maratea to the car park (first hr €5, each subsequent hr €3) where you'll have to leave your vehicle and take a shuttle bus (round trip €1). You can also get to the statue on foot from Maratea Superiore via a 15-minute walk through the ruins.

★ **Maratea Superiore** RUINS
(Map p149, B3) It's not uncommon to resort to hyperbole in travel guides, but the view over the Gulf of Policastro from here, as from the statue of Christ, is, without exaggeration, truly incredible. Strolling through the ruins of this ancient village (known also as Castello) with a history dating back thousands of years – recent excavations have unearthed artefacts and coins from the Roman era – you can let your imagination fly by picturing it in its former splendour with small, thin houses, gardens and sophisticated systems of terracotta pipes for chanelling rainwater into tanks. You might also think to disagree with those who chose to abandon a place of such beauty after the Napoleonic looting of 1806.

Basilica di San Biagio BASILICA
(Map p149, B3 ☑ 0973 87 82 11; Località Castello; ⊙ 9.30am-12.30pm & 4-8pm daily Jun-Aug, Sun only rest of the year, or by reservation) Built, apparently, by Basilian monks between the 6th and 7th centuries, on the site of a pagan temple to the goddess Minerva, this basilica opposite the Redeemer statue, appears today as an amalgamation of several structures, including a tower. Inside it houses marble bas-reliefs and the remains of Maratea's patron saint, San Biagio, who legend holds arrived miraculously aboard a ship surrounded by divine light in 732.

★ Festivals & Events

Festa di San Biagio MAY
The feast day of Maratea's patron saint falls on the second Sunday in May (even if events kick off eight days earlier) and is celebrated with a ceremony governed by a centuries-old protocol. On the Saturday preceding the first Sunday of the month, a silver bust of the saint is paraded through the streets of Castello, covered by a red cloth. The following Thursday, the bust is brought down from the basilica, taken to Capo Casale, where the drape is removed, and carried on to Santa Maria Maggiore (p150). At this point the celebrations begin. They last all weekend until, on the second Sunday of May, the statue is taken back to the basilica.

Marateale JULY
(www.marateale.com) An international film award which includes a green section and one dedicated to Lucanian short films. Also debates, meetings and masterclasses.

Maratea Scena JULY, AUGUST
Held in Maratea's historic centre or nearby hamlets, this summer event always provides something to do. Get the programme at the tourist office and you'll see there's something for everyone, from meetings with authors and fashion shows to exhibitions, dance evenings, theatre performances and concerts.

⌷ Sleeping

Maratea is one of southern Italy's most elegant tourist resorts. Consequently the standard of accommodation is generally good (if far more expensive than elsewhere in the region). During the Easter period and summer season you'll need to book well in advance. In winter, most places are closed. The prices here are for high season – by avoiding this period you can save up to 50% or more.

Marabea B&B €€
(Map p151; ☑ 0973 87 76 38, 339 752 88 39; www.marabea.it; Via La Rosa 15; s/d €100/130; 🛜) Some 50m from Piazza Buraglia, the two rooms of this B&B, named after Escher and Magritte and equipped with all the home comforts, stand out for their bold colour scheme – black and white punctuated by a few dashes of fiery red. The first room has size as its added value, the second a terrace overlooking Maratea's rooftops. The design is modern while the welcome smacks of times past.

COASTAL TOWERS

Standing testimony to the territory's former strategic importance, the six towers set along Basilicata's coastal stretch add a poetic and martial air to the landscape. They were built by the viceroy Pietro da Toledo in the second half of the 16th century to protect the Maratea coast against Saracen raids. Although they can't be visited, they're such a familiar presence to drivers on the state road they can almost be considered attractions in their own right. Starting in the north, on the regional border with Campania, there's the Torre del Crivo, dominating the Mezzanotte canal; the Torre di Acquafredda, on a small promontory; and the colourful Apprezzami l'Asino, whose name derives from the path that cut through the coastal strip before the construction of the SS18 and was so narrow that two animals couldn't pass by in opposite directions. Next up is the Torre Santavenere, the largest tower, which once presided over the defense of the valley behind it; the Torre di Filocaio, which guards the port; and finally the Torre Caina, which dominates the Piana di Castrocucco and accompanies visitors along the last stretch of the Lucanian coast as it runs down to Calabria.

POTENZA PROVINCE MARATEA

La Locanda delle Donne Monache
HOTEL €€€

(Map p151; ☑ 0973 87 61 39; www.locandamo nache.com; Via Mazzei 4; d €185; late Apr-early Oct; ❋ ☎ P ☎) We doubt the nuns who lived here in the 1700s fared as well as the guests of today. Whoever stays at this finely restored convent will enjoy a luxurious setting, styled with contemporary wall art and smatterings of antique furniture, as well as charming rooms and a lovely swimming pool. One of the most beautiful accommodation options in Maratea and environs.

 Eating

You eat well in Maratea and, of course, there's no better place in Basilicata for a succulent seafood feast.

Panza
PASTRIES €

(Map p151; ☑ 0973 87 76 24; Via Angiporto Cavour 9; ⊙8.30am-1.15pm & 4.30-7.30pm daily) The specialty of this renowned pastry shop are its bocconotti, variations on the theme of Pugliese pasticciotti with shortcrust pastry filled with cream and black cherries. But it's also worth a stop for its walnut desserts and array of dry almond pastries, something you'll never find lacking at a Lucanian festival.

Avigliano
BAR, PASTRIES, GELATO €

(Map p151; ☑ 0973 87 31 77; Piazza Buraglia 1; ⊙7am-1.30pm & 2.30pm-midnight) This crowded bar-pastry shop serves all kinds of croissants for breakfast and good homemade ice cream, making it the perfect place to start or end the day. Don't miss the chocolate and lemon cassatine.

La Merenderia
APERITIFS €

(Map p151; ☑349 147 19 18; Traversa Dietro l'Annunziata 12; platters for 1/2 people €12/18; ⊙7.30-11.30pm Jun, 7.30pm-midnight Jul, 7.30pm-1.30am Aug, 7.30-10.30pm Sep) The wooden tables of this delightful, tiny tavern are just a stone's throw from the promenade of Via San Pietro, but in a corner that's quiet enough to savour the delicious platters of cold cuts and cheeses, with pezzente sausage and spiced goat cheese.

La Taverna di Zu Cicco
RESTAURANT €€

(Map p151; ☑ 0973 87 32 96; www.latavernadizu cicco.it; Via Dietro il Trappeto 32; meals €30-35; ⊙7-11pm daily) There are those who stay late into the evening chatting at the outside tables, and there are those who come to dine on traditional dishes, such as salted cod and podolica steak. In all cases, this is a good option in the heart of Maratea.

Taverna Rovita
RESTAURANT €€€

(Map p151; ☑ 0973 87 65 88, 333 922 17 90; www. tavernarovitamaratea.it; Via Rovita 13; meals €40; ⊙7-10.30pm) The decor of this small restaurant is captivating, with an 18th-century kitchen corner, and Vietri ceramics. The attentive service and above-average food justify the expense. Excellent wine list.

🔒 Shopping

La Farmacia dei Sani
FOOD & WINE

(Map p151; ☑ 347 832 65 50, 349 147 19 18; Via Cavour 10; ⊙9.30am-1pm & 5-7.30pm Fri-Wed Mar-May, Oct & Dec, 9.30am-1pm & 5-7.30pm Fri-Wed Mar-May, Oct & Dec, closed Nov & Feb) Giovanna Rinaldi's historic treasure chest has been a riot of Lucanian and Calabrian products since 1981. Among the Amaro Maratea (made according to a secret recipe), four-grain flours, sausages, dried pastas, and bean jams, you're sure to find something to fill your backpack.

Acquafredda

This small hamlet north of Maratea on the border with Campania features spectacular stretches of open coastline punctuated by small coves.

Beaches

Coming from the north, the first beaches you'll come to are the intimate Spiaggia di Mezzanotte and the Spiaggia dei Crivi, both backed by overhanging limestone walls and reachable only by boat. Decidedly larger, more accessible and better equipped are the Spiaggia Anginarra and Spiaggia Luppa, two stretches of fine shingle separated by a promontory; both are particularly suitable for families with children. Then there's the dark, rocky Grotta della Scala beach, just below the station, which will appeal to people who'll enjoy the counterpoint between the noise of the trains and that of the waves. Finally, there's a string of beaches: Spiaggia di Porticello, situated near to the fresh water source that gave its name to the hamlet; the difficult-to-reach Spiaggia Pietra Caduta (Fallen Stone Beach) with its unreassuring name; and the Spiaggia della Monaca, accessible via a very steep path.

🛏 Sleeping

La Casa del Gelso　　　　　　B&B €€
(☎ 0973 87 81 08, 338 523 03 90, 340 838 28 98; www.lacasadelgelso.it; Via Timpone 47; d €105; ☺ Mar-Jan; ﹡ P �☏) The double rooms (one of which can serve as a triple) are pleasant and welcoming, but what makes the difference here is the garden with its centuries-old trees and the helpfulness of the owners. Definitely recommended.

Nonna Vincenza　　　　　　B&B €€
(☎ 331 806 09 84; Via Nitti 16; d €100; P ⊙ ﹡) The garden, the portico where breakfast is served, the sea that peeps through the trees – all these go to make this B&B one of the most romantic on the coast. Clean rooms with some touches of class.

Hotel Gabbiano　　　　　　HOTEL €€€
(☎ 0973 87 80 75; www.hotelgabbianomaratea.it; Via Luppa 24; r €200; ☺ Apr-Oct; ﹡ ⊙ P ⚓) Some

complain that this hotel isn't great value for money, but its location on the promontory that separates the Spiaggia Anginarra from the Spiaggia Luppa is extraordinary, and the views from the sea-facing rooms are magnificent. The holiday atmosphere in the refined patio and the private beach with blue and white umbrellas are additional bonuses.

★**Villa Cheta**　　　　　　HOTEL €€€
(☎ 0973 87 81 34; www.villacheta.it; Via Timpone 46; d €250; ☺ Apr-Oct; ﹡ ⊙ P ⚓) The most aristocratic hotel in Maratea will leave you speechless thanks to its antique-furnished rooms, fine fabrics and Art Nouveau glassware, its large terrace with spectacular views of the Gulf of Policastro, its swimming pool and fairy-tale restaurant (meals €45-50). A stairway across the road leads to the Spiaggia di Porticello. They also organise yoga and cooking classes.

🍴 Eating

Da Peppe　　　　PIZZERIA, RESTAURANT €€
(☎ 0973 87 80 00, 338 286 03 02, 347 859 74 31; Via Luppa 1; meals €25; ☺ lunch & dinner Tue-Sun, always open in summer) There aren't many options in Acquafredda, but this airy, spartan, restaurant-pizzeria, serves decent pizzas and hearty seafood antipasti which you can wash down with a half-litre of house wine.

Cersuta

This idyllic village between Acquafredda and Fiumicello consists of a small grouping of houses and villas scattered among the oak trees from which it takes its name (*cersa* in the local Maratea dialect means 'oak'). And it's here, less than a kilometre south of the village (just before the tunnel on the state road), that the amazing Skywalk has been built, a panoramic glass-floored terrace hanging over the sea.

🏖 Beaches

The only objection tourists sometimes have to staying in Cersuta is that there aren't any beaches here. In reality, you can go down aromatic paths to the coast where you'll find rocks that you can sunbathe on. A short way to the south is one of the coast's most beautiful beaches, the prize-winning Rena d'u Nastru (so called, because in times past a conveyor belt from the railway yard used to dump debris into the sea here). Unfortunately, though, it has been declared out of bounds due to dangers caused by erosion and the difficulties of accessing it.

🛏 Sleeping

La Torretta
B&B €€

(📞 329 791 95 52, 349 259 47 16; www.beblatorretta.it; Via Cersuta, d €140; ❄ 🛜 P) This B&B takes its name from its enchanting terrace, which extends between the surrounding houses to command a sublime view of Maratea's sea. In summer you'll have breakfast in the courtyard adorned with flowering plants; in winter it's served in a living room with fireplace. Clean and comfortable rooms.

Nefer
B&B €€

(📞 0973 87 18 28, 339 732 07 98; www.bbnefer.it; Via Cersuta 27; r €120; P 🛜 ❄) Although many accommodation providers on this part of the coast offer gardens and sea views, this B&B in a 19th-century residence still stands out. Its rooms are tastefully furnished and curated in every detail, and the owners' kindness is something you won't forget in a hurry.

Le Chiane
B&B €€

(📞0973 87 18 64; Via Cersuta; r €120; ⊙Mar-Nov; ❄ 🛜 P) This B&B offers four rooms that smell of summer, blaze with colour courtesy of the owner's handmade fabrics, and are, above all, very clean. The lawn with agapanthus, hibiscus, bougainvillea and jasmine plants is the perfect place to lie back on a deck chair and enjoy the beauty of travelling.

Mariposa
B&B €€

(📞338 836 65 72; Via Cersuta 23; r €120; 🛜 P ❄) Yet another spectacular accommodation option, with a flowery terrace overlooking the sea (some rooms have a private terrace), a breakfast of champions, refined furnishings and a luxuriant avocado tree where squirrels play in the branches. One of the most popular choices in the area.

🍴 Eating

Da Cesare
RESTAURANT €€

(📞0973 87 18 40; Via Cersuta; meals €30-35; ⊙12.30-2.30pm & 7.30-10.30pm daily summer, closed Sun winter) Frequented by locals all throughout the year, this 250-seat restaurant is popular for its no-frills cuisine of always-fresh fish and its jovial terrace overlooking the state road. This is the place for those who prefer authenticity to the somewhat contrived sophistication of the tourist restaurants.

Fiumicello

The hamlet adjacent to the port sits on the beach of the same name, the epicentre of the 1950s tourist boom. And still today, holiday cheer pervades its small square which, in the evening, becomes a meeting point for local kids.

🏖 Beaches

Fiumicello beach is perhaps the most emblematic on the entire coast. Its form is typical of the area, with an expanse of sand and shingle sandwiched between rocky walls and a crystalline sea. And with its considerable dimensions and the local love of beach-going, deep-rooted over the decades, it's very popular not only with tourists but also with thoroughbred Maratea folk. There are two serviced lidos: Le Pergole (📞 339 604 07 30) and L'Approdo (📞 328 602 39 11) as well as free stretches. Continuing south, before the port, you'll come to the pebbly beaches of Cent'ammari, near the Torre Santavenere (see boxed text p153), and Cala Tunnara, as well as an old bathing pool (shown on Google Maps as a 'natural pool'), accessible on foot via a staircase.

LITERARY MARATEA

It's inevitable – you need only immerse yourself in Maratea's atmosphere for a few hours and your imagination will start coming up with the germ of ideas and thoughts. And given how many travellers have experienced the same thing, it's hardly surprising that Maratea appears as a setting for various novels and poems. In some of Giorgio Bassani's poems, for example, we can detect an inspired tribute to this sublime coastal stretch. Francesco Saverio Nitti once took refuge in Villa Nitti (Località Acquafredda; ⊙ open only for special events) to ponder his European trilogy. Even Cesare Pavese in Fuoco Grande and, more recently, Michele Serra in Tutti al Mare imbued pages of their works with the charm of this land. Good luck with your future ideas.

🛏 Sleeping

Da Zio Pino GUESTHOUSE €€
(☎0973 87 72 93/329 219 92 72; www.ziopinoma
ratea.it; Via Santavenere 17; s/d €72/112; ☺year-
round; ﹡ ☞) This place has certainly seen
better days, but the hospitality it offers is still
unrivaled. If you also like an environment
where the elderly play cards and old friends
come for coffee, then Da Zio Pino could be
the place for you.

La Dimora di Alfonso B&B €€
(☎0973 87 73 86, 338 959 48 45; www.ladimora
dialfonsomaratea.com; Via Santavenere 151; d €130;
﹡ ☞ P) Everything you need is here – large,
bright rooms, an abundant breakfast, and an
excellent location a few steps from Fiumicello's small centre and within walking distance
of the hamlet's beaches.

Hotel Murmann HOTEL €€€
(☎0973 87 31 95, 379 266 44 04; www.hotelmur
mann.it; Via Fiumicello 1; d €159-399; ﹡ ☞ P ﹡)
Suitable for those who prefer the comforts
of a hotel, even if it's a little anonymous, to a
family atmosphere. That said, the hotel has
a certain minimalist charm, the rooms are
bright and modern, and the swimming pool
is a welcome bonus.

Hotel Villa delle Meraviglie HOTEL €€€
(☎0973 87 13 19, 0973 87 74 53, 348 079 92 98,
331 133 51 25; www.hotelvilladellemeraviglie.com;
Contrada Ogliastro; r €200; ☺May-Sep; ﹡ ☞
P ﹡) The name might seem pretentious
(Hotel Villa of Wonders) and in high season
the prices are considerable, but the garden
overlooking the Gulf of Policastro, a beautiful
spectacle of oleanders, pines, geraniums, and
wrought-iron furniture merits unambiguous
praise. The rooms are very elegant.

Hotel Santavenere HOTEL €€€
(☎0973 87 69 10; www.santavenere.it; Via Conte
Stefano Rivetti 1; d superior €700; ﹡ ☞ P ﹡)
Set in a large private park of centuries-old
Mediterranean flora directly on the sea,
this is southern Italy's first five-star hotel.
It opened its doors in the 1950s and is still
internationally prestigious. You'll have to
take out a mortgage to spend a night here,
but you'll have a great night.

🍴 Eating

La Bussola Pizzeria PIZZERIA €
(☎339 893 77 28; Via Conte Stefano Rivetti 12, ex Via
Santa Venere 42; meals €15; ☺7.30-11pm Tue-Sun
winter, 7.30pm-midnight daily summer) This little

pizzeria is always recommended by locals.
As well as pizzas, it also serves antipasti and
various appetizers. It's open year-round, but
only in the evening.

La Cambusa RESTAURANT €€
(☎340 971 46 23; www.lacambusamaratea.it; Via
Santavenere; meals €40; ☺12.30-2pm & 7.30-
10.30pm Wed-Mon) This fish restaurant stands
out for its refined dishes and welcoming
atmosphere. The pasta dishes are amazing
and the Purp' fiction starter (with octopus
and saffron-infused cauliflower cream) is a
guaranteed delight. Best to book, whatever
the season.

Porto di Maratea

The trendiest spot on the coast, Porto di
Maratea unfolds around the piers and docks
of what was once a classic fishing village.
The fishermen's houses have long since been
converted into restaurants and small yachts
now moore where once small fishing boats
waited to sail. On summer nights, the piazza-
salon is the ideal place to whisper romantic
sweet-nothings or chat with friends.

🍴 Eating

Zà Mariuccia RESTAURANT €€€
(☎0973 87 61 63, 335 165 23 82; www.zamariuccia.
it; Via Grotte 2; meals €45; ☺7.30-10.30pm daily
summer, Tue-Sun Jun-Sep, Tue-Sat Mar-May) The
quality of the food is obvious, as evidenced by
the raw fish dishes, as is the refined creativity
behind the pasta courses. A terrace jutting
out over the sea and an elegant setting that
retains its seafaring identity complete the
picture.

Lanterna Rossa RESTAURANT €€€
(☎331 914 78 74; www.darioamaro.it; Via Porto
Arenile; meals €50; ☺noon-4pm & 7.30pm-midnight
Thu-Sun, 7.30pm-midnight Mon & Wed Easter-Nov,
daily Jun-Sep) Given the charm of the terrace,
the freshness of the fish and the bold culinary combinations, the hefty bill is justified.
Particularly superb are the *foie gras* with
raw shrimp and ravioli with braised duck
and bitter chocolate. It's advisable to book.

🍷 Drinking & Nightlife

Il Clubbino BAR
(☎328 282 21 59; Via Porto Arenile 16; ☺noon-11pm
Easter-Jun & Sep-Oct, noon-2am Jul-Aug) Here
you'll breathe that holiday air typical of piazzas overlooking ports, where people arrive

showered and perfumed for the evening after a day out in the sun. As well as drinks, they serve a mean hamburger.

Marina di Maratea

Between the slopes of Monte Serra and a wide inlet lies yet another of Maratea's tiny hamlets, complete with a train station and a string of beaches lapped by enchanting sea waters. Off-shore you can make out the silhouette of the uninhabited Isola di Santo Janni, where legend holds that Ulysses made a stop. According to hagiographies, Armenian believers landed there with the remains of San Biagio (St. Blaise), while archaeological research has documented the supply of Roman merchant ships on the island.

☉ Sights

Grotta delle Meraviglie   CAVE
(Map p149, C4; ☑ 331 915 06 95; SS18 Km 236; €5; ☉ 10.30am-1pm & 3.30-6.30pm Jun-Sep, year-round by reservation) Basilicata's 30km Tyrrhenian coastline is full of natural caves, many of which are flooded by sea water and so accessible only by boat. However, this fantastical 70m-deep grotto adorned with enigmatic stalactites and stalagmites, is near the state highway and conveniently accessible to anyone who has left their dinghy at home. The cave is well lit and the visit, which lasts about 30 minutes, requires no special precautions.

🏖 Beaches

Marina di Maratea is home to the greatest number of coves and sandy beaches on the entire coastal stretch. Of these, the large and very black Cala Jannita (also called Spiaggia Nera or Black Beach) stands out for the way its black sand contrasts with the blue of the sea and for the burns your feet will suffer if don't wear a pair of sandals. From the beach, which is partly occupied by two private lidos, you can swim (if you're moderately fit) to the wild Spiaggia d'I Vranne, recently recognised by Legambiente as Italy's most beautiful beach, and, to the south, to the Grotta della Sciabella, which has a small beach inside. Continuing southwards you'll come to the Spiaggia Illicini, which is totally occupied by an elegant tourist complex (☑ 0973 87 90 28; www.illicini.com; Località Illicini; Via Malcanale 6) and which has umbrellas and sunbeds, as well as a restaurant and guesthouse. In addition to the beaches, there are also areas,

cliffs and rocks where you can sunbathe. Further south is the Spiaggia di Macarro (known also as Cala 'i Don Nicola), which is situated in a bay backed by a shady pine forest where day-trippers picnic on Sundays, and which is largely occupied by two lidos. And thanks to the presence of shallows along its flanks, it's perfect for snorkelling. Then there's Calaficarra, an inlet with sand and shingle that's decidedly lighter and less hot than those of the coves further north, and, further on, Santa Teresa, where you can explore small caves on the northern side and meet romantic travellers even on melancholy winter afternoons. To get there, take the road that goes under the railway.

🛏 Sleeping & Eating

Hotel Martino   HOTEL, RESTAURANT €€€
(☑ 0973 87 91 26; www.hotelmartino.net; Via Citrosello 16; SS18 Km 239; standard/classic/superior rooms €165/180/200; 🛜 ✳ ♿ P) Book a room with a sea view, because that's the hotel's real strong point. But if there are none available, you can still admire the panorama from the common terrace. Views apart, you can pamper yourself in the heated indoor pool and wooden sauna. The hotel's very popular restaurant, the Locanda di Nettuno (meals €30), serves excellent fish dishes.

Cala del Citro   HOTEL €€€
(☑ 331 854 26 44; www.caladelcitro.it; Via Rovina; d €200; ✳ P 🛜 ♿) Immersed in greenery, the building that houses the eight rooms (each with a balcony overlooking the garden or the stretch of sea facing the Isola di Santo Janni) enjoys an elevated position, as does the splendid swimming pool. The delightful private beach can be reached by a staircase.

White Horse   PIZZERIA, RESTAURANT €€
(☑ 0973 87 90 09, 0973 87 92 35; www.whitehorse.it; Via Vallone Arenara 3; meals €30; ☉ noon-3.30pm & 7pm-midnight, closed Wed mid-Oct–mid-May) This is one of the few restaurants in the Marina di Maratea area and affords the usual splendid view of the Gulf of Policastro. A huge bougainvillea shades the outdoor terrace, where you can dine on classic seafood dishes and good pizzas. Given its 270-seat capacity, it's worth considering even in busy periods.

Castrocucco

Just before the regional border with Calabria, Castrocucco marks a decisive turning point in the landscape. Against a backdrop of dunes, reed beds and a land where vines and citrus fruit have been cultivated for centuries, the coast smoothes out its rough edges, evoking views like those on the Adriatic coast.

🏖 Beaches

Castrocucco is home to the long, broad Spiaggia A Gnola, the widest beach on the gulf. Easily accessible from a nearby car park, it's covered by rows of umbrellas belonging to the Approdo beach club (☑ 393 840 49 75; www.lapprodomaratea.com). If long beaches aren't your thing, you can opt for La Secca, set in a splendid inlet enclosed by a promontory a little further to the north. Here there are two very renowned lidos: La Secca (☑ 0973 87 17 19; Via Secca; umbrella & 2 sunbeds Aug €25, Sep-Jul €20-23, parking Aug €10, Sep-Jul €5-8) and Mirto Solarium (☑ 340 931 50 76; www.mirtomaratea.it; Via Secca; umbrella & 2 sunbeds Aug €25, Sep-Jul €18-20, parking Aug €7, Sep-Jul €5-6). Nestled amid trees above a steep cliff, this is considered one of the more refined options on the Maratea seafront.

🛏 Sleeping & Eating

Villaggio-Camping Maratea   CAMPING €
(☑ 0973 87 16 80, 393 801 14 90; www.villaggiocampingmaratea.it; Via del Mare 1/2; pitches per day €36-50) This, the only campsite in Maratea, has pitches – gold ones by the sea, standard ones further back – caravans, and 24 sq m mobile homes with all the comforts of a small cottage. There's also a minimarket, a restaurant-pizzeria, a bar and a toilet block with hot showers. There is entertainment, but it's usually quite discreet. Prices plummet outside the central weeks of August.

Borgo La Tana   HOTEL €€€
(☑ 0973 87 17 20, 328 336 53 00; www.latana hotelmaratea.it; Via dell'Amicizia 22; d/tr €180/240; ❋ 🛜 🅿 ❄) Spread on both sides of the road, the elite rooms, the suites, the breakfast area and the swimming pool are all in the upper part; the standard rooms and restaurant in the lower sections. The hotel's cleanliness and general efficiency, the fitness area, restaurant and availability of boats, cars and scooters to hire are also worth a mention. In August there's a six-night minimum stay.

Massa

If, by magic, you were suddenly transported to Massa, you'd think you were anywhere in Basilicata but Maratea. The hamlet furthest

from the sea appeals to visitors for the cool mountain air you can breathe on its hiking trails, for the chance to experience a decidedly unusual corner of the territory, and, most all, for its foodie products: tomatoes, cured meats, mozzarella and caciocavallo cheeses.

🍴 Eating

Il Giardino di Epicuro   RESTAURANT €€
(☑ 0973 87 01 30; Via Massa Piano dell'Orco; meals €30-35; ☺ daily Apr-Nov) After you've feasted on tons of fish, this delightful little restaurant surrounded by greenery will reconcile you with land-based cuisine: *lagane* pasta and chickpeas, pappardelle with truffles, kid and Podolico beef ribs. If you really can't do without your seafood fix, pre-order the extraordinary fish soup. And to finish up, seasonal fruit tarts.

ℹ Information

TOURIST INFORMATION
Maratea's official website, www.welcomemaratea .it, has plenty of information, as does the useful www.maratea.info.

Maratea's municipal authority has set up five IAT tourist offices (☑ 0973 87 41 11). The main ones are in Maratea Inferiore (Map p151, C2; Piazza Vitolo; ☺ 9am-2pm Mon-Fri & 3-6pm Tue & Thu Sep-Jun, also Sat & Sun Jul-Aug) and Fiumicello (Piazza del Gesù; ☺ 9am-2pm Mon-Fri, & 3-6pm Tue & Thu Sep-Jun, daily Jul-Aug). Those at the Port, the Redentore and the Spiaggia di Fiumicello are open only in the summer, every day.

ℹ Getting There & Away

BUS
The difficulty of getting around Basilicata by public transport is attested to by the fact that you can't go from Maratea, the region's second most important tourist destination, to Matera in a day. SITASUD buses (☑ 0971 50 68 11; www.sitasud trasporti.it) run twice a day to Lagonegro (45 minutes), where you can change for Potenza.

CAR & MOTORCYCLE
Parking in Maratea is not so easy, and in a lot of places you have to pay. Rates vary: on most beaches you'll pay €5 per day but near the Redentore it's €3 per hour.

From Rome, take the A3/A2, then join the SS585 at the Lagonegro Nord exit. After another 20km you'll reach the turn-off for Maratea.

From Bari and Potenza, follow the westbound SS407 until you reach the A2 at Sicignano. Alternatively, you can take a short cut by exiting the SS407 at Tito, 16km west of Potenza, and continuing south on the SS95 to Brienza where you head west on the SS598 until you reach the A2 at Atena Lucana. Once on the A2, follow signs for Reggio Calabria and exit onto the SS585 at Lagonegro Nord.

From Calabria, take the northbound A2 and exit at Lauria Sud or Lauria Nord, where you'll find signs for Maratea.

ⓘ Getting Around

A meager bus service operated by **SITASUD** (☎0971 50 68 11; www.sitasudtrasporti.it) and **Rocco Autolinee** (☎0973 229 43; www.roccoauto lines.it) connects Maratea Inferiore's Piazza Europa with Castrocucco to the south and Acqua-fredda to north, passing through various hamlets. Services generally increase slightly in summer. For a taxi, call **EuroTravel** (☎339 699 18 78; www.eurotravelweb.it) or **Cab Mar** (☎327 164 63 67; www.cabmar.com).

TRAIN
The station is between Fiumicello and Maratea, from which it's about 3km away. Regional and intercity trains connect with Naples (from €12.05, 2½ hours). There are also a few direct trains to Reggio Calabria (from €18, three hours), but most require change in Sapri or Paola. For Potenza (from €10.70, 3½ hours) you'll need to change at Battipaglia.

THE HINTERLAND

Given Maratea's extraordinary appeal, even the most petulant of visitors will have to refrain from criticising those who spend their days on the beach and neglect the remarkable cultural attractions in the interior. However, it's worth noting that some of the region's most evocative villages are actually only a few kilometres away. So, if the sky's cloudy or you get sunburnt, all you have to do is jump in your car and head up the SP3 and your day will prove equally as captivating as those spent on the beach.

Trecchina
POP 2159 / ELEV 500M
The first town you come to out of Maratea, after about 10 kilometres, is a pleasant and graceful place, slumbering between the still invisible coast and the looming mountains. Trecchina features several characteristics typical of the area's provincial towns. Its history is tortuous, involving destruction by the Saracens at the end of the 10th century, reconstruction under the Normans and

Swabians, and several fateful earthquakes. Then it has a medieval core perched on the rockside (with intricate alleyways and the remains of an ancient baronial palace) as well as quarters developed over subsequent centuries. Vestiges of its past are carved onto the stone portals of its 19th-century buildings in the form of friezes and coats of arms.

But having said all this, the atmosphere on lively Piazza del Popolo is far from low-key, especially on summer days. The piazza is where the locals go to see out the end of the day at bar tables set in the shade of trees. And it's here you can try the town's signature walnut and chestnut pastries, perhaps while eavesdropping to try and recognise the Gallo-Italic inflections of the local dialect. A kind of Lucanian-Piedmontese mix, this possibly emerged in the 13th century when migrants from the north encountered the local community. Also on the square is the town's most important church, the 19th-century Chiesa Madre, dedicated to the Archangel Michael. Finally, when you've had your fill of coolness, calories and chatter, you can head off to visit the town's main attraction, the Santuario della Madonna del Soccorso (p160).

⭐ Festivals & Events
Rievocazione Storica Medievale   AUGUST 13-14
Once a year, the town immerses itself in its medieval past with costumed figures, flag-wavers, shops where old trades come to life, music and traditional products. A festival dedicated to street artists is held in the days leading up to the event.

🛏 Sleeping
La Valle degli Ulivi   B&B €€
(☎0973 82 01 56, 338 955 01 76, 338 540 85 45; www.lavalledegliuliviagriturismo.it; Contrada Ortigliolo 7; €40 per person; ⊙year-round; P 🛜) Surrounded by olive trees and accessible via a bridge over a small river, this property is a picture of rural serenity. It's made up of five apartments equipped with kitchens and outdoor terraces.

L'Aia dei Cappellani   AGRITURISMO €€
(☎0973 82 69 37, 339 890 07 93, 333 993 59 92; www.laiadeicappellani.com; Contrada Maurino; set menu €28; ⊙Sat & Sun winter, daily Easter-Nov) There's always a fixed menu here, but it changes daily: lasagna with chickpeas, *strascinate alla lucana* (Basilicata-style

SPIRITUALITY & ADRENALINE

After a few days travelling around Basilicata, you'll almost certainly have got used to the great views. However, the panorama from the Santuario della Madonna del Soccorso, a twisting 6km south of Trecchina atop the Serra Pollino (1089m), is exceptional even by local standards. The isolated position, the view of the surrounding valleys and long coastal stretch, and the wild terrain all combine to shroud the church in a spiritual aura that even the most secular of travellers will feel. Thus, the recent inauguration of the Parco delle Stelle (☑389 992 32 71; www.parcodellestelletrecchina.it; adult/reduced €5/3, admission plus attractions adult/reduced €25/18; ☉daily in summer, check the website) has not been without controversy. Its detractors argue that the construction of this kind of amusement park in such a place is an act of brutality, that the *Big Bang* (a large swing with a 360° rotation angle) disfigures the landscape, and that the cries of children shooting down the *Synestia* slide on rubber rings shatter the mystical silence that has always characterised the area. Supporters, on the other hand, stress the potential for development that such an attraction represents and the fact that you only have to move a few hundred metres to find a more meditative atmosphere. What is not up for debate, however, is the fact that the walk up from Trecchina is truly wonderful. From Piazza del Popolo, head to the old core of the village, and from there, continue along the paved road for a few hundred metres until you get to the start of the 4km path. This heads up through thick woods offering a succession of dazzling mountain and sea views.

pasta), ricotta ravioli, gnocchi with tomato sauce, and then various roast meats, cold cuts and local cheeses. What never changes is the quality of the ingredients. In summer, the tables are immersed in the greenery of a well-kept garden and there are games for children. Always best to book.

❶ Getting There & Away

SITASUD (☑0971 50 68 11; www.sitasudtrasporti.it) buses between Lagonegro and Maratea stop in Trecchina. There's also one daily bus to Rivello. It is decidedly easier to arrive by car, via the SP3 from Maratea and the SS585 for Rivello and Lagonegro.

Rivello

POP 2591 / ELEV 479M

Of the problems that afflict Basilicata, one you certainly couldn't include would be a lack of postcard-pretty villages. One such village, Rivello, is absolutely unique, sprawled unevenly across the tops of three hills (the Motta, Serra and Poggio); one side of the village dominates the Valle del Noce, the other looks up to highest peaks of the Sirino. The soft-contours of the village's layout are certainly unforgettable and the state of preservation of the houses, rebuilt after the 1998 earthquake, is decidedly better than you'll find in many other provincial towns. The absence of any modern high-rise buildings to mar the village's silhouette is another not

inconsiderable bonus for the local residents. In addition to an abundance of fine ornamental details, from balconies and arches to noble coats of arms and ornate friezes, Rivello is also home to one of the region's most artistically significant monuments, the Convento di Sant'Antonio. Ideal for a day trip from Maratea.

History

Rivello has a curious past. Because of its strategic position it was fought over for centuries by the Lombards and the Byzantines, with no one side ever managing to gain the upper hand. So a compromise was reached – the Lombards would take the lower part of the village, and the Byzantines the upper part. The result was the development of two distinct centres with two different cultures and different religious rites: Latin in the upper part, dominated by the Chiesa di San Nicola, and Greek in the lower part, centred on the Chiesa di Santa Maria del Poggio. The division lasted until the 17th century, when the Greek rite was abolished. But still today, and despite subsequent baroque makeovers, many churches retain details typical of Byzantine architecture.

❍ Sights

★ Convento di Sant'Antonio   MONASTERY
(☑380 360 99 92; Via Monastero) This, the most important monument in Rivello and indeed

in the whole hinterland, is situated in the eastern part of town. The reason for its importance lies in its quadrangular cloister frescoed by Giovanni and Girolamo Todisco in the mid-16th century. Other than this prestigious calling-card, the 17th-century style church houses an interesting 17th-century wooden choir, the work of a Benedictine monk, Ilario da Montalbano. On the first floor of the convent, there's also a small archaeological exhibition, entitled *Greci ed indigeni tra Noce e Lao* (Greeks and natives from Noce to Lao), which exhibits finds from Serra Città and the Piano del Pignataro. The complex is often closed, so it pays to call ahead. If you forget to do so, you can still admire the frescoed entrance porch, which features a panel illustrating the *Martyrdom of the Christians of Japan* (1597). Also of note is the imposing stone portal framed by two lions, and the carved wooden door.

Chiesa Madre di San Nicola CHURCH
(Via San Nicola) Rivello's main church, which dates to the 9th century, is located in the narrow lanes of the upper village, which only serve to make it seem bigger. Subsequent enlargements, due to population growth, and various revamps (including after earthquakes), have defined its current appearance. It features a monumental staircase, a Latin cross layout with three naves and 18th-century paintings in the side altars.

Chiesa di Santa Maria del Poggio CHURCH
(Via Santa Maria) Still inaccessible today after the 1980 earthquake, this was perhaps the last church in Rivello to abandon the Greek rite. Its current look is the result of two facelifts, one in the 18th century (to which some works inside also date), and one in the 19th century at the hands of a Neapolitan architect who redecorated the interior with elaborate stucco work. Outside, the structure is characterised by the scenic position of the apse, overhanging a small cliff. Byzantine traces can also be seen in the small tiled domes of the churches of San Michele dei Greci (Via San Michele), which today serves as a theatre space, and Santa Barbara (Corso Vittorio Emanuele), with its distinct semi-cylindrical apse.

🎎 Festivals & Events

Notte della Transumanza AUGUST 23-24
A night of celebrations dedicated to transhumance with dancing, music and food. In recent editions there have also been walking

(or horseback) tours, traditional activities (sheep shearing), and a barbecue on the river.

🛏 Sleeping & Eating

Lo Straniero B&B €€
(🖄 330 440 47 69; www.beb-lostraniero.it; Via Pace 67; d €80; 🛜) The poetry of the alley in which this B&B is located augurs well for a pleasant stay. Initial impressions are confirmed inside the warm and welcoming 19th-century residence whose small rooms look onto a verdant garden and beyond to the entire valley. Very interesting food and wine evenings are also held.

Trattoria del Pellegrino PIZZERIA, RESTAURANT €€
(🖄 0973 466 17, Corso Vittorio Emanuele II 2; meals €25; ⏲ 8.45-11pm Fri-Wed, daily in summer) It's a bit of a struggle to get here, with all those steps to the top of the village, but at least you'll work up an appetite. In the afternoon old folk play cards here, but in the evening it's the warmth of the owners, and of the wood-burning oven, that animates the splendid square where a few covered tables are laid out. As you admire the valley view, you can enjoy homemade ravioli and fusilli pasta with locally produced ricotta, or a good pizza.

Il Rifugio del Cavaliere RESTAURANT €€
(🖄 339 730 61 54, 335 816 28 18; www.ilrifugiodel cavallo.it; Contrada Molinguiolo; meals €25, fixed-price menu €30; ⏲ 12.30-3pm & 7.30-10pm Sat & Sun Oct-May, 12.30-3pm & 7.30-10pm daily Jun-Sep) This agriturismo situated in the countryside between Rivello and Lagonegro tops the locals' restaurant charts. The food is simple but genuinely good, the starters are superb, and the service is friendly. It also has an area for RVs.

Coccovello AGRITURISMO €€
(🖄 0973 42 80 25, 329 22 39 318; Contrada Carposcino 2; meals €25; ⏲ noon-3pm & 8-11pm Tue-Sun, daily in summer) In a hamlet near Rivello, this is another agriturismo where they get everything right – homemade salamis, vegetables, bean soup, cavatelli pasta, and mixed grilled meats in a lively setting that smacks of tradition. In late summer, you'll see dozens of chains of drying crusco peppers.

🍷 Drinking & Nightlife

Bar One BAR
(🖄 348 012 55 04; Piazza Umberto I 10; ⏲ 7.30am-1.30pm daily, 4pm-midnight Mon, Tue & Thu, 4pm-2am Fri-Sun) The little square, where a few

CYCLING ON A FORMER RAILWAY

One of the most spectacular ways to get to know this part of the territory is undoubtedly to cycle it. In fact, a spectacular bike path has recently been built on the former Calabro-Lucana railway line, linking Lagonegro to Castelluccio Inferiore by way of 32km of tunnels and great views. If you're not in great shape, it would be best to avoid the first uphill section and start at Rivello station (6km north of the village centre).

trucks stop to sell fruit and vegetables in summer, is truly delightful. The bar comes alive on July and August evenings, and sometimes offers musical entertainment.

Shopping

Yamuna Cuoio LEATHERWARE

(✉ 0973 463 02, 338 178 58 72; www.yamunacuoio.it; Via Zanardelli 50; ⊙ 9.30am-1pm Mon-Sat, 4-8pm Mon-Wed, Fri & Sat) If you're passionate about leatherware, this family-run workshop will satisfy your every craving with everything from bags and belts to diaries and key rings.

Information

Despite the village's tourist potential, to date there's no tourist information service. You can go to the **town hall** (✉ 0973 42 80 42; www.comune.rivello.pz.it; Via Roma) and flash your best smile to try and get information and get them to open the churches for you. Alternatively, call the **Pro Loco** (✉ 380 360 99 92).

Getting There & Away

SITASUD (✉ 0971 50 68 11; www.sitasudtrasporti.it) runs a daily bus from Maratea (35 minutes), which continues on to Lagonegro (15 minutes). By car, take the SS585 towards Lagonegro. From Rome or Potenza, take the A3 south and exit onto the SS585 at Lagonegro Nord. From Rotonda head north on the A2 and take the Lauria turn-off to join the SS585.

Lauria

POP 12,166 / ELEV 430M

Very few travellers make it as far as Lauria, which is accessible from Maratea on the extension of the SP3 and the SS585. It's actually no more than a 45-minute drive from

the lovely coastal resort and while, in terms of attractions, Lauria is no New York, it does merit a certain attention, despite its share of architectural blots. First of all, its townscape is curious, with two clearly distinct centers (distinct also in terms of spirit) – Borgo Superiore and Borgo Inferiore, known locally as 'Castello' and 'Borgo'. As proof of the rivalry, it's said that until not long ago marriages between the inhabitants of the two districts were frowned upon. Secondly, the town's profile, which follows the contours of the mountain close to the woods, produces a certain melancholic harmony. Finally, there are the town's typical wrought iron railings, its archaeological collection and the exhibitions of Palazzo Marangoni (✉ 347 354 99 96; www.lauriacultura.it; Via Cairoli 60; ⊙ 5.30-7.30pm Fri-Sun) [FREE], several interesting churches with bell towers and oriental-style majolica tiles, and the ruins of the medieval castle of the Aragonese admiral Ruggiero. For centuries political prisoners were confined here and on dark nights it seems you can still hear their laments. In front, the Chiesa dell'Assunta houses a 14th-century wooden statue adorned with a quilted robe of stars. The subject of great devotion, this is the protagonist of a religious festival held every August 15. From outside the church, you can savour the amazing view over the whole town.

Lauria is known in the area for being the birthplace of the Beato Domenico Lentini who supposedly performed various miracles between the 18th and 19th centuries. His house (✉ 0973 82 33 73; Via Lentini) [FREE] can be visited by appointment.

Sleeping & Eating

Isola di Lauria HOTEL €€

(✉ 0973 82 39 06; www.hotelisoladilauria.it; Piazza Insorti d'Ungheria 6; s/d €65/90; 🖥) This hotel is in a good location but it has certainly seen better days. Despite the worn carpeting, it's still a good option with its very clean rooms and hearty breakfast.

Over Dream RESTAURANT €€

(✉ 0973 82 74 51, 338 293 21 50; www.over-dream.com; Contrada Piano Cataldo 223; meals €25; ⊙ noon-3pm & 7pm-midnight Mon-Sun) This is one of the most popular venues for weddings and birthdays in the area, surrounded as it is by greenery, but it's also perfect for a holiday meal with a view of the mountains. You can eat everything, from fish and meat dishes to robust pizzas.

ℹ Information

Pro Loco office (☑ 320 823 46 28, 320 899 98 53; www.prolocolauria.it; Via Roma 104; ☉ variable hrs)

ℹ Getting There & Away

The five daily buses to Lagonegro (35 minutes) are operated by **SITASUD** (☑ 0971 50 68 11; www. sitasudtrasporti.it). There's also one daily bus to Rivello (one hour) and one to Potenza (2½ hours). For those coming by car, Lauria can be reached via the two exits (north and south) on the A2 motorway, or, from the coast, on the SP3 and SS585.

Lagonegro

POP 5192 / ELEV 666M

Lagonegro is one of the main road hubs in the region – the Salerno-Reggio-Calabria autostrada passes through, as do the SS19 and SS585 state roads. So, drive here at rush hour, and despite its small size, the town can gift you the unusual (for these parts) thrill of being in traffic. The old part of town, founded by Byzantine monks between the 9th and 10th centuries on the classic rocky outcrop, has kept its original configuration made up of skinny alleys, narrow lanes and stairways. The entry point is the Porta di Ferro, which features the post-feudal town coat of arms showing St Michael killing the dragon. To reach it, take Piazza del Purgatorio as your point of reference and walk along the long staircase, which replaces the drawbridge of the past.

Lagonegro's modern town is less cramped and not without a certain grace.

Lagonegro is also Basilicata's main ski resort, although the facilities are extremely limited compared with those found elsewhere.

◎ Sights

Piazza Grande   PIAZZA
The focal point of the 19th-century town is this stately tree-lined square which stands

out for its size, its animated atmosphere when the local schoolkids go home for lunch, and its patched-up elegance. On its eastern flank, the Chiesa della Santissima Trinità houses the effigy of the Madonna del Sirino (1758), which is carried to the Cappella della Madonna della Neve, on the homonymous mountain, in late spring. Adjacent to the square, on the southern side, the Chiesa di Sant'Anna (Piazza Sant'Anna) impresses with its interesting Tuscan Renaissance-style facade, baroque features, and a 15th-century wooden sculpture of the Madonna that's kept inside.

Chiesa di San Nicola   CHURCH
(Contrada Colla) This church, which dominates the oldest part of town, dates to the 9th to 10th centuries, although it was rebuilt after the 1836 earthquake. It's known not so much for its artworks it houses, although some wooden sculptures from the school of Altobello Persio merit attention, but because popular tradition, or rather a theory set out in an improbable biography of Leonardo da Vinci, holds that Lisa del Giocondo (aka the Mona Lisa) is buried here. Allegedly she died of malaria in Lagonegro in 1506 while she was returning to her homeland in Calabria. If you want to learn more, check out the Mona Lisa Museum (☑ 0973 413 30; Palazzo Corrado, Piazza Bonaventura Picardi; ☉ variable) FREE . The Palazzo Corrado, the nerve centre of Lagonegro's cultural scene, also hosts exhibitions.

🏃 Activities

Monte Sirino   SKIING
(☑ 0973 89 00 04, 333 572 95 95; www.montesirinosci.it; Località Lago Laudemio; daily ski pass €20) Although it's not far from the sea, Lagonegro is an essential stop for ski enthusiasts in southern Italy. The efficient ski area on the slopes of the mountain has four ski lifts, seven pistes and a cross-country circuit.

FLAVOURS OF THE HINTERLAND

There might be no sea, and in winter it can get pretty cold, but when it comes to the pleasures of the table, you'll find nothing to fault the towns of the hinterland. Fish lovers will even find satisfaction courtesy of Laudemio and Sirio lakes and the plentiful eels and trout that swim in their waters. However, the area's most iconic product is probably the chestnut, which abounds in the woods around Lagonegro and Trecchina. Just as sublime is Rivello's *soppressata* (salami), made with prime cuts of pork, lard, pepper and salt. For lovers of fresh pasta, Lauria is the place to go.

THE LAKES OF LAGONEGRESE

The town's name (Lagonegro) refers to a dark-watered lake that has disappeared without trace. There are, however, two other lakes in the area. First up is Lago Laudemio, which is known for its proximity to the ski slopes (p163). To get there from Lagonegro, take the SP26 for 4km, then follow the signs right and continue for a further 10km. Europe's southernmost glacial lake, it sits at an altitude of 1525m in the homonymous nature reserve, and is good for a visit any time – in summer to enjoy the fresh air; in spring and autumn to admire the stunning colours of the surrounding woods; and in winter to ski the slopes that snake around its banks. Then there's Lago Sirino, 8km south of town along the SS19. It's less wild here, more suitable for a walk with an ice cream or a family Sunday outing. On its west bank, the Microworld theme park (🖉0973 406 32; www.ilmicromondo. com; Via Di Lascio 13; adult €5-11, reduced €4-9; ⊙10am-1pm & 4-7pm Sun Mar-mid–Jul & Sep-Oct, 10am-1pm & 3.30-7.30pm daily mid-Jul–Aug, year-round by reservation), shines a light on the earth's geological processes.

🛏 Sleeping & Eating

Lulugiù   B&B €
(🖉392 716 88 32, 334 886 38 77; Via Roma; d/tr €65/80; 🛜) This B&B still smells new, is beautifully located in the town centre, and doesn't disappoint in its simplicity. The spaces are large and comfortable.

Da Federico   RESTAURANT €
(🖉0973 217 42, 328 220 42 78; www.locandadafederico.it; Via Carmine 2; meals €10-15; ⊙12.30-3pm & 7.30-11pm) Truth be told, the seafood pasta dishes aren't amazing, but the place is pleasant, always full, the helpings are generous, and the pizzas do the job nicely. What's more, we challenge you to find a cheaper restaurant in all of Basilicata.

Valsirino   RESTAURANT €€
(🖉0973 415 65, 338 815 84 96, 338 529 09 28; www.valsirino.it; Contrada Ceraso; s/d €30/60; meals €25; ⊙noon-3.30pm & 7-11pm daily in summer, Wed-Mon rest of year; 🛜 🅿) Those heading to the ski slopes can stop here for a good meal and a restful night's sleep. The restaurant is rustic and offers traditional Lucanian dishes accompanied by local Aglianico wines. Don't overdo it with the salami starters or you can forget any hope of sport.

ⓘ Information

There's no tourist office in Lagonegro. For information, contact the **town hall** (🖉0973 413 30; Piazza dell'Unità d'Italia).

ⓘ Getting There & Away

Lagonegro can be reached by car from Potenza (98km, about one hour 20 minutes) via the SS95 and A2; from Maratea via the SS585 (26km, about 35 minutes). The rare bus services to/from Potenza and Maratea are operated by **SITASUD** (🖉0971 50 68 11; www.sitasudtrasporti.it; two hours for Potenza, 45 minutes for Maratea). Buses to Lauria are more frequent (40 minutes).

Understand Basilicata

History

"That other world...which no one can enter without a magic key:" Carlo Levi, forced into confinement in Aliano, perceived the dark and powerful aura of paganism that surrounded him in this mysterious, profound, unsettling land – a land whose history is made up of a few glorious moments punctuated by scourges and suffering faced with tenacity and pride.

Prehistoric Man

In recent times, a system of National Archaeological Museums has been established to showcase the complex archaeological reality of a region that for centuries was a meeting place for different ethnic groups and cultures. You'll find museums in Matera, Metaponto, Policoro, Grumento Nova, Melfi, Venosa, Muro Lucano and Potenza.

The first inhabitants of whom traces have been found settled around Venosa, and in the Valle del Bradano and Murgia Materana, during the Paleolithic period. At the time, the area was also populated by huge animals including 'ancient elephants', the remains of which have been unearthed in Venosa and near Rotonda. Later, in the Neolithic period, agricultural villages (characteristic for their 'entrenched' shape) developed around Matera and in the Melfese area. These marked a significant stage in the growth of the region, which during the Bronze Age became an important strategic link between the Ionian and the Tyrrhenian seas. In the Iron Age, from the 9th century BCE onwards, people started settling in the hinterland: first the Lycians, a people of Illyrian origin from whom we perhaps get the name 'Lucania', then Greek colonists, who established settlements whose treasures are still found in the region.

Founded from the 8th century BCE onwards, Metaponto, Siris and Heraclea were the main Greek colonies. They were later weakened when a profound crisis hit Greece's mainland cities, resulting in the Peloponnesian war (431–404 BC), and they became targets for the increasingly expansionist ambitions of neighbouring peoples. The Oscians began to press from the north, and the Samnites and Sabines later set out to conquer Basilicata's Apennine plateaus. But it was the Lucanians who enjoyed the greatest success and in the 5th and 4th centuries BCE they established themselves across the region. When the Romans appeared on their northern borders, the Lucanians, who were organised in small independent units and were capable of uniting in the face of an external threat, decided that an alliance was more convenient. The resulting pact,

TIMELINE	5th Millennium BCE	1300–1200 BCE
	Neolithic settlements are established in the Murgia Materana. Remnants of these fortified villages survive in the Murgecchia area and Murgia Timone.	In the Bronze Age, the Lycians arrive from Anatolia and settle in the Lucanian region.

signed in 298 and strengthened by the conversion of some important settlements into colonies (the first being Venusia in 291 BCE), was, however, short-lived. Just a few years later the Lucanian tribes defected and sided with Pyrrhus, the ambitious king of Epirus, when he invaded southern Italy with his own fierce army.

Roman Lucania

Lucania was the scene of a crushing defeat for the Romans as Pyrrhus vanquished them at the battle of Heraclea (280 BCE). The victory, however, didn't benefit the king of Epirus as he'd hoped and five years later the Romans took their revenge, defeating him at Benevento and putting an end to the Lucanians ambitions of autonomy. Over the following 200 years, revolts broked out but they achieved little and were all put down by the Romans. Matera, in particular, was hit hard – it had already been devastated by Pyrrhus and Hannibal's Carthaginians during the second Punic war, when it was destroyed by the Romans during the Social War at the start of the 1st century.

In the northeast of the region Grumentum (now Grumento) was founded and connected to Venusia by Via Herculia. Then, around 190 BCE, the Appian Way (Via Appia), which had been conceived to link Rome and Brindisi, reached Venosa. More or less contemporarily, Potenza was founded. Elsewhere, intense deforestation began in Lucania's vast woods to create space for agriculture – an unexpected consequence of this was the spread of malaria, a disease which would plague the region throughout the following centuries.

The territorial reorganisation of Italy commissioned by Augustus at the beginning of the 1st century CE saw Lucania merged into Brutium. Matera and the territory on the left bank of the river Bradano were, however, incorporated into a neighbouring region called Apulia et Calabria. By this stage, Lucania's economy was based on timber and animal farming, in particular pig farming, a sector in which it was unrivalled in Italy. Good land and river communication routes also favoured trade which flourished until the fall of Rome.

For an ethnologist's take on Basilicata's culture and magic rituals, start with the classic *Sud e Magia* (*Magic: A Theory from the South*) by Ernesto De Martino, first published in 1959, and translated into English in 2015.

From the Lombards to the Normans

At the beginning of the 5th century, the Western Roman Empire entered a crisis from which it would never recover. In 476, Odoacer, a Roman army general of Germanic origin, was recognised as governor of Italy by the Eastern emperor Zeno and the Roman Senate. However, in 493 he was defeated and assassinated by Theodoric's Ostrogoths.

Theodoric died in 526 and the following year Justinian became the Eastern emperor. A period of conflict ensued and from 535 Italy was devastated by war between the Byzantines (who, in Lucania, controlled the

8th Century BCE	330 BCE	867 CE
Siris, one of the first Greek colonies in the region, is founded. After two centuries of prosperity it is destroyed by an alliance of Metaponto, Sibari and Crotone.	Early contacts are made between the peoples of Basilicata and the Romans, mainly to ally against the Samnites.	Matera is besieged and destroyed during a war which pits the Lombards and Imperial forces against the Saracens. The Saracens lay siege to the city again in 994, this time without success.

coastal centres) and the Goths (who controlled the inland settlements). After 25 years of bitter conflict, the Byzantines emerged victorious.

The situation changed once again with the arrival of the Lombards in Italy and the foundation, in around 570, of a southern duchy with Benevento as its capital. This survived for two centuries until the Lombards were ousted by the Franks and it was converted into a principality, prior to being split into two states – Lucania was largely incorporated into a state governed by Salerno as its capital. The political situation, however, remained unstable. The local nobles distrusted a central power that appeared to them weak and inadequate, and the local populace lived in fear of the Saracens, whose raids terrorised the coasts and countryside. In the 10th century, the Byzantines made a brief re-appearance in Italy, reconquering the southern regions and establishing a province called *thema* in Lucania. However, less than a hundred years later, Italy's complex political situation was thrown into turmoil as the Normans burst onto the scene.

Basilicata has a long history of serious seismic events. Earthquakes with magnitudes measuring more than 6.0 have occurred in the Vulture area (1851), along the Lucanian Apennines (1561, 1826, 1857), in the Lagonegro area (1831, 1836), and in nearby Irpinia (1694, 1930, 1980). In earlier centuries, a violent earthquake hit Potenza in 1273, destroying a large part of the city.

As early as the year 1000, Norman adventurers and mercenaries had begun to appear in Italy, offering their services to the various potentates in perpetual conflict and establishing small autonomous domains. One such, the fiefdom of Melfi, was granted to Guglielmo Braccio di Ferro (William Iron Arm) of the house of Hauteville by the lord of Salerno. Recognised as direct vassals of the Holy Roman Empire, these Normans of Melfi went on to take over increasingly larger territories. In 1053 they defeated papal forces at Civitate, in the Foggia area, and took Pope Leo X prisoner.

At this point the Altavillas and the pope joined forces against Byzantium and the Empire – an important agreement, stipulated in Melfi in 1059, assigned the title of Duke of Apulia and Calabria (including Lucania) to Robert Guiscard (aka the Astute; c.1015–1085), in exchange for his support and his recognition of the pope's sovereignty. The Normans thus began to establish themselves as a major Mediterranean power, a development that was subsequently reinforced by their conquest of Sicily and further expansions into mainland Italy. And it's to this period that the first documentary attestations of the name Basilicata date, probably in reference to a Byzantine official, the *basilikós*, who administered the *thema* of Lucania.

Federico II, Wonder of the World

It was the Swabians who eventually consolidated the kingdom and made it great. In particular, it was Federico II, Stupor mundi (Wonder of the World), king of Sicily and Holy Roman Emperor who starred in this period, one of the greatest in the history of southern Italy. Thanks to the union of the two crowns in 1220 Federico ruled a vast territory that

1041	1137	1299
The Normans establish Melfi as capital of their territories in Puglia and Lucania. The city, formerly a bishopric controlled by Byzantium, is enlarged and fortified.	Potenza welcomes Pope Innocent II and Emperor Lothair for an important meeting. In 1149, Roger II of Hauteville will receive Louis VII, king of France.	Roger of Lauria, an admiral in the service of the Aragonese, defeats the Sicilians at the Battle of Cape Orlando.

encompassed much of central Europe and southern Italy and included the flourishing Kingdom of Sicily and the remnants of the Byzantine world. To govern this immense kingdom, and reset relations with the riotous local aristocracies – an absolute imperative for Federico – a set of rules known as the *Assizes of Capua* (1220) was issued. This marked a radical turning point in the internal politics of the Swabian state. Controls were strengthened over internal drives for autonomy, many noble privileges were abolished, and fiefdoms and properties of the aristocracy and clergy were confiscated.

During his reign, Federico maintained quite close relations with Basilicata. He stayed in Melfi on several occasions and various provisions were issued there. An important example was the *Constitutiones Regni Siciliæ* (1231), or *Constitutions of Melfi*, which dealt with public and feudal law, the magistracy, and legal procedures. Notable for its sense of justice, balance and capacity to combine tradition with modernity, it formed the basis of southern Italy's legislative system throughout the modern age.

Federico died on 13 December 1250 in Castel Fiorentino, near today's Torremaggiore in the Foggia area. A titanic character, of extraordinary culture and brilliant intelligence, he provoked overwhelming passions and implacable hatreds. But in the following years, his children failed to build on his work. Conrad, the only son of Federico's marriage to Yolande of Brienne, tried to gain control of southern Italy, but he died young of malaria in 1254 at Lavello in Basilicata. Four years later the crown of Sicily passed to Federico's natural son, Manfred. Manfred enjoyed initial success but in so doing he rekindled the hostility of the papacy and in 1263 Pope Clement IV granted Sicily as a fiefdom to Charles of Anjou, lord of Provence and brother of the king of France. Then, in 1266 Charles won a decisive victory over Manfred in Benevento.

The Normans in Italy (Laterza, 2008) focuses on the highlights of the kingdom that unified southern Italy, from Roger II of Hauteville to the splendours of Emperor Federico II of Swabia.

HISTORY THE ANGEVINS & ARAGONESE

The Angevins & Aragonese

The pope's support for the Angevins was no accident. Rome had an interest in seeing the Kingdom of Sicily ruled by a dynasty close to the Guelph cause, which supported the papacy against the Ghibellines who were close to the Empire. The reign of Charles of Anjou brought no benefits to the southern populations, who quickly made their feelings clear, rising in the revolt of the Sicilian Vespers (1282) to protest against their heavy tax burden, the abuses committed by royal officials, and the introduction at court of many French knights to the detriment of the local barons. The insurrection, which began in Palermo, quickly spread across the continent in the form of a war between the Angevins and the Aragonese for control of southern Italy. Basilicata, which was suffering a serious demographic crisis at the time, was dragged into the war: the Aragonese invaded the region and conquered several important strongholds and urban centres,

1514	1663	1806
Giovanni Carlo Tramontano, governor of Matera, is killed by a local citenzry incensed by the heavy taxes he had imposed on them.	Matera becomes capital of the Justiciarate of Basilicata, a province of the Kingdom of Naples. Until then, the city had been administered by the Terra d'Otranto.	Napoleonic troops besiege Maratea, where a pro-Bourbon contingent has taken refuge. After a week of fighting, the garrison surrenders in exhange for military honours and the safeguarding of their lives and property.

DOMUS REGIAE, CASTLES & FORTIFIED FARMHOUSES

At the time of Federico II's reign, Basilicata was dotted with *domus regiae* (royal residences) and castles (29 in all, out of a total of 225 in Frederick's entire kingdom) as well as fortified farmsteads. These had originally been conceived as defensive in nature but after the *Constitutions of Melfi* were instituted in 1231, they became imperial residences and places of social gathering, as well as political-administrative centres (as in the case of the Castle of Melfi, for example). Important castles, many of which now lie in ruins, were located at Muro Lucano, Brienza, Brindisi di Montagna, Pescopagano, San Fele, Abriola, Anzi, Calvello, and Matera. Raffaele Licinio's book *Castelli medievali. Puglia e Basilicata: dai normanni a Federico II e Carlo I d'Angiò* (CaratteriMobili, Bari 2010) examines the 'castle system' that was established by the first Norman king, Roger II, and which was later restructured and reinforced by Federico II and, in part, by the Angevin Charles I.

such as Scalea and Lagonegro. Maratea, however, remained in Angevin hands despite repeated attempts to conquer it. The war dragged on for 90 years until, in 1372, the Treaty of Avignon assigned Sicily to the Aragonese and the rest of the south to the Angevins. However, the new arrangement lasted little more than 60 years, and in 1434 King Alfonso of Aragon overthrew the Angevins and reunited the territories of the old Norman–Swabian kingdom. This didn't please some of the Lucan aristocracy, who were determined to defend their feudal privileges. In the second half of the 15th century the barons of Basilicata conspired and rebelled against the Aragonese on two separate occasions, but they were defeated both times and many lost their lives. The conflict between the crown and the feudal lords didn't let off, though, especially as the Spanish presence in Italy became progressively stronger throughout the 16th century, and the conditions of the peasantry continued to worsen, amid exploitation and taxes.

From the 17th Century to the Risorgimento

The Thirty Years' War, which devastated Europe between 1618 and 1648, had strong social repercussions in southern Italy as Spain, strenuously engaged in the conflict, exploited the Kingdom of Naples' and Basilicata's human and agricultural resources to the point of exhaustion. In 1647, social tensions led to a revolt in Naples. Led by a rabble-rouser called Masaniello, the uprising spread from the city to the countryside before eventually being put down. In Basilicata, brave insurgents, led by Matteo Cristiano, fought hard but couldn't avoid defeat and reprisals, and

1863	1904	1943
The parliament of the Kingdom of Italy overwhelmingly approves the Pica Law, authorising exceptional measures for the fight against brigandage in the southern regions.	The second Giolitti government passes a package of special measures in favour of Basilicata.	Between 16 and 24 September, 18 civilians are killed by retreating Germans in Rionero in Vulture.

Cristiano himself ended up on the scaffold. At the beginning of the 18th century, the Kingdom of Naples found itself at the centre of a struggle, both diplomatic and bellicose, between the Bourbons of Spain and the Habsburgs of Austria. The Spaniards finally prevailed and in 1734 they added the throne of Naples and Sicily to their possessions.

Despite its peripheral position, its essentially peasant vocation, and its thinly spread bourgeoisie, Basilicata played a role of some importance during the Enlightenment. The region also served as a laboratory for some experimental Catholic reforms, thanks in the main to the bishop of Potenza Giovanni Andrea Serrao.

In 1799 revolution broke out in the Kingdom of Naples. A republic was proclaimed but within a few months it was suppressed by the Bourbons. A few years later the region was conquered by Napoleonic forces, paving the way for new rebellions and French reprisals. When Napoleon eventually fell, the Congress of Vienna placed the Bourbons back on the throne. But the situation in the kingdom, which had by now been renamed the Kingdom of the Two Sicilies, continued to simmer. Liberal uprisings in 1820 induced King Ferdinand to grant a Constitution but it was abrogated the following year after intervention by forces of the Holy Alliance. An almost identical replay then took place in 1848, the year of revolutions across Europe. The end of the Bourbon reign finally came in 1860, when Giuseppe Garibaldi's red shirts conquered Sicily and continued towards Naples. The successes of Garibaldi's forces gave courage to those hostile to the Bourbons and to liberals supporting the cause of Italian unification. An insurrection broke out in mid-August and on 2 September Garibaldi crossed the region's borders and took control of it. The annexation of southern Italy to the Kingdom of Italy was sanctioned by a plebiscite held on 21 October 1860: the percentage of favourable voters in Naples' provinces, which included Basilicata, exceeded 99%.

The Unification of Italy & Banditry

Basilicata's first years as part of Italy were very difficult. Problems caused by the transition, many of which were aggravated by mistakes made by the new rulers, led to an exponential increase in the phenomenon of banditry. Harsh fiscal policies, an increase in the cost of living, and a lack of agrarian reform in favour of the peasantry combined with widespread pro-Bourbon sentiments and other factors to push thousands of people into joining brigand gangs. The state authorities weren't ready to counter this phenomenon and chose to treat it as a simple problem of public order. This was a serious mistake, for while the brigands were mostly crooks and common criminals, they also reflected the feelings of injustice and discontent that the population often felt and which should have elicited a more articulated response than indiscriminate repression. As such, the

"Death to the king, long live the Universal Republic, long live Orsini." This was the message attached to the knife used by the Basilicata anarchist Giovanni Passannante in his attempt on the life of King Umberto I in 1878.

1952	1986	1993–4
Alcide De Gasperi signs a law ordering the complete evacuation of Matera's Sassi districts, where living conditions have become unsustainable. The population is transferred to newly built neighbourhoods and the Sassi district becomes a ghost town.	The government approves law 771 entitled *Conservation and Recovery of Matera's Sassi Districts*. This begins the long process of reclaiming and restorating the Sassi areas.	Unesco declares Matera a World Heritage Site. Production begins at the Fiat plant in Melfi, one of the Turin company's flagship factories.

struggle against banditry in Basilicata played out between characters who had become almost legendary and against a backdrop of terrible bloody episodes. Among the most feared local gang leaders were Carmine Crocco, Ninco Nanco, and Rocco Chirichigno, who the army hunted for years without quarter, often without sparing the civilian population. By 1865, banditry had largely been defeated, even if the problems that had unleashed it remained – in the second half of the 19th century almost 200,000 people chose to emigrate to escape the misery and degradation that afflicted the region.

The 20th Century

World War I cost the lives of almost 7500 inhabitants of Basilicata, a very high figure in relation to its overall population. The spread of fascism in the region was largely due to the actions of squads from nearby Puglia. There were many episodes of violence, one of which, in 1921, resulted in the death of the socialist mayor of Ferrandina, Nicola Montefinese. After the establishment of the dictatorship, a massive plan of public works and land reclamation was announced – and partially implemented before the regime fell. The region also became a place of confinement for the regime's political opponents: in Pisticci a proper penal colony was created which, in 1941, counted more than 500 prisoners. During World War II some centres, such as Potenza, Maratea and Lauria, were bombed by the Allies. But Basilicata's position proved to be an advantage after the armistice of 8 September 1943: the German occupation only lasted for a few weeks and already by October it was effectively over. Matera was the first city to rise up against the Nazi fascists, who withdrew on 21 September having killed 15 people (11 others fell in the clashes). In the institutional referendum of 2 June 1946, the republic prevailed, but in Basilicata, as in almost all of southern Italy, the majority of voters supported a monarchy – almost 60% in the Potenza–Matera district. After the war, some work was carried out on the road and water networks, for the main financed by the Cassa per il Mezzogiorno fund (established in 1950), but the economic miracle of the 1950s and 1960s failed to bridge the stark gap between Italy's north and south. The situation has improved in more recent times with the region recording significant development, thanks to the opening of large industrial complexes (the FIAT factory in Melfi), the exploitation of natural resources such as oil, and the downsizing of sectors like the chemical sector affected by the crisis.

In 1970 Basilicata's first regional elections were won by the Christian Democrats, as were the next four elections. However, during the Second Republic Basilicata's Regional Council has always had a centre-left majority, until the elections of March 2019 were won by Vito Bardi, an exponent of the centre-right.

Emilio Colombo, born in Potenza in 1920, is the only person born in Basilicata to have served as Prime Minister (1970).

1998	2014	2020
ENI and the Basilicata Region agree on terms for the extraction of oil in the Val d'Agri. A protocol of intent outlines measures to limit the environmental impact.	On 17 October, Matera is designated European Capital of Culture for 2019. It is the second Italian city after Genoa to win this prestigious accolade.	The Covid-19 pandemic deals a serious blow to the regional economy, hitting a recovery fuelled by increased tourist flow to Matera after the city's designation as Capital of Culture.

Society & Culture

Basilicata is a land of great contrasts. Walking in a semi-deserted village you might feel yourself enveloped in an imperceptible veil of melancholy, only for that to be suddenly shaken off by the elegiac beauty of the landscape or by finding one of the infinite fragments that make up the mosaic of its fascinating culture.

Behind the open windows of the region's historic centres, you'll often only find elderly people, the only people who have remained here. Their children and grandchildren, whose return in August is joyfully greeted, have long since emigrated to other parts of the country, to Europe or even further afield. Emigration remains a deep, open wound in these parts and in the kindness you receive from local people, you may perhaps glimpse a hope of knowing that their children, relatives and grandchildren will receive the same treatment wherever they are.

And so there are few young people left, probably fewer than in other regions of the south. But when you meet them you will feel the energy and passion with which they speak of their land. They usually study at the University of Potenza or perhaps they have chosen to return after studying elsewhere to work as craftsmen, artists or guides. Some may have started their own business in Matera, now a firmly established Italian tourist destination after its designation as European Capital of Culture in 2019. Others may work as hiking guides in the Pollino National Park, inexhaustible in their eagerness to show you every corner of the wild landscape, or be members of the cooperatives and associations in Irsina and San Fele, Aliano and Barile that are trying to keep alive and promote Basilicata's cultural and artistic heritage, as well as its natural resources and food and wine. They work as musicians attempting to revive the sounds of ancient instruments or as councillors in small villages. In some corners of its territory, Basilicata has therefore succeeded in that rare and precious task of preserving the ever thinner thread that links the past and present, and of reviving, in isolation, those rites and traditions that make this such a unique land.

Emigration & Immigration

The serious economic crises that struck the Mezzogiorno (southern Italy) after the unification of Italy and in the two post-war periods caused great waves of migration. The heaviest period of emigration was between 1900 and the outbreak of World War I, when floods of southern labourers left for America. The reasons for the territory's impoverishment can be traced back decades and have been well articulated. The end of the feudal system had an adverse impact on the economy as lots of not-always productive land were unfairly divided between the local farm-labourers. These plots became increasingly fragmented as they were passed down through the generations, and still today families can be divided by issues relating to inheritance and the division of property. The lack of an entrepreneurial class and the cumbersome presence of absentee landlords also led to the failure of any attempted land management strategy. Further exacerbating the situation was the fact that the job of

Emigration peaked in 1913, when 872,598 people left Italy.

a farm-labourer was not held in high regard in southern Italian society, despite it being the main source of income for the local economy. Thus, of the 400,000 Italians who found themselves in New York in 1920, a considerable number came from Basilicata. The drama of emigration is told today in the Museum of Lucanian Emigration (p121) in Castel Lagopesole.

After the new waves of migration that followed World War II and land reform, emigration fell sharply, but it didn't stop altogether. Today, emigration routes have changed, but young Lucanians continue to leave their homeland in search of fortune, and the small villages of the interior continue to empty.

Fulvio Wetzel's film *Mineurs* (2007) centres on a group of emigrants from Basilicata who leave their homeland in 1961 to work in Belgium's coal mines. Gruelling shifts, accidents, and illnesses such as silicosis await them.

Religion, Folklore & Festivities

"The air over this desolated land and among the peasant huts is filled with spirits. Not all of them are mischievous and capricious gnomes or evil demons. There are also good spirits in the guise of guardian angels." In *Christ Stopped at Eboli*, Carlo Levi, a writer, painter and doctor from Turin as well as a member of the anti-fascist Justice and Freedom movement, describes a society with a strong mystical, semi-pagan element, in which people still nurtured an unshakable faith in magical practices.

The world described by Levi (and by other authors such as Ernesto De Martino) may no longer exist, but many of the rites still celebrated in the region have their roots in traditions that far pre-date Christianity. This is the case of the *taranta*, which in Basilicata is strongly rooted in the Tricarico area, but also of many Christian traditions and events which are, in fact, adaptations of ancient pagan rites. Chief among these is Carnival, which Catholics now hold to mark the start of Lent, and which in Basilicata is celebrated in different ways in Montescaglioso, Aliano, Satriano di Lucania and Tricarico.

However, the Christian feast celebrated with the greatest pomp is Easter. To mark it, many towns stage rites and events that continue throughout Holy Week. And there are people who will pay handsomely for the privilege of participating in the solemn processions and carrying the heavy statues that represent the characters from the Passion. Each town also celebrates its patron saint every year with concerts, performances and plenty of eating and drinking, often accompanied by bonfires, exploding fireworks and spectacular illuminations. Then there are the festivals and rituals related to agricultural life, from those celebrating transhumance to those propitiating the harvest. A prominent role is also played by arboreal rituals, the best known of which is the Maggio di Accettura (see boxed text p81), which stages the symbolic marriage between a turkey oak tree and a holly.

Riprendiamoci la storia. Dizionario dei lucani ((Mondadori Electa, Milan 2012) by Angelo Lucano Larodonta is a passionate and engaging collection of stories that re-explores and questions the image of Basilicata's intellectual misery and creative poverty.

Arts

Music & Dance

Italy's south is a land of music, and its popular festivals often showcase the music and dance that testify to the region's exuberance and passion. The hypnotic and obsessive cadences of the taranta, the solemn and melancholy marches of municipal bands, the explosive rhythms of local reggae – these all serve as soundtracks to the many events on the annual calendar. Pop is as important as traditional music and interesting mixes are often created between the two genres. There is also a classical music tradition, driven by the school of Viggiano (p132), which counts among its illustrious former graduates the composer Gesualdo da Venosa (1566–1613), the subject of one of the late singer-songwriter Franco Battiato's most beautiful and unforgettable songs: 'La Cura' (1995).

Taranta, Pizzica & Traditional Music

Black-and-white photographs of tarantism ceremonies show women lying on the ground with their skirts billowing and their bodies tensed in unnatural poses, as if in the throes of a convulsive fit. Such performances are rarely seen nowadays, but the *taranta* and *pizzica* (from *pizzico* or 'bite') are still played at many folk festivals, their vigorous, hypnotic rhythms making people want to get up and dance. *Taranta* music constituted the ritual cure for tarantism – dancing was thought to nullify the effect of the spider's poisonous bite – and accompanied religious celebrations. It's possible that this type of dance derives from practices in force in ancient Greece. When certain symptoms appeared, it was thought that the peasants working in the fields (particularly women cutting grain) had been bitten by a spider, though it's possible they were suffering from convulsive seizures or psychological disorders and so the dance would have a cathartic effect. The ritual was subsequently incorporated into Christianity, and St. Paul (himself a survivor of a spider bite) was chosen as its patron saint, with the power to heal women. Among the groups to have rediscovered and revived this cultural musical heritage are the Tarantolati di Tricarico (www.tarantolatiditricarico.org) and Istamanera from Terranova del Pollino.

Bands and Popular Music

In Basilicata each village has its own song or typical melody. Folk music ensembles perform the melancholic songs sung by the shepherds and peasants of old. The Albanian villages of Pollino boast an Albanian musical tradition inspired by the Arbëreshë culture, characterised mainly by religious or satirical songs sung by female voices accompanied by bagpipes.

Jazz & Contemporary Music

There are a number of blues and rock bands in Basilicata, including, for example, **Le Mani** (www.myspace.com/lemaniband) from Matera; the **Esquelito Band** (www.esquelito.com) from Bernalda; an alternative rock group that won Italia Wave Basilicata 2012; **Fuoco Vivo** (www.fuocovivo.net) from Satriano di Lucania; and **Aeguana Way** (http://aeguanaway.wordpress.com) from Brienza. **Krikka Reggae** (www.krikkareggae.com) perform the warm sounds of Jamaican rhythms, while **Musicamanovella** (www.musicamanovella.it) play folk-rock music. The Lucanian band, which took the stage at Rome's Primo Maggio concert in 2014, takes its inspiration from a famous Irpinian native of Calitri (right on the border between Campania and Basilicata), Vinicio Capossela.

The jazz scene is centred on Matera, where a music festival has been held every year since 1985 (for more details see www.onyxjazzclub.it). It's in Matera that you'll find the **Casa Cava Collective**, a Pugliese-Lucanian group, and musicians like **Rino Locantore**, who has revived the tradition of southern friction drums such as the *cupa cupa*. **Arisa**, who grew up in Pignola and made her debut on the Sanremo stage in 2009, winning in the youth section and again topping the podium in 2014, preforms songs of yesteryear along with pop and jazz. In the pop sphere, the Mediterranean sounds of **Pino Mango**, known artistically by his last name and who sadly passed away in autumn 2014, has enjoyed great success in recent years.

If your soul is dark, there's no shortage of heavy metal sounds in Basilicata. The Agglutination festival is dedicated to it and groups include **Walkyrya**, **Nefertum** and **Omnia Malis Est**.

SOCIETY & CULTURE ARTS

The website www.sassiweb.it is full of up-to-date information on cultural and musical events in Basilicata.

Architecture

Basilicata has been devastated several times by tragic natural disasters, and earthquakes have demolished many superb buildings from its glorious past. However, plenty have survived, ranging from great medieval religious buildings in Romanesque–Gothic style, such as the Cathedral of Acerenza, the Sanctuary of Anglona, the Abbey of San Michele Arcangelo in Montescaglioso, and the frescoed church of the Sanctuary of San Donato in Ripacandida, to the baroque churches of Castelluccio Inferiore, Irsina and Matera.

In architectural terms, Basilicata has two key characteristics: its rock churches and its Norman, Swabian, Angevin and Aragonese fortifications.

The multi-coloured Gravina of Matera makes a strong impression on visitors with its natural scenery. It's a kind of spur that reaches up to the city of Matera, home to the famous sassi which have been declared a Unesco World Heritage Site thanks to their unique historical and architectural value. The Sassi, a veritable urban gem, are the result of a complex stratification of streets, small squares and stairways that took place between the early Middle Ages and the 18th century. Of particular note is the civil architecture, a well-balanced blend of structures dug into the rock and made with materials from the digs, of isolated, overlapping and juxtaposed houses and small palazzi connected by communal inter-linking courtyards. But Matera is just the best-known of a series of rock-hewn settlements created across the Murgia in the Middle Ages. Rock churches dot Basilicata with many in and around Matera featuring decorative Byzantine-inspired paintings.

Successive rulers transformed the area from the late medieval period to the end of the 16th century by building impressive fortifications – counts and barons expanded pre-existing Longobard and Byzantine forts or constructed new strongholds and castles. Many of these are today in ruins or have been extensively re-modelled, but their presence is still discernible in the form and structure of numerous villages, from Brienza and Moliterno to Irsina and Tricarico. Some, however, have survived in good shape and serve as fine examples of fortified architecture from the Norman (Miglionico), Swabian (Melfi and Lagopesole), Angevin (Venosa and Brienza) and Aragonese (Bernalda and Miglionico) periods.

If you're interested in the Sassi of Matera, their history, and how they came to be designated as a Unesco World Heritage Site, check out *Giardini di pietra* by Pietro Laureano (Bollati Boringhieri, Turin 2012).

Sculpture

A little-known chapter of the already little-known history of Lucanian art, sculpture in Basilicata finds its most impressive form in the religious-themed wooden statuary that adorns many of the region's churches. Look for crucifixes, for example, in Irsina's Cathedral, in Miglionico's Chiesa Madre, and in Tursi's Collegiata. Even more numerous are representations of the Madonna. The object of special devotion, these are often housed in villages in the winter months and in mountain shrines in the summer. You'll find them in Viggiano (p133), San Severino Lucano (p144), Abriola (p112) and many other towns.

THE NORMAN CASTLE SYSTEM

Some of the most important castles scattered around Basilicata were built by the Normans, who fortified their kingdom by reinforcing pre-existing structures and, more frequently, by building new ones. A tour of these castles would make an excellent itinerary. Significant stops could include the castles of Castel Lagopesole (Federico II; 13th century; p121, Melfi (Henry VI, late 12th century, and Federico II, 13th century; p125) and Valsinni (11th century; p90). And if you're into the architecture of fortified castles, don't miss those built by Federico II (see boxed text, p170).

There are also some fine examples of stone sculpture. One such is the statue of St. Euphemia in Irsina's cathedral (p73). An authentic Lucanian jewel, albeit an imported one, the work is attributed to Andrea Mantegna, making it the only known sculpture by the Renaissance painter. Matera's cathedral has a stone nativity scene by Altobello Persio (1507–93) of Montescaglioso, creator of the portal of the Abbazia di San Michele in Montescaglioso and statues in the Chiesa di San Nicola in Lagonegro and Ferrandina's Chiesa Madre. Stone sculpture subsequently underwent a more 'artisanal' phase of development as represented by the portals crafted by Lucanian stonemasons to adorn churches and stately palaces – good examples of this include the baroque decor in Castelluccio Inferiore, p143) – and the fountains made for village streets (as in the case of Rotonda, p140). Finally, it should also be mentioned that Matera is home to an important museum dedicated to contemporary sculpture, the MUSMA (p55).

Maternità Divine, an exhibition dedicated to wooden sculpture from Basilicata from the Middle Ages, was hosted at the Basilica di Santa Croce complex in Florence from 2017 to 2018. The catalogue is available from Aska Edizioni (www. askaedizioni.it)

Painting

The Byzantine and medieval frescoes that decorate the walls of the many chapels that lie scattered across the region, often in remote places, are among Basilicata's most interesting art forms. In fact, the history of Lucanian art conventionally takes the frescoes of the Crypt of Original Sin (p68) as its start point. The paintings that adorn the region's rock churches, many of which date to the 10th and 11th centuries, inspired and defined Christian worship in Basilicata. There are many in and around Matera, including extraordinary examples in the monastic complex of Madonna delle Virtù and San Nicola dei Greci (p49) and in the churches of Murgia Timone (p69). But you'll also find superb works of rupestrian art in the Potenza area, in Melfi and Oppido Lucano.

Less relevant is Renaissance painting, which has left very few indigenous traces (such as the remains of frescoes in the Abbazia di San Michele Arcangelo in Montescaglioso) or even imported ones. Standout examples of the latter include Cima da Conegliano's polyptych in the Chiesa di San Francesco in Miglionico and, perhaps, Leonardo Da Vinci's self-portrait in Vaglio di Basilicata. More numerous are works from the late 16th and early 17th centuries, when talented local painters emerged in Basilicata, such as Giovanni Todisco of Abriola, creator of various works that you can still see in his hometown and across the region (including the frescoes in the Convento di Santa Maria in Orsoleo); Giovanni de Gregorio, known as il Pietrafesa, whose works can be found in Potenza, Brindisi di Montagna, Satriano di Lucania and other places in the region; and Pietro Antonio Ferro, famous for the wonderful frescoes in the Cappella del Crocifisso in Tricarico (p78).

Splendori del barocco defilato. Arte in Basilicata e ai suoi confini da Luca Giordano al Settecento (edited by Elisa Acanfora) is the catalogue of an exhibition hosted in Matera in 2009 and dedicated to Basilicata's baroque and rococo visual arts.

Basilicata's baroque art has recently been the subject of studies aimed at enhancing this still little-known heritage. Key to its significance was the presence of artists of the Neapolitan school, such as Gaspare Traversi (some of whose paintings are preserved in Matera at Palazzo Lanfranchi).

The finest exponents of 19th-century Lucanian art were local artists who trained in Italy and abroad but dedicated intense works to their home region. Chief among them was Giacomo Di Chirico (1844–83), an artist from Venosa whose painting *Sposalizio in Basilicata* was exhibited in Paris, Vienna and Munich in the 1970s and 1980s, and Michele Tedesco from Moliterno (1834–1917), who, in 1903, painted *Visita di Zanardelli in Basilicata* to mark a visit by the Italian Prime Minister.

Contemporary Art

Twentieth-century art went through a period of great intensity in the wake of World War II, when Basilicata became the focus of debate on the southern question and a forum for cultural exchanges between personalities such as Carlo Levi and Rocco Scotellaro (see boxed text, p79), Manlio Rossi Doria and Tommaso Pedio. In fact, Carlo Levi's paintings, which can be seen in Matera at Palazzo Lanfranchi (p57) and in Aliano (p95), represent one of the most important artistic chapters of the century. Alongside the northern painter and intellectual, there were also artists who had grown up or matured on Lucanian soil. Among these was Maria Padula (1915–87) from Montemurro who produced neorealist paintings and writings such as *Il vento portava le voci (Story of a Lucanian Girl;* 1985) that were of great interest for understanding Lucanian society and culture. One of the artist's main sources of inspiration was her love for and artistic and cultural collaboration with the adopted Lucanian Giuseppe Antonello Leone (1917–2016). Protagonists of the latter 20th century include the Potenza artist Nino Tricarico (b. 1938), who since the 1980s has worked in 'abstract lyricism'.

You can find interviews with Gaetano Cappelli and Mariolina Venezia at www.letteratura.rai.it – simply go to the site and type the author's name into the search box.

In terms of contemporary sculpture, the Lucanian centre of operations is undoubtedly Matera, where MUSMA (p55) exhibits many works by local artists and international talents. Among these is José Ortega (1921–90), a Spanish painter and sculptor, a student of Picasso and leading exponent of papier-mâché art who was forced to wander around Europe after being sentenced to death by the Franco regime. He arrived in Matera in the 1960s and fell in love with the ancient techniques of working with papier-mâché and terracotta as well as with the Sassi, where you can still find his former home (p51). The Puglia-born sculptor Antonio Paradiso, animator of La Palomba Sculpture Park, also chose Matera (p71). In general, interest in new trends is on the rise, and you'll find exhibitions and expositions being organised in even the smallest towns.

Handicrafts

Pollino Arte is an amazing initiative that attracts big names from the world of contemporary art while also involving local communities. Held at various locations in the park, it features remarkable installations, such as *Earth Cinema* by Anish Kooper in Latronico.

Artistic handicrafts are well represented in Matera. In its workshops (p66) you can buy decorated plates, hand-painted terracotta whistles (*cucú* in the local dialect), often in the shape of cockerels, wooden bread stamps, sculptures in calcarenite, and papier-mâché nativity scenes set in the sassi.

Also of note is the production in Maratea of goods made from the various plant fibres that grow in the area, even if there is no shortage of painted ceramics with the form and colours more typical of nearby Campania. Thus, figurines, jugs, plates and various baskets abound: small containers for fresh ricotta cheese, cane grates used to sun-dry figs and tomatoes and season cheeses, and *cernicchi* (sieves) used for separating pulses from the chaff.

The mix of local Basilicata culture and Arbëreshë traditions (of Albanian culture) has proved fruitful on the eastern side of the Pollino National Park. The custom of making bagpipes (in San Paolo Albanese) and *surduline* (smaller bagpipes, different in structure and different to play, in Terranova di Pollino), as well as shawms and tambourines has been complemented by ancient Albanian methods of spinning cloth and lace. Music lovers will also appreciate Viggiano, which is known for the production of harps (called 'viggianese harps').

Literature

Basilicata's literary tradition originates with the Latin poet Quintus Horatius Flaccus (born in Venosa in 65 BC, died in Rome, 8 BC), aka Horace, author of the *Epodes*, the *Satires*, the *Odes* and the *Epistles* and one of the most celebrated writers of classical antiquity. After the so-called 'dark ages', during which Basilicata actually gave rise to some of Federico II's intellectual and political works, the main literary figure of the Renaissance was the noblewoman and poetess Isabella Morra (p90; 1516–45). She was murdered by her brothers and her ghost is said to wander her former home, the Castello di Valsinni (p90).

The 19th century saw the arrival of politically- and socially-committed writers such as Ferdinando Petruccelli della Gattina, who was born in Moliterno in 1815, and, later, Tommaso Claps of Avigliano, a scholar, journalist and author of many novellas.

In the 20th century Basilicata became a source of inspiration for writers such as Carlo Levi, who in 1945 published *Christ Stopped at Eboli*, as well as home to several poets and writers whose fame extended beyond its regional borders. Among them was the poet Albino Pierro (1916–95), a native of Tursi, who wrote both in Italian and in the archaic dialect of his hometown (among his works is *Ci véra turnè. Poesie nel dialetto di Tursi*). A contemporary of Pierro, Leonardo Sinisgalli (1908–81) was born in Montemurro but emigrated after graduating from secondary school. To learn about his poetry, in which he fused humanistic and scientific culture (he was called 'the poet of the two muses'), geometry and art, mathematics and poetry, look up *Vidi le muse, Horror vacui, L'indovino. Dieci dialoghetti, Intorno alla figura del poeta* and *L'odor moro*. This 'impure' poetry contaminated by social themes and realism seduced Rocco Scotellaro (Tricarico, Matera, 1923–53; see boxed text, p79), whose dazzling poetic oeuvre is contained in the collection *Tutte le poesie 1940–53*. He also wrote *L'uva puttanella. Contadini del sud*. Another interesting figure was Pasquale Festa Campanile (1927–86), a director, screenwriter and writer from Melfi, who published, among other titles, *La strega innamorata*.

Perhaps the most widely read of Basilicata's current authors is Raffaele Nigro (born in Melfi in 1947), a journalist, screenwriter and writer of dialect poems. His *I fuochi del Basento* is an award-winning historical novel with an unconventional literary form. Set between 1784 and 1861, it deals with the themes of peasant life, brigandage and popular devotion. Then there is Gaetano Cappelli (born in Potenza in 1954), author of the award-winning *Storia controversa dell'inarrestabile fortuna del vino Aglianico nel mondo* (2007), *Parenti lontani* (2008), and more recently *Floppy disk* (2018), the story of a bewildered and jobless young man in 1980s Rome. Also an immediate success was the novel *Mille anni che sto qui* (Einaudi, 2006) by Mariolina Venezia (born in Matera in 1961), a family saga set in Grottole. And while the novel won the 2007 Campiello prize, the author (a screenwriter as well as a writer) tried her hand at a detective story by publishing *Come piante tra i sassi* (Einaudi, 2009), set in Matera, and *Maltempo* (2013). Also belonging to the same generation are Giuseppe Lupo (born in 1963), who in 2008 won the Carlo Levi prize for his historical novel *La carovana Zanardelli*, set at the time of the Italian president's visit to Basilicata, and Mimmo Sammartino, who in 2004 published *Vito ballava con le streghe* for the Sellerio publishing house. Inspired by the oral traditions of Castelmezzano, it gave rise to the 'seven stone path' (p110). Basilicata has also inspired works by non-Lucanian writers, ranging from Carlo Levi to Cesare Pavese with his *Fuoco grande* (1959), and Giuseppe Catozzella, one of the best-known voices in contemporary Italian literature and author of *E tu splendi* (Feltrinelli, 2018).

The celebrated ex-pression *carpe diem* (seize the day) and *dulce et decorum est pro patria mori* (it is sweet and fitting to die for one's country) were coined by the Latin poet Horace, who was born in Venosa, on the border between Puglia and Basilicata, on 8 December 65 BCE.

The journalist Raffaele Nigro, who now lives in Bari, is famous for his poems in Melfi dialect. Don't miss his historical novel *I fuochi del Basento* (BUR, Milan 2008), which is set in Puglia, Basilicata and Calabria between 1784 and 1861.

SOCIETY & CULTURE ARTS

Cinema

Matera's cinema debut could hardly be described as triumphant. The town overlooking the Gravina first appeared on the big screen as a symbol of misery and backwardness in southern Italy in Carlo Lizzani's 1949 documentary *Nel Mezzogiorno qualcosa è cambiato* (with a run-time of 22 minutes, it is available to watch at www.cinemadipropaganda. it). Then, in 1953, it provided the location for a tragic neorealist film set in a bleak and primitive southern Italian town, Alberto Lattuada's *La Lupa (The Devil is a Woman)*, based on Giovanni Verga's novella of the same name. About a decade later, in Luigi Zampa's 1962 film *Anni ruggenti (Roaring Years)*, the sassi are used to depict an unspecified place in Puglia, where an insurance agant (Nino Manfredi) is mistaken for a fascist official and showered with attention and favours. The year 1964 saw the birth of a visual correlation that was set to endure, that of the sassi landscape with Palestine. Pier Paolo Pasolini first used this in *Il Vangelo secondo Matteo (The Gospel according to St. Matthew)*, filmed in Matera and Barile. Two decades on and it was the turn of Bruce Beresford's *King David* (1985), followed 20 years later by Mel Gibson's *The Passion of the Christ* (2004). But Matera's fortunes as a film location go beyond the 'religious strand' – in the 1974 film *Allonsanfan* the Taviani brothers use the timeless sassi landscape to set a story that takes place in early 19th-century southern Italy. In 1979 Francesco Rosi's *Christ Stopped at Eboli* was released, starring an introspective Gian Maria Volonté as Carlo Levi. Matera also pops up in some scenes in Francesco Rosi's 1981 film *I tre fratelli (The Three Brothers)*, which features the Italy of the *anni di piombo* (years of lead) and its many contradictions, and in Giuseppe Tornatore's 1995 *L'Uomo delle Stelle (Man of the Stars)*. More recently, Matera finally got to play itself in Federica di Giacomo's 2006 documentary *Il lato grottesco della vita (The Grotesque Side of Life)*, which tells of two unauthorised tour guides who roam the alleyways, inventing new stories about the city every day, and in Matteo Rovere's 2016 *Veloce come il Vento (Italian Race)*, where it sets the stage for a reckless rally race. However, its success as a location for major films continues and it appeared in the 2016 remake of *Ben-Hur* and Patty Jenkins' *Wonder Woman* (2017). Its crowning glory, though, came in 2021, when the sassi provided the backdrop for *No Time to Die*, and James Bond's legendary Aston Martin hurtled around the city's narrow alleyways.

The rest of Basilicata also appears on the big screen in a film that leaves no room for optimism. *I basilischi (The Lizards)* by Lina Wertmül-ler (who at the time, in 1963, had already worked with Fellini) tells of the meaningless lives led by three young people in a provincial town (it was filmed in Palazzo San Gervasio in Basilicata and the Pugliese towns of Minervino Murge and Spinazzola). Decades later, Gabriele Salvatores released *Io non ho paura (I'm Not Scared)* in 2003. Based on the book of the same name by Niccolò Ammanniti, it's set in the wheat fields of Vulture, where the golden colours of the semi-deserted landscape frame a dramatic story and a mesmerising sequence of images. Decidedly more light-hearted, though no less compelling, is the portrait of the Lucanian land that emerges from *Basilicata Coast to Coast* (2010) by Rocco Papaleo (born in Lauria in 1958). The film follows a group of friends as they set out to walk to Maratea and, amid guitars and fishing rods, falling in love and quarrelling, get as far as Scanzano Jonico by way of Trecchina, Lauria, Tramutola, Aliano and the ghost town of Craco. Craco itself deserves a mention as the place of choice for Lucanian cinema outside Matera, having hosted filming for Fabio Segatori's gripping 1999 film *Terra Bruciata (The Wasteland)* and Dagen Merril's *Murder in the Dark* (2011). Also worthy of mention is the 2012 TV miniseries *Il generale dei briganti* by Paolo Poeti, which plunges into Lucanian history and highlights the exploits of the brigand Carmine Crocco in and around Melfi, Venosa, San Fele and Castel Lagopesole, and Massimo Gaudioso's 2015 *La Grande Seduzione* (with Silvio Orlando and Fabio Volo) which was filmed in the small village of Castelmezzano (in the Lucanian Dolomites).

Environment

The Italian peninsula is shaped like a boot with Basilicata forming the arch of the foot. Its distinct and varied landscapes offer opportunities for nature enthusiasts to visit and explore in every season of the year.

Half mountain, half hill – this is how you can divide Basilicata, which covers an area of just under 10,000 sq km. Extending south of the volcanic area of Vulture, the Apennine zone includes some of the highest massifs in the southern Apennines. Five groups can be distinguished: the ridge of the Monti di Muro, Bella and Avigliano, south of which begins the minor group of the Monti Li Foi di Picerno; west of these, the Maddalena range only partially touches Lucanian territory; the Valle del Melandro and the upper Valle dell'Agri separate the Maddalena chain from the Vulturino mountain complex; further south, the Apennine ridge rises to form the Monti del Lagonegrese with the two summits of Monti del Papa and Madonna del Sirino and, on the border with Calabria, the peaks of Monte Pollino.

Basilicata's entire eastern flank is occupied by a hilly area, which, thanks to the particular composition of its soil, is constantly being reshaped by erosive phenomena. The result of this is the presence, in the Lower Val d'Agri and Matera area, of extensive badlands where vegetation finds it hard, sometimes even impossible, to survive.

The main flat areas are to be found in the Metaponto plain, which was itself formed by the continuous accumulation of eroded material brought downstream by Basilicata's numerous rivers. The name is of Greek derivation and comes from the union of the words *meta* and *pontos*, meaning 'beyond the sea,' or 'overseas'.

Thanks to its varied topography, Basilicata has a rich and articulated river network. Among the watercourses that originate in Lucanian territory, some lie entirely within the region (Agri, Basento, Bradano, Cavone and Sinni) and flow into the Ionian Sea, while others, such as the Noce, Ofanto, and some tributaries of the Sele, cross it only in part and continue beyond the region to the Tyrrhenian or Adriatic seas. The total length of Basilicata's coastline is 70km, of which 30km skirt the Tyrrhenian Sea, while the other 40km extend gently along the Ionian Sea.

Lay of the Land

Over the centuries, human activity has transformed uncultivated land into fertile vineyards, olive groves and citrus orchards, and extensive woodlands into wheat fields and pasture land. Elsewhere, the region displays the strange characteristics of its nature in its original form. A volcanic imprint is evident at Monte Vulture, where an extinct crater is now occupied by the Laghi di Monticchio and lush vegetation thrives on its slopes. In the Matero area, multicoloured reflections come off the clay hills that make up the arid, lunar and fascinating landscape of the badlands, while the signs of erosion and landslides are evident in the ghost village of Craco.

In the Murgia, water has furrowed deeply into the rock to create a landscape of caves and grottoes, some of which (such as Matera's famous sassi) have been inhabited since prehistoric times.

Basilicata's mountains are not especially high, but there are still several imposing peaks. The highest is Monte Pollino (2248m), which is pitted by deep valleys, karst caves and volcanic gorges. Topping off at 2000m is the Sirino Massif, where evidence has been found of the last glaciation.

South of Potenza, wind and water erosion has created bizarre karst formations and carved deep fissures in the Apennine sandstone. In this astonishing landscape, remote stone villages cling precariously to the high rocky spires of the Lucanian Dolomites, providing the perfect setting for folk legends populated by sprites and werewolves.

Climate

The region's climate varies enormously – you can head to the beach between spring and autumn and ski in autumn and winter. The mountains have a typical continental climate, while that of the Ionian and Tyrrhenian coasts is more typically Mediterranean. Linking the two zones is the Matera hinterland, particularly the area around Vulture. Rainfall in Basilicata is very erratic, meaning that streams can quickly fill with water and then run dry just as fast.

Natural Environments

The low population density of some inland areas, determined by the harsh character of the land, has enabled nature to remain largely un-spoiled. Some of the most important areas of natural interest have been included in the Natura 2000 Network. A European Union initiative to conserve biodiversity, this is an EU-wide ecological network aimed at ensuring the long-term survival of natural habitats and threatened or rare species of flora and fauna. The Natura 2000 Network in Basilicata today consists of 54 Special Areas of Conservation, 1 SCI (Site of Community Importance) and 17 SPAs (Special Protected Areas), covering 17.1 percent of the regional area.

Animals

On the Natura 2000-Regione Basilicata website (http://natura 2000basilicata.it) you can find fact sheets on every type of plant, amphibian, mammal and bird in Basilicata, as well as nature itineraries and audio guides for learning about the region.

Basilicata's diverse habitats have given rise to a rich and varied fauna. Needless to say, it's in the areas of the Natura 2000 Network that you'll find the species of greatest conservation interest. The term Lucania, by which this region rich in protected areas is identified, is sometimes linked to the Greek word for wolf. And this large carnivore is, in fact, one of Basilicata's most representative species. It was from here that the wolf set out to reconquer other parts of Italy where it had almost become extinct in the early 20th century.

Other significant mammals include the elusive wildcat and, in hilly forests, the porcupine with its crepuscular and nocturnal habits. A special regional project has been set up to protect the endangered otter, which is also present.

The spectacled salamander is one of Basilicata's most important, and rarest, amphibians. It can be distinguished by its black and white body, the vivid red colouration of its undertail, and a light spot on the head between its V-shaped eyes. It lives in environments ranging from Mediterranean scrubland to damp beech groves, fir woods and oak forests, from areas a few metres above sea level to 1500m above sea level, and especially in hilly areas between 300 and 900m.

Also present are many birds, fish and invertebrates. Notable among its birdlife are some of Italy's most important birds of prey, including the short-toed eagle, Egyptian vulture, kestrel, lanner falcon and red kite.

Flora

The historical name of Lucania derives from the word '*lucus*' meaning forest, and it is the *pino loricato* (Heldreich's pine; see boxed text p184) that best symbolises the region's forests. The tree colonised southern Italy when the European continent was still covered with glaciers and so it is a true arboreal patriarch, capable of adapting to wind and the cold by contorting its trunk.

Beech forests are common in Apennine mountain areas while white oak forests thrive in Mediterranean parts and tamarisks flourish along the region's rivers and streams. Dunes and estuaries host plenty of vegetation in coastal areas. In total, Basilicata boasts some 2350 plant species, a large number given its modest surface area. Of particular note is the number of endemic plant species, 168, which represents 6.8 percent of the region's total flora, one of the highest values in Italy.

Parks & Protected Natural Areas

In addition to the areas that are part of the European Natura 2000 Network, Basilicata boasts two national parks, three regional parks, eight state reserves and seven regional reserves, covering a total area of 198,047 hectares.

Located near the national parks of Pollino (between Basilicata and Calabria) and Cilento (Campania), and covering and area of 68,996 hectares, **Parco Nazionale Lucano Val d'Agri-Lagonegrese** (www.parco appenninolucano.it) represents an area of connection and environmental continuity. It includes some of the highest peaks in the Lucanian Apennines, and closes off the upper Agri river valley like a fan. Its extensive length accommodates various environments, from forests of beech and characteristic silver fir to expanses of woods punctuated by meadows and pastures.

The Parco Nazionale Lucano Val d'Agri-Lagonegrese is Italy's youngest national park: it was established in 2007.

The presence of vast cultivated areas testifies to long-standing human activity in the area. Visitors can immerse themselves in the area's traditions, art and culture by exploring the archaeological area of Grumentum and various destinations of religious interest as well as its natural attractions.

From the 300m-high Murgia di Sant'Oronzo to the 2005m Monte Papa, the landscape boasts a diverse and species-rich flora. The most interesting areas lie between 1000 and 1800m. Here the dominant tree is the beech. In the park's northernmost reaches, the slopes of Monte Surranetta are cloaked in a vast forest where beech trees thrive alongside Turkey oaks, hazels, and some species of maples and hornbeams at lower altitudes. The most impressive forest stands atop the crown of peaks formed by the Serra di Calvello, Volturino, Madonna di Viggiano, Sant'Enoc and Caldarosa mountains. High-altitude grasslands host valuable endemic species, while lower down, in the hilly belt up to 500m, Mediterranean vegetation and holm oak dominate. Depending on altitude and exposure, holm oaks may give way to mixed groves of Turkey oaks and downy oaks, often with other deciduous species. In areas of gentler terrain, holm oaks rise to form small woods rich in junipers.

Of particular value are the oak woods of the Fieghi-Cerreto Regional State Forest, located in Piano dei Campi at the foot of Mt. Raparo.

Oak forests rich in mushrooms and truffles surround Lago di Pietra del Pertusillo. Further species of oak, holm oak, mastic, juniper, phillyrea, cistus and broom enrich the valley's outer edges. Beneath, the Agri river flows through the valley, its waters feeding a forest that's particularly impressive in spring with its blooming poplars, willows and viburnums.

Parco Nazionale del Pollino (www.parcopollino.it), the largest protected area in Italy at 192,565 hectares, comprises elements of a mosaic

HELDREICH'S PINE

Heldreich's pine (*Pinus leucodermis*) is the institutional symbol and iconic image of the Parco del Pollino. It characterises the mountain and high-altitude vegetation of the Pollino in a unique way, growing either in groups or in isolation on inaccessible crests and rock faces, far from the sun-facing plains, where they struggle tenaciously against the wind and weather. The pine arrived in the Calabrian-Lucanian area in ancient times and it can generally be observed at altitudes between 550m and 2200m above sea level. Its bark is light grey in colour, particularly on young plants, while on mature examples it is fissured into irregular plates, called *loriche*, which resemble ancient Roman armour. During its long life it can reach heights of 40m and diameters of more than one metre. The properties of the wood allow the stem and branches to survive beyond their natural life, transforming the plant into a veritable sculpture. In the past, its wood was used for the construction of boats and furniture. It was also used, in the first half of the 20th century, to create the trunks with which emigrants left Pollino in search of their fortune in America.

in which history and human action have conspired to create emotions, stories and landscapes of great allure. The Lucanian side of the park is soft and wooded, unlike the Calabrian side which is far more rugged. The park's tallest peak, from which it takes its name, is also Basilicata's highest point. Its lower reaches are traversed to the north by the Sinni river, which carries eroded material from the massif's uppermost slopes.

From the park's highest mountains, the western Tyrrhenian coasts of Maratea, Praia a Mare, and Belvedere Marittimo are all visible to the naked eye, while to the east, you can see the Ionian coast stretching from Sibari to Metaponto. The park boasts a wealth of plant species, as well as some rare ecosystems, and together these combine to make the area unique in the Mediterranean basin. In the areas closest to the coast and up to 700m to 800m above sea level, Mediterranean scrubland prevails, with holm oaks, mastics, various species of juniper, myrtle, strawberry tree, downy oak, Montpellier maples and common broom. On sandy and rocky soils, the vegetation is low-lying and sparse and takes the name 'garrigue.' It's characterised by the presence of cistus, thyme and arboreal wall germander. Elsewhere, tracts of 'Mediterranean steppe' are cloaked in perennial grass species. It should also be noted that in certain areas of the park, for example along the sunniest faces of the San Lorenzo, Cassano and Porace mountains, the Mediterranean scrubland sports some juniper specimens up to 900m altitude. This is due to microclimatic conditions caused by the rock's capacity to accumulate heat. Above 800m and up to 1100m, different varieties of oak prevail: downy oaks, Turkey oaks and Hungarian oaks, often growing together or in mixed forests with oriental hornbeams, maples, chestnuts and Neapolitan alders. Other notable forest formations include the maple woods on the Ionian slopes of Monte Sparviere. Here five species co-exist extraordinarily well: the field maple, sycamore maple, Lobel's maple, Hungarian maple and Norwegian maple.

In higher areas, forests are largely made up of beech trees, either growing on their own or alongside chestnuts, Turkey oaks and maples. At lower altitudes the beech thrives with holly and Hungarian maples; at higher altitudes and in ravines, beeches grow with Lobel's maples and, on the northern slopes of the protected area, white spruces. On the southern slope of the massif, up to about 1700m, formations of black pine appear. Grasslands and high-altitude pastures extend around the mountains' karst plateaus and upper reaches. The wealth and variety of the area's flowers provides a stunning spectacle in spring. Among the most common species you'll see are the common yarrow, great yellow gentian, mountain asphodel, poet's narcissus, spring crocus, woolly buttercup and various types of orchid.

Other Parks

The **Parco Regionale di Gallipoli Cognato e Piccole Dolomiti Lucane** (p81), rises in the heart of Basilicata, spanning the provinces of Potenza and Matera, and highlighting the contrast between the dense Gallipoli Cognato Forest on one side and the rocky spires and sandstone peaks of the Lucanian Apennines overlooking the Valle del Basento on the other. The other regional park is the **Parco della Murgia Materana** (p68), which is pitted with prehistoric caves, rocky monastic settlements, precipices and stony ground. Birdwatchers might also enjoy a visit to the inland Ionian wetlands of the **Riserva Naturale Bosco Pantano di Policoro** (p88) and the **Riserva Naturale Oasi di San Giuliano** (p76).

Basilicata's Cuisine

"Better to go to bed hungry than get up in debt". This ancient regional proverb tells of a harsh land where in times past it wasn't uncommon to go to sleep on an empty stomach. This certainly won't be your problem these days.

Food festivals in Basilicata are mainly held in summer and during the Christmas and Easter holidays, when emigrants return home and villages repopulate for a few weeks. They are cheerful and lively events (though far less crowded than similar festivals in neighbouring Puglia), with stalls of local specialties, live music, wine and traditional dancing.

Today people come to Basilicata not only for its stunning landscapes and artistic beauty, but also for its cuisine – for its wine and oil and its many land and sea products. What's more, the prices in many places, even in high season, compare very favourably with those in other, more touristy destinations in Italy. The flavours, aromas and recipes of Lucanian cuisine will often remind you that the history of this region is also one of struggle and hardship, of poverty even. Many traditional dishes are based on modest ingredients that could be found in the kitchens of even the humblest of peasants – bread and legumes, some vegetables and the poorest cuts of meat. In this land of conquest and passage, culinary richness comes from the people who passed through: the Swabians are credited with introducing radishes and horseradish, and the Arabs with citrus fruits and almonds. The Spanish promoted the cultivation of tomatoes and potatoes while the stewed octopus of the Metaponto area distinctly recalls the flavours of Greek cuisine. A poor food culture, then, but one that's varied and mixed, and which today benefits from the territory's great resources and a renewed attention to typical local products. These include PGI-designated (Protected Geographical Indication) foodstuffs like Sarconi beans, sweet peppers from Senise, canestrato cheese from Moliterno and bread from Matera; PDO-designated (Protected Designation of Origin) products such as pecorino cheese from Filiano, red aubergines from Rotonda and olive oil from Vulture; and Slow Food recognised foods, which in Basilicata are *caciocavallo podolico* cheese, the Pantano di Pignola red bean, Ferrandina's baked olive, the signora pear from the Valle del Sinni, and the *pezzente* sausage from the Matera mountains. And then there are cardoncelli mushrooms, eaten since Roman times, that flourish on the Pugliese and Lucanian Murgia; *lampascioni* (wild onions); salt cod in all its variations; fresh and aged cheeses; and goat, lamb and pork meat. Pork also provides the raw material for the *lucanica* or *luganega* sausage, whose flavours were praised by the ancient writers Apicius, Cicero, Martial and Varro. Tasty, Mediterranean, but hardly light, Lucanian cuisine is decidedly earthy, the ideal partner for mineral waters from the Vulture and the king of Lucanian red wines, his majesty, Aglianico.

Specialities
Bread & Baked Goods
Like Altamura's famous bread, *pane* (bread) from Matera (which is less than 20km from Puglia's baking capital) is tasty and crunchy, its ancient recipe calling for the exclusive use of durum wheat semolina. When cut in half, it can serve as a basket for *ciambottella,* a succulent mix of onion, peppers and sausage. Once stale it can be used in the preparation of

recipes such as *pan cotto* (a kind of bread soup), *cialledda* (a traditional salad) and *muddica fritta* (fried breadcrumbs added to enrich fresh pasta sauces). Matera is also home to *friselle*, slices of crusty bread that are eaten topped with tomato and oil. The production centre of biscuits, however, lies to the west towards the Tyrrhenian coast – stop in Bernalda to taste *scorzetta* (a typical sweet made of hazelnuts and egg whites); in Trecchina to try walnut biscuits and chestnut cakes; and in Maratea for the Lucanian version of *bocconotti* (sweet pastries).

Pasta

You could say that everything was born in Basilicata (at least from a documentary point of view) in that the first record we have of Italian food par excellence was written by Horace, a citizen of the Lucanian town of Venosa.

You'll be spoiled for choice when it comes to homemade pasta. Typical of the region are *frizzuli* (fusilli), which are usually seasoned with sautéed bread crumbs and sweet bell peppers (in Pietrapertosa, they traditionally add chopped walnuts to the dish on Palm Sunday), and which are particularly tasty with the addition of pecorino and horse-radish. Then there are *capunti*, so called because they are hollowed out with four fingers and not with an iron; *manate di Vaglio*, a fesh pasta prepared with eggs; and *mischiglio*, which takes its name from the mix of fava bean and chickpea flour typical of the Chiaromonte area. The Maratea area, on the other hand, favours *lagane*, a wide ribbon pasta typically served with chickpeas or beans.

Cheese

Basilicata is strong on cheese. It's difficult to choose from the wide range of fresh and aged cheeses. Famous varieties include *cacioricotta*, the salty and intensely flavoured *pecorino di Filiano*, *canestrato di Moliterno* (named after the custom of storing it in reed baskets), and *caciocavallo*, whose name is perhaps a reference to the mare's milk with which it was once prepared or to the fact that it used to be carried hanging over a horse's back. The most popular variety here is made in small quantities from the milk of Podolica cows which graze wild on the region's meadows. But if you prefer soft, stringy fresh cheeses to aged cheeses, don't miss Massa's tasty braided mozzarella, *casieddu* (fat, fresh, and wrapped in fern leaves), and Paddaccio del Massiccio del Pollino, an excellent goat's cheese that can only be enjoyed between June and September.

Meat

It has been ingrained since ancient times not to waste anything and use even the least prized parts of the animal (the head, tail, cow, pig or sheep hooves) as well as the offal. Tasty and succulent, offal can be divided into red meats (liver, heart, lungs, kidneys, spleen, tongue) and white

The most wide-spread cattle breed in Basilicata is the *podolica*, which is hardy and able to withstand the tough environmental conditions. Its milk is used to produce *caciocavallo* cheese, an icon of the southern dairy tradition, which lends itself to prolonged aging (especially large pieces can be aged for up to four or five years).

TIPS FOR TASTING THE LOCAL CUISINE

➡ Never decline something offered by friends or relatives, even if you're well beyond being full. The offense would be terrible.

➡ Eat lamb with your hands.

➡ When you order wine, keep it local; ideally go for majestic Aglianico.

➡ If you're vegetarian, take it philosophically. Ask about ingredients but don't be shocked if your host fails to see how a little lard and a couple of pieces of bacon to flavour the sauce and vegetable side dish might bother you.

GASTRONOMIC CALENDAR

⇒ **January** The flavours of the beautiful season are resurrected in the form of dried legumes and preserves. Look out for *crusco* peppers and *cardoncelli* (king trumpet mushrooms) from the previous autumn and aubergines marinated in olive oil. It's also the period for *lampascioni* (bitter wild onions), which are excellent in olive oil, and winter truffles.

⇒ **February** The main focus is the preparation of dried and smoked meats, and once again pork takes centre stage in Basilicata. The region is famous for its salami and sausages (local pigs are fed natural foods such as acorns). Chief among these is the *lucanica* or *luganega*, which is flavoured with fennel, pepper, salt and chilli. There's also *soppressata* and *pezzente*, a cured meat much loved by gourmets and aficionados of local food that's prepared with pork scraps and sweet or spicy peppers from Senise. In the Potenza area it's also used to prepare a meat sauce called *ndrupp'c*, to which a grating of horseradish is added at Carnival. Others to try include *rafanata* (a sweet black pudding) and *chiacchiere* (ribbons of fried dough).

⇒ **March** The spring months and Easter are ideal for lamb. Nothing is thrown away: the innards are used in the preparation of *gnummareddi*, meat rolls that are excellent but not to everyone's taste. If you prefer the more refined cuts, Basilicata has some of the best lamb in Italy. Meat sauces pair triumphantly with fresh pastas, especially the ragù prepared with lamb, pork and kid, and flavoured with herbs. If you find yourself in Rotondella you could also sample a succulent *pastizz*, a golden calzone (typical of Easter festivities) stuffed with ricotta cheese, eggs, herbs and pork and lamb meat. Another seasonal highlight are Ferrandina's baked olives, which reach the end of their processing in this period.

⇒ **April** Spring arrives and with it come vegetables such as chicory and wild asparagus. Noteworthy among the region's fresh cheeses is mozzarella from Massa (a tiny hamlet near Maratea), *stracciatella*, *casieddu* from Moliterno, and *burrino* (or manteca) made from *podolico* cow's milk and widespread around Vulture and in the Lucanian Dolomites. Don't miss Filiano's interpretation of *fave e pecorino* (fava beans and pecorino cheese), with its hard, crumbly, and somewhat spicy texture. Ricotta abounds, fresh and seasoned, and enriches desserts with ancient flavours, such as *falagone*. This sweet of Turkish origin uses goat ricotta mixed with eggs, mint and sugar to fill a simple pastry made from yeast, lard, flour and milk.

⇒ **May** While enjoying a foretaste of summer on the Lucanian coast, take the chance to eat some fish. This is the ideal time to try some freshly caught octopus, cuttlefish or squid (it's the breeding season so they're easier to catch). Try Maratea's soup and fried fish, and attend an arboreal ritual (p81) to fill up on cured meat, cheese, stuffed calzones and fried sweets, which abound during the festivities. If the weather is good you'll find it's time for peaches and apricots. Strawberries, especially the Candonga variety, are already in full season.

⇒ **June** It's the beginning of the tomato season. In the countryside, you'll see branches laden with ripe cherries, peaches, apricots, plums and pears – the San Giuvan variety ripens in this, the very month dedicated to the saint (San Giovanni or St John) and has a fresh, sweet taste

meats (brain, bone marrow, sweetbreads from salivary glands, thymus and pancreas, tripe). Regional offal dishes include *gnummareddi*, rolls of liver, lung and kidney tightly wrapped in lamb or kid intestine, and, of course, *pezzente* sausage, prepared with finely chopped throat, gristle, various harder-to-cook muscles, stomach, and leftover fat. Traditionally, nothing is ever thrown away from a pig. The slaughtering of a pig was often an occasion for a family reunion (especially in Basilicata) and to mark the event the pig's cleaned head would be displayed in the family window with a large orange in its mouth. Still today you'll find many delicious pork-based cured meats on Basilicata's tables, ranging from sausage (perhaps seasoned with sweet red bell peppers and fennel seeds) to *soppressata* (a type of salami). Meat lovers should also try *cutturidd*, a hearty stew of ancient pastoral tradition that's made with mutton (or that goes perfectly with salty, spicy pecorino. You'll also get a spicy aftertaste from the wild rocket that adds flavour to bruschetta, pasta dishes, salads and pizzas.

➡ **July** The long harvest of the peppers that blaze across Senise's landscape begins. In the fields, aubergines have also reached maturity. In Rotonda, in the Pollino area, are red eggplants, probably imported from Africa in the 19th century, which look like a mix between an aubergine and a tomato . You'll find them throughout the year canned or in jars with oil or vinegar, but now is the time to consume them fresh. Try them grilled or stuffed with stale bread, garlic, percorino cheese, eggs and capers.

➡ **August** It's time for figs, perhaps the pink figs of Pisticci, which you can taste reduced in syrup (*ficotto*) together with aged cheese. It's also the period for hot chilli peppers, which inflame many summer preparations. In August, strawberries, raspberries and Basilicata's red fruits ripen. This is also the month to taste street food classics such as focaccia and calzoni or, in Matera maybe, a cold *cialledda* (salad of dried bread, tomatoes, olive oil and salt).

➡ **September** It's time for the grape harvest, but in Vulture it's still early for the Aglianico grapes. Better to turn your attention to snails (or *uddratieddri*, the stars of an August festival in Irsina) and mushrooms, the most popular of which are the fragrant, meaty, wild *cardoncelli* (king trumpet mushrooms), so called because they grow near wild thistles (*cardi* in Italian). The legume harvest that began in August continues, and in the Pollino area there's nothing better than a plate of *patane e vajane* (potatoes and bean pods or mashed green beans).

➡ **October** The weather is still mild, but sometimes the air cools – a good time for a bowl of grain and pulse soup, such as Matera's *crapiata*. In October the Aglianico grapes are harvested, and the first cold weather brings chestnuts, which can be savoured roasted over a fire or on a griddle. Nothing that can top the warm, welcoming atmosphere of a chestnut festival in a little village set amid chestnut-clad hills.

➡ **November** Once the olive harvest has finished, it's time to extract the liquid gold that enriches so many Lucanian dishes. Now's also the time to taste those cherry tomatoes that have been conserved to give some colour and flavour to the grey winter months. Left hanging since summer, they're packed with flavour and, with oil, make the ideal topping for bruschetta. Kiwis are also coming into maturity in this period.

➡ **December** The popularity of *baccalà* (dried salted cod) makes it possible to eat fish even when the weather makes fishing difficult, and to eat it inland (it's not for nothing that it's called 'mountain fish'). Many Lucanian dishes use it, and in the Christmas period it's often prepared with *crusco* peppers. Christmas is also the time for sweets, which in the Lucanian tradition, as in almost all poor cuisines, abound during festivities. There are *cartellate* and *pettole* (fried dough sweetened with vincotto or honey); walnut cakes from Trecchina; *calzoncelli* (fried ravioli stuffed with chestnuts); *mostaccioli* (pastries made with chocolate, almonds, cinnamon and cloves); and Santa Lucia's *cuccia* (wheat cooked for a few hours with honey).

lamb) slowly cooked in an earthenware pot with vegetables, mushrooms, tubers and perhaps a few chunks of old salami and cheese. And then there are meat sauces, which are ideal to serve with all kinds of pasta and are generally prepared with three different meat (lamb, pork and kid). Sometimes *pezzente* sausage is added to enrich the sauce, as is typical in the Potenza area.

Fish

Lucanian cuisine was and remains predominantly land-based, but on the Tyrrhenian and Ionian coasts (where fishing is more developed) you'll come across plenty of fresh fish dishes. In Roman times Maratea was famous for the preparation of *garum*, a sauce similar to today's *colatura* (anchovy fish sauce), while today it's its fish soup that reigns supreme.

Over in the Metaponto area, it's not uncommon to find *sarde in scapece* (fried sardines marinated in vinegar). More widespread is *baccalà* (dried salted cod), which is prepared in many ways but is traditionally paired with sweet *crusco* peppers. You can also enjoy freshwater fish, such as trout from Nemoli or eels fished in the region's lakes. These are usually cooked with chillies, tomato, mint and bay leaves as per the recipe for a dish called *anguilla di pantano*.

Fruit & Vegetables

Basilicata produces many vegetables. Of particular note are the tomatoes from Massa (they're also grown in Castrocucco), which are large and purplish-red in colour. The same area is also known for its spicy cherry or cornetto peppers, which are conserved in bunches or braids. Another regional star is the Senise bell pepper, which you'll find sold everywhere and which features in many local dishes – its thin skin and low water content make it ideal for natural drying and for it to be cooked *crusco* (fried in oil and served crispy). Eggplants are red in Rotonda and purple in the rest of Basilicata. The former, a designated Slow Food presidium, are eaten fresh: they're conserved in jars of oil or vinegar or, like tomatoes and peppers, tied in clusters and placed to dry under the roof. Most of Basilicata's fruit is produced on the Metapontine plain – in addition to *staccia* oranges from Tursi, pink figs from Pisticci and apricots from Rotondella, you can also bite into red fruit (especially strawberries and raspberries), kiwis, peaches, pears and grapes.

Sweets

Traditional Lucanian desserts are simple preparations. They are made with few ingredients but sometimes feature daring combinations. A case in point is sweet black pudding (now rarely prepared according to the traditional recipe) which is made with pig's blood, cooked must, dark chocolate, raisins, lemon peel, cinnamon and sugar. Chestnut cakes and *paparotta*, made with wine must, flour, sugar and spices (usually cinnamon and cloves), often appear on autumnal tables, while fried sweets (honey *crustole*, *cartellate*, *pettole*) feature in village festivals throughout the year, and especially at Carnival. Biscuits abound, too: among the best-known are walnut biscuits from Trecchina and Bernalda's *scorzette*. Made with almonds, hazelnuts, egg whites and sugar, these were created in 1977 by a pastry chef from Salerno, Vincenzo Spinelli, who then went on to trademark them in 2013 to stave off imitations. Also on the menu are various recipes imported from neighbouring regions and then reinvented, such as *pastiera* (a sweet tart made with eggs and ricotta cheese) and *bocconotto* (a type of stuffed pastry).

Ferula Viaggi (www. ferulaviaggi.it), in Matera, is an excellent agency that organises tastings and food-themed tours on which you can see mozzarella being made and taste local wines.

Wine

Wine production in Basilicata dates back to ancient times and the region's best vineyards occupy the steep, volcanic slopes of the Vulture area. This is where Lucania's most prized red wine is produced from the Aglianico grape variety, which was perhaps introduced by the Greeks but is now found across the region. The wine's distinctive characteristics owe much to the volcanic soil of Monte Vulture, which gives it a harmonious, velvety flavour that pairs perfectly with Lucanian meats. Basilicata's other DOC (*denominazione di origine controllata*) wines are less renowned and less widespread, but still enjoyable: Matera white, rosé and red from the Terre dell'Alta Val d'Agri, and Grottino di Roccanova (red, white or rosé).

Survival Guide

Directory A-Z

Accessible Travel

Basilicata isn't well furnished with infrastructure to meet the needs of travellers who use wheelchairs. Only a few museums provide wheelchair access, and only a few high-end hotels are equipped with adequate facilities. Roads are often cobbled, and it's worth mentioning that the region's terrain is almost entirely hilly and mountainous.

However, the public administration is looking at accessibility for residents and visitors, and is considering establishing a Disability Manager role dedicated to this important subject. To keep up with the latest news, check out the following sites, which contain practical information for people with reduced mobility and are continuously updated:

- www.isassidimatera.com/ guida-matera/itineraries/ visiting-matera-with-disabilities

- www.handysuperabile. org/property/guida-turistica-di-matera-con-info-accessibilita-disabili (download the photo report)

Lonely Planet's *Accessible Travel Online Resources* lists numerous online resources useful for trip planning and and organising stays around the world. You can download

it for free at media.lonely planet.com/shop/media/ accessible-travel-online-resources.pdf.

Useful Websites

Accessible Europe (accessi bleeurope.com)

Accessable Tourism Italy (accessibletourism.italy.com/en/)

Disabili.com (www.disabili .com)

LP Tour (www.lptour.it)

Matera Welcome (matera welcome.it/en/tourismo -accessibile/)

Places of Culture For information see www.accessibi litamusei.beniculturali.it/ luoghi-cultura/index?catego riald=&denomitazione=

Parking For information see www.aci.it/i-servizi/per-la -mobilita/aci-per-il-sociale/ contrassegno-disabili.html

Getting Around

Trenitalia's (train travel) assistance service for passengers with disabilities and reduced mobility can be contacted by calling the **toll-free number** (🖉800 906 060, from fixed line only; ⊙6.45am-9.30pm daily), or the **RFI national number** (🖉02 32 32 32, ordinary rate, from fixed line or mobile; ⊙6.45am-9.30pm daily). For more information, visit www. trenitalia.com and follow the links for 'Info and assistance' > 'Assistance and contacts' > 'For people with reduced mobility'. If you're travelling with

Italo (www.italotreno.it) you'll find information at 'Traveling with Italo' > 'Assistance for people with reduced mobility'.

Accommodation

Basilicata's accommodation is constantly improving. There's an increasing number of B&Bs and agriturismi (farm stays), as well as more luxurious establishments, particularly in Matera and Maratea. Over time, the concept of the *albergo diffuso* has also taken root, leading to the revival and redevelopment of many old, sometimes abandoned, buildings, villages and quarters which

DISCOUNT CARDS

DISCOUNT CARDS	CONTACT	PRICE
Camping Card International	www.campingcardinternational.com; ☑055 88 23 91; www.federcampeggio.it	€40 two-adult family digital card; €43 one-adult family paper card; €45 two-adult family paper card valid until December 31 of year of issue
Carta Giovani Nazionale (National Youth Card)	https://giovani2030.it/iniziativa/carta-giovani-nazionale/	Digital card available through the IO App for young people aged between 18 and 35 resident in Italy. It provides discounts (for people aged up to 35 years on the national circuit, up to 30 on the EYCA circuit – www.eyca.org) on goods, services, activities and opportunities.
Hostelling International	www.hihostels.com	€20 digital card valid for one year from the date of issue
International Student/ Youth/Teacher Identity Card	www.isic.org	€13 digital card valid for one year from the date of issue
IoStudio – Student Card	http://iostudio.pubblica.istruzione.it	Distributed free of charge by schools to all high school students; valid for the duration of the pupil's school career

are restored and converted into apartments and guest rooms, managed by a single, centralised reception.

Campgrounds in Basilicata are mostly large complexes with swimming pools, restaurants, and supermarkets. They usually offer bungalows and/or apartments, in addition to tent pitches and RV sites. Almost all campgrounds are only open between April and October, and some only open from June to September.

In this guide, accommodation listings in the Sleeping sections are listed in ascending order of price and then by author preference within the price categories. Prices quoted are the maximum high season rates.

Useful Websites

Azienda di Promozione Turistica della Basilicata www.aptbasilicata.it – click on the Where to Sleep link.

Agriturismi and B&Bs www.agriturismo.It or www.agriturismo.net; www.bed-and-breakfast.it.

Albergo Diffuso www.alberghidiffusi.it.

Campgrounds www.camping.it, www.touringclub.it.

Hostels www.hihostels.com/it.

Mountain Refuges www.cai.it.

Eating

The flavours and authentic aromas of Basilicata's rich culinary tradition will make your meals here a delight. You'll also enjoy great snacks thanks to the vast array of breads (including Matera's fabulous *pane*), breadsticks, artisanal cured meats and cheeses, all accompanied

by a glass of excellent wine. You'll be spoiled for choice.

Eating options reviewed in this guidebook are listed in ascending order of price, from cheapest to most expensive, and, within each price category, by author preference.

Useful Websites

Associazione Italiana Celiachia (Italian Coeliac Association; www.celiachia.it)

Restaurants for Coeliacs (www.ristorantiperceliaci.net)

Vegetarian and vegan restaurants (www.iomangioveg.it; www.ristorantiveg.com; www.veganhome.it)

Emergency

At the time of research, a single **Unique Emergency Number** (NUE ☑112) was being introduced to cover the following contacts:

Ambulance ☑118

Carabinieri ☑112

State Forestry Corps (Wildfire Emergency) ☑1515

Coast Guard ☑1530

Police ☑113

Alpine and Speleological Rescue (Mountain Rescue) ☑118

Fire Brigade ☑115

LGBTIQ+ Travellers

While openness to diverse sexual orientations has always been difficult in Basilicata, especially in inland villages, things are changing, and in 2017 the region hosted its first ever Gay Pride in Potenza.

Useful websites include **Arcigay** (www.arcigay.it), **Gay. it** (www.gay.it) and **Quiiky** (www.quiiky.com).

Media

Local newspapers include *La Gazzetta del Mezzogiorno* (www.lagazzettadel novem-bre.it) and the Basilicata edition of *Il Quotidiano del Sud* (www.quotidianodelsud. it/basilicata), as well as the online *Basilicata24* (www. basili cata24.it).

Medical Services

You'll find a list of on-duty pharmacies at www.pharm acies diturno.org portal. You can search the directory by entering the municipality.

Tourist Information

Two excellent websites are those of the **Basilicata Tourist Board** (www.aptbasilicta .it) and the **Basilicata**

Territorial Promotion Agency (www.basilica taturisti ca.com), which has informative brochures you can download. Both have useful information for trip planning.

There's an extensive network of tourist and Pro Loco offices in the region, but they are only reliable in the most important centres where you can get maps, brochures and help for all your needs. In less touristy places, you can't always rely on the stated hours. Important contacts:

Potenza - IAT (☑0971 41 50 80; www.comune.potenza. it – click on the tourism link; Palazzo del Turismo e della Cultura, Via Cesare Battisti 22; ⊙9am-6pm).

Matera-Basilicata Open Space (☑0835 40 88 16; Palazzo dell'Annunziata, Piazza Vittorio Veneto; ⊙9.30am-6.30pm).

Maratea–APT (☑0973 03 03 66; Piazza Vitolo 1; ⊙8am-2pm Mon-Fri & 3-6pm Tue & Thu).

Transport

GETTING THERE & AWAY

Air

Airports

Karol Wojtyla International Airport (✆080 580 02 00; www.aeroportidipuglia.it; Bari) is about 70km from Matera. The **Salento International Airport** (✆080 580 02 02; www.aeroportidipuglia.it; Brindisi) is more distant, about 140km away.

Naples Capodichino Airport (✆081 789 62 59; www.aeroportodinapoli.it) is about 160km from Potenza.

Land

Bus

The bus lines indicated below connect Basilicata with other regions in Italy. Refer to the companies' websites or the **iBus** site (✆051421 05 30; www.ibus.it) for information on routes, stops, timetables and ticket purchases.

Autolinee Liscio (✆0971 546 73; www.autolineeliscio.it) Rome-Potenza-Matera, Perugia-Rome-Potenza.

Flixbus (✆02 9475 9208; www.flixbus.it) Connects Potenza and Matera with many Italian towns via Naples, Rome, Milan or Bologna.

Marino Autolinee (✆080311 23 35; www.marinobus.it) Has

an extensive route network with connections to many destinations in Basilicata and numerous cities in central and northern Italy.

Marozzi-SITA (✆080 579 02 11; www.marozzivt.it) Turin-Potenza-Ferrandina.

Miccolis (✆0835 34 40 32; www.miccolis-spa.it) Connects Potenza, Metaponto, Ferrandina, Matera, Salandra with various destinations in Campania and Puglia.

Moretti (✆097 22 45 90; www.autolineemoretti.it) Connects several Lucanian villages with major cities in southern, central and northern Italy.

Car & Motorcycle

Useful websites for planning a road trip include:

ACI - Automobile Club d'Italia (✆06 499 81, roadside assistance ✆803 116; www.aci.it).

Autostrade per l'Italia (www.autostrade.it) Real-time traffic and toll calculation.

CCISS Viaggiare Informati (toll free✆1518; 24 h; www.cciss.it) Realtime traffic updates.

Google Maps (maps.google.co.uk) For route planning.

Isoradio ((FM 103.3; www.raiplaysound.it/isoradio) Advisory radio service from Italy's national broadcaster providing transport information.

ViaMichelin (www.viamichelin.co.uk/web/Itineraries) For route planning.

Bicycle

If you're a passionate cyclist and plan to explore the area by bike, you can get advice on the **FIAB – Federazione Italiana Ambiente e Bicicletta** (fiabitalia.it, www.bicitalia.org) websites.

If you want to transport your bike with you on a train, check out **Trenitalia's website** (www.trenitalia.com) – follow links to 'Services' > 'On board' > 'Bike on board'; or **Italo** (www.italotreno.it).

Train

Trenitalia's high-speed **Frecciarossa** trains connect Turin, Milan, Bologna, Florence, Rome and Naples with Salerno, from where **Frecialink** buses run on to Potenza and Matera. Get more information at www.trenitalia.com; click

TRAIN CARDS

Trenitalia (www.trenitalia.com) provides discounted fares, promotions and offers of various kinds. To get the most out of them, it may be useful to obtain – depending on your requirements – one of the cards issued by Trenitalia. These include the **Green Card** (for people aged between 12 and 26) and the **Silver Card** (for those over 60), both of which provide discounts on domestic and international tickets. The **CartaFRECCIA** enables you to accumulate points and take advantage of services and benefits throughout the country.

To find out about Trenitalia's full offers, go to www.trenitalia.com then click on 'Offers'. Here you'll find a heading 'Green and Silver Card'.

on 'Frecce' and then 'Servizio Frecce+bus' (in Italian only).

At the time of research, an equivalent service offered by **Italo** (www.italotreno. it): high-speed trains from Turin, Milan, Reggio-Emilia, Bologna, Florence, Rome, Afragola, and Naples to Salerno to connect with an **Italobus** shuttle to Potenza, Ferrandina, and Matera, had been suspended.

Trenitalia operates interregional trains which connect Maratea (Salerno–Paola line), Castel Lagopesole and Melfi (Potenza–Foggia line), and Metaponto (Potenza–Taranto line) to the broader rail network.

For information on connections and to purchase tickets, contact **Trenitalia** (☏8920 21; www.trenitalia.com; ⏰24) or **Italo** (☏0607 08; www.italotreno.it); for Trenitalia reservation changes, contact **CartaFRECCIA assistance** (☏0630 00; www.trenitalia. com, select the 'Main Solutions' search box).

To follow the progress of trains in Italy you're interested in, and for real-time updates on possible line interruptions, cancellations and eventual replacement services, check **Viaggiatreno Trenitalia** (www.viaggia treno.it).

Ferrovie Appulo Lucane (☏800 050 500; ferrovieappu lolucane.it) trains and buses connect Bari with Potenza and Matera and other locations in Puglia and Basilicata. Note that journey times can be lengthy.

TRAIN STATIONS

Stations are generally served by public transport from surrounding towns. The Getting There & Away sections in individual city/town entries list the bus companies that serve them and provide websites where you can get route and timetabling information.

GETTING AROUND

To/From the Airport

There are no airports in Basilicata. Details for connections to/from Bari, Brindisi, and Naples airports are provided on p195.

Bus

There are several transport companies that operate both buses and trains in Basilicata. You can reach many places by local bus, but journeys can be very slow and complicated. Services between the main centres might be frequent during the week, but they're significantly reduced on Sundays and holidays. It's also not uncommon for smaller towns and villages to have no bus services. Bear this in mind so you don't get stuck in remote places, particularly at the weekend. However, even travelling between Maratea and Matera, the region's two

main tourist destinations, can take a full day.

You can usually find bus timetables at local tourist offices or posted near stations and stops. In cities, some companies offering intercity bus services operate through travel agencies which can be a bit disorienting for first-time visitors to the region. In some smaller towns, tickets are sold at bars or directly on the bus.

Listed below are the main transport companies and the main routes they offer. For more details on timetables and destinations see their websites. See also the individual Getting There & Away sections of the towns and cities covered in this book.
SITASUD (☏0971 50 68 11; www.sitasudtrasporti.it) Offers extensive public transport services in Basilicata, Puglia and Campania.

Ferrovie Appulo Lucane (☏800 050 500; www.ferrovie appulolucane.it) Operates in Puglia and Basilicata; connects Bari, Matera and several other locations by bus and train.

Cotrab (www.cotrab.eu) A website providing information on regional transport connections.

Car & Motorcycle

The easiest way to get around Basilicata is with your own car. This will guarantee you maximum freedom and enable you to discover the region's most enchanted corners. State roads are not always in good condition, so it pays to be very careful, especially if you see signs warning of potholes (which can be veritable pits).

Provincial roads are sometimes little more than country lanes, but they make it possible to reach some of the more picturesque locations and many smaller towns.

Hire

It's advisable to choose full insurance which will cover you for theft and damage. New drivers are advised to check requirements in advance, particularly those relating to a minimum age and date of licence issue. Hire firms operating in the region have offices in Basilicata's main towns and cities.

Avis (☑06 452 108 391; www. avisautonoleggio.it)

Budget (☑199 30 73 73; www. budgetautonoleggio.it)

Europcar (☑199 30 70 30; www.europcar.it)

Hertz (☑02 696 82 445; www. hertz.it)

Maggiore (☑199 15 11 20; www.maggiore.it).

Bicycle

The beauty of Basilicata's landscape will make you want to visit by bike. But bear in mind that the terrain is largely mountainous.

You can download a free brochure **Cicloturismo in Basilicata** (in Italian only)

from the website of **Tourist Basilicata** (www.basilicataturistica.it) – click on 'Sport e outdoor' then 'Cicloturismo'. It outlines itineraries of various degrees of difficulty taking in the region's most important tourist destinations, as well as lesser known villages. Details are given of the route's elevation profile and 'cycle-friendly' accommodation options.

You can take your bike on any Trenitalia regional train marked with the appropriate icon on the timetable and on daytime intercity trains that provide the service. The bike supplement on intercity trains costs €3.50 and is valid for 24 hours; alternatively, you can buy a second-class ticket for the same route,
but note that this must be validated before boarding the train. It's always worth checking the rules for regional trains as they can vary from region to region. Disassembled bikes in bike bags and folding bicycles can be carried free of charge on Trenitalia trains (one bicycle per person; dimensions no larger than 80x110x45cm) and Italo trains.

Regarding carrying bicycles on local public transport, you should check the regulations with the individual operating company, as each company applies its own rules.

For help planning your bike itinerary, contact **FIAB-Federazione Italiana Ambiente e Bicicletta** (fiabitalia

.it). Ot try **Albergabici** (www. albergabici.it), a dedicated search engine that will help you find accommodation for your chosen route. Bike-friendly accommodation options are listed by location and details are provided of rates and the services each place offers.

Hire

It's not easy to find places offering bike hire (or repair shops) in Basilicata. Better to plan ahead and ask your accommodation provider in advance. Alternatively, you could contact a specialised agency such as **Ferula Viaggi** (www.bikebasilicata.it).

Train

The regional rail network serves only a few places of tourist interest.

For a complete overview of rail connections, check **Trenitalia** (☑89 20 21; www. trenitalia.com) and the **Ferrovie Appulo Lucane** (☑800 050 500; http://ferrovieappulo luca
ne.it), or even travel agencies.

LOCAL TRANSPORT

Only the main centres have good public transport systems, though in most places it's easy to find your way around on foot. Throughout this guidebook, information about each individual location is provided in the 'Getting There & Away' sections.

Behind the Scenes

SEND US YOUR FEEDBACK

We love to hear from travellers – your comments keep us on our toes and help make our books better. Our well-travelled team reads every word on what you loved or loathed about this book. Although we cannot reply individually to your submissions, we always guarantee that your feedback goes straight to the appropriate authors, in time for the next edition. Each person who sends us information is thanked in the next edition – the most useful submissions are rewarded with a selection of digital PDF chapters.

Visit **lonelyplanet.com/contact** to submit your updates and suggestions or to ask for help. Our award-winning website also features inspirational travel stories, news and discussions.

Note: We may edit, reproduce and incorporate your comments in Lonely Planet products such as guidebooks, websites and digital products, so let us know if you don't want your comments reproduced or your name acknowledged. For a copy of our privacy policy visit lonelyplanet.com/legal.

OUR READERS

Many thanks to the travellers who used the last edition and wrote to us with helpful hints, useful advice and interesting anecdotes:

Fabrizio Ciani, Federica and Fabio, Francesco Soliani, Giuliana Cesari, Luca Perri, Luca Settembre, Maria Martinelli, Olga Milsey, Serena Gallo, Tiziana Conti, Tiziana Meucci.

WRITERS' THANKS

Remus Carulli

In light of my travels in Basilicata, the list of people to thank would spill over the pages of this guidebook. I was constantly made to feel welcome, and to give credit to everyone who helped make my trip possible would require me to go over every detail of long weeks' worth of travel. For the sake of brevity, I'll focus my gratitude on Francesco Foschino, who remains an amazing source of knowledge on the Matera area, even after multiple visits to the city. On a personal level, I'd like to thank Angelo Pittro and Silvia Castelli for their trust in me, and the superlative Cristina Enrico for the competence and patience with which she continues to tolerate me.

THANKS

Thanks to Adriano Auleta and Giulia Grimaldi for their kind permission to use their photographs.

THIS BOOK

This first English-language edition of *Basilicata* is a translation of the third edition of the Italian-language *Matera & Basilicata* guide. Remo Carulli, who conducted the research and wrote this edition is also the author of the previous edition.

The English-language translation was produced by the following:

The third edition of the Italian-language guide was produced by the following:

Managing Editor Silvia Castelli

Destination editor Darren O'Connell

Translator Duncan Garwood

Production editor Lauren O'Connell

Thanks to Melanie Dankel, Karen Henderson, Claire Rourke

Coordination Christine Henry

Updates & adaptations Luciana Defedele, Annarosa Sinopoli

Editors Annalisa Bruni, Cristina Enrico

Layout Tiziana Vigna

Colour cover & pages Alessandro Pedarra, Tiziana Vigna, Sarah Viola Cabras

Cartographer Ivo Villa

Production Alberto Capano

Index

INDEX T-Z

NOTES

Map Legend

Sights
- Beach
- Bird Sanctuary
- Buddhist
- Castle/Palace
- Christian
- Confucian
- Hindu
- Islamic
- Jain
- Jewish
- Monument
- Museum/Gallery/Historic Building
- Ruin
- Shinto
- Sikh
- Taoist
- Winery/Vineyard
- Zoo/Wildlife Sanctuary
- Other Sight

Activities, Courses & Tours
- Bodysurfing
- Diving
- Canoeing/Kayaking
- Course/Tour
- Sento Hot Baths/Onsen
- Skiing
- Snorkelling
- Surfing
- Swimming/Pool
- Walking
- Windsurfing
- Other Activity

Sleeping
- Sleeping
- Camping

Eating
- Eating

Drinking & Nightlife
- Drinking & Nightlife
- Cafe

Entertainment
- Entertainment

Shopping
- Shopping

Information
- Bank
- Embassy/Consulate
- Hospital/Medical
- Internet
- Police
- Post Office
- Telephone
- Toilet
- Tourist Information
- Other Information

Geographic
- Beach
- Gate
- Hut/Shelter
- Lighthouse
- Lookout
- Mountain/Volcano
- Oasis
- Park
- Pass
- Picnic Area
- Waterfall

Population
- Capital (National)
- Capital (State/Province)
- City/Large Town
- Town/Village

Transport
- Airport
- Border crossing
- Bus
- Cable car/Funicular
- Cycling
- Ferry
- Metro/MRT/MTR station
- Monorail
- Parking
- Petrol station
- Skytrain/Subway station
- Taxi
- Train station/Railway
- Tram
- Underground station
- Other Transport

Note: Not all symbols displayed above appear on the maps in this book

Routes
- Tollway
- Freeway
- Primary
- Secondary
- Tertiary
- Lane
- Unsealed road
- Road under construction
- Plaza/Mall
- Steps
- Tunnel
- Pedestrian overpass
- Walking Tour
- Walking Tour detour
- Path/Walking Trail

Boundaries
- International
- State/Province
- Disputed
- Regional/Suburb
- Marine Park
- Cliff
- Wall

Hydrography
- River, Creek
- Intermittent River
- Canal
- Water
- Dry/Salt/Intermittent Lake
- Reef

Areas
- Airport/Runway
- Beach/Desert
- Cemetery (Christian)
- Cemetery (Other)
- Glacier
- Mudflat
- Park/Forest
- Sight (Building)
- Sportsground
- Swamp/Mangrove

OUR STORY

A beat-up old car, a few dollars in the pocket and a sense of adventure. In 1972 that's all Tony and Maureen Wheeler needed for the trip of a lifetime – across Europe and Asia overland to Australia. It took several months, and at the end – broke but inspired – they sat at their kitchen table writing and stapling together their first travel guide, *Across Asia on the Cheap*. Within a week they'd sold 1500 copies. Lonely Planet was born.

Today, Lonely Planet has offices in the US, Ireland and China, with a network of over 2000 contributors in every corner of the globe. We share Tony's belief that 'a great guidebook should do three things: inform, educate and amuse'.

OUR WRITERS

Remo Carulli

Remo's passion for travel has been evident since the age of five, when he won a gummy candy in a bet with his sister for correctly identifying the capital of Mongolia. As a psychotherapist, however, he deals with another type of journey: that of people who want to know themselves more deeply. He holds writing courses, knowledge groups on meditative techniques, and teaches Clinical Psychology at the IUSTO University of Turin. His published works include the novels *Pensieri di un ternetno sinister* (Zona Editrice, 2009) and *Viaggio al termine di un amore* (Gesualdo Edizioni, 2021), and essay *La letterarietà del mestiere di psicologo. Meditazioni tra narrativa, retorica e poesia* (Libreria Universitaria, 2020). Remo is the author or co-author of various Lonely Planet guides to the Italian regions.

Duncan Garwood

Based in Rome, Duncan is a travel writer and guidebook author specialising in Italy and the Mediterranean. Duncan translated the third edition of the Italian-language *Matera e Basilicata* for the first English-language edition of *Basilicata*.

Roger Bontempi

Environment Roger is a naturalist and journalist who collaborates on environmental research projects. He is the author of publications dedicated to environmentally-friendly sport.

Stefano Cena

History Stefano is an editor at EDT.

Anita Franzon

Basilicata's Cuisine Anita is a sommelier and writes for various food and wine blogs.

Jacopo Tomatis

Society and Culture Jacopo is a journalist, musicologist and DIY enthusiast. He has been editor of *Il Giornale della Musica* since 2008.

Published by Lonely Planet Global Limited
CRN 554153
1st edition – July 2024
ISBN 978-1-83758-585-4
© Lonely Planet 2024   Photographs © as indicated 2024
10 9 8 7 6 5 4 3 2 1
Printed in China